The Internet For Canadians For Dummies, 2nd Edition Starter Kit

Cheat Sheet

Useful Web Pages

www.yahoo.com	Yahoo! Web directory
www.yahoo.ca	Yahoo! Canada Web Directory
www.altavista.com	AltaVista Web search page
www.google.com	Google Web search page
www.tucows.com	The Ultimate Collection of Windows Software (also for Macs)
cws.internet.com	Stroud's Consummate Winsock Applications
www.infobeat.com	Sign up to get news via e-mail
home.netscape.com	Netscape Communications home page
www.microsoft.com/ie	Microsoft Internet Explorer home page
www.operasoftware.com	Opera home page
canada411.sympatico.ca	Canadian phone directory to find people and businesses
www.liszt.com	Liszt Directory of E-mail Mailing Lists
www.unitedmedia.com/comics/dilbert	Dilbert comics
www2.uclick.com/content/db.html	Doonesbury comics
people.yahoo.com	Yahoo People Search phone and e-mail directory
www.ragingbull.com	Investment Web site and online community
weather.ec.gc.ca	Canadian weather information
www.canada.gc.ca	Canadian government home page
www.canadapost.ca	Canada Post rates, postal codes, and locations
mail.yahoo.com and www.hotmail.com	Free e-mail via the Web
www.us.imdb.com	Internet Movie Database
net.gurus.com	Updates to this book

Types of URLS

file://pathname	File stored on local comput...
ftp://hostname/pathname	File on FTP server
http://hostname/pathname	World Wide Web page
mailto:address	E-mail address
telnet:hostname	Computer to log in to using t...

D1227611

...For Dummies®: Bestselling Book Series for Beginners

The Internet For Canadians For Dummies, 2nd Edition Starter Kit

Cheat Sheet

Netiquette Tips

- Remember that everyone else on the Net is human, too.
- Don't respond in anger or insist on getting the last word.
- DON'T TYPE IN ALL CAPS! It's shouting.
- Don't post messages to mailing lists if you don't have something new to add.
- Don't pass along chain letters (even virtuous-looking ones), online petitions, make-money-fast messages, avoid-this-virus warnings, or other bogus mail.

Hostname Zones

This list shows you the three-letter last word of Internet hostnames.

ca	Canadian federal, provincial, local government, or nonprofit organization
com	Company or individual
edu	Educational institution
net	Network organization
int	International organization
org	Nonprofit or other noncommercial organization

Acronyms Worth Knowing

BTW	By the way
RTFM	Read the manual
IMHO	In my humble/honest opinion
ROFL	Rolling on floor, laughing
TIA	Thanks in advance
YMMV	Your mileage may vary
TLA	Three-letter acronym
LOL	Laughing Out Loud

E-Mail Mailing Lists

To find a list, go to www.liszt.com

To subscribe, send a message to the administrative address (usually with username LISTSERV, ListProc, or Majordomo) containing the line subscribe listname yourname (for Majordomo, omit yourname) in the text of the message.

Read and save the welcome message you receive.

To sign off, send a message to the administrative address containing the line signoff listname (for LISTSERV and ListProc) or unsubscribe listname (for Majordomo) in the text of the message.

Fill In Information about Your Internet Account

Your e-mail address:

_____

Your Internet Service Provider's data phone number (the number your software dials):

_____

Your Internet Service Provider's technical support phone number (if you want to talk to a human being):

_____

Your Internet Service Provider's technical support department's e-mail address:

_____

...For Dummies®: Bestselling Book Series for Beginners

TM

References for the Rest of Us!™

BESTSELLING BOOK SERIES

Do you find that traditional reference books are overloaded with technical details and advice you'll never use? Do you postpone important life decisions because you just don't want to deal with them? Then our *...For Dummies®* business and general reference book series is for you.

...For Dummies business and general reference books are written for those frustrated and hard-working souls who know they aren't dumb, but find that the myriad of personal and business issues and the accompanying horror stories make them feel helpless. *...For Dummies* books use a lighthearted approach, a down-to-earth style, and even cartoons and humorous icons to dispel fears and build confidence. Lighthearted but not lightweight, these books are perfect survival guides to solve your everyday personal and business problems.

Already, millions of satisfied readers agree. They have made *...For Dummies* the #1 introductory level computer book series and a bestselling business book series. They have written asking for more. So, if you're looking for the best and easiest way to learn about business and other general reference topics, look to *...For Dummies* to give you a helping hand.

TM

CDG BOOKS

C A N A D A

8/99

The Internet
For Canadians

FOR

DUMMIES®

2ND EDITION
STARTER KIT

The Internet For Canadians

FOR DUMMIES®

2ND EDITION

STARTER KIT

by Andrew Dagys
John R. Levine
Carol Baroudi
Margaret Levine Young

CDG BOOKS CANADA

CDG Books Canada, Inc.

◆ Toronto, ON ◆

The Internet For Canadians For Dummies 2nd Edition Starter Kit®

Published by
CDG Books Canada, Inc.
99 Yorkville Avenue
Suite 400
Toronto, ON M5R 3K5
www.cdgbooks.com (CDG Books Canada Web Site)
www.idgbooks.com (IDG Books Worldwide Web Site)
www.dummies.com (Dummies Press Web Site)

Canadian Cataloguing in Publication Data

The Internet for Canadians for dummies starter kit : [kit]

2nd ed.

Includes index.
ISBN: 1-894413-27-X

1. Internet (Computer network). I. Dagys, Andrew.

ZA4201.I565 2001   004.67'8   C00-933242-1

Printed in Canada

1 2 3 4 5 TRI 05 04 03 02 01

Distributed in Canada by CDG Books Canada, Inc.

For general information on CDG Books, including all IDG Books Worldwide publications, please call our distribution center: HarperCollins Canada at 1-800-387-0117. For reseller information, including discounts and premium sales, please call our Sales department at 1-877-963-8830.

This book is available at special discounts for bulk purchases by your group or organization for resale, premiums, fundraising and seminars. For details, contact CDG Books Canada, Special Sales Department, 99 Yorkville Avenue, Suite 400, Toronto, ON, M5K 3K5; Tel: 416-963-8830; Email: spmarkets@cdgbooks.com.

For press review copies, author interviews, or other publicity information, please contact our Marketing department at 416-963-8830, fax 416-923-4821, or e-mail publicity@cdgbooks.com.

For authorization to photocopy items for corporate, personal, or educational use, please contact Cancopy, The Canadian Copyright Licensing Agency, One Yonge Street, Suite 1900, Toronto, ON, M5E 1E5; Tel: 416-868-1620; Fax: 416-868-1621; www.cancopy.com.

Trademarks: For Dummies, Dummies Man, A Reference for the Rest of Us!, The Dummies Way, Dummies Daily, and related trade dress are registered trademarks or trademarks of IDG Books Worldwide, Inc. in the United States, Canada and other countries, and may not be used without written permission. All other trademarks are the property of their respective owners. CDG Books Canada is not associated with any product or vendor mentioned in this book.

is a trademark under exclusive license to CDG Books Canada, Inc., from International Data Group, Inc.

CDG BOOKS
C A N A D A

About the Authors

Andrew Dagys is a professional accountant (CMA) and business advisor to government. He first used a computer in 1986 to crunch and analyze complex numbers and to write business reports. Today, he puts computers to use mostly in writing books and columns related to technology and personal finance. He also enjoys using the Internet for investment purposes, and invests almost exclusively in technology stocks.

Andrew is a regular guest on TV and radio shows about finance or technology. He enjoys speaking publicly about how the Internet is changing the world's business and social landscape. He views computers as a tool to harness, and often reminds people he meets never to allow technology to displace the human, spiritual, and interpersonal side of life.

Consistent with his interests, Andrew has written several books on investing, personal finance, and the Internet — among them, *Investing Online For Canadians For Dummies* and CliffsNotes *First-time Investing Online for Canadians*. He is a frequent contributor of related articles to *Canadian Living Magazine,* and *Forever Young.* But his greatest joy is his wife Dawn-Ava, and their three children — Brendan, Megan, and Jordan.

John R. Levine was a member of a computer club in high school — before high school students, or even high schools, had computers, where he met Theodor H. Nelson, the author of *Computer Lib/Dream Machines* and the inventor of hypertext. (Nelson reminded us that computers should not be taken seriously and that everyone can and should understand and use computers.)

John wrote his first program in 1967 on an IBM 1130 (a computer somewhat less powerful than your typical modern digital wristwatch, only more difficult to use), and became an official system administrator of a networked computer at Yale in 1975. He began working part time, for a computer company, of course, in 1977 and has been in and out of the computer and network biz ever since. He got his company on Usenet (the Net's worldwide bulletin-board system) early enough that it appears in a 1982 *Byte* magazine article on a map of Usenet, which then was so small that the map fit on half a page.

Although John used to spend most of his time writing software, now he mostly writes books (including *UNIX For Dummies* and *Internet Secrets,* both published by IDG Books Worldwide, Inc.) because it's more fun and because he can do so at home in the tiny village of Trumansburg, New York, where he is the sewer commissioner (Guided tours! Free samples!) and play with his small daughter when he's supposed to be writing. John also does a fair amount of public speaking (see `iecc.com/johnl`, to find out where he'll be). He holds a BA and a PhD in computer science from Yale University, but please don't hold that against him.

Carol Baroudi first began playing with computers in 1971 at Colgate University, where two things were new: the PDP-10 and women. She was lucky to have unlimited access to the state-of-the-art PDP-10, which taught her how to program, operate the machine, and talk to Eliza. She taught Algol and helped to design the curricula for computer science and women's studies courses. She majored in Spanish and also studied French, both of which, thanks to the Internet, she now has the opportunity to use every day.

In 1975, Carol took a job doing compiler support and development, a perfect use for her background in languages. For six years she developed software and managed software development. For a while she had a small business doing high-tech recruiting (she was a headhunter). Though she wrote her first software manuals in 1975, her job since 1984 has been writing. Carol has described all kinds of software, from the memory-management system of the Wang VS operating system to e-mail products for the PC and Mac. For the past several years, she has been writing books for lay people who want to use computers. She enjoys speaking to academic, business, and general audiences about the impact of technology on society and other related topics. (Check out her home page at iecc.com/carol to see what she's up to.)

The mother of a fantastic eight-year-old, Carol loves acting and singing and will fly to Europe on any excuse. She believes that we are living in a very interesting time when technology is changing faster than people can imagine. Carol hopes that as we learn to use the new technologies, we don't lose sight of our humanity, and feels that computers can be useful and fun but are no substitute for real life.

Unlike her peers in that 40-something bracket, **Margaret Levine Young** was exposed to computers at an early age. In high school, she got into a computer club known as the R.E.S.I.S.T.O.R.S., a group of kids who spent Saturdays in a barn fooling around with three antiquated computers. She stayed in the field throughout college, against her better judgment and despite her brother John's presence as a graduate student in the computer science department. Margy graduated from Yale and went on to become one of the first microcomputer managers in the early 1980s at Columbia Pictures, where she rode the elevator with big stars whose names she wouldn't dream of dropping here.

Since then, Margy has co-authored more than 16 computer books about the Internet, UNIX, WordPerfect, Microsoft Access, and (stab from the past) PC-File and Javelin, including *Dummies 101: The Internet For Windows 98*; *Dummies 101: Netscape Communicator*; *Internet FAQs: Answers to Frequently Asked Questions*; *UNIX For Dummies* and *WordPerfect 8 For Windows 95 For Dummies* (all published by IDG Books Worldwide, Inc.). She met her future husband, Jordan, in the R.E.S.I.S.T.O.R.S. They live in Middlebury, Vermont (see www.gurus.com/margy for some scenery), with her other passion: her children, Meg and Zac. She loves gardening, chickens, reading, and anything to do with eating.

Dedication

Andrew dedicates his part of *The Internet For Canadians For Dummies*, 2nd Edition Starter Kit, with all his love, to Dawn-Ava, his wife; and their three children — Brendan, Megan, and Jordan.

John dedicates his part of the book (the particularly dumb jokes) to Sarah Willow, who still doesn't sleep after two-and-a-half years and is impressively articulate when explaining why not, and to Tonia, who, when not staying up with her, reminded him ever so politely that he really did have to finish revising this book.

Carol dedicates her part of the book to Joshua, with all her love, and to her friends, who remind her that there's more to life than writing books.

Margy dedicates this book to Jordan, Meg, and Zac, who make life worth living.

Authors' Acknowledgements

Melanie Rutledge found many thoughtful and creative ways to add value to this second Canadian edition. In the process of going the extra mile, she made us look like better writers than we are. We appreciate her insights, thoroughness, and lighthearted humour during the important editorial stage.

Andrew thanks Robert Harris, who provided opportunity and guidance for his writing career, as well as to the direction of this book. He also thanks Joan Whitman, who always had timely and decisive answers to his endless stream of questions. He appreciates the many things he has learned from both Robert and Joan over the years, and counts them as friends. Andrew also thanks the rest of the hard-working crew at CDG who are listed on the Publisher's Acknowledgements page.

Margy thanks Jordan and the Cornwall Elementary School. John likewise thanks Nancy Fuhr, who provided vital and high-quality attention and care to the aforementioned nonsleeping person.

We edited and submitted the entire contents of this book to the publisher using the World Wide Web; practising what we preach.

ABOUT CDG BOOKS CANADA, INC. AND
IDG BOOKS WORLDWIDE, INC.

Welcome to the world of IDG Books Worldwide and CDG Books Canada.

IDG Books Worldwide, Inc., is a subsidiary of International Data Group, Inc., the world's largest publisher of computer-related information and the leading global provider of information services on information technology. IDG was founded more than 30 years ago and now employs more than 9,000 people worldwide. IDG publishes more than 295 computer publications in over 75 countries (see listing below). More than 90 million people read one or more IDG publications each month.

Launched in 1990, IDG Books Worldwide is today the #1 publisher of best-selling computer books in North America. IDG Books Worldwide is proud to be the recipient of eight awards from the Computer Press Association in recognition of editorial excellence and three from *Computer Currents'* First Annual Readers' Choice Awards. Our best-selling *...For Dummies®* series has more than 55 million copies in print with translations in 31 languages. In record time, IDG Books Worldwide has become the first choice for millions of readers around the world who want to learn how to better manage their businesses.

In 1998, IDG Books Worldwide formally partnered with Macmillan Canada, a subsidiary of Canada Publishing Corporation, to create CDG Books Canada, a dynamic new Canadian publishing company. CDG Books Canada is now Canada's fastest growing publisher, bringing valuable information to Canadians from coast to coast through the introduction of Canadian *...For Dummies®* and *CliffsNotes™* titles.

Every one of our books is designed to bring extra value and skill-building instructions to the reader. Our books are written by experts who understand and care about our readers. The knowledge base of our editorial staff comes from years of experience in publishing, education, and journalism — experience we use to produce books to carry us into the new millennium. In short, we care about books, so we attract the best people. We devote special attention to details such as audience, interior design, use of icons, and illustrations. And because we use an efficient process of authoring, editing, and desktop publishing our books electronically, we can spend more time ensuring superior content and spend less time on the technicalities of making books.

You can count on our commitment to deliver high-quality books at competitive prices on topics you want to read about. At IDG Books Worldwide and CDG Books Canada, we continue in the IDG tradition of delivering quality for more than 30 years. You can learn more about IDG Books Worldwide and CDG Books Canada by visiting www.idgbooks.com, www.dummies.com, and www.cdgbooks.com.

Eighth Annual
Computer Press
Awards ≥1992

Ninth Annual
Computer Press
Awards ≥1993

Tenth Annual
Computer Press
Awards ≥1994

Eleventh Annual
Computer Press
Awards ≥1995

IDG is the world's leading IT media, research and exposition company. Founded in 1964, IDG had 1997 revenues of $2.05 billion and has more than 9,000 employees worldwide. IDG offers the widest range of media options that reach IT buyers in 75 countries representing 95% of worldwide IT spending. IDG's diverse product and services portfolio spans six key areas including print publishing, online publishing, expositions and conferences, market research, education and training, and global marketing services. More than 90 million people read one or more of IDG's 290 magazines and newspapers, including IDG's leading global brands — Computerworld, PC World, Network World, Macworld and the Channel World family of publications. IDG Books Worldwide is one of the fastest-growing computer book publishers in the world, with more than 700 titles in 36 languages. The "...For Dummies®" series alone has more than 50 million copies in print. IDG offers online users the largest network of technology-specific Web sites around the world through IDG.net (http://www.idg.net), which comprises more than 225 targeted Web sites in 55 countries worldwide. International Data Corporation (IDC) is the world's largest provider of information technology data, analysis and consulting, with research centers in over 41 countries and more than 400 research analysts worldwide. IDG World Expo is a leading producer of more than 168 globally branded conferences and expositions in 35 countries including E3 (Electronic Entertainment Expo), Macworld Expo, ComNet, Windows World Expo, ICE (Internet Commerce Expo), Agenda, DEMO, and Spotlight. IDG's training subsidiary, ExecuTrain, is the world's largest computer training company, with more than 230 locations worldwide and 785 training courses. IDG Marketing Services helps industry-leading IT companies build international brand recognition by developing global integrated marketing programs via IDG's print, online and exposition products worldwide. Further information about the company can be found at www.idg.com.   8/24/99

Publisher's Acknowledgments

We're proud of this book; please register your comments through our IDG Books Worldwide Online Registration Form located at http://my2cents.dummies.com.

Some of the people who helped bring this book to market include the following:

Acquisitions and Editorial

Editorial Director: Joan Whitman

Associate Editor: Melanie Rutledge

Copy Editor: Allyson Latta

Production

Director of Production: Donna Brown

Production Editor: Rebecca Conolly

Layout and Graphics: Kim Monteforte, Heidy Lawrance Associates

Proofreader: Pamela Erlichman

Indexer: Belle Wong

Special Help

Michael Kelly

General and Administrative

IDG Books Worldwide, Inc.: John Kilcullen, CEO; Bill Barry, President and COO; John Ball, Executive VP, Operations & Administration; John Harris, CFO

CDG Books Canada, Inc.: Ron Besse, Chairman; Tom Best, President; Robert Harris, Vice President and Publisher

IDG Books Technology Publishing Group: Richard Swadley, Senior Vice President and Publisher; Mary Bednarek, Vice President and Publisher, Networking and Certification; Walter R. Bruce III, Vice President and Publisher, General User and Design Professional; Joseph Wikert, Vice President and Publisher, Programming; Mary C. Corder, Editorial Director, Branded Technology Editorial; Andy Cummings, Publishing Director, General User and Design Professional; Barry Pruett, Publishing Director, Visual

IDG Books Manufacturing: Ivor Parker, Vice President, Manufacturing

IDG Books Marketing: John Helmus, Assistant Vice President, Director of Marketing

IDG Books Online Management: Brenda McLaughlin, Executive Vice President, Chief Internet Officer

IDG Books Packaging: Marc J. Mikulich, Vice President, Brand Strategy and Research

IDG Books Production for Branded Press: Debbie Stailey, Production Director

IDG Books Sales: Roland Elgey, Senior Vice President, Sales and Marketing; Michael Violano, Vice President, International Sales and Sub Rights

◆

The publisher would like to give special thanks to Patrick J. McGovern, without whom this book would not have been possible.

◆

Contents at a Glance

Cartoons at a Glance

By Rich Tennant

page 77

page 41

page 7

page 289

page 161

Fax: 978-546-7747

E-mail: richtennant@the5thwave.com

World Wide Web: www.the5thwave.com

Table of Contents

Introduction

*W*elcome to *The Internet For Canadians For Dummies*, 2nd Edition Starter Kit. Although lots of Canadian books are available about the Internet, most of them assume that you have a degree in computer science, would love to know about every strange and useless wart of the Internet, and enjoy memorizing unpronounceable commands and options. We hope that this book is much different.

This book describes what you actually do to become an *Internaut* (someone who navigates the Internet with skill) — how to get started, what you really need to know, and where to go (aside from this book) for help. And we describe it in plain old English.

When the Internet first started to become a household name — about seven years ago — a typical Canadian Net user was a student who connected from university or a technical worker who had access through work. Today, the Net has grown like crazy to include millions of (dare we say it?) normal people connecting on their own time from computers at home, along with students ranging from elementary school to adult education. This book focuses on the parts of the Net that are of the most interest to typical users. It introduces you to the World Wide Web and shows you how to find what you're looking for there. It shows you how to use Netscape Communicator, Internet Explorer, and Opera (the most popular and/or useful Web programs). You also find out how to send and receive electronic mail (e-mail), how to shop and chat online, and how to download interesting stuff from the Net.

We needed to write this, the second edition, a mere year after the first one, to keep up with the rapid growth of the Internet. There's simply so much more that you can do on the Net today than you could a year ago. Instant messaging is one Internet application that really took off this past year. Music downloaded from the Net, just a curiosity 12 months ago, is now forcing the music industry to rethink the way it does business. And Internet video and radio broadcast technology continues to become more viable as a greater number of Canadians embrace high-speed Internet access. We discuss these and other exciting new developments in *The Internet For Canadians For Dummies,* 2nd Edition Starter Kit.

About This Book

One of the great things about ...*For Dummies* books is that you don't have to sit down and read through the whole thing (although it should be fine reading material for the bathroom). When you run into a problem using the Internet ("Hmm, I *thought* that I knew how to find somebody on the Net, but I don't seem to remember . . ."), just dip in to the book long enough to solve your problem.

Pertinent sections include:

- ✔ Understanding what the Internet is
- ✔ Knowing how to get connected to the Net
- ✔ Climbing around the World Wide Web
- ✔ Finding people, places, and things
- ✔ Communicating with e-mail (electronic mail)
- ✔ Getting stuff off the Net
- ✔ Finding services and software
- ✔ Dabbling in the latest and coolest Internet bells and whistles

How to Use This Book

To begin, please read the first three chapters. They give you an overview of the Net and provide some important tips and terminology. Besides, *we* think that they're interesting.

When you're ready to get yourself on the Internet, turn to Part II and pick the option that best suits you and your circumstances.

Parts III, IV, and V spur you on and provide extra support.

Although we try hard not to introduce a technical term without defining it, sometimes we slip. Sometimes, too, you may read a section out of order and find a term we defined a few chapters before that. To fill in the gaps, we include a glossary.

Because the Internet is constantly changing, this book has been expanded to include an online area to help keep it up-to-date. Whenever you see the special Whoosh icon, it means that there's more up-to-the-minute information available on our Web site, at

`net.gurus.com`

When you have to type something, it appears in the book like this: `Hello, Internet!` Or else it shows up on a line of its own, like this:

```
cryptic command to type
```

Type it just as it appears. Use the same capitalization we do — many systems care deeply about CAPITAL and small letters. Then press the Enter or Return key. The book tells you what should happen when you give each command and what your options are.

If you have to follow a complicated procedure, it's spelled out step-by-step wherever possible, with what you have to do highlighted in **boldface**. We then tell you what happens in response, and what your options are.

When you have to choose commands from menus, we write File⇨Exit. This means that you choose the File command from the menu bar and then choose the Exit command from the menu that appears.

Who Are You?

In writing the book, we assumed that:

- ✔ You have or would like to have access to the Internet.

- ✔ You want to get some work done with it. (We consider the term "work" to include the concept "play.")

- ✔ You are not interested in becoming the world's next great Canadian Internet expert — at least, not this week.

How This Book Is Organized

The Internet For Canadians For Dummies, 2nd Edition Starter Kit has five parts. The parts stand on their own. However, although you can begin reading wherever you like, you should at least skim Parts I and II first to get acquainted with some unavoidable Internet jargon and find out how to get your computer on the Net.

Here are the parts of the book and what they contain:

In **Part I, Welcome to the Internet**, you find out what the Internet is and why it's interesting. Also, this part has details about vital Internet terminology and concepts that help you as you read through the later parts of the book. Part I discusses how you get on the Internet, gives some thoughts about children's use of the Net, and talks about the latest rage in corporate intranet technology.

For the nuts and bolts of getting on the Net, read **Part II, Internet, Here I Come**. For most users, by far the most difficult part of using the Net is getting to that first connection, with software loaded, configuration configured, and modem modeming. After that, it's (relatively) smooth sailing.

Part III, Web Mania, dives into the World Wide Web, the part of the Internet that has powered the Net's leap from obscurity to fame. Part III discusses how to get around on the Web, how to find what you're looking for (which is not as easy as it should be), how to shop and invest online, and how to add your own home page to the Web.

Part IV, Essential Internet, looks at the other important and useful Net services: sending and receiving electronic mail, sending instant messages, chatting, and getting stuff off the Net. You find out how to exchange electronic mail with people down the hall or on other continents, how to use electronic mailing lists to keep in touch with people of similar interests, and how to download from the Net. We also cover the use of the Net from AOL Canada and WebTV, two popular online services that offer Canadians access to the Internet.

A compendium of ready references and interesting facts is in **Part V, The Part of Tens**. (Does this suggest that the rest of the book is full of *uninteresting* facts? No way — the stuff in The Part of Tens is just super easy to find. It's a staple of ...*For Dummies* books.)

The appendix provides all the information you need to install the programs on the CD-ROM.

What's on the CD-ROM

Here are some of the programs on the CD-ROM, with the chapters that describe them. To find out how to install the programs, see the "About the CD" Appendix.

> ✔ **Netscape Communicator 4.7** (for Windows 95/98 and the Mac) and **Microsoft Internet Explorer 5.5** (for Windows 95/98) and 5.0 (for the Mac), the two most popular Web browsing programs. Chapters 6 and 7 explain in some detail how to use them.

> ✔ **AOL Canada 6.0** (for Windows) and **4.0** (for the Mac) signs you up for AOL Canada. Chapter 17 discusses AOL Canada's services in detail.

> ✔ **Eudora Light 5.0.2** (for Windows) and **5.0.1** (for the Mac) is our favorite electronic mail program; see Chapters 11 and 12 for how to use it.

> ✔ **Netscape Messenger** and **Microsoft Outlook Express** are e-mail and news reading programs that are also on the CD-ROM. For more on how to use these and other e-mail programs, see Chapters 11 and 12.

- **Free Agent 1.21** (for Windows 95/98) and **InterNews 2.02** (for the Mac) are newsreaders, which enable you to participate in Usenet newsgroups (discussion groups). See this Web page for more info:

    `net.gurus.com/news`

- **WS_FTP Pro** (for Windows 95/98) and **Interarchy 4.0** (formerly called Anarchie) (for the Mac) are for downloading programs, graphics, and other files from the Net; see Chapter 16.

- **mIRC 5.82** (for Windows 95/98) and **Ircle 3.0.4** (for the Mac) let you participate in Internet Relay Chat (IRC), a bunch of real-time worldwide conversations. See Chapter 15 for how to use these programs to get chatting.

    `net.gurus.com/irc`

- **NCSA Telnet 2.6** (for the Mac) lets you log in to other computers on the Net. See this Web page for more info:

    `net.gurus.com/telnet`

- **HotDog Professional 6.0** (for Windows 95/98) and **BBEdit Lite 4.6** (for the Mac) help you to create your own Web pages, as we describe in Chapter 10.

- **WinZip 8.0** (for Windows 95/98), **StuffIt Expander 5.5**, and **DropStuff 6 with Expander Enhancer** (for the Mac) can expand the zillions of compressed files you'll find on the Net. See Chapters 16 and 21.

- **Paint Shop Pro** (for Windows 95/98) and **GraphicConverter 4.0.1** (for the Mac) let you create pictures for your Web site or look at pictures that you download from the Net.

- **Adobe Acrobat Reader 4.0** (for Windows 95/98 and the Mac) lets you read and print documents formatted as Portable Document Format files, such as the Eudora Light manual on the CD-ROM.

Icons Used in This Book

Lets you know that some particularly nerdy, technoid information is coming up so that you can skip it if you want. (On the other hand, you may want to read it.)

Indicates that a nifty little shortcut or time-saver is explained. Or, it might be some advice on conducting yourself on and around the Net (Netiquette!).

Gaack! We found out about this information the hard way! Don't let it happen to you!

Points out a (usually Canadian) resource on the World Wide Web that you can use with Netscape Navigator, Internet Explorer, or other Web software.

Points you to more up-to-the-minute information on our very own Web site, net.gurus.com. Hey, this book is *alive.*

The CD-ROM in the back of the book includes this program.

What Now?

That's all you need to know to get started. Whenever you hit a snag using the Internet, just look up the problem in the table of contents or index in this book. You'll either solve the problem in a flash or, at least, know where to go to find some expert help.

Because the Internet has been evolving for almost 30 years, largely under the influence of some extremely nerdy people, it was not designed to be particularly easy for normal people to use. Don't feel bad if you have to look up a number of topics before you feel comfortable using the Internet.

Feedback, Please

We love to hear from our readers. If you want to contact us, please do!

To contact the publisher or authors of this or other ...*For Dummies* books, visit the publisher's Web site, at www.cdgbooks.com, www.idgbooks.com, or www.dummies.com. You can also send an e-mail to info@cdgbooks.com, or regular mail to the following address:

CDG Books Canada, Inc.
99 Yorkville Avenue, Suite 400
Toronto, Ontario, Canada
M5R 3K5

Part I
Welcome to the Internet

"IT HAPPENED AROUND THE TIME WE SUBSCRIBED TO AN ON-LINE SERVICE."

In this part . . .

The Internet is an amazing place. But because it's full of computers, nothing is quite as simple as it ought to be. That's why you've got this book. "Simple" is this book's middle name. This part first looks at what the Internet is and how it got that way. You find out what's happening, what people are doing, and what it means to you. It highlights issues related to the Internet that are of concern to Canadian families, and lists online resources to help them. It takes a brief look at intranets and extranets, which are Internet technologies gone corporate.

Chapter 1

What Is the Net?

*W*hat is the Internet? It depends (an answer you'll be seeing in this book more often than you might expect). The Internet and the technologies that make it work are changing faster than anyone can keep track of. This chapter begins with the basics. What is the Internet? And, just as important, how has it changed during the past couple of years?

If you're just encountering the Internet for the first time, and especially if you don't have much computer experience, *be patient with yourself.* Many of the ideas here are completely new. Allow yourself some time to read and reread. It's a world with its own language, and it takes some getting used to. Many people find it helpful to read through the entire book once quickly, to get a broader perspective on what we're talking about. Others plow through one page at a time. Whatever your style, remember that it's cutting-edge stuff — you're not *supposed* to understand it just like that. Even for many experienced Internet users, it's a brave new world.

Even if you're an experienced computer user, you may find the Internet unlike anything you've ever tackled. The Internet is not a software package, and doesn't easily lend itself to the kind of step-by-step instruction you can get for a single, fixed program. This book is as step-by-step as can be, but the Internet resembles a living organism that's mutating at an astonishing rate. In that sense, it's a far cry from Microsoft Word or Excel, which sit quietly on your computer and mind their own business. After you get set up and get a little practice, using the Internet seems like second nature. In the beginning, however, it can be daunting.

The Internet — also known as the *Net* — is the world's largest computer network. "What is a network?" you may ask. Even if you already know, you may want to read the next couple of paragraphs to make sure that we're speaking the same language.

A computer *network* is basically a bunch of computers hooked together somehow. In concept, it's sort of like a radio or TV network that connects a bunch of radio or TV stations so that they can share the latest episode of *The X-Files*.

Don't take the analogy too far. TV networks send the same information to all the stations at the same time (it's called *broadcast* networking); in computer networks, each particular message is usually routed to a particular computer. Unlike TV networks, computer networks are invariably two-way: when computer A sends a message to computer B, B can send a reply back to A.

Some computer networks consist of a central computer and a bunch of remote stations that report to it (a central airline-reservation computer, for example, with thousands of screens and keyboards in various airports and travel agencies). Others, including the Internet, are more egalitarian and permit any computer on the network to communicate with any other.

In fact, the Internet isn't just one network — it's a network of networks, all freely exchanging information. The networks range from the big and formal (such as the corporate networks at Bell Canada, Nortel Networks, and Canadian Pacific) to the small and informal (such as the one in Andrew's home office, with a couple of old PCs bought through the *Buy & Sell Newspaper*) and everything in between. Community college and university networks have long been part of the Internet, and now high schools and elementary schools across Canada are joining up. In the past year or two, Internet usage has been increasing at a pace equivalent to that of television in the early '50s; the Net now has an estimated 125 million computers and something like 350 million users, growing at 40 to 45 percent per year.

So What's All the Hoopla?

Everywhere you turn, you hear people talking about the Net — almost as though they're on a first-name basis with it. Radio shows give you their e-mail addresses, businesses give you their Web sites (starting with "www" and ending with the ubiquitous "dot com") and strangers ask whether you have a "home page." People are "going online and getting connected." Are they really talking about this same "network of networks"? Yes, *and* there's more.

With networks, size counts for a great deal, because the larger a network is, the more stuff it has to offer. Because the Internet is the world's largest interconnected group of computer networks, it has an amazing array of information — all potentially at your disposal.

The Internet is communications technology that is affecting our lives on a scale comparable to that of the telephone and television. Some have said that when it comes to disseminating information, the Internet is the most significant invention since the printing press! If you use a telephone, write letters, read a newspaper or magazine, or do business or any kind of research, the Internet can radically alter your entire world view.

When people talk about the Internet today, they're usually talking about what they can do, what they have found, and whom they have met. The Internet's capabilities are so extensive that there isn't room to give a complete list in this chapter (indeed, it would fill several books larger than this one), but here's a quick summary:

- **Electronic mail (e-mail):** This service is certainly the most widely used — you can exchange e-mail with millions of people all over the world. People use e-mail for anything for which they might use paper mail, faxes, special delivery of documents, or the telephone: gossip, recipes, rumours, love letters — you name it. (We hear that some people even use it for stuff related to work.) Electronic mailing lists enable you to join group discussions with people who have similar interests and meet people over the Net. *Mail servers* or *mailbots* (programs that respond to e-mail messages automatically) let you retrieve all sorts of information. Chapters 11, 12, and 13 have the details.

- **The World Wide Web:** When people talk these days about surfing the Net, they often mean checking out sites on this (buzzword alert!) multimedia hyperlinked database that spans the globe. In fact, people are talking more about the Web and less about the Net. Are they the same thing? Technically, no. Practically speaking, for many people, yes. These similarities and differences are mapped out in Chapter 6.

  The Web, unlike earlier Net services, combines text, pictures, sound, and even animation, and lets you move around with a click of your computer mouse. New Web sites (sets of Web pages) are growing faster than you can say "Quarter Pounder with cheese," with new sites appearing every minute. In 1999, when the first edition of this book was written, the Internet had a few million Web sites. Today, it has many many millions, and statistics indicate that the number is doubling every few months.

  The software used to navigate the Web is known as a *browser*. The most popular browsers today are Netscape Navigator and Microsoft Internet Explorer. We tell you all about them in Chapters 6 and 7, along with some other less popular but worthy competitors.

✔ **Chatting:** People are talking to people all over the globe about every-thing under the sun. They enter chat rooms with several other people or one special someone. They're using the AOL Canada chat facility, SympaticoLycos's version of the same thing, or Internet Relay Chat (IRC), a chat facility available to almost anyone on the Internet. Chapter 15 tells you how. Chapter 15 also discusses paging programs, such as AOL Instant Messenger, that let you send messages that "pop up" on the recipient's screen.

✔ **Information retrieval:** Many computers have files of information that are free for the taking. The files range from Supreme Court of Canada decisions and library card catalogues, to the text of old books, digitized pictures (nearly all of them suitable for family audiences), music, and an enormous variety of software, from games to operating systems.

Special tools known as search engines, directories, and indexes help you find information on the Net. Lots of people are striving to create the fastest, smartest search engine and the most complete Net index. We tell you about three of the most useful search tools — AltaVista, Google, and Yahoo — so that you get the picture. As mentioned in the introduction to this book, you see a Web icon here and there; it points to resources you can retrieve from the Net, as described in Chapter 16.

✔ **Electronic commerce:** This term is just a fancy word for buying and selling stuff over the Net. It seems that everybody's doing it, and now the software is available to make the process of sending your credit card number over the Net safe and secure. You can buy anything from books to stock in Bombardier. Keep reading for more on relevant issues surrounding this topic, or turn to Chapter 9.

✔ **Intranets, extranets, and business-to-business marketplaces:** Wouldn't ya know? Businesses have figured out that this Internet stuff is really useful. They're using e-mail and Web technologies on their own internal networks and calling them *intranets*. Intranets make communication and data processing more efficient. After companies figured out that Internet technology could be used internally, some quickly cottoned on to the idea that they could use this same stuff to work with their customers and suppliers, and other companies with which they have business relationships. Intranets make business between companies run more smoothly. Because this technology goes outside their companies, they called the new permutation *extranets*.

Then businesses figured out that they could share one common virtual Web site, and began putting their products and services together in a sort of one-stop business mall. The result was the creation of an online *business-to-business marketplace* or *business-to-business exchange* with all the convenience and amenities of being in the thick of business. Whether or not you currently use these terms, chances are this will be your year to experience at least one of them. Intranets, extranets, and business-to-business marketplaces are dealt with in Chapter 2.

> ✔ **Games and gossip:** A type of multi-user game called a *MUD* (*Multi-User Dimension* or *Multi-User Dungeon*) can easily absorb all your waking hours and an alarming number of what otherwise would be your sleeping hours. In a MUD, you can challenge other players who can be anywhere in the world. Lots of other multi-user games are available on the Web too. MUDs are discussed in Chapter 15.

A Few Real-Life Stories

In several Canadian elementary schools, students use the Internet to exchange letters and stories with kids in countries as far away as Israel and Scotland. Although it's partly just for fun and to make friends in a foreign country, a sobre academic study reported that when kids have a real audience for their stuff, they write better. (Big surprise.)

For many purposes, the Internet is the fastest and most reliable way to move information. In July 2000, when the Air France Concorde crashed, millions of people followed the minute-by-minute developments on the Web. Many other breaking events are also first discovered through the Web.

During the 1991 Soviet coup, members of a tiny Internet provider called RELCOM sent out stories that would have been in newspapers, statements from Boris Yeltsin (hand-delivered by friends), and their personal observations from downtown Moscow.

Medical researchers around the world use the Internet to maintain databases of rapidly changing data. People with medical conditions use the Internet to communicate with each other in support groups and to compare experiences.

The Internet has more prosaic uses, too. Here are some from our personal experience:

When we began writing our Internet books, we posted notices on the Net asking for contributions. We got responses from all over the world. Many of these contributors became our friends. Now we have people to visit all over the world. It could happen to *you*.

We get mail every day from all over the world from readers of our *...For Dummies* books, and are often the happy recipients of readers' first-ever e-mail messages.

The Internet is its own best source of software. Whenever we hear about a new service, it usually takes only a few minutes to find software for our computers (various computers running various versions of Windows and a Power Macintosh), download it, and start it up. Most of the software available on the Internet is free or inexpensive *shareware*. You download the shareware program for a trial period, and see whether it appeals. If you like it and want to keep it, you're expected to send a payment to the shareware provider specified in the program.

The Internet has local and regional parts, too. When Andrew wanted to sell his feisty six-cylinder "steed," a note on the Internet in the local for-sale area found a buyer within five days. Margy's husband sold his used computer within a half-hour of posting a message in the relevant Usenet newsgroup.

Why Is This Medium Different from Any Other Medium?

The Internet is unlike any other existing communications media. People of all ages, colours, creeds, and countries freely share ideas, stories, data, opinions, and products.

Anybody can access it

One great thing about the Internet is that it's probably the most open network in the world. Thousands of computers provide facilities that are available to anyone who has Net access. This situation is unusual — most networks are extremely restrictive in terms of what they allow users to do, and require specific arrangements and passwords for each service. Although pay services exist (and more are added every day), most Internet services are free for the taking. If you don't already have access to the Internet through your company, your school, your library, or a friend's attic, you probably have to pay for access by using one of the Internet access providers. More about them in Chapter 4.

It's politically, socially, and religiously correct

Another great thing about the Internet is that it is what one might call "socially unstratified." That is, one computer is no better than any other, and no person is any better than any other. Who you are on the Internet depends solely on how you present yourself through your keyboard. If what you say makes you sound like an intelligent, interesting person, that's who you are. It doesn't matter how old you are or what you look like or whether you're a student, a business executive, or a construction worker. Physical disabilities don't matter — you can correspond with people who are blind or deaf. If they don't feel like telling you, you'll never know. People become famous in the Net community, some favourably and some unfavourably, but they get that way through their own efforts.

The Net advantage

Maybe it's obvious to you that Internet technology is changing so quickly that you barely had time to crack the spine of the first edition of *The Internet For Canadians For Dummies* Starter Kit — and here you are holding the second edition. "Could it possibly be all that different?" you ask yourself. Well, the answer is a resounding "yes." It's *that* different again this year. This year, the Internet is totally mainstream, and you're falling farther behind the curve faster if you haven't yet gotten started. Increasingly, news gets out on the Internet before it's available in other media, and the cyber-deprived are losing ground.

The Internet can be used for many things — too many to count or even imagine. However, at the most basic level, the Net can be used to find information, get digital files, communicate with people, and buy and sell things. For example, you can do research or educate yourself on a topic of interest. You can find people, products, or services. You can get music from the Net for playback on your computer. You can make friends on the Net. Anything you find in a store or at an auction can probably be bought through the Net. As you read chapter-to-chapter, you'll see many more examples of how the Net can be used. You can also take a summary approach and turn to Chapter 21 for 10 ways Canadians really love to use the Net.

Electronic Commerce

We hear many new buzzwords and phrases aimed at confounding the innocent and filling the pockets of would-be consultants. We hear about "digital commerce," "electronic commerce," "digicash," "virtual cheques," and "smart cards." If you care, entire books are being written about these subjects. The one topic in this area that you need to know about is buying stuff over the Net. (If you plan to set up your own business and sell products or services over the Net, you need more info than we have pages in this book to cover it.) Chapter 9 introduces you to it.

The earth-shattering, startling new idea of how to buy things over the Net is hidden between the lines of the following phrase: "Enter your credit card number." We're not saying that you shouldn't exercise caution, but our experience of buying over the Net in the past couple of years indicates that you have no great cause for alarm. What have we bought? Books, CDs, clothing, software, groceries, videotapes, encyclopedia subscriptions, and matchmaking subscriptions. Here's what you need to know.

Every continent?

Some skeptics, after reading the claim that the Internet spans every continent, may point out that Antarctica is a continent, even though its population consists largely of penguins, who (as far as we know) are not interested in computer networks. Does the Internet go there? It sure does. A few machines at the Scott Base on McMurdo Sound in Antarctica are on the Net, connected by radio link to New Zealand. The base at the South Pole is supposed to have a link to the United States, but it doesn't publish its electronic address.

Security in general

Some folks seem particularly wary of sending their credit card numbers over the Net. On the other hand, every day, people hand their actual physical cards with their handwritten signatures to gas station attendants, to servers at restaurants, and to clerks at all sorts of stores. Do you know what they do with the card before they give it back to you? Do you worry about it? We don't. We do know someone who used to run a restaurant and later ran an online store, who assures us that he had far more credit card trouble at the restaurant.

If you use a credit card, remember that the credit card companies are even more concerned than you are about the idea of any kind of credit card fraud, on or off the Net. All cards have a limit on the amount of fraudulent use for which you're liable; if you're a Canadian resident, the limit is $100 or less.

If possible, use credit cards rather than cheques when ordering over the Net. If you have a dispute with the vendor, you can ask your credit card company to reverse the charge or to refuse further charges from that company.

The point is, if you're comfortable using a credit card for other uses, you don't have to get really scared about using it over the Net just because it's new. Chapter 9 talks about shopping on the Net, with or without a credit card, and outlines the precautions you can take.

Security in specific

To avoid the possibility of bad guys or gals electronically listening to the bits of your private information whirring across the Net, stripping them off, and redirecting them to purchase their dream vacations, schemes have been invented to encode info sent over the Net; even if the villains intercept the info, it doesn't do them any good. The information gets all mixed up and hidden in such a way that only the legitimate recipient can decode it. The software that processes this information safely, hiding everything from possible perverse perusal, is known as *SSL* (Secure Sockets Layer) or a *secure server*. Most Web browsers (you can read more about them in Chapter 6) have SSL built right in. If you're the least bit antsy about sending your card number over the Net, stick to secure servers.

Software that takes your credit card number (or any other information) over the Net without encoding it is known as *insecure*. Insecure services are perfectly adequate for many transactions, as long as you know that the business behind the server is reliable. If you don't know the business behind the server, its reliability should be of more concern to you than the flavour of server they use.

Some Thoughts about Safety and Privacy

The Internet is a funny place. Although it seems completely anonymous, it's not. People used to have Internet usernames that bore some resemblance to their true identity — their name or initials or some combination, in conjunction with their university or corporation, gave a fairly traceable route to an actual person. Today, with the phenomenon of screen names and multiple e-mail addresses, revealing your identity is definitely optional.

Depending on who you are and what you want to do on the Net, you may, in fact, want different names and different accounts. Here are some legitimate reasons for doing so:

- ✔ You're a professional — a physician, for example — and you want to participate in a mailing list or newsgroup without being asked for your professional opinion.

- ✔ You want help with an area of concern that you feel is private, and would not want your problem known to people close to you; if your name were associated with it, they might find out.

- ✔ You do business on the Net, and you socialize on the Net. You may want to keep those activities separate.

To those who might consider abusing the anonymous nature of the Net: Most Net activities can be traced. If you start to abuse the Net, you'll find you're not so anonymous.

Safety first

The anonymous, faceless nature of the Internet has its downside, too.

Do not use your full name or ever provide your name, address, and phone number over the Net to someone you don't know. Never believe anyone who says that he is from "AOL Canada or SympaticoLycos tech support" or some such authority and asks you for your password — especially if they called you! Legitimate entities rarely ask you for your password. Be especially careful about disclosing information about kids. Don't fill out profiles in chat rooms that ask for a kid's name, hometown, school, age, address, or phone number, since they are invariably used for "targeted marketing" (a.k.a. junk mail).

Though relatively rare, horrible things have happened to a few people who have taken their Internet encounters into real life. On the other hand, many wonderful things have happened, too. We've met some of our best friends over the Net. And some people have even met and gotten married — no kidding! We just want to encourage you to use common sense when you set up a meeting with a Net friend. Here are a few tips:

✔ Talk to the person on the phone before you agree to meet. If you don't like the sound of the person's voice or something makes you feel nervous, don't pursue it.

✔ Depending on the context, try to check the person out a little. If you've met in a newsgroup or chat room, ask someone else whether they know this person. (Women, be sure to ask another woman before meeting a man.)

✔ Meet in a well-lit public place. Don't be shy to take a friend or two with you.

✔ If you're a kid, never, ever meet someone from the Net without your parents' explicit consent. If a first meeting is arranged, always take a parent with you.

The Net is a wonderful place, and meeting new people and making new friends is one of the big attractions. Just exercise a little caution.

Protect your privacy

Here in Canada, we've grown up with certain attitudes about freedom and privacy, many of which we take for granted. We tend to feel that who we are, where we go, and what we do is our own business, as long as we don't bother anyone else. Well, it seems that a whole bunch of people are extremely interested in who we are, where we go (on the Net, at least), and, most especially, what we buy. Here are a few hints to control how much or how little info you give them.

Please pass the cookies

To enhance your online experience, the makers of Web browsers such as Netscape and Internet Explorer have invented a type of special message that lets a Web site recognize you when you revisit that site. They thoughtfully store this info, called a *cookie,* on your machine, to make your next visit to the same site smoother.

Usually this info can, in fact, make your next transaction more efficient. When you're using an airline-reservation site, for example, the site uses cookies to keep the flights you're reserving separate from the ones other users may be reserving at the same time.

On the other hand, suppose that you use your credit card to purchase something on a Web site and then the site uses a cookie to remember your credit card number. Suppose that you provide this information from a computer at work, and the next person to visit that site uses the same computer. That person could, possibly, make purchases on your credit card. *Oops.*

It may be true that cookies can make your life more convenient. You have to be the judge. Every Web server can offer you cookies. You need to know that this kind of software exists so that if you're concerned about your privacy, you can take steps to protect it.

Cookie files usually have the name *cookie* associated with them — cookies.txt on Windows and MagicCookie on a Mac, for example. You can delete your cookie files — your browser will create a new, empty one. Modern browsers tell you about cookies and ask you whether to accept them as servers offer them to you. When Carol checked her Macintosh, she found two cookie files — one from Netscape and one from Internet Explorer. If she hadn't been looking for them, she never would have known that they were there.

Contrary to rumour, cookie files cannot get other information from your hard disk, give you a bad haircut, or otherwise mess up your life. They collect only information that the browser tells them about.

In addition to the cookie file, Internet Explorer keeps a history file of where you've been on the Web. (Look in your Windows folder for a subfolder called History.) If anyone other than you uses your home or work computer, you may want to delete its contents after your use, unless you don't care who sees it. North American courts have ruled, by the way, that companies own their computers and their contents. You have no "right to privacy" at work, even though most of us find the idea creepy. Companies can eavesdrop on phone calls, read your e-mail (going and coming), and read anything on your computer, including a history file detailing where you've searched. This can be problematical if you've done a little too much "unofficial" surfing.

Encryption and pretty good privacy

When you send information through the Internet, it gets relayed from machine to machine, and along the way, if someone really cares, she may be able to take a look at what comes across the wire. Whether you're sending your credit card number or sending e-mail love letters, you may feel more comfortable if the absolute secure nature of the transmission is guaranteed.

You can guarantee security by using encryption. *Encryption* is high-tech-ese for encoding — just like with a secret decoder ring. You know — codes, spies, secret messages. Software exists that helps you package up your message and send it in such a way that nobody except the intended recipient can read it. Encryption is the virtual envelope that defies prying eyes. In practice, we rarely encrypt e-mail, though we're happy to know that the option exists. One reason we don't encrypt it is that, at this point, it's too darn cumbersome. Some e-mail software comes with encryption built in, notably Microsoft Outlook Express, so many more people will end up using it by default. Also check out PGP, which stands for *pretty good privacy*, the most widely used encryption scheme on the Net. Because it's complicated enough to require pages of explanation, we don't have room in this book to go into the details; check out *E-mail For Dummies,* 2nd Edition and *Internet Secrets,* 2nd Edition, which provide you with the blow-by-blow details. New, easier-to-use versions of PGP come out every month or two, so a PGP add-in is probably available for your favorite e-mail program.

Where did the Internet come from?

The ancestor of the Internet was the ARPANET, a project funded by the United States Department of Defense (DOD) in 1969, both as an experiment in reliable networking and to link DOD and military research contractors, including the large number of universities doing military-funded research. (ARPA stands for Advanced Research Projects Administration, the branch of the DOD in charge of handing out grant money. For enhanced confusion, the agency is now known as DARPA — the added *D* is for Defense, in case anyone had doubts about where the money was coming from.) Although the ARPANET started out small, connecting four computers with one another, it quickly grew to span the continent.

In the early 1980s, the ARPANET grew into the early Internet, a group of interlinked networks connecting many educational and research sites funded by the United States National Science Foundation (NSF), along with the original military ones. By 1990, it was clear that the Internet was here to stay, and DARPA and the NSF bowed out in favour of the commercially run networks that comprise today's Internet. Some of the networks are run by familiar companies like Rogers Communications, Worldcom/MCI, IBM, and Britain's Cable and Wireless; others belong to specialist companies like PSI and Metronet Networks. No matter which one you're attached to, they all interconnect, so it's all one giant Internet.

For yet more Internet history and gossip, visit our Web site at net.gurus.com/history.

Chapter 2

So Much to Do on the Net, So Little Time

*W*e think that one reason some Canadians haven't found themselves on the Internet until now is that they haven't had good enough cause. They might not be familiar with some of the bazillion ways that the Internet can be of use to them. This chapter gives you some big hints. So keep reading. You may actually want to try some of this stuff.

At Home with the Internet

The Internet is changing how we live our lives in countless ways. If you're looking for a new apartment or house, for example, the Internet can really help you out. From near or far, you can look at real estate listings, apply for a mortgage, and get step-by-step driving instructions so you don't get lost trying to find the property. You can check the weather, search for a new job, and locate businesses you're interested in.

Once you get to your new home on the range, you can even decorate it with furnishings you can find right on the Internet. You can find folks to paint, repair, and even deliver cords of wood.

The Internet can help with your home finances, too. You can get spiffy accounting software right on the Web — without having to install it on your own machine. You can download tax forms from the Canada Customs and Revenue Agency without having to spend hours on the phone or driving to an office.

You can shop for everything from food to footwear, and have stuff delivered right to your doorstep. You can find recipes, news, and helpful hints on any subject under the sun (or beyond it, for that matter). Log on to your local library to see what books are available.

At Work with the Internet

This year just might be the year you have to learn about the Internet 'cause, like it or not, it's part of your job. More and more offices are using the Internet and Internet-associated stuff to do everyday office tasks. E-mail has replaced memos; the human resources manual is online; you file your expense reports online; you even book travel, order supplies, send flowers, and gossip — you guessed it — all online. In the name of efficiency, you talk to your colleagues over an intranet, you talk to your customers over an extranet, and you do business at a business-to-business exchange or marketplace. Say what?

Now that lots of people have warmed up to the idea that the Internet is pretty cool, clever individuals are adapting all the cool features and putting them to work inside companies, outside companies, and even between companies. You may get the sense that even though the jargon keeps changing, everybody's really talking about the same thing. You would be right. Here are some formal definitions so that you can't be bamboozled by jargon-slinging cybersnobs, and so you can sling some jargon yourself, if the occasion arises.

Intranets and what they're good for

Intranet? Are you sure that that's spelled right? Sure is. Now that everyone knows about the Internet, the marketroids have invented intranet, which is just the same except different. The idea is simple: Take all that swell technology that's been developed for the Internet during the past 20 years and use it directly inside your company on the company's own network.

An *intranet* is, specifically, a bunch of services, such as Web pages, that are accessible only within an organization. The World Wide Web works over the Internet with tens of thousands of Web servers (computers that store Web pages) serving up Web pages to the public. An intranet works over an organization's internal network, with Web servers serving up Web pages to folks within the organization. An intranet is sort of a private World Wide Web — an Organization Wide Web. (OWW! — another acronym!)

What's the big deal?

In one sense, intranets aren't very interesting, because anything you can do on an intranet, people have probably been doing on the Internet for years. Departments in your organization create Web pages that other people in the organization can see. So what?

In fact, intranets can be an extremely big deal. In many, if not most, companies, a mountain of important information about the business is locked up in big old databases on big old mainframes or minicomputers. The information would be of great use to people all over the company, if only they could get at it. Another mountain of stuff is stuck in spreadsheets and word-processing files on people's computers. Intranets offer a new way to make that locked-up information available to everyone in the company.

Once people within a company have a basic set of Web browsers (which we discuss in Chapters 6 and 7) and other Internet-style software on an intranet, it's surprisingly easy to write software glue, often known as *middleware* (as described in the upcoming sidebar, "You, too, can be an intranet consultant!"). Middleware lets people get at the formerly locked-up information. Lots of people can make information available in weeks or months on an intranet that they would have had to spend months or years providing by using older software tools. There are also nifty little projects called "skunkworks": small but useful intranets that have been created quickly and with little or no budget by using a few spare PCs.

After an organization has an intranet — its own Web server and some Web pages — anyone in the organization can see the Web pages by using a browser. Product information, human resources information, and other tidbits are suddenly easy to find, read, and print by using the intranet.

Using intranets

What your organization can do on an intranet is limited only by the imaginations of the people in the organization. (We realize that this limitation is more severe in some organizations than in others, but we're optimists.) Here are some examples:

- Nearly all the paper memoranda circulated around a company can be sent more effectively as e-mail messages or as Web pages. This method saves paper and makes the information easier to file and find, and it keeps everyone up-to-date.

- Those big, dusty company manuals moldering on the shelf, or perhaps holding up one corner of your rickety desk, work much better as Web pages. They're easier to search through to find the page you want. Also, the authors can update them as often as necessary so that everyone instantly has access to the most current version.

✔ Catalogues, parts lists, and the like are relatively easy to put on the Web by using database publishing, a technique that automatically creates Web pages that contain the information from the legacy system in which the information is stored.

✔ If several people are working on a project, putting the project information on the Web lets each person look at and update the status of parts of the project, with everyone seeing up-to-date information. That's how the four authors and the editors of this book, who live in different cities, tracked our progress in updating the book and kept all of us moving in roughly the same direction — using a little Web application one of the authors whipped up in an afternoon.

✔ If your company has a flair for multimedia, now you can have animation, video, and sound right on your desktop. Slightly less dramatic but perhaps more useful are new integrated intranet products that let you put "live" links to Web pages in your e-mail messages. Now you can send around a memo that refers to different types of material with a link directly to that material. Your readers just have to click the link to see the information you're referencing.

✔ Filing time cards and expense reports is becoming a pretty routine intranet task. Keeping forms online certainly cuts down on the paper shuffle and allows you to change the forms when necessary without having to toss the obsolete ones into the recycling bin.

All in all, this technology flows both ways. As Internet technology, particularly e-mail and Web technology, combines with traditional databases, the ways that companies manage information are bound to change. Paper memoranda will become about as common as the IBM Selectric, and large, metal file cabinets won't fill to busting the way they used to.

Extra, extra net, net net

Anything worth doing is worth doing in any number of ways. We start with the Internet; we bring it into the company — we get an intranet; we take the intranet out of the company, and — *voilà* — we get an *extranet*. Not that this net is extra, mind you: we mean extra as in "outside," as in *extra*terrestrial.

Here's the idea: Now that people are successfully using Internet technology (browsing, creating Web pages, and using e-mail, for example) *inside* companies, the logical extension is to expand these internal networks to include a company's customers, suppliers, and business partners. After intranets expanded outside the boundaries of one organization to include other entities, someone ingenious created a brand-new buzzword: *extranet*. As is the case with intranets, it's all the same technology — it's just used in a different way.

You, too, can be an intranet consultant!

A rule of thumb in the computing industry says that a consultant is anyone more than 120 kilometres from home. Although we can't offer transportation, here are some handy buzzwords you will want to use if you want to sound like an intranet expert. (See if you can use all of them in one sentence.)

✔ **Client/server:** A type of computer system in which one program, the client, runs on your computer so that you can work with it directly; a separate program, the server, runs on another computer and manages all the important data. A computer network connects the two. Although the Internet has always worked this way, it took the special insight of the large-scale business data-processing industry to realize that you could make a great deal of money in the process.

✔ **Database publishing (DP):** The process of taking a company's information that used to be locked away in databases where only the DP types and a few managers could see it, and making it available to a large number of people inside and even outside the company. DP makes it much easier to get your job done — but makes managers nervous ("If they know everything I know, how can I keep my job?").

✔ **Drill down:** To throw away all the confusing but important details and reduce something to one or two simple ideas that a customer can understand; or conversely, to look at the underlying data from which a simple idea or number came. Yes, these are practically opposite definitions, which gives you a lot of room to improvise.

✔ **Legacy:** Referring to something that's obsolete but still essential. "I'm looking for a pair of recapped whitewalls for my legacy vehicle here." It's usually called a *legacy system*, a computer system that has been nursed along for the past 25 years, and everyone who remembers how it was originally put together has retired.

✔ **Middleware:** Software that connects one piece of software to another piece of software that nobody ever dreamed it would work with, but now does. If you saw the movie *Apollo 13*, remember the scene in which the air scrubbers in the command module are exhausted? The astronauts have to use spares from the lunar module, only the spares are a completely different shape, so the astronauts concoct something from duct tape and wire and who-knows-what to make it fit. (If you didn't see the movie, you're now well and truly lost.) Well, the concoction they came up with was "middleware."

✔ **Platform:** The underlying computer hardware or software on which a system runs ("We're targeting a Netscape platform on a Windows 98 Pentium platform.")

✔ **Solution:** A software package, or a bundle of hardware and software, that is designed to streamline a company's business process(es). For example, an inventory control software solution could help trigger the automatic purchase of raw materials in a manufacturing company when certain production levels are reached.

Really, you care

Once again, you may be asking yourself, "What does this stuff have to do with me?" Well, Internet technology is changing the way our world operates. For example, you may notice that you're talking to your favorite companies over the Net instead of picking up the phone. Smart companies are realizing that they can cut costs in the areas of customer service, marketing, and sales by using Internet technology. Dell Computer Corporation was a pioneer in this "business-to-business" side of the Internet, and is one example of the way the Internet is changing how companies do business.

Some of what you see from the outside will seem just like the Internet to you. The glue that's connecting the Internet site you see to the company or companies that are handling your transactions, however, is really an extranet — the linking of internal systems with the outside.

Another important aspect of extranets is that they can be designed with security in mind and allow only people with legitimate access to use them.

Let us count the ways

Here are some of the ways folks are using extranets. Your imagination can no doubt pick up where we leave off:

- ✔ Newsletters, press releases, product announcements, and any other information that a company would send out by snail-mail (the kind that uses paper and a postage stamp) or fax can be e-mailed and put on a Web site.

- ✔ Catalogues and brochures can be placed on the Web to radically reduce printing costs and enable materials to be easily updated.

- ✔ Customers can place and track orders.

- ✔ Answers to frequently asked questions can be posted on a Web site to eliminate unnecessary and time-consuming phone calls.

A virtual flea market

Another way industries — and individual businesses within them — are trying to chart virtual territory is to create centres of trade activity on the Internet. These *business-to-business exchanges* or marketplaces (you call them "B2B," if you're in the know) are electronic exchanges on the Net where businesses can go to buy and sell products and services at the best price and quality. The corporate owners of these exchanges — such as VerticalNet or FreeMarkets — want to keep you within the confines of their site to better serve you — based on the theory that you'll spend all your money in one place. Not surprisingly, they get a commission.

We have to admit that some of the ways businesses are coming together online are pretty cool, and you might well find that a lot of the things you used to do by phone and fax are simpler and easier to do on the Net. It seems to us that it's just a matter of time before this way of conducting business becomes the norm — so you might as well get with the tour now.

At School with the Internet

The Internet is finding its way into educational institutions of all levels, though we're not entirely convinced of its benefit to the youngest of our citizens. (We talk about this more emphatically in Chapter 3.) Aside from the obvious research opportunity on the Net, we see the Internet being used to facilitate parent–teacher communication and teacher–student communication. We know of a university where teachers can look up pictures and profiles of all their students (and vice versa), and coursework is routinely distributed online. In some cases, the Net *is* the university or community college. More about this in Chapter 3.

At Play with the Internet

If you ask some people, the Internet is one big cyber-playground. And the ways in which we can play on the Net are increasing exponentially. You can meet people and just hang out; you can play all kinds of interactive games; you can discuss your favorite sport, hobby, or medical malady (well, this is some people's idea of recreation). You can enter virtual realities and get three-dimensional. You can speak different languages (if you already speak different languages) and meet people from all over the globe. Or you can just surf. Throughout this book, we'll introduce you to Web sites with this very thing in mind!

Chapter 3

The Net, Your Kids, and You

. . . .

In This Chapter

▶ The Internet and family life: How the Net can benefit you

▶ Some concerns about the Internet

▶ Parental guidelines for using the Internet

▶ Mailing lists and Web sites for kids

▶ Help for parents whose kids have problems

▶ The Internet in schools

. . . .

*W*ith more than a million Canadian kids already online, we think that a discussion of families online is critical. Obviously, if this isn't your concern, just skip this chapter and go to the next.

Stop Making Sense

Most parents are trying to make sense of the Internet and what it means for them and their families. Although no one has the ultimate answer, we can talk about some of the major issues being raised, the benefits we see, and the problems. The Net has dramatic implications in the education, entertainment, and socialization of our children. The more we know and the more actively involved we are, the better choices we can make.

What's in it for us?

We're just beginning to discover the myriad ways that the Internet can be exciting in the context of family life. Here are some of the ways we think it enhances our lives:

✔ It provides information about every topic imaginable.

✔ It provides personal contact with new people and cultures.

> ✔ It helps develop and improve reading, writing, research, and language skills.
>
> ✔ It provides support for families with special needs.
>
> ✔ It is an exciting new outlet for artistic expression.

Not everything new is wonderful, and not everything wonderful is new. In talking about children, we have to make distinctions. Are they preschoolers, preteens, or university kids? Because what makes sense for one group in this case usually doesn't map to another, the remainder of this section considers how the Internet works for different age groups.

The Internet for young children and preteens

We have to say up front that we are strong advocates of allowing children to be children, and we believe that children are better teachers than computers are. None of our kids watch commercial TV. Now that you know our parental predisposition, maybe you can guess what we're going to say next: We are not in favour of sticking a young child in front of a screen. How young is young? We believe that younger than age 7 is young. Many Canadian educators believe that unstructured computer time for kids aged 12 or younger is inappropriate. We recommend that children get as much human attention as possible, and we believe that computers are not meant to be babysitters. At a young age, a child benefits far more from playing with trees, balls, sand, crayons, paint, mud, monkey bars, and bicycles — not to mention other kids and adults.

Even if you do want to let your small kids use the Internet, frankly, there's not much out there for the pre-reading set anyway.

The Internet for JK–12

JK–12 is the label given to all the education that happens in Canada between preschool (nursery school or daycare) and university or community college. It's a broad category. We use it here because many mailing lists and newsgroups use the JK–12 designation, and it seems to be common ground for many Canadians. We think that Internet access is more appropriate for somewhat older children (grade 5 and older), but your mileage may vary.

Even so, we think you should limit the amount of time your kids spend online. We who (despite our good looks) have been playing with computers for the better (and worse) part of 30 years want to tell you that what happens to kids that are allowed to stay glued to their computers for unlimited chunks of time is not good. Kids need to be able to communicate with other human beings. It's one of those ironies that kids who have difficulty in the communication area often prefer to interact with a computer screen rather than another human. This definitely doesn't help them to develop their social skills. Instead, it compounds the problem. Limit the time your kids spend on the computer (online or off). Schedule time for baths or showers, and ensure they have meals and conversations on a regular basis with real live people.

You should also make sure your kids know the safety rules for using the Net:

- ✔ Your kids should never reveal exactly who they are. They should use only their first name, and never provide their address, phone number, or the name of their school. They should never tell anyone their password.

- ✔ Your kids should never agree to talk to someone on the phone or meet someone in person without checking it out with you.

- ✔ Your kids should never assume that people are telling the truth. That "kid" who apparently shares their interests and hobbies might actually be someone completely different, with rather questionable interests and hobbies.

- ✔ Your kids should always let you know if someone is scaring them or making them uncomfortable (especially if the person tells them *not* to let you know).

All that said, the Internet is an incredible way to expand the walls of a school, and the learning process itself. The Net can connect kids to other schools and to libraries, research resources, museums, and other people. They can visit the Louvre; practice their French or Spanish or Cantonese or Russian or Japanese (using online chat); hear new music; and make new friends.

School projects such as the Global Schoolhouse connect Canadian kids to other kids around the world by working collaboratively on all types of projects. The first annual global learning project drew more than 10,000 students from 360 schools in 30 different countries. Since then, annual cyberfairs have brought together more than 500,000 students from hundreds of schools in at least 37 countries!

You can send an e-mail message to the Global Schoolhouse at helper@gsn.org or check out the foundation's Web site at www.gsn.org. (We explain these funny-looking locations in Chapter 6, so you can come back here later and follow up on them.) From the Global Schoolhouse Web site, you can subscribe to lots of mailing lists. If you don't have Web access, you can subscribe to the Global Watch mailing list (Chapter 13 has all the details) by sending an e-mail message to lists@gsn.org that contains this single line in the body of the text: subscribe global-watch.

University, community college, and the Net

Although the Internet has had a home in universities for a long time, what's happening with the World Wide Web is new for everyone. Much of the inspiration and perspiration of the volunteers who are making information available to everyone is coming from universities, both students and faculty, who see the incredible potential for learning.

Many campuses provide free or low-cost access to the Internet for their students and staff. Campuses that enable you to register early sometimes give you that access when you register, even months in advance. If you're going to go anyway, you can get a jump on your Internet education before you even get to campus.

The Internet (more specifically, e-mail) is a great way for parents and kids away at university or community college to stay in touch. It's much cheaper than phoning and easier than coordinating schedules. Forwarding mail to other family members allows for broader communication. We noticed another surprising benefit: In our experience, families tend to fight less when they're communicating by e-mail. Somehow, when folks have time to think about what they're going to say before they say it, it comes out better.

When the Net is university

It's no exaggeration to say that many people are learning more on the Net than they ever did in school. And while the Net might require a bit more personal motivation on the part of the learner, since you're not learning under a tight, pre-set schedule, this virtual classroom has plenty of advantages. The Net

Checking out universities and community colleges on the Net

Most Canadian universities and community colleges have Web sites. You can locate the Web sites of many of them from the Yahoo! Canada home page at www.yahoo.ca. Using Yahoo! Canada's search tool, simply type in the name of the Canadian university or college that interests you. The search results will lead you to the respective Web site, containing program information, online application forms, and other essential information. Some schools provide snazzy, PC-based multimedia campus tours that you can take in the comfort of your home.

After you're a little more adept at using the Net, you can research classes and professors to get a better idea of what appeals to you.

provides equal opportunity beyond the imagination of those locked in physical settings. It's open to people of any colour, height, belief, and description. People previously shut out of educational opportunities by physical handicap, economic need, conflicting work schedules, or geography find the Net an empowering, life-altering experience.

Beyond the informal education that's already available, organizations are actively working to establish formal online colleges and universities. The Globewide Network Academy (at `www.gnacademy.org`) may have been the first completely virtual incorporated educational institution. It serves as a clearinghouse for online courses available throughout the world.

Finding a job through the Net

The Net is a very useful tool if you're looking for a job. It's especially good for students because it provides a powerful, economical way to conduct a real job search. You can publish your résumé online for prospective employers, and browse a list of job postings on the Net. You may want to pay an online visit to CareerMosaic Canada (`www.canada.careermosaic.com`), an impressive compilation of job-related information that enables you to research companies to find ones you may want to work for. Students can check out its CampusConnection feature, which highlights job opportunities geared to Canadian students.

Companies have found that posting their jobs on the Net is an effective, economical way to recruit talented people. Check out the home pages of companies that interest you, and look for their open positions. Many Canadian community colleges and universities have career office home pages, many of which are grouped together for you on the Web. Ask a Web search engine such as AltaVista (which we visit in Chapter 8) to look for "career office home pages," to get community college and university listings grouped by geography.

Of Paramount Concern

High on the list of parents' concerns about the Internet is the question of children's access to inappropriate material, including businesses trying to market and sell directly to children. This concern is a legitimate one: As time has gone by, both the good stuff and the grody stuff on the Net have increased dramatically. We have no simple answers. One thing is crystal clear to us, though: parents *have* to be involved. And considering the direction of education, *kids will be involved* with the Internet, as schools hook up at a rapid clip.

Hey, Mom, what's on?

Parents who take the time to learn about access issues may find that, on one hand, the threat is not as great as some would have you believe, while some of the proposed solutions create severe problems of their own. Parents who have thought about the issues on a larger scale are extremely concerned that reactionary sentiment and hyperbole pose a real threat to our freedom of expression and that those reactions are ultimately a great danger to our children. On the other hand, a great deal of garbage lurks online. Parental involvement is absolutely essential; we talk about family Internet use strategy a little later in this chapter. If you're interested in thrashing out these issues, you can subscribe to the CACI (Children Accessing Controversial Information) mailing list by sending an e-mail message to majordomo@cygnus.com with the words subscribe caci in the body of the message. (We talk about sending e-mail in Chapter 11.)

Sell, sell, sell!

Another problem that has surfaced that *should* be of concern to parents but doesn't get much press is the targeting of children by marketing organizations. Children of middle- and upper-income families are considered the most lucrative target market, and businesses view the Net as another way to capture this audience.

Targeting children isn't new. If you have ever walked into Toys R Us, you've seen the unmistakable link between television shows (or movies) and toys. And you probably weren't surprised to have witnessed the huge *Star Wars* toy promotion frenzy following the release of *The Phantom Menace*.

You should know that astute marketing types have already designed kid-friendly, fascinating, captivating software to help them better market to your kids. Delightful, familiar cartoon characters deftly elicit strategic marketing information directly from the keyboard in your home. As we mentioned before, you should be aware of this situation and instruct your children to never give out any personal information over the Net.

Who's there?

We strongly encourage all family members using the Net for personal reasons (distinct from businesspeople using the Net for business purposes) not to use their full or real names and never to disclose names, addresses, phone numbers, Social Insurance Numbers, or account information — such as a password — to anyone who asks for it online or off. If you're dealing with your

Internet Service Provider's (ISP's) tech support area and are asked for your password, state that you would prefer to give out an alternative piece of validating information — such as date of membership. (An Internet Service Provider, by the way (ISP for short), is a company that has arranged for ongoing Internet access with telecommunications carriers, and in turn provides its customers with Internet access through its own network backbone or infrastructure. Various types of ISPs are discussed more fully in Chapter 4.) But if you absolutely feel compelled to give out your password in such a case, ask for the person's name and call her right back. This advice applies whenever you receive information requests from people claiming to be in positions of authority, such as the instant messages AOL Canada users have received from people claiming that they're from AOL Canada tech support and need your password information. They're not — and they don't.

People with real authority never ask those types of questions.

More than ever, children need to develop critical thinking skills. They have to learn how to evaluate what they read and see — especially on the Web.

Regrettably, we have to report that we have seen a great deal of trashy e-mail *(spam)* lately. This situation is likely to get worse until someone figures out an effective way to deal with unsolicited e-mail. Again, you have to be involved and teach your children what to do. Find out more about e-mail and dreaded spam in Chapters 11 and 12.

Parental Guidance Required

Parents, educators, and free-speech advocates alike agree that there's no substitute for parental guidance when it comes to the subject of Internet access. Just as you, as parents, want your children to read good books and see quality films, you also want them to find the good stuff on the Net. If you take the time to find out these things with your children, you have the opportunity to share the experience and to impart critical values and a sense of discrimination that your children need in all areas of their lives.

The good stuff on the Net vastly outweighs the bad. Software aids are being developed almost daily to help parents and educators tap the invaluable resources of the Net without opening Pandora's box. Remember that every child is different and that what may be appropriate for your children may not be appropriate for someone else's. You have to decide what's right for you.

Establish rules for your family's use of the Net. Outline areas that are off-limits and within the limits; restrict the time that can be spent online; and be explicit about the types of information kids can give out over the Net.

Using the Internet, like watching television, is a solitary experience, so it takes extra effort from you to establish limits and at the same time give your child the freedom he needs to explore the cyberworld. Some families prefer to keep their computers in a family space as opposed to in kids' bedrooms. Wherever they are, check often; *never let the computer screen be your babysitter.*

Kids need explicit rules about talking with and meeting people they meet on the Net. As we mentioned before, never let your kids meet a cyberfriend in person by themselves. Keep an eye on your phone bill for charges for unusual calls.

Setting limits

Now that most Canadian Internet Service Providers (ISPs) charge a flat rate for service, you can't rely on economic incentives alone to curb your Internet use. You don't let your children watch unlimited television, right? By the same token, you don't want to let them have unlimited computer access either. Don't buy in to the hype that just because it's on a computer, it's educational. We're reminded of the cartoon featuring wishful parents reading the newspaper's Help Wanted section and finding that Nintendo players are making $70,000. Everyone knows kids whose lives have become sedentary, and who seem to be lost if they're not in front of a screen. Don't let your kid be one of them.

Rating the ratings

Several schemes have been proposed for rating Internet content. Who will rate the material, and whose ratings will you trust? Is the author of a Web page or other online material the best person to assign the ratings? Probably not. Internet software designers have added provisions for third-party ratings so that you can choose or exclude material based on the ratings — although the guidelines the raters use may not be the ones you would choose.

In an attempt to address the concern of controlling access while not caving in to censorship, the World Wide Web Consortium (W3C) has designed a standard for marking Web content so that third parties can rate the material. You can read all about the standard, called PICS (Platform for Internet Content Selection), at this Web address:

```
www.wellesley.edu/CS/JimMillerTalk/9601PICS/slide1.htm
```

Or see the W3C Web page about PICS, at

```
www.w3.org/PICS
```

Other software under development eventually will let parents limit access using their own criteria. A parent who feels strongly about, say, warthogs and asparagus, will be able to block all material about those subjects. More realistically, they'll be able to block heavy fictionalized violence, yet permit access to medical information about sexually transmitted diseases.

Consumer's choice

Because parents are paying for online services, services that want to remain competitive are vying for parental dollars by providing features to help families control Internet access. AOL Canada, for example, enables you to block access to chat rooms that may not be appropriate for children and to restrict access to discussion groups and newsgroups based on keywords you choose. Parental blocking is available at no extra cost. WebTV enables the master account holder to restrict the material that sub-account holders can view.

Software sentries

More and more products are appearing on the market to help parents restrict access or monitor usage through some sort of activity report. If you choose to use one of these systems, remember that they're not a substitute for your direct involvement in your child's Internet experience; they all filter based on keywords and fixed lists of systems that the programs' authors believe to contain objectionable material. None of them tells you exactly what they block, and furthermore your idea of what's appropriate and inappropriate may well not be the same as theirs. Many software sentries seem to have political agendas, blocking sites whose political opinions don't conform to those of the program's authors. In the final analysis, the best approach is to *prevent* undesirable surfing — not to detect it after the fact.

You can try before you buy by downloading evaluation copies of software-blocking packages. (You see how to do that when you find out how to navigate the Web in Chapters 6 and 7.) We recommend that you go to www. smartparent.com, where they keep a list of current links to dozens and dozens of filtering software sites. They also list Internet Service Providers (you'll be hearing more about those in the next chapter) who are actively trying to make the Net safe for kids. And what's more, SmartParent.com also lists kid-friendly sites.

Internet Resources for Kids

As you may have guessed, the Internet is replete with resources for kids — and parents, by the way. As we have learned from writing this book, however, nothing is as ephemeral as a Net address. To help keep information as accurate as possible, we're putting our lists of resources on our Web site, both to keep them up-to-date and because they're too long to list here completely. From there, you can get right to the source. We do our best to keep the sources current.

Visit net.gurus.com/kids, which puts you one click away from the pages described in this section.

Mailing lists for parents and kids

Chapter 13 tells you how to subscribe to mailing lists. Lots of mailing lists for and about kids are listed on our Web page.

Web sites for kids

Okay, we admit it. Web sites can be the coolest thing since sliced bread. To get to them, though, you have to know how to use a browser, such as Netscape Navigator, Internet Explorer, or Lynx. We tell you how in Part III of this book, Web Mania. (But watch out — when your 10-year-old finds a Web site that lists 1,000 knock-knock jokes, you'll be saying, "Who's there?" for weeks on end!)

Help for parents of kids with problems

One of the most heartening experiences through the Net is the help that total strangers freely offer one another. The bonds that form between people sharing their experiences, struggles, strengths, and hopes redefine what it means to reach out and touch someone. We encourage everyone who has a concern to look for people who share that concern. Our experience of partici-pating in mailing lists and newsgroups related to our own interests compels us to enthusiastically encourage you to check things out online. You can do so with complete anonymity, if you want. You can watch and learn for a long time, or you can jump into the fray and ask for help.

Remember, though, that not everyone who gives advice is an expert. You have to involve your own practitioners in your process. Many people have derived enormous help, however, from others who have gone down similar paths before them. For many of us, it has made all the difference in the world.

A mailing list or group specific to your needs almost certainly exists, and new groups are added every day. If you're using a commercial provider, such as AOL Canada or SympaticoLycos, it has special discussion forums that may interest you as well.

Notice that some lists are talk lists, which feature free-flowing discussion; some lists have focused discussions; and some lists are almost purely academic. The type of discussion is not always obvious from the name. If it looks interesting, subscribe and see what sort of discussion is going on there. It's easy enough to un-subscribe if you don't like it.

The Internet in Canadian Schools

As hundreds of schools across Canada continue to hook up to the Net, they are actively debating Internet access for their students. Find out as much as you can and get involved. The more you know, the more you can advocate for appropriate access.

Contractually speaking

Many kids are smart. Smart kids can find ways around rules, and smart kids can find ways around software systems designed to "protect" them. Many institutions rely successfully on students' signed contracts that detail explicitly what is appropriate and what is inappropriate system use. Students who violate one of these contracts lose their Internet or computer privileges.

We believe that this approach is a good one. In our experience, kids are quicker and more highly motivated, and have more time to spend breaking into and out of systems than most adults we know, and this method encourages them to do something more productive than electronic lock-picking.

Real education

Used effectively, the Internet is a terrific educational resource. Used ineffectively, it's a terrific waste of time and money. The difference is research and planning. We were chatting with our local elementary school principal who'd just spent four hours one weekend afternoon searching the Net to help her son, who teaches grade 3 in a nearby district, develop a unit on a foreign country. She found plenty of useful information. Once you get more familiar with the Web and the ways to find things online (which we cover in Chapter 8), offer to help your teachers look for material to bolster their teaching.

Part II
Internet, Here I Come

The 5th Wave
By Rich Tennant

"SINCE WE GOT IT, HE HASN'T MOVED FROM THAT SPOT FOR ELEVEN STRAIGHT DAYS. ODDLY ENOUGH THEY CALL THIS 'GETTING UP AND RUNNING' ON THE INTERNET."

In this part . . .

When you're ready to get started, *where* do you start? Probably the hardest part of using the Internet is getting connected. We help you figure out which kind of Internet service is right for you and help you get connected. We also introduce new ways to get connected.

Chapter 4

Picking Your Internet Service

. . . .

In This Chapter

▶ Choosing a computer for Net access

▶ Picking a modem

▶ Considering various types of Internet accounts

▶ Comparing the speed of Internet connections

▶ Deciding where to get an account

▶ Figuring out what kind of software you need

. . . .

"*G*reat," you say. "How do I get to the Internet?" The answer is "It depends." Well, the Internet isn't one network — it's more than 100,000 separate networks hooked together, each with its own rules and procedures — and you can get to the Net from any one of them. We have heard from many people who say that one thing they really want to see in an Internet book is step-by-step directions on how to get on. Here, we make them as step-by-step as we can.

You need four things to connect to the Internet:

1. **A computer (unless you use WebTV, which we talk about in a minute).**

2. **A modem (a piece of computer equipment that's either inside your computer or is a separate box) to hook your computer to the phone line or cable system.**

3. **An account with a commercial online service or Internet Service Provider (ISP), to give your modem somewhere to call.**

4. **Software to run on your computer.**

We look at each of these items in turn.

Do You Have a Computer?

We have always said that there's really no way around this one. In fact, it's still true. Because the Internet is a computer network, the only way to hook up to it is by using a computer. But computers are starting to appear in all sorts of disguises, and they may well already be in your home, whether you know it or not. If you have a computer at work, particularly if it's already set up to handle electronic mail, you may already have an Internet connection (see the sidebar, "Are you already on the Internet?").

Yup! I got this old beige box in the closet

Almost any personal computer made since 1980 is adequate for at least some type of connection to the Internet. But unless you have a really good friend who is a computer geek and wants to spend a lot of time at your house helping you get online, it isn't worth fooling with that old clunker — unless, of course, you're interested in the geek spending a lot of time at your house. (But that's your business.) If you can possibly afford it, we strongly encourage you to buy a new one, or at least to not use one that's more than a year old. New computers come with Internet software already installed and are configured for the latest in Web technology. If you own an older computer, you'll spend much more time and energy, and ultimately just as much money, just trying to get the thing to work the way you want it to. New computers are getting cheaper and cheaper, and you can now get a downright good one for $1,000 or less.

Yup! Just got a brand new Thunderstick 2002

Ah, you do have a computer. (Or maybe you're thinking about buying one.) Most Internet users connect to the Net by letting their computer dial in to an Internet service (this is the method that Margy uses). When you first turn your computer on, or when you run one of the Internet programs that come installed, your computer will offer to call an Internet provider and set up an account right then and there.

Don't dial (or let your computer dial) until you've read the rest of this chapter. There are some other options we think you ought to consider first.

A snazzier way to connect, not yet available everywhere, is a broadband connection. Your local cable or telephone company brings nifty equipment and connects your computer to a high-speed connection while you sit back and watch. Andrew and Carol like this approach best. We tell you why later in the chapter. Ask your cable company (Rogers, Cabletron, Shaw, or another provider) if it offers cable modem Internet access. You can also ask your phone company if it offers something called *DSL* in your area (Digital Subscriber Line). DSL services work over your existing phone line and in-house wiring to provide a very fast connection to the Internet. More on DSL later. If either provider says yes, consider getting a fast broadband connection.

No, but I can't wait to buy one

People argue at great length about the advantages and disadvantages of various types of computers. We don't do that here. (If you'll buy the beer, though, we'll be happy to argue about it after work.) It's usually safer to talk about politics or religion. The most popular computers are ones running Microsoft Windows 98 or 2000 (usually called *IBM-compatible* or just *PC*s (Personal Computers)) and Apple Macintoshes. Apple's new iMacs and iBooks are particularly easy to set up. Both Windows and Macintosh computers offer the spiffiest type of Internet connection with the nicest point-and-click programs to get pictures, sounds, and even movies from the Net.

If you have a knowledgeable friend who is willing to help you get on the Internet, consider getting the same type of computer she has. That way, if you have a problem, she might even be able to help you solve it!

No way! I even had to borrow this book!

If you don't have a computer, you still have some options.

A convenient place to find Net access might be your public library. More and more libraries are transforming themselves into local Internet access centres and have found these services to be quite popular. Call ahead to reserve time or find out which hours are less crowded.

Another possibility is a local university or community college, continuing-education centre, or high school, many of which often have short, inexpensive Introduction to the Internet courses. You may ask, "What kind of loser book tells people to go out and take a course?" A course can offer two things you can't possibly get from any book: a live demonstration of what the Internet is like and, more important, someone to talk to who knows the local Internet situation. You can certainly get on the Net *without* a class (we did, after all); if an inexpensive class is available, though, take it.

Are you already on the Internet?

If you have access to a computer or a computer terminal, you may already be "on" the Internet. Here are some ways to check.

If you have an account for an online service, such as AOL Canada or SympaticoLycos, you already have a connection to the Internet. At the least, you can send mail — and some online services provide relatively complete Internet connections.

If your company or school has an internal e-mail system or a local area network (LAN), it may also be directly or indirectly connected to the Internet. Ask a local e-mail expert.

If you're trying to avoid buying a computer and you already own a television you're fond of, think about buying WebTV (a small computer in disguise). This option is cheaper than buying a computer, because it isn't a general-purpose computer and it uses your existing TV as a monitor. Although this option has drawbacks, it may be just what you need, at least for your first date. None of us likes this particular approach, though we know people whom we respect who do. We describe how to get connected using WebTV in the next chapter.

Dem Modems

A *modem* is the thing that hooks your computer to the phone line. Because the usual way to hook up to the Internet is over the phone, you need a modem. Modems come in all sorts of shapes and sizes. Some are separate boxes, known as *external* modems, with cables that plug in to the computer and the phone line. Others are inside the computer, with just a cable for the phone. Some of the newest ones are tiny credit-card–size things you stuff into the side of your computer. (They still have a cable for the phone — some things never change.)

Matching the variety of physical sizes is an equally wide variety of internal features. The speed at which a modem operates (or the rate at which it can stuff computer data into a phone line) ranges from a low of 2,400 bits per second (*bps*, commonly but erroneously called "baud") to 56,000 bps (usually abbreviated 56K, and the bps part is dropped). Some modems can act as fax machines, and some can't. Some have even more exotic features, such as built-in answering machines.

Pretty much any modem made in the past ten years is adequate for an initial foray on the Net, and most computers sold in the past couple of years come with built-in modems. If you already have a modem, use it. If you have to buy a modem, get a 56K, since anything less won't be much cheaper. Be sure to get a cable to connect the modem to your computer, and be sure that it has connectors that *match* the computer — three different types of plugs may be on the back of a computer.

Note to laptop computer owners: If your computer has credit-card–size PC Card slots but no built-in modem, get a PC Card modem that fits in a slot so that you don't have to carry around a separate modem when you take your computer on the road. Although it costs more, it's worth it.

Providing That . . .

Unless you have wangled a free account somehow, you have to subscribe to an Internet Service Provider to get your Internet connection. You use your computer and modem to call in to the ISP's system, and it handles the rest of the details of connecting to the Internet.

You can choose from (no, how did you guess?) many different types of ISPs, with a trade-off among ease of use, ranges of features, and price:

- Online service providers
- Internet Service Providers (ISPs)
- WebTV
- High-speed providers
    - Cable Internet access
    - DSN
    - ISDN

We take you through all of these options so you can pick the one best suited to your needs. Oh, and another point: Throughout this book, we use the term *Internet Service Provider (ISP)* to refer to *all* types of Internet accounts, even though in the chapter the term also refers to a specific type of account. We do this because *Internet Service Provider* really has entered the vernacular over the past little while; people use it to describe any kind of Internet service. Whew! Now that that's explained, let's get on with describing the different types of accounts.

Big ol' commercial providers

You can choose a big, commercial online service, such as AOL Canada, SympaticoLycos, or Microsoft Network Canada (MSN Canada). Each has its own software package that you run on your computer and that connects you to the service. AOL Canada has versions of the packages for Windows, Mac, and even DOS. AOL Canada requires that you use its software, and Sympatico and MSN Canada require that you have Windows 95 or Windows 98. Some commercial providers have introduced high-speed Internet access, which is discussed later in this chapter. Here are some good things about the big commercial services:

✔ They're relatively easy to get connected to and use.

✔ They claim to have lots of helpful people you can call when you get stuck. (Our firsthand experience doesn't necessarily substantiate these claims.)

✔ They offer flashy screen- and mouse-oriented programs to help you use them (see Figure 4-1).

✔ They offer proprietary services and information not available elsewhere on the Net (although much of the material that used to be available solely via these services has now moved to public areas on the Net).

✔ Many give you a way to limit the material that your kids can access.

Figure 4-1: The AOL Canada Today page offers many online destinations.

How much does all this cost?

You can spend a great deal of money on your Internet connection. Or you can spend practically none. Here are a few small-print items to look out for.

Provider charges

Pricing schemes are all over the map. Most providers charge about $20 per month and give you either unlimited hours or a large monthly allotment of 80 to 100 hours. Often there is a cheaper $10 rate that only includes 8 or 10 hours, with time beyond the included amount charged at $2/hour or so. Most people prefer a flat rate, or at least a large enough allotment that they're unlikely to use it up. If you decide to pick one with limited free hours, keep in mind that studies have shown that the average Internet user in Canada eats up about 17 hours per month.

If you or your kids become regular online users, you will discover that time seems to stand still while you're online and that you use much more online time than you think you do. Even if you think that you will be online for only a few minutes a day, if you don't have a flat-rate plan, you may be surprised when your bill arrives at the end of the month.

Phone charges

If you're not careful, you can end up paying more for the phone call than you do for your Internet service. One of the things you do when you sign up for an online service is determine the phone number to call. *If at all possible, use a provider whose number is a free or untimed local call.* If you use a local or regional Internet service provider, that provider will have a short list of phone numbers you can use.

If you cannot find a provider that's a local call for you, your options are limited. If you have a long-distance plan, such as the ones offered by Bell, Sprint, and AT&T Canada, your provider's phone number can be included in that plan and, as a result, you will get a low rate that should be less than 10 cents per minute. (Keep in mind, though, that that's still more than $5 per hour.) Be sure to compare rates for in-province and out-of-province calls, because an out-of-province call is cheaper in many cases even though it's farther away. Beware of 800 numbers, which almost always levy a stiff hourly surcharge.

Some providers give you software that automatically selects a local phone number to dial. Usually it chooses correctly, but we've heard enough horror stories that we'd recommend you always verify that the number your computer is calling is in fact a local call. Check the front of your phone book or call the local business office.

Free access

To provide some relief from Internet access costs, a company called NetZero (`www.net-zero.com`) will be offering Canadians free unlimited Internet access in the fall of 2000. All that subscribers are asked to do is provide NetZero with demographic and geographic data, as well as information about their hobbies and interests, in exchange for free Internet services. Funcow.com (`www.funcow.com`) has already entered this market space with a similar free service.

Warning: You should be aware that there's a pretty good chance this information will be passed on to other marketers who will study it, size you up, and stick you on *their* mailing list. Keep this in mind before you go the free access route. You may decide that your loss of privacy is too high a price to pay — even if it is "free."

Subscribers are also usually asked to tolerate what is considered by many to be intolerable: banner ads! Banners ads can be annoying, especially those that emit sounds and have silly-looking animated objects that move across the screen.

Here are some bad things about the big commercial services:

- Many people complain that the screens are too crowded with banner ads.
- They limit you to whatever specific set of Internet services they choose to offer; if you want something else, you're out of luck.
- They make it more difficult, or in some cases impossible, to get to parts of the Net that are considered controversial. (Some people, of course, think of this restriction as an advantage.)

ISPs: The Internet, the whole Internet, and nothing but the Internet, so help us . . .

An *Internet Service Provider*, often abbreviated *ISP* (we computer types just love TLAs — three-letter acronyms), is similar to a commercial service, but with the important difference that its primary business is hooking people to the Internet. Because almost all ISPs buy their equipment and software from a handful of manufacturers, the features and services that one ISP offers are much like those of another, but with important differences such as price, service, and reliability. Think of it as similar to choosing between a Ford and a Buick, with the differences between your local Canadian dealers being at least as important in the purchase decision as the differences between the cars.

It's terminal

The older, dying-breed type of ISP account is *UNIX* shell access. Although it's less flexible than PPP, it's easier to set up. For shell access, the only software you need on your computer is a *terminal emulator*, a simple program found on nearly any computer shipped since 1970. Windows 95/98 users can use Hyperterminal.

With shell access, your ISP's computer is considered part of the Internet, but your computer isn't. When you connect to your ISP, you type commands to its system that tell it what Internet or other functions you want to perform. The program on your ISP's computer that receives and acts on the commands is known as a *shell*

(hence the name). The shell and the programs it runs for you send back to your computer some text that is displayed on-screen. You don't get graphics, but for text-only e-mail and Web browsing, shell access can be quite adequate.

Almost without exception, shell access ISPs are running some version of UNIX system software (such as the fast-growing Linux operating system), so it eventually helps to understand a little about UNIX systems. We shamelessly recommend our *UNIX For Dummies* and *MORE UNIX For Dummies* (both published by IDG Books Worldwide, Inc.). Check around your area to see which Canadian ISPs offer shell access.

TIP

Internet on the run

Everywhere you go these days, people are carrying laptop computers. But staying connected on the road can be a challenge. One way to get your Internet fix is to plug your modem into the hotel phone and dial your ISP or online service. Check with your ISP to see if it has local numbers that you can call from your various ports of call.

A fancier way is to buy a radio modem. It's kind of like giving your laptop its own cell phone. You should know, however, that radio modem connections can be breathtakingly slow — typically 9,600 bps — and the connection charges breathtakingly expensive.

The standard type of connection to the Internet is known as *PPP* access. (An older, obsolete scheme called SLIP works similarly to PPP, but PPP is better.) When you connect to your provider with PPP, your computer becomes part of the Internet. You type stuff directly to programs running on your computer, and those programs communicate over the Net to do whatever it is they do for you.

An ISP account lets programs running on your computer take full advantage of your computer's facilities so that the programs can draw graphics, display windows, play sounds, receive mouse-clicks, and otherwise do all the fancy footwork that modern computer programs do. If your computer system can handle more than one running program at a time, as Mac and Windows can do, you can have several Internet applications running at a time, which is quite handy. You may be reading your e-mail, for example, and receive a message describing a cool new home page on the World Wide Web. You can switch immediately to your Web program (Netscape Navigator or Internet Explorer, most likely), look at the page, and then return to the mail program and pick up where you left off. Most new e-mail programs highlight *URLs* (Web addresses) and enable you to go straight to your browser by clicking the URL in your e-mail message. Another advantage of PPP is that you're not limited to running programs that your Internet provider gives you. You can download a new Internet application from the Net and begin using it immediately — your provider just acts as a data conduit between your computer and the rest of the Net.

Couch potatoes, ho! It's WebTV!

The cheapest entry to the Internet for people with a TV and no computer is WebTV. If you're already a computer aficionado, this solution will probably leave you wanting the real thing. If you're a whiz with the remote control, however, and aren't ready to plop down a grand to buy a computer, this method may just be the ticket. You buy a WebTV box in an electronics or department store, follow the directions to sign up for an account, and pay a monthly fee to WebTV. We tell you all about it in Chapter 18.

High-Speed Connections: The Beauty of Bandwidth

If you're the type of person who likes to live on the edge, technologically speaking, you'll want the fastest Internet connection available so that you can play with all the fancy graphics, and download sound and video. Graphics, video, and sound are all bits of information — lots and lots of bits of information — too many, in fact, for most dial-up connections to handle. High-speed connections can provide greater *bandwidth,* the amount of data transferred in a specific amount of time. The good news is that high-speed connections are becoming available — courtesy of companies such as Nortel Networks — and affordable by mere mortals.

After you get used to having a high-speed connection, you will never be able to tolerate an ordinary dial-up connection again. It's that good.

Cable connections

Canadian cable-television companies such as Rogers Communications and Shaw Cable have been working to provide Internet access and are successfully providing service in many areas. If cable Internet access is available in your community, it's worth checking out. It's really fast, nominally 1.5 million bits per second, with downloads in practice often exceeding 150,000 bps.

In most areas where cable connections are available, you simply call the cable company. The technician comes and installs a network connection doozus (technical term) where your cable comes into your house, installs a standard network card in your computer if you don't already have one, brings a cable modem (which can look like a laptop computer with a spike hairdo), and hooks them together. Like magic.

If you have cable television, the cable is split, and one segment goes to your computer. If you don't have cable television, the cable company may have to install the actual cable, too. By the time the technician leaves, however, you have a permanent, high-speed connection to the Internet (as long as you pay your bill, about $40 a month). In addition to the advantages of speed and constant access at a fixed price, you aren't tying up a phone line.

Cable access comes in two forms: the older one-way and the newer two-way. With one-way cable, incoming data comes from the Net to your computer at high speed via the cable, but outgoing data still uses a modem and a phone line. With two-way cable, everything goes over the cable. Your cable company can tell you which kind it offers.

DSL connections

Phone companies have a broadband type of connection, too: *DSL (Digital Subscriber Line)*. DSL service is supposed to use your existing phone line and in-house wiring. But DSL often works better if the phone company runs a new wire from outside your building to where you use your computer. (Bell Atlantic calls this a "home run.") For DSL to work, you have to live within a couple of miles of your telephone company's central office, so DSL is unavailable in many rural areas.

DSL is available at different speeds. The higher speeds cost more (surprise, surprise!). The lowest speed (usually 640Kbps) is fast enough for most users.

If DSL service *is* available, you call your phone company. A phone installer comes with a network connection box (similar to a cable modem) and hooks it up to your computer.

Who's on first?

Your phone company may soon offer video on your DSL, and your cable company may offer local phone service via your cable modem. Confusing, isn't it? The original idea behind DSL technology was to provide video on demand — any movie or TV show, any time. But old habits die hard: when customers wanted to watch a movie, they tended to just flick on HBO or run down to the video store, instead of using DSL. Oh, well. DSL has now been reborn as yet another high-speed Internet gateway, but the video capability is still in there.

A hidden cost in getting either cable or DSL Internet access is having to take a day off from work to wait for the installers. Sometimes it takes them two trips to get things working — try to make the first appointment in the morning. Also, usually, the cable company or phone company *is* your ISP (unless you pay extra), so you won't have a choice of ISPs.

TIP

If you're a student

Most colleges and universities provide some type of Internet access for their students. The type of access, however, varies a great deal. In some cases, it's just a few text-only terminals in a lab somewhere on campus. In other cases, it's a complete dial-up Internet service comparable to what you would get from a commercial provider, often with direct Internet access into every dorm room.

In all cases, Internet access is inexpensive or free. If you're a student or otherwise affiliated with a college or university, check out what's available on campus before you look elsewhere. In some areas, becoming a student is cheaper than paying for long-distance Internet access.

Some Canadian institutions even let alumni use their systems; if you live close to your alma mater, it's worth seeing whether it offers alumni access.

ISDN and other four-letter words

In the early 1980s, AT&T developed what was supposed to be the next generation of telephones, called *ISDN*, alleged to be short for I Still Don't Know or Improvements Subscribers Don't Need. ISDN uses the same phone wires (which is important because phone companies have about 100 million of them installed) and puts boxes at each end that transmit *digital* data rather than the older *analog* data. With this arrangement, an ISDN line can transmit 128K bits per second, a considerable improvement over the 33K or 56K that a regular line permits.

Although the idea was good, phone companies utterly botched the way they made ISDN available. For one thing, the method used to install ISDN is fantastically complicated, so much so that we know full-time telecom managers who have been unable to find anyone at their local phone company who knows how to install it. For another thing, ISDN is overpriced in most places. In Toronto, for example, an ISDN line costs about twice as much as a regular Bell Canada phone line. For this reason, unless you have a local Internet provider that arranges the details of an ISDN connection for you, ISDN probably isn't worth the bother. If DSL is available in your area, don't even consider getting ISDN.

Picking an ISP

After you've decided that you want to go with an ISP, the next question is *which* ISP. Answering this is relatively complicated — you have several hundred ISPs from which to choose. A few large ISPs, such as AOL Canada, SympaticoLycos and AT&T WorldNet, have loads of dial-in numbers. These numbers can be handy if you travel, and often have support staff to guide you along. Their price is usually about $25 per month. You can usually get a good deal from a regional or local ISP. These tend to compete in pricing, and in many cases because they stick to one geographic area, they also offer community-oriented online materials. When you're doing your comparison shopping, consider these factors:

- ✔ **Price:** Ask about unlimited or at least 100-hours pricing if you plan to use the Net frequently, or lower pricing for a limited number of hours.

- ✔ **Support:** Call and talk to members of the support staff before you sign up. We think that good support means 1) support available outside 9 to 5 office hours; 2) not being put on hold for long periods; and, most important, 3) support people who don't think that your questions are stupid and who can actually answer them. (You can't take this one for granted.)

- ✔ **Load:** What is response time like at peak times, and do you get busy signals when you call?

- ✔ **Access numbers:** Ask what phone numbers your computer can call to establish a connection. Make sure that at least one of them is a local call from your home or office.

- ✔ **Modem speed:** Some providers haven't upgraded their equipment in a long time. It does you no good to have a fast modem if your provider's modem speed can't match it.

A few lines about Linux

Linux is a free UNIX-style operating system that runs on PCs. Because most servers on the Net run UNIX, most server software also runs on Linux or can be easily adapted for it by someone with a little programming experience. Although the process of getting Linux installed can be a pain, it is the system to use if you find yourself wanting to put your computer on the Net many hours a day or to test out a set of interrelated Web pages that you have written. By using advanced system-software techniques known since 1961 (but not yet fully implemented in Windows — even in Windows 98), Linux protects running programs from each other; if one program crashes, it almost never takes the system with it. Nobody thinks it at all unusual when Linux systems run continuously for a month or more without having to be restarted.

Although Linux is not as easy to set up as Windows, it's considerably cheaper and much more reliable for use as a server. Check out *Linux For Dummies*, 2nd Edition, by Jon Hall (published by IDG Books Worldwide, Inc.) for details.

How to find a local Internet Service Provider

An important topic to consider in choosing your Internet Service Provider is the cost of the phone call, because calls to online systems tend to be long ones. You want to find an ISP that has a local phone number. Although a few ISPs have toll-free numbers, their hourly rates have to be high enough to cover the cost of the call. To dial direct and pay for the call yourself is almost invariably cheaper than to use a toll-free access number; someone has to pay for the call, and that someone is you. Some local ISPs have local numbers for day-to-day use and a more expensive toll-free number for you to use while traveling, or they belong to a network called iPass, which lets you use dial-in numbers of other ISPs when you're out of town.

Here are the best ways we know to find an ISP close to home:

- Check the business pages of your local newspaper for advertisements from local-access providers.

- Ask your public library's research librarian or online services staff.

- Look in your local *Yellow Pages* under Internet Services.

- Ask anyone you know in your area who already has access what she's using and whether she likes it.

Many Canadian cities also have *freenets*, a type of local community computer system that usually has a link to the Internet. Freenets are indeed free (although they don't turn down contributions if you want to support them). If you know anyone who already has access to the Web, or if you can use an Internet computer at the local library, check out the following location, which provides a list of freenets around the world:

```
www.lights.com/freenet/
```

Signing up

Many ISPs list two numbers: a voice number and a modem number. We think that it's useful, if you're new at this stuff (nothing personal — some of us are new at it for *years*), to call and talk to the live human beings on the other end of the phone line to get their helpful guidance. Talking to a person enables you to ask questions and in many cases goes a long way toward calming the trepidation that often accompanies this step. For an ISP account, talk to your ISP about which software it provides or expects you to have. If you don't get understandable answers, or the person you're talking to sounds as if he has better things to do than answer customer questions, look for a different ISP.

Fire at the wall

Lots of PCs in big companies are loaded up with Internet software and have network connections with a hookup to the Internet. If you're so blessed, can you run programs on your computer and hook right up to the Net? Not quite.

If you're in a large organization that has (not altogether unreasonable) concerns about confidential company secrets leaking out by way of the Internet, a *firewall* system placed between the company network and the outside world may limit outside access to the internal network.

The firewall is connected to both the internal network and the Internet, so any traffic between the two must go through the firewall. Special programming on the firewall limits which type of connections can be made between the inside and outside, and who can make them.

In practice, you can use any Internet service that is available within the company; for outside services, however, you're limited by what can pass through the firewall system. Most standard outside services — such as logging in to remote computers, copying files from one computer to another, and sending and receiving e-mail — should be available, although the procedures, involving something called a *proxy server,* may be somewhat more complicated than what's described in this book.

Often, you have to log in to the firewall system first and from there get to the outside. It's usually impossible for anyone outside the company to get access to systems or services on the inside network (that's what the firewall is for). Except in the case of the most paranoid of organizations, e-mail flows unimpeded in both directions.

Keep in mind that you will probably have to get authorization to use the firewall system before you can use *any* outside service other than e-mail.

Most ISPs now have sign-up programs that come on a CD-ROM or pre-installed on your computer. Windows 98 comes with sign-up software for AOL Canada and a few national ISPs (choose Start⇨Programs⇨Online Services from the taskbar). If you choose a local ISP, ask them for their sign-up CD-ROM. It includes both a program that signs you up for an account, as well as other programs you can use when connected to the Internet (such as an e-mail program and a Web browser).

Signing up for an account with an ISP generally involves providing your name, address, and telephone number, along with billing information, almost invariably including a credit card number. Access is often granted immediately, or the service may call you on the phone to verify that you are who you said you were. If you don't use credit cards, call the ISP and find out if you can prepay your account by cheque.

Back to Software

The type of Internet account you have is intimately related to the type of software you need.

- **Commercial accounts:** All commercial providers (such as AOL Canada and SympaticoLycos) give you program disks with software that works with their particular systems. Chapter 17 describes AOL Canada. We tell you how to use AOL Canada and how to get and install the software required to access it.

- **ISP accounts:** If you use an ISP with a dial-up account (also called a PPP — point-to-point protocol — account), you need dial-up software. You also need programs for the various types of information you want to use over the Internet: an e-mail program for sending and receiving e-mail, a Web browser for looking at Web pages, and other programs. Chapter 5 tells you how to get and install the programs you need, with sections on Windows 98, Windows 95, and Mac.

- **WebTV:** Since you don't need a computer for WebTV, you don't need programs, either! Chapter 5 tells you how to set up a WebTV box.

- **High-speed accounts:** To connect to an ISDN account, you use the same programs used for other dial-up accounts (see Chapter 5). For a DSL or cable account, you use the kind of network software you'd use to connect to a *local area network (LAN)*. A technician from your phone or cable company usually does this part for you, as part of the hookup service.

Some phone numbers

Here are the voice phone numbers for some of the national providers we have listed in this chapter:

AOL Canada: 888-265-4357

SympaticoLycos: 310-7873 (in Ontario and Quebec), 800-773-2121 (elsewhere in Canada)

Chapter 5

Online and On Your Way

In This Chapter

▶ Getting ready to connect to the Internet

▶ Connecting from Windows 98 and Windows 95

▶ Connecting from Windows 3.1

▶ Connecting from a Mac

▶ Connecting to AOL Canada

▶ Connecting with WebTV

C hapter 4 explains the types of accounts that can connect your computer to the Internet. This chapter shows you what you actually have to do to make that connection happen. We describe The Real Thing: an honest-to-goodness Internet account, with instructions for connecting from a Windows 98, Windows 95, Windows 3.1, or Mac computer. If you're interested in using AOL Canada or WebTV to access the Internet, skip ahead to the sections "Connecting to AOL Canada" or "I Want My WebTV!"

The Real Thing: An ISP Account

When you dial into an ISP to connect to your Internet account, your computer technically becomes part of the Internet. Your computer communicates (if you care) using *PPP (Point-to-Point Protocol)*, which enables your PC to connect to the Internet not as a terminal but as a full-fledged member of the Net, at least while your computer is on the phone to its Internet Service Provider. PPP (and its predecessors, *SLIP (Serial Line Internet Protocol)* and *CSLIP (Compressed SLIP)* are versions of *IP (Internet Protocol)*, the underlying part of *TCP/IP (Transmission Control Protocol/Internet Protocol)*, which is the way all computers on the Internet communicate with each other. By the way, we promise there won't be any other paragraphs in this book with this many acronyms.

You provide the programs

To use a PPP account, you need two types of programs:

✔ **A program to get you connected to the account:** The technical term for this type of program is a *TCP/IP stack,* although normal mortal human beings usually call it something like an *Internet connection program.* Windows 95, 98, and NT (a version of Windows used mostly by large companies, and ideally suited to intranet and extranet computer environments) come with one, called Dial-Up Networking. Windows 3.1 users have to get an Internet dialer from somewhere; we tell you how, in the section "Connecting, for Windows 3.1 Users" later in this chapter. Macintoshes have the basic TCP/IP stuff, called MacTCP, built in as of System 7 and later (see "Connecting, for Mac Users" further ahead in this chapter). Linux comes with a connection program called, strangely, ppp.

✔ **Programs to use various Internet services:** These programs give you access to e-mail, the Web, and information over the Internet. They're known as *client programs* because they're part of a two-part strategy: Part of the programs run on your computer; the other part, the *server programs,* run on your ISP's computer and other Internet host computers. You want an e-mail program to read and send e-mail, and a Web browser to surf the Web. Or you can get a program, such as Netscape Navigator, that does both. Windows has a standard way (called Winsock) for Internet client programs to work with your Internet dialer. If you use a Mac, you can use any MacTCP-compatible program.

Winsock? Like at an airport?

No, Winsock is short for Windows sockets. It's like this: Back in the dark ages of PC networking (about 1990), several different software vendors wrote PC Internet packages. Each package sported functions that enabled other people to write Internet applications of their own that worked with the vendor's package. But because each vendor's functions were slightly different, even though functionally they all did the same thing, applications that worked with one package didn't always work with another.

In 1991, all the network vendors were gearing up to produce Windows Internet packages. One day, a bunch of them got together at a trade show and thrashed out a standard set of functions for Windows Internet applications. Every Internet software vendor, even Microsoft, quickly agreed to support this Windows sockets standard, or Winsock. (It's called sockets because its design is based on a well-established UNIX package by that name.)

Any Windows Internet application you find that uses Winsock (whether it's commercial, shareware, or free) should work with any Windows Internet package. In the annals of software development, this degree of compatibility is virtually unprecedented, so let's hope that it's a harbinger of things to come.

Many ISPs give you a CD full of programs when you sign up for your account. The CD usually contains connection software and client programs — you may find everything you need. Be sure to tell your ISP what kind of computer you use, so you get the right CD.

Cool programs you can use

All the cool Internet programs you have heard about are either Winsock- or MacTCP-compatible, and many work on both Windows and Macs. Here are some famous programs available for Windows NT/98/95/3.1, and the Mac:

- **Netscape Navigator, Internet Explorer, and Opera:** The two rivals for World's best Web browser and a dark horse candidate. (Chapters 6 and 7 tell you how to use them.)

- **RealAudio and Shockwave:** You have to be running Netscape Navigator or Internet Explorer to use these and lots of other cool plug-in programs for Netscape Navigator and Internet Explorer (see Chapter 7).

- **Eudora, Netscape Messenger, and Outlook Express:** Eudora remains our favorite e-mail program. Netscape Messenger and Outlook Express are other good e-mail programs that share the advantage of being free. (Chapters 11 and 12 describe how to use them.)

- **Free Agent (for Windows) and Newswatcher (for the Mac):** These programs are great for reading Usenet newsgroups; see our Web site for an introduction to newsgroups:

  ```
  net.gurus.com/usenet
  ```

- **mIRC (for Windows) and Ircle (for the Mac):** These programs let you participate in Internet Relay Chat (IRC) for online, real-time, flying purple conversations with lots of people at the same time. These programs are discussed in Chapter 15, or you can look at our Web site:

  ```
  net.gurus.com/irc
  ```

Where does all this software come from?

Here's where to look for the Internet connection program that connects your computer to the Internet:

- **Your operating system may supply it.** Windows 95, 98, and NT already have all the software you need to connect with an Internet account. Newer versions of MacOS have it too.

✔ **Your ISP may offer it on a disk.** If your ISP gives you software, use it. That way, when you call for help, your ISP knows what to do (you hope!). Note that the software your ISP gives you may be shareware — which means that if you use it, you're honour-bound to send a donation to the author, who is probably on the other side of the world in Tasmania (yes, really).

✔ **You can buy it.** If you buy Netscape Navigator in a box from a store, for example, the program (a Web browser) comes with an Internet connection program. But we can save you that trip to the store; Netscape Navigator 4.7 is included in the CD-ROM in the back of this book. Aren't we nice!

✔ **You can get someone to download it from the Internet for you.** If you have a friend with an Internet account, beg him or her to download the programs you need, copy them on one or more diskettes, and give them to you. Then buy your friend lunch.

Read the rest of this chapter to find out exactly which programs you may need, depending on which type of computer system you use (Windows 95, Windows 98, Windows 3.1, or the Mac).

Getting Connected

Internet accounts are easy to use, but unless your ISP gives you a good, automated sign-up program, they can be tricky to set up. In fact, connecting for the first time can be the most difficult part of your Internet experience. Installing and setting up Internet connection software used to require you to type lots of scary-looking numeric Internet addresses, host names, communications ports — you name it. These days, sign-up programs are pretty humane, and don't require all that arcane information.

Make sure that your ISP is helpful and available, or choose another ISP. If you can bribe or coerce a friend or relative into helping you, do so. (**Hint:** Look for someone roughly between the ages of 12 and 16, who can be very knowledgeable and very patient, after you get past your humiliation. Chocolate chip cookies always help.)

Because each ISP is just a tad different from the next, we can't go into exact step-by-step directions for everyone. We give the usual steps, help you understand the terms, and coax you through the whole process. If you find this process totally impossible and have no one you can press into service or just don't like the thought of doing it, don't despair. Consider using AOL Canada or another account that comes with an automated sign-up program.

The big picture, sign-up-wise

To connect your Windows PC to an Internet account, follow these steps:

1. **Arrange for an Internet account from an ISP with a local access phone number.**

   In Chapter 4, we give you ideas about how to choose an ISP. Most ISPs give you a software disk when you sign up for an account; ask for one if they don't send it automatically.

2. **Get the basic Internet connection software loaded into your computer somehow, either from a disk, or arranged over the phone.**

   Later in this chapter are sections about Internet connection software for Windows 98, Windows 95, Windows 3.1, and the Mac.

3. **Type about a dozen setup parameters, if you're not lucky.**

   Your ISP (if it provided the software) or the software vendor should have given you instructions for when to type what. If you're lucky, your software has an automatic configuration program to set most or all of the setup parameters. In the following section, "Many mysterious numbers," we tell you as much as we know about the parameters you may encounter.

4. **Crank up your Internet connection program and fiddle with it until it works.**

   Miracles have been known to happen and sometimes it works the first time. If it doesn't, call and ask your ISP to help you. Having only one phone line and having to hang up to call your provider may be difficult and frustrating. We can only sympathize and tell you that this is the worst part — bar none. Once your connection is set up, the fun begins.

Many mysterious numbers

Your TCP/IP program uses a bunch of scary-looking technical information to connect to your Internet account. Although in theory you should never need any of this information after your account is first set up, we find that it's useful to have on hand, particularly if you have to call your provider for help. Feel free to write it all down in Table 5-1 (except for your password — just store that one in your head).

Make sure that your phone line doesn't have call waiting. If it does, you (or your Internet connection program) have to type U70 or 1170 at the beginning of your Internet Service Provider's phone number to tell your phone company to turn off call waiting for this call; otherwise, an incoming call will sever your Internet connection.

Table 5-1	Information about Your Internet Connection	
Your Information	*Description*	*Example*
Domain name _____	The name of your ISP's domain. It's the last part of your Internet address and usually ends with `.ca`, `.net`, or `.com`.	`gurus.com`
Communications port _____	The communications port on your own PC to which your modem is attached, usually COM1 or COM2. (Mac owners don't have to worry about this stuff.) Even if your modem lives inside your computer and doesn't look as though it's connected to a port, it is.	COM1
Modem speed _____	The fastest speed that both your modem and your ISP's modem can go. If your modem can go at 56 Kbps or 33.6 Kbps, for example, but your ISP can handle only 28.8 Kbps, choose 28.8 Kbps.	28.8.Kbps
Modem _____	The type of modem you have. Windows 95/98 has info on about 15 million modems, but most dialer packages are only dimly aware of the details of different types of modems. A regular PC-type modem is probably similar enough to a Hayes model to fool the programs you use if your modem isn't on the list.	Hayes
Phone number _____	The number you call to connect to your ISP, exactly as you would dial it by hand, including 1 and the area code, if needed. If you have to dial 9 and pause a few seconds to get an outside line, include 9, at the beginning. (Each comma tells your modem to pause for two seconds, so stick in extra commas as necessary to get the timing right.) Many modems have speakers so that you can hear them dialing. The noise is useful when you're trying to figure out whether you have succeeded in getting an outside line when you dial out.	1-905-555-1234
Username _____	The name on your account with your ISP, also called a *login name*.	`myoung`

Your Information	Description	Example
User password	The password for your account. (But don't write it down here!)	3friedRice
Start-up command	The command your ISP should run when you call in. Your ISP can tell you this command. Many packages start automatically, so you can probably leave this entry blank.	PPP
Domain name server (DNS) address	The numeric Internet address of the computer that can translate between regular Internet addresses and their numeric equivalents. Your ISP should give you this address, although the software may set it automatically when your computer connects.	123.45.67.99
Interface type	The exact type of interface your ISP uses. The three choices are PPP, CSLIP, and SLIP. Some TCP/IP packages can't handle them all. If your software and ISP handle PPP, use it; the next-best choice is CSLIP; the worst (but still okay) choice is SLIP.	PPP
Your own host name	The name of your computer. Although most ISPs don't give each user's computer a name, if yours does, make it short and spellable and (perhaps) cute.	meg

A home for your programs

Before you begin filling your computer's hard drive with network software, make a folder in which to put it. (Windows 3.1 users, make a directory.) You can use this folder for the programs you download in this chapter in addition to useful little programs you find on the Net.

✔ In Windows 95 or 98, run My Computer or Windows Explorer, move to the Program Files folder, and choose File➪New➪Folder from the menu.

✔ In Windows 3.1, run File Manager, move to the directory in which you want to create the new directory (probably the root, a. k. a. C:\), and choose File➪Create Directory.

✔ On a Macintosh, choose New Folder from the File menu.

If you don't already have a folder or directory for storing things temporarily, you should make one. You need it when you install the software you download from the Internet. On a PC, we recommend calling the directory C:\temp.

Sign in, Please

To connect to the Internet once you've signed up for an account, you run the connection program that works with your account. Before you can use the account, you must sign in, or log in. When you're done, you don't have to log off, in most cases, but you do need to hang up the phone.

Who are you, anyway?

Three hundred million people are on the Internet. Because only one of them is you, it would be nice if the other 299,999,999 couldn't go snooping through your files and e-mail messages. No matter which type of Internet account you have, you use a security procedure to prove that you are who you say you are.

Your provider gives each user an account, kinda like a bank account. The account has your user name and a secret password associated with it.

Your user name (or user ID or login or logon name) is unique among all the names assigned to your provider's users. It's also your e-mail address, so don't pick a name like *snickerdoodle* unless that's what you want to tell your friends and put on your business cards.

Your password is secret, and is the main thing that keeps bad guys from borrowing an account. Don't use a real word or a name. A good way to make up a password is to invent a somewhat memorable phrase, and turn each word in the phrase into a single letter or digit. "Computers cost too much money for me" turns into Cc2m$4m, for example. *Never tell anyone else your password.* Particularly don't tell anyone who claims to be from your ISP; they're not.

How to get off the Internet

After you've gotten yourself connected to the Internet, you're inevitably placed in the position of having to disconnect. You can do this in more and less graceful ways — and, depending on how far "into" the Net you've gone, you may have layers of systems to exit from.

The most common exit sequences include the ones in this list:

- ✔ Click the Disconnect button in the program you used to connect.
- ✔ Double-click on the Dial-up Networking icon in the system tray and then click on Disconnect in the dialog box that appears (for Windows 95/98/NT users with Dial-Up Networking).
- ✔ Choose File⇨Disconnect from the menu bar.
- ✔ Type **exit**, **logout**, or **bye** or press Ctrl+D in a terminal emulator.

If you use an ISP account, you may have a bunch of programs running, including your Web browser and your e-mail program. Only one of these programs, however, is the program that connects you to the Internet. That's the one you have to talk to when you're disconnecting from the Internet. In Windows 95/98, you disconnect using the Dial-Up Networking program.

Connecting, for Windows 98 Users

Amazingly, Windows 98 comes with all the software you need to connect to an Internet account, using its Dial-Up Networking program. Windows 98 also comes with automated sign-up programs for several Internet service providers (in the United States, anyway). To sign up for an account or to use an existing account with one of these services, click the Start button and choose Programs⇨Online Services, and then choose the service.

If you want to use an account other than the ones with automated sign-up programs (and the service didn't send you an automated sign-up CD), you can run the Internet Connection Wizard to configure Dial-Up Networking to work with your account. Run the wizard by clicking the Connect to the Internet button on your Windows desktop, if there is one, or by clicking the Start button and choosing Programs⇨Internet Explorer⇨Connection Wizard, which should display a window similar to Figure 5-1. (This is the Internet Explorer 5.0 version of the wizard; your version may look somewhat different.)

If you have no account set up and want Windows to look for an ISP in your area, click the top button. If you've already arranged for an account, click the middle button whether or not you've set it up on another computer before. If you tried the middle button and your ISP is not in the list that Microsoft suggests, quite likely if you're using a local ISP, click the bottom button. Setting up your account manually isn't as scary as it sounds; it mostly means that you have to type in the provider's phone number and your login and password yourself. (Wow, makes our fingers hurt just to think about it. Not.)

When you're done, you have an icon for your ISP in your Dial-Up Networking folder. Open the My Computer folder on the desktop, then open the Dial-Up Networking folder, and you'll see it. To call your account, run the Dial-Up Networking program and click the Connect button.

Windows 98 comes with Microsoft Internet Explorer, a reasonably good Web browser. (Chapter 6 explains how to use it.) Windows 98 also comes with a capable e-mail program called Outlook Express. See Chapter 11 for instructions. You can also use Netscape Navigator, Eudora, and other programs — you're not stuck with Microsoft's offerings.

To make your ISP connection icon more convenient, make a shortcut to it on your desktop. Drag the ISP's icon from the Dial-Up Networking folder to the desktop, and Windows creates a shortcut. You can even add your Internet connection program to your Start menu: right-click the Start button and choose Open to display the Start menu items in a window. Drag your ISP's icon from the Dial-Up Connection window to the Start menu window. Way cool!

Figure 5-1: Windows tries to help you get connected.

Connecting, for Windows 95 Users

The good news is that Windows 95 comes with Dial-Up Networking. The bad news is that at least three major sub-versions of Windows 95 exist, and what they call Dial-Up Networking varies a lot.

Except in the earliest version of Windows 95, you get the Internet Setup Wizard, which helps you configure Dial-Up Networking to work with your account. You may be able to run the wizard by clicking the Start button and choosing Programs➪Accessories➪Internet Tools➪Internet Setup Wizard (if you don't see the wizard there, look around your Programs menus for it). If you can start the wizard at all, it'll work like the Windows 98 wizard, described previously, although perhaps without some of the options.

Later versions of Windows 95 come with Microsoft Internet Explorer 4.0, a Web browser, and Microsoft Exchange, an e-mail program we consider rather confusing. If you have Internet Explorer 3.0, you should download a later version. We also recommend that you download a better e-mail program, such as Eudora Light or Outlook Express (the latter comes with Internet Explorer 4.0 and 5.0); see Chapter 16 to find out how to download and install programs, and Chapter 11 for instructions for using Eudora.

To sign up for and connect to an account, of course, you can always use the automated sign-up CDs that you can get from AOL Canada, and other services.

Connecting, for Windows 3.1 Users

Windows 3.1 lacks the software you need to connect to a PPP account. Most ISPs give you a copy of the Trumpet Winsock shareware TCP/IP package or else the Shiva TCP/IP package that comes with Netscape. Trumpet Winsock is freely available shareware (we thought you'd like that, although you should register and pay for it if your provider hasn't done so for you). They may also give you a copy of Eudora, the freeware version of the popular Eudora e-mail program, and possibly Netscape Navigator or Internet Explorer.

Some Internet providers give you an automated sign-up program. Otherwise, your Internet provider should give you detailed installation and configuration instructions. If they do the latter, plan to spend some time on the phone getting your software set up correctly.

After you're done setting up Trumpet Winsock, you have a Trumpet icon in one of your Windows program groups. Double-click the Trumpet icon and follow the instructions your Internet provider gave you to get connected.

Your provider should also have given you, at the very least, an e-mail program and Web browser. If your provider gave you Netscape Navigator (Version 2.0 or later), you have an excellent Web browser and an acceptable e-mail and newsreader program. Because Microsoft Internet Explorer also runs on Windows 3.1 and is free, your provider may give it to you along with Outlook Express, an e-mail program. Parts III and IV of this book tell you how to use these programs.

Using a UNIX shell account

In the early days of the Internet, before Netscape, before America Online, before the World Wide Web itself (can you remember back that far? — we're talking about 1989), intrepid Internet explorers dealt with the Internet by using UNIX accounts. UNIX is an operating system that, in its purest form, requires you to type short, cryptic, and totally unmemorable commands to get anything done. Although UNIX is a powerful system and programmers love it, most mere mortals find it a pain in the neck to use. Because most of the computers on the Internet run UNIX, however, early Internet users didn't have any choice. UNIX accounts are also called *shell accounts*, for the name of the part of UNIX that listens to the commands you type.

UNIX accounts used to be widely available, before PPP accounts took the world by storm. Some ISPs can still give you one, if you ask specifically.

One big advantage of UNIX accounts is that you don't need any fancy programs on your computer to get connected. All you need is a *terminal emulator* program, one that dials the phone and pretends to be a terminal attached to the UNIX

computer at the other end of the phone line. Almost every computer comes with a terminal emulator program; Windows 3.1 comes with Windows Terminal, Windows 95 and Windows 98 come with HyperTerminal, and Macs come with MacTerminal.

When you use a UNIX account, all the programs you run (except for the terminal emulator) run on the Internet provider's computer, not on your computer. To read your e-mail, you run a UNIX e-mail program on your Internet provider's computer; the most popular UNIX e-mail program is called Pine, which we describe in Chapter 11. To browse the Web, you run a UNIX browser, usually one called Lynx, which we describe in Chapter 6. To read Usenet newsgroups, you run a UNIX newsreader program, such as trn or tin. Because these programs don't do graphics and you don't use your mouse, you end up learning lots of one-letter commands.

If you run a version of UNIX such as Linux or FreeBSD on your PC, you have the equivalent of a shell account on your own PC. You can also run Lynx and other UNIX shell programs locally, and you don't need a terminal emulator.

Connecting, for Mac Users

Mac users already have most of the software they need to connect to the Internet because System 8 comes with MacTCP. Upgrade to System 8 to get it. You also need a Mac TCP/IP modem program, such as FreePPP, MacPPP, or InterSLIP, which your ISP should be able to give you. (If not, consider finding an ISP that has more of a clue about Macs or else you'll be on your own when you have problems.) Most newer Macs come with modem software installed.

Connecting to AOL Canada

AOL Canada is the Canadian offspring of the world's largest online service — America Online, located in the United States. AOL Canada provides access to both the Internet and its own proprietary services. The features offered by AOL Canada are similar to those offered by AOL in the United States, but content and links to other sites are more Canadian in nature. AOL and its international services combine for more than 25 million members and are still growing. To use AOL Canada, you use software it provides. (Windows 98, Windows 95, and Mac versions are available.) You can also use other software with your AOL Canada account, such as Netscape Navigator and Microsoft Internet Explorer. This chapter describes the AOL Canada Internet-related capabilities, including e-mail and the World Wide Web.

This section applies to Version 6.0 of the AOL Canada software for Windows, and Version 4.0 for the Mac. Because AOL Canada updates its software and the graphics that appear in its dialog boxes all the time, your screen may not match exactly the figures in this chapter.

Signing up for AOL Canada

Ready to sign up? No problem! If you have Windows 98, click Start and choose Programs⇨Online Services⇨AOL; otherwise, in the unlikely event that you don't have a CD-ROM lying around, call 888-265-4357 and ask for a trial membership. Specify whether you want the CD-ROM or a floppy disk with the Windows version (Windows 95 or Windows 98) or the Mac version. The introductory package has instructions and a CD-ROM or disk containing the AOL Canada software program. After you have the introductory package, follow the instructions on its cover to install the program and sign up for an account. You need a credit card to sign up.

Note: AOL Canada members can use their account in more than 100 countries. As well, AOL Canada members can connect to their account without roaming surcharges through AOL access numbers while travelling throughout North America. You can also use AOL Canada from other parts of the world, but you pay a roaming surcharge and the amount varies from city to city.

Running AOL Canada from Windows and the Mac are similar processes. Although we took pictures of the Windows version, we don't think that it matters much. You can always tell that you're on the correct Mac screen.

The installation program creates a cute triangular icon named AOL Canada. If you have trouble installing the AOL Canada software, call 888-265-4357.

The pros and cons of AOL Canada

AOL Canada is easier to use than most commercial online services and Internet accounts because one big AOL Canada access program does it all for you. AOL Canada also does a nice job of providing members with online software updates — it can update your AOL Canada access software for you right over the phone, and connect-time is usually free when it does so.

Signing up for an AOL Canada account is easy, too — many magazines come with free AOL Canada sign-up CDs. AOL Canada also has lots of discussion groups and information available only to its members. And as part of the world's largest Internet online community, you can access great content from 16 countries, in 8 languages, including France, Germany, Sweden, Switzerland, Austria, Japan, Australia, the UK, the US, Hong Kong, Mexico, Argentina and Brazil.

AOL Canada offers unlimited and limited-use price plans, designed to appeal to a broad range of consumers and provides both AOL-specific content and features plus access to the Internet.

On the other hand, getting connected may be difficult at certain peak usage times, usually around 10 pm, when access lines get a bit busy. If you do sign up for an AOL Canada trial membership and decide to cancel your account later, it can be difficult. Cancellations must be done by calling AOL Canada Member Services and cannot be handled by sending an e-mail.

Setting up your AOL Canada account

After you've installed the AOL Canada software, you can use it to sign up for an account. When you sign up, you have to tell it which screen name (account name) you want to use and how you want AOL Canada to bill you after you've used up your free hours.

Follow these steps to set up your account:

1. **Double-click the AOL Canada icon.**

2. **Follow the instructions on-screen.**

   First, AOL Canada calls up an 800 number to find out the local-access number closest to you. Then it asks for your *registration number and password*, which comes with AOL Canada disks and CD-ROMs. The registration number is a long number with a couple of dashes, and the password is two words joined by a hyphen (ours was *SPECS-RICHES*, and our editor's was *ANGER-PASTRY*. Who or what thinks up these things?). If AOL Canada was already installed on your computer when you got it, you may not need to enter these.

3. **Choose an account name (which AOL Canada calls a screen name —
   sounds glamourous).**

   Your screen name can be as long as 16 characters and can contain spaces.
   The length of the screen name will probably be longer by the time you
   read this book. The screen name length may even be longer by now!
   Read the instructions on-screen to find out. You can use a combination
   of capital and small letters, as in MargyL or LoveAOL. When AOL asks
   you to enter your screen name, it checks its list of existing names. If
   someone is already using that name (John Smith, for example), you have
   to invent another one. By now, the 25 million most obvious names have
   been taken, so get creative. If the screen name you want is already taken,
   try adding a number to the end to make it unique. For example, if NetHead
   is taken (and we're sure that it is), you can be NetHead3236.

4. **Enter a credit card number and expiration date.**

   When you finish, you see the Sign On window in the AOL Canada window,
   as shown in Figure 5-2. You're ready to boogie!

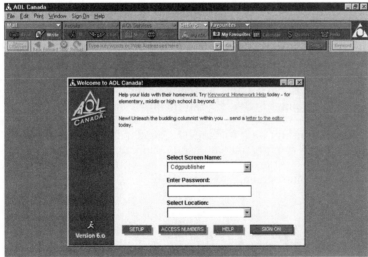

Figure 5-2:
The AOL
Canada
Welcome
window
suggests
that you log
right in!

GO Canada GO!

To connect your computer to AOL Canada:

1. **Type your password in the Enter Password box.**

   The AOL Canada window always displays the menu bar and, underneath
   it, the toolbar (a row of cute little icons).

2. **Click the SIGN ON button.**

   A window appears, showing the progress of the connection. The graphic changes as the AOL Canada program dials the phone, establishes a connection with the big AOL computer in the sky, and logs you in.

   You see the AOL Canada Welcome Screen and AOL Canada channel line-up menu. Now you're connected to AOL Canada. You can click the various headlines and/or photos to read the day's news stories. If e-mail is waiting for you, you can click the You've Got Mail icon.

3. **Minimize the AOL Today screen by clicking its Minimize button (in the upper-right corner of the window).**

If your PC has a sound board or you're using a Mac, don't be surprised if your computer suddenly says "Welcome to AOL Canada!" when you sign on. If you have e-mail, it says, "You've got mail!" Try not to jump right out of your chair when you hear this message.

For more information about using your AOL Canada account, see Chapter 17.

I'm outta here!

To get out of AOL Canada, choose Sign Off⇨Sign Off from the menu (yes, it's a little redundant). You'll have to choose Sign Off one more time on the next screen, then the AOL Canada program hangs up on your connection with the big AOL computer in the sky. Exit the program if you're done.

The next time you want to use AOL Canada, double-click the AOL Canada icon, choose your screen name and fill in your password, and click the SIGN ON button or just press Enter. You're ready to explore when you see the AOL Today Welcome Screen.

I Want My WebTV!

If you don't have a computer, you can get connected to the Internet in another way and reap some of (but not all) the benefits. It's called WebTV, the brand name of a system that includes both hardware and service. The hardware includes a box you connect to your television set, a remote control, and a remote keyboard (optional, but indispensable unless you are an extremely patient person); the service consists of an Internet connection for which you pay a monthly fee. After you connect the WebTV box to your TV and your telephone line — *voilà* — you're online. The box includes a computer, of course, but don't tell anybody. The computer basically runs one program, the WebTV program, and uses your TV as the monitor. WebTV became available in 1996, and, although it hasn't exactly caught on like wildfire yet, it may be right for you. Microsoft bought the company, so who knows what will happen. This section tells you how to get WebTV and connect it. Chapter 18 tells you in some detail how to use it and what its advantages and drawbacks are.

Getting started with WebTV

Before you buy WebTV, you should check to make sure that you can connect to the service through a local telephone number. If you have access to the Web already through a friend or work, you can go to the WebTV Web page, at www.webtv.com, to look up your local Canadian WebTV access number. Or, alternatively, if you already have an ISP (Internet Service Provider), you can use that connection, which WebTV calls OpenISP. This option reduces your monthly service charge by $10.

If you don't have a TV, don't buy WebTV unless you really want to buy a TV and can't admit that to yourself. Colour is best, for the same reasons that having a colour monitor on your computer is best — not only do things look snazzier in colour but designers also use colour to convey information.

To buy the WebTV equipment, go to a consumer electronics store and, while you're there, get a demonstration of the product. Because you have only a couple of options from which to choose, this process isn't quite as bad as, say, picking out a new car. There are two versions of the box, the Classic, for about $150, or the Plus, for $300. Plus offers some extra features such as on-screen TV schedule listings, and the monthly service is about $35 rather than $30.

The next choice you have is whether to buy a keyboard for about $120. If you don't buy a keyboard, you can use the remote control to navigate your way around the screen and bring up a picture of a keyboard on-screen. You can then navigate around the keyboard and press a key when you land on it. This technique is not unlike the way that Gutenberg set type, a hideously painful way to operate the product, especially if you want to send e-mail or type URLs. Get the keyboard. Even if you can't type, you can hunt and peck infinitely faster than moving a selector across the grid of a keyboard image. (Some of us can't type properly either, despite many years — going back to the days of punched cards — of hanging around keyboards.) The keyboard is small and light, about the size of this book, and wireless. It communicates with the WebTV box by infrared light, just like all those remote controls sitting in your TV room. You can also use a regular $20 computer keyboard (it plugs into a socket in the back of the WebTV box), but then you have to buy an extension cable for the keyboard or sit close to the TV.

Because the WebTV box connects to your TV set by using RCA jacks — those cables with round things on the end that just push in — the box has to be close to the TV. If your TV isn't in a giant entertainment centre unit that has plenty of room for more black boxes, put the box on the floor or on top of the TV. It has to be in the line of sight of the place (the couch) from where you want to use it. The hardware comes with a usable set of instructions that tell you how to connect it to your TV, either directly or through the VCR you already have connected. If you have any difficulty setting everything up, ask the teenager at the store where you bought the product for advice.

You have to connect your telephone line to the WebTV box. A phone jack splitter and phone cable come in the WebTV package. Find the nearest phone jack in your house, remove the phone cable from it, insert the splitter, and then put the phone cable back in. Then run the new phone cable from the other side of the splitter over to the WebTV box and plug it in around back. All you're doing is adding your WebTV to your phone system like an extension phone. When you're using WebTV, of course, you can't use the phone. You can easily disconnect from the Internet to make a phone call while you're running WebTV, then reconnect when you're done by just pushing a button on your keyboard or remote control.

Beam me up, Scotty!

All right, you've connected all the wires, and now you're sitting on the couch (the best thing about WebTV) with the remote control and keyboard in front of you, the popcorn within easy reach, and no one in the house using the phone. What to do next? It's as easy as pie: Point your remote control in the general direction of your TV and push the green TV button and then the WEB button. This step turns on the power to everything. You may have to press the TV/Video button to get your TV set to listen to the box rather than to the television programs. When you see the WebTV logo and hear its soothing music, you're all set.

The first time you use the system, you go through a sign-up procedure with the folks at WebTV. Your WebTV connects to home base by dialing an 800 number. Then they ask you your name, address, credit card number, and so on, and find a local telephone number to call. (Without a keyboard, the sign-on phase takes a long time.) After you're registered, WebTV disconnects from the 800 number and calls the local number, and you're on your way.

You may want to call your phone company to confirm that the "local" number for WebTV is really local for you, before spending hours surfing the Net. They've been known to guess wrong. If there's no local number but you love WebTV anyway, try the OpenISP plan with a local ISP that really is a local call.

Part III
Web Mania

The 5th Wave   By Rich Tennant

In this part . . .

No doubt about it, the Web's *the* happenin' place. For many Canadians, the Web *is* the Internet. In this part, we explain what the Web is and how to get around. We give you great tips about how to actually find Canadian and other stuff you're looking for. We also tell you about Web shopping so you can confidently spend your money online. Finally, we've added a chapter about how to make a home page so that you, too, can be "on the Web."

Chapter 6

The Wild, Wonderful Wacky Web

*P*eople talk about the *Web* today more than they talk about the *Net*. The World Wide Web and the Internet are not the same thing — the World Wide Web (which we call the Web because we're lazy typists) lives "on top of" the Internet. The Internet's network is at the core of the Web, and the Web is like a benevolent parasite that requires the Net for survival.

Okay, enough gross metaphor — so what is it already? The Web is a bunch of "pages" of information connected to each other around the globe. Each page can be a combination of text, pictures, audio clips, video clips, animation, and other stuff. (We're vague about naming the other stuff because new types of other stuff are added every day.) What makes Web pages interesting is that they contain *hyperlinks,* usually just called *links* because the Net already has plenty of hype. Each link points to another Web page, and when you click a link, your *browser* fetches the page that the link connects to. (Stay calm — we talk about browsers in a couple of pages. For now, just think of your browser as the program that talks to the Web.)

Each page your browser gets for you can have more links that take you to other places. Pages can be linked to other pages anywhere in the world, so after you're on the Web, you can end up looking at pages from Nova Scotia to Calgary, from Sydney to Buenos Aires, all faster than you can say "Jack's your uncle." Give or take network delays, you're only seconds away from any site, anywhere in the world.

This system of interlinked documents is known as *hypertext.* Figure 6-1 shows a Web page (our Web page, in fact). Each underlined phrase is a link to another Web page.

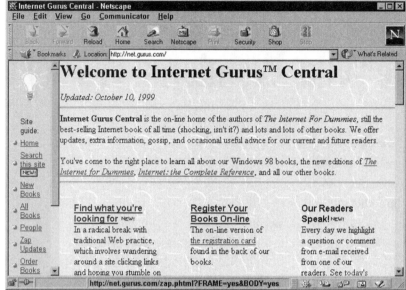

Figure 6-1:
Underlined
phrases on
Web pages
are links to
other pages.

Hypertext, the buzzword that makes the Web go, is one of those simple ideas that turns out to have a much bigger effect than you would imagine. With a hypertext system, people can create connections among pieces of information that let you go directly to related information. As you draw connections among the pieces of information, you can begin to envision the web created by the links among the pieces. What's so remarkable about the Web is that it connects pieces of information from all around the *planet,* on different computers and in different databases, all pretty much seamlessly (a feat you would be hard-pressed to match with a card catalogue in a brick-and-mortar library). We sometimes think of the Web as an extremely large but friendly alien centipede made of information.

The other important thing about the Web is that the information in it is searchable. For example, in about ten seconds, you can get a list of Web pages that contain the phrase *domestic poultry,* or your name, or the name of a book you want to find out about. You can follow links to each page on the list, to find the information you want.

Name That Page

Before you dive in and hit the Web (hmm, that metaphor needs work), you need one more basic concept. Every Web page has a name attached to it so that browsers, and you, can find it. Great figures in the world of software engineering named this *URL,* or *Uniform Resource Locator.* Every Web page has a URL, a string of characters that begins with an `http://` or `www.` Some people pronounce each letter ("*U-R-L*"), and some think that it's a word ("*URL*"). Most people we know pronounce each letter — but it's your choice. Now you know enough to go browsing. (For more entirely optional details about URLs, see the sidebar "Duke of URL.")

Browsing Off

Now that you know all about the Web, you undoubtedly want to check it out for yourself. To do this, you need a *browser,* the software that goes and gets Web pages and displays them on your screen. Fortunately, if you have Internet access, you probably already have one. One probably came from your Internet Service Provider (ISP), and you installed it when you installed the rest of your Internet software. If you don't have a browser or want to get a copy of Netscape Navigator or Internet Explorer (most likely because you have one but want to try the other), see the section "Getting and Installing Netscape Navigator, Internet Explorer, or Opera," later in this chapter.

We discuss three of the most popular Web browsers: Netscape Navigator, the world's most popular graphical browser; Internet Explorer, Microsoft's response to Netscape; and Opera, a small, fast, lesser-known browser. We also deal with Lynx, the text-only browser for the UNIX shell account crowd. AOL Canada's software has a built-in browser, as we explain in Chapter 17. They all work similarly.

Where did the Web come from?

The World Wide Web was invented in 1989 at the European Particle Physics Lab in Geneva, Switzerland, an unlikely spot for a revolution in computing. The inventor is a British researcher named Tim Berners-Lee, who is now the director of the World Wide Web Consortium (W3) in Cambridge, Massachusetts, the organization that sets standards and loosely oversees the development of the Web. Tim is terrifically smart and hardworking, and is the nicest guy you would ever want to meet. (Margy met him through Sunday school — is that wholesome or what?)

Tim invented *HTTP* (*HyperText Transport Protocol*), the method that Web browsers use to communicate with Web servers; *HTML* (*HyperText Markup Language*), the language in which Web pages are written; and *URLs* (*Uniform Resource Locators*), the codes used to identify Web pages and most other information on the Net. He envisioned the Web as a way for everyone to both publish and read information on the Net. Early Web browsers had editors that let you create Web pages almost as easily as you could read them.

For more information about the development of the Web and the work of the World Wide Web Consortium, visit its Web site, at `www.w3.org`.

Essentials of hypertext thought

If you can get a handle on the fundamental structure of the Web, you can use it better, not to mention thinking about all the other ways it can be used. *Hypertext* is a way of connecting information in ways that make it easy to find — in theory. Traditional libraries (both the kinds with books and the kinds in computers) organize information in an arbitrary way, such as alphabetical order or the Dewey decimal system. This order reflects nothing about the relationships among different pieces of information; it just reflects the limits of manual indexing. In the world of hypertext, information is organized in relationship to other information. The relationships between different pieces of information are, in fact, often much more valuable than the pieces themselves.

Hypertext can arrange the same set of information in multiple ways at the same time. A book in a conventional library can be on only one shelf at a time; a book about mental health, for example, is shelved under medicine or psychology, but not in both places at once. With hypertext, it's no problem to have links to the same document from both medical topics and psychology topics.

Suppose that you're interested in what influenced a particular historical person. Start by looking at her basic biographical information: where and when she was born, the names of her parents, her religion, and other basic details like that. Then you can expand on each fact by finding out what else was happening at that time in her part of the world, what was happening in other parts of the world, and what influence her religion may have had on her. You draw a picture by pulling together all these aspects and understanding their connections — a picture that's hard to draw from just lists of names and dates.

Surfing with Netscape Navigator, Internet Explorer, and Opera

When you start Netscape Navigator (which comes as part of the Netscape Communicator 4.7 suite), you see a screen similar to the one shown in Figure 6-2. The Internet Explorer window looks very similar. Opera 3.6 displays a browser window shown in Figure 6-3. Which page your browser displays depends on how it's set up; many providers arrange to have a browser display their home page; otherwise they tend to display the Netscape or Microsoft home page, respectively, until you choose a home page of your own. Opera starts with three Opera Software pages, each its own little window.

At the top of the browser window are a bunch of buttons and the rectangular "box" that contains the *Uniform Resource Locator*, or *URL*, for the current page. Netscape calls this the Location; Internet Explorer calls it the Address line. (Netscape sometimes labels the box Netsite for reasons that doubtless make sense to someone. Internet Explorer sometimes calls it Shortcut.)

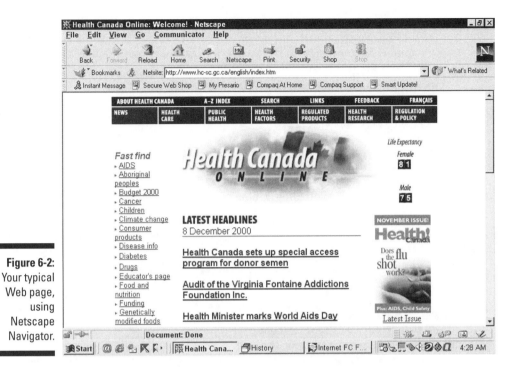

Figure 6-2: Your typical Web page, using Netscape Navigator.

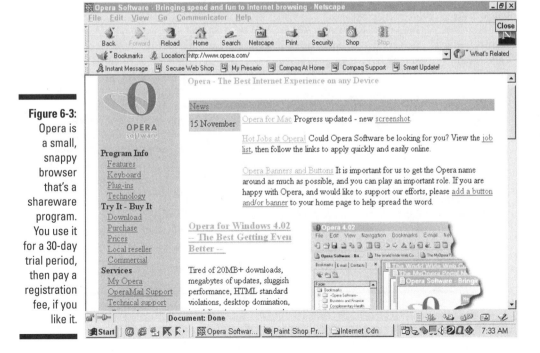

Figure 6-3: Opera is a small, snappy browser that's a shareware program. You use it for a 30-day trial period, then pay a registration fee, if you like it.

Opera, a bit of a maverick, puts the box at the bottom of the window. Remember that URLs are an important part of Web lore because they're the secret codes that name all the pages on the Web. For details, see the sidebar "Duke of URL," on the next page.

Getting around

You need two very simple primary skills (if we can describe something as basic as a single mouse-click as a skill) to get going on the Web. One is to move from page to page on the Web, and the other is to jump directly to a page when you know its URL (see "Going places" later in this section).

Hypertext: A reminiscence

John writes:

The term and concept of *hypertext* were invented around 1969 by Ted Nelson, a famous computer visionary who has been thinking about the relationship between computers and literature for at least 30 years now — starting back when most people would have considered it stupid to think that such a relationship could exist. Twenty years ago, he claimed that people would have computers in their pockets with leatherette cases and racing stripes. (I haven't seen any racing stripes yet, but otherwise he was dead-on.)

Back in 1970, Ted told me that we all would have little computers with inexpensive screens on our desks, with superwhizzo graphical hypertext systems. "Nah," I said. "For hypertext, you want a mainframe with gobs of memory and a high-resolution screen." We were both right, of course, because what we have on our desks in 2000 are little computers that are faster than 1970s mainframes and that have more memory and better screens.

Various hypertext projects have come and gone over the years, including one (of which Ted was a part) at Brown University, and one at the Stanford Research Institute (which was arguably the most influential project in computing history because it invented screen windows and mice).

Ted's own hypertext system, Project Xanadu, has been in the works for close to 20 years, under a variety of financing and management setups, with many of the same people slogging along and making it work. The project addresses many issues that other systems don't. In particular, Ted figured out how to pay authors for their work in a hypertext system, even when one document has pieces linked from others and the ensuing document consists almost entirely of a compendium of pieces of other documents. For a decade, I have been hearing every year that Xanadu, and now a smaller Xanadu Light, which takes advantage of a great deal of existing software, will hit the streets the next year. This year, I hope that they're right.

Now that the World Wide Web has brought a limited version of hypertext to the masses, Ted is building a Xanadu system on the Web. Visit www.xanadu.net to see what he's up to!

TECHNICAL STUFF

Duke of URL

Part of the plan of the World Wide Web is to link together all the information in the known universe, starting with all the stuff on the Internet and heading up from there. (This statement may be a slight exaggeration, but we don't think so.)

One of the keys to global domination is to give everything (at least everything that could be a Web resource) a name, and in particular a consistent name so that no matter what a hypertext link refers to, a Web browser can find it and know what to do with it.

Look, for example, at this typical URL:

```
http://net.gurus.com/index.phtml
```

The first thing in a URL — the word before the colon — is the *scheme*, which describes the way a browser can get to the resource. Although ten schemes are defined, the most common by far is *HTTP,* the *HyperText Transport Protocol* that is the Web's native transfer technique. (Don't confuse HTTP, which is the way pages are sent over the Net, with HTML, which is the way the pages are coded internally. We get to that in Chapter 7.)

Although the details of the rest of the URL depend on the scheme, most schemes use a consistent syntax. Following the colon are two slashes (always forward slashes, never reverse slashes) and the name of the host computer on which the resource lives; in this case, `net.gurus.com`. Then comes another slash and a *path*, which gives the name of the resource on that host; in this case, a file named `index.phtml`.

Web URLs allow a few other optional parts. They can include a *port number,* which specifies, roughly speaking, which of several programs running on that host should handle the request. The port number goes after a colon following the host name, like this:

```
http://net.gurus.com:80/index.
   phtml
```

Because the standard HTTP port number is 80, if that's the port you want (it usually is), you can leave it out.

Finally, a Web URL can have a *search part* at the end, following a question mark, like this:

```
http://net.gurus.com:80/index.
   phtml?plugh
```

Although not all pages can have search parts, in those that do, the search part tells the host, uh, what to search for. (You rarely type a search part yourself — they're often constructed for you from fill-in fields on Web pages.)

Three other useful URL schemes are mailto, ftp, and file. A mailto URL looks like this:

```
mailto:internet6@gurus.com
```

That is, it's an e-mail address. When you choose a mailto URL in Netscape, it pops up a window in which you can enter an e-mail message to the address in the URL. In Internet Explorer, clicking a mailto URL runs the Outlook Express program or whatever you've designated as your default mail program. (Outlook Express is described in Chapter 11.) Mailto URLs are most commonly used for sending comments to the owner of a page.

A URL that starts with ftp lets you download files from an FTP server on the Internet (see Chapter 16 for information about FTP servers). An FTP URL looks like this:

```
ftp://ftp.netscape5.com/pub/
   communicator/4.6/english/
   mac/README.TXT
```

(continued)

(continued)

The part after the two slashes is the name of the FTP server (`ftp.netscape5.com`, in this case). The rest of the URL is the pathname of the file you want to download.

The file URL specifies a file on your computer. It looks like this:

`file:///C|/www/index.htm`

On a Windows or DOS computer, this line indicates a Web page stored in the file `C:\www\index.htm`. The colon turns into a vertical bar (because colons in URLs mean something else), and the reverse slashes turn into forward slashes. File URLs are useful mostly for looking at graphics files with .gif and .jpg filename extensions, and for looking at a Web page that you just wrote and stuck in a file on your disk.

Moving from page to page is easy: Click any link that looks interesting. That's it. Underlined blue text and blue-bordered pictures are links. (Although links may be a colour other than blue, depending on the look the Web page designer is going for, they're always underlined — unless the page is the victim of a truly awful designer.) You can tell when you're pointing to a link because the mouse pointer changes to a little hand. If you're not sure whether something is a link, click it anyway; if it's not, clicking it won't hurt anything. Clicking outside a link selects the text you click, as in most other programs.

Backward, ho!

Web browsers remember the last few pages you visited, so if you click a link and decide that you're not so crazy about the new page, you can easily go back to the preceding one. To go back, click the Back button (its icon is an arrow pointing to the left; a pair of arrows in Opera) or press Alt+←.

All over the map

Some picture links are *image maps,* which use illustrations instead of text to provide a visual hint at the information available behind the links. In a regular link, it doesn't matter where you click; on an image map, it does. Some image maps are actual maps, while others are pictures that contain many buttons to go various places.

As you move the mouse cursor around a Web page, whenever you point at a link, the URL of the place it links to appears in small type at the bottom of the screen, or in a little box that "floats" over the mouse pointer. If the link is an image map, it shows the link followed by a question mark and two numbers that are the X and Y positions of where you are on the map. The numbers don't matter to you (it's up to the Web server to make sense of them); if you see a pair of numbers counting up and down when you move the mouse, however, you know that you're on an image map.

Going places

These days, everyone and his dog has a home page. A home page is the main Web page for a person or organization. Chapter 10 shows you how to make one for yourself (and your dog). (For an example, check out `users.aimnet.com/~carver/cindy.html`.) Companies advertise their home pages, and people send e-mail talking about cool sites. When you see a URL that you want to check out, here's what you do:

1. **Click in the Location or Address box, near the top of the Netscape or Internet Explorer window or the bottom of the Opera window.**

2. **Type the URL in the box. Most browsers conveniently let you leave out the `http://` part.**

   The URL is something like `www.altavista.com`.

3. **Press Enter.**

If you receive URLs in e-mail, Usenet news, or anywhere else on your Windows PC or Macintosh, you can use the standard cut-and-paste techniques to avoid retyping:

1. **Highlight the URL in whichever program is showing it.**

2. **Press Ctrl+C (⌘+C on the Mac) to copy the info to the Clipboard.**

3. **Click in the Location or Address box to highlight whatever is in it.**

4. **Press Ctrl+V (⌘+V on the Mac) to paste the URL into the box, and then press Enter.**

Eudora and many other mail programs highlight any URLs in e-mail messages. All you have to do is click the highlighted link, and it'll switch to your browser and open the Web page.

You can leave the `http://` off the front of URLs when you type them in the Location or Address box. Your trusty browser can figure out that part!

Where to start?

You'll find out more about how to find things on the Web in Chapter 8; for now, here's a good way to get started. Go to the Yahoo! page. (Yes, the name of the Web page includes an exclamation point — it's very excitable. But we'll leave it out for the rest of the book because we find it annoying.) Type this URL in the Location or Address box, then press Enter:

```
www.yahoo.ca
```

You go to the Yahoo page, which is a directory of millions of Web pages organized by topic. Just nose around, and you're sure to find something interesting.

This page looks funny

Sometimes a Web page gets garbled on the way in, or you interrupt it (by clicking the Stop button on the toolbar). You can tell your browser to get the information on the page again. In Netscape, click the Reload button or press Ctrl+R; in Internet Explorer, click the Refresh button or press F5. In Opera, click the Reload button.

Get me outta here

Sooner or later, even the most dedicated Web surfer has to stop to eat or attend to other bodily needs. You leave your browser in the same way that you leave any other Mac or Windows program: by choosing File➪Exit (File➪ Close for Windows Internet Explorer, we were surprised to find) or pressing Alt+F4. In Windows 95/98/NT/2000, you can also click the Close button in the upper-right corner of the window.

You can do a few things to speed up Netscape Navigator and Internet Explorer; we'll address these in Chapter 7. (That's a ploy to keep you reading.)

Getting and Installing Netscape Navigator, Internet Explorer, or Opera

With luck, Netscape Navigator or Internet Explorer is already installed on your computer. The two programs are so similar that if you have one of them, we suggest that you stick with it (for now, anyway). Without luck, you don't have either program — but they are, fortunately, not difficult to obtain and install.

Netscape Navigator comes in several varieties: Windows 3.1 (the 16-bit version), Windows 95/98/NT (the 32-bit version), Mac, and versions for a bunch of UNIX workstations. Netscape also comes as part of a suite of programs called Netscape Communicator (we talk about the mail programs in Chapter 11). Netscape Navigator 4.7 includes a Web page editor, too, in case you want to create your own Web pages. (See Chapter 10 to find out how to create Web pages.)

Although Internet Explorer used to be available only for Windows 95, Microsoft now has versions for Windows 98, 3.1, the Mac, and a few versions of UNIX.

Even if you already have a copy of Netscape or Internet Explorer, new versions come out every, oh, 20 minutes or so, and it's worth knowing how to upgrade because occasionally the new versions fix some bugs so that they're better than the old versions. The steps are relatively simple:

1. **Get a copy of the Netscape Navigator or Internet Explorer installation package on your computer.**

2. **Unpack the installation package.**

3. **Install the software.**

Because computers are involved, each of these steps is, naturally, a little more difficult than necessary.

Getting the package

Your Internet provider may have given you a copy of Netscape Navigator or Internet Explorer on a disk.

Because Internet Explorer comes as part of Windows 95/98/NT/2000, you may already have it, but it may be an elderly version. Microsoft gives away Internet Explorer, so you may as well upgrade to the current version if you have an old one. (One can complain about many aspects of Internet Explorer, but not its price, unless you worry about software monopolies.)

You can also download any of these browsers from the Net. If you have access to any Web browser, try one of these Web sites:

- ✔ **TUCOWS (The Ultimate Collection of Internet Software):** www.tucows.com

- ✔ **The Consummate Winsock Applications page:** cws.internet.com

- ✔ **Netscape home page (for Netscape Navigator):** home.netscape.com/download

- ✔ **Microsoft home page (for Internet Explorer):** www.microsoft.com/windows/ie for Windows and www.microsoft.com/mac/products/ie for Macs

- ✔ **Opera Software (for Opera):** www.operasoftware.com (Opera is shareware; you should pay the $35 USD registration fee if you use it for more than 30 days.)

Use your Web browser to go to the page, then follow the instructions for finding and downloading the program. You may also want to consult Chapter 16 for more information about downloading files from the Internet.

Another option is to stroll into a software store and buy Netscape Internet Essentials, a boxed version of Netscape — you get a manual and the phone number for tech support, something you *don't* get when you download Netscape or install it from this book.

We're home — let's go

After you have the program, you have to install it. If you get Netscape (Navigator or the whole Communicator suite) or Internet Explorer, which come on the CD-ROM in the back of this book, follow the accompanying instructions. Opera also comes with instructions, which you should read carefully.

If you have the Netscape, Internet Explorer, or Opera distribution file on your hard drive, follow these instructions (assuming that you use Windows 3.1, 95, 98, or NT). Macintosh users, check the tips at the end of this section.

To avoid excess user comprehension, the thing that Microsoft called a *directory* in MS-DOS and Windows 3.1 is called a *folder* in Windows 95, 98, and NT. We use the official newspeak term; if you're a Windows 3.1 user, however, pretend that we said *directory* wherever you read *folder*.

1. **The distribution file contains a program — run it.**

   The program begins installing Netscape, Internet Explorer, or Opera. First, it extracts a bunch of files that it needs for the installation, and then it proceeds to the installation process.

2. **Follow the instructions on-screen.**

   Although the installation program asks a bunch of questions, the default answers for all of them are usually okay. If the Internet Explorer installation program asks whether you want to select optional components, choose Yes, and select the additional programs you want to install. (They may include Outlook Express, the Microsoft e-mail program; see Chapter 11 to find out how to use it.)

   The Internet Explorer installation program is actually just a "stub" that requires you to have your Net connection active when you run the program, because it goes out over the Net and fetches the rest of the program. The installation program is about 400 kilobytes, so you can download it in two or three minutes; after the installation starts, however, it has to download between 10 and 25 megabytes more, which takes a couple of hours. Consider starting the installation program and then going out for pizza (a lot of pizza).

   When the Internet Explorer installation is done, you may have to restart your computer; if so, you see a message offering to restart it now. Click Yes, unless you're in the middle of other work, in which case you should save your work and restart your computer.

3. **Connect to your Internet provider or online service if you're not already online.**

The first thing your new browser wants to do is to display a Web page, so you had better be connected to the Internet.

4. **Try out your new browser.**

Click the browser's attractive new icon.

The first time you run Netscape, you see a bunch of legal boilerplate stuff describing the licence conditions for Netscape. If you can stand the conditions (many people can), click to indicate your acceptance. Netscape then starts up. It may want to connect to the Netscape Web page so that you can register your copy of Netscape — follow its instructions.

The first time you run Internet Explorer, it may run the Internet Connection Wizard, which offers to help you get connected to the Internet. If so, follow the instructions on-screen. If you already have an Internet connection that works, you have a chance to tell it so.

When you run Opera, it opens a nagging window to encourage you to register your copy. To use it without registering, click Evaluate. If you use Opera regularly, do register it via its Web page at `www.operasoftware.com`.

Mac users: The installation tips for a Mac are almost exactly the same. If you download your browser from the Net and you're lucky, the browser should arrive as an executable program in your download folder. Click it and follow its directions in order to install it. The program may arrive as a StuffIt file that self-extracts if you have StuffIt installed.

If you're upgrading from an older version of Netscape to a newer one, you can install the new version to replace the old one. The installation program may even be smart enough to remember some of your old settings and bookmarks (favorites).

Upgrade magic

After you have installed either Netscape Navigator or Internet Explorer, your software vendor would really, really, REALLY like you not to switch to a competing product. (Opera isn't so pushy.) Toward this end, Netscape and Microsoft have both invented more or less automated schemes to upgrade from one version of their software to the next, and to help you figure out what needs upgrading in the first place.

✔ Netscape has a Smart Update feature. Fire up Netscape, go to `home.netscape.com/download`, click Smart Update, and follow the instructions on the page. Once the download of the newer version of the program has begun, Netscape opens a small window listing what it's doing, with detailed directions on what to click and when. Follow them exactly (which can be a little confusing), and it downloads the new programs and installs them, one at a time. Some of the programs are large (new versions of Navigator and Communicator can be more than 20 MB), so the downloads may take awhile.

✔ Internet Explorer is included in Microsoft Windows' Windows Update command. Choose Start⇨Windows Update or Start⇨Settings⇨Windows Update on the taskbar. Microsoft's programs are even bigger than Netscape's, so the downloads can take a long time.

✔ Opera doesn't have an automated upgrade system as such. To see what it has available, run Opera; then, on the menu, select Lists⇨Opera Software⇨Download page.

Life with Lynx

The graphical browsers we've been discussing require PPP connections. What if you're stuck with a UNIX shell account? Those of you living a mouse-free existence can still do some serious Web surfing by using Lynx.

Because Lynx is a text-only browser, it can't do some things, such as show pictures, play audio and video clips, or display news-ticker-style moving messages at the bottom of your screen (a real advantage, in this last case). Within those limitations, though, it's a good program.

In fact, because Lynx *is* text-only, it's much faster than the graphics-based browsers, leaving you at least one thing to feel good about. And if you are sight-impaired, Lynx is definitely the way to go, because special programs can take Web page text and blow it up to huge sizes or even read it aloud.

All UNIX shell providers should have Lynx available, because it's free. To start it, you type lynx at the UNIX shell prompt. It starts up and displays a home page on-screen, as shown in Figure 6-4, which shows one of our friends' Web pages.

Because most text screens can't do underlining, the links are shown in reverse video. Bracketed text or the word [IMAGE] appears where a picture would be displayed. One link on the screen is *current* and is highlighted in a different colour. (On our screen, it's yellow rather than white text, which doesn't show up on a black-and-white page. Use your imagination, or go get a yellow highlighting pen.) Lynx thoughtfully puts some help information on the bottom two lines, which makes it much easier to use.

```
                    TeamFlow - Team-based Process Flowcharting (p3 of 8)
        software products. Through an alliance, we also provide computer
        hardware, installation, and support in Northern Illinois.
      * Creative Learning Technologies uses TeamFlow's scheduling features
        to support Team-based project management for a variety of clients.
        TeamFlow is The Project Manager for the Rest of Us(TM).
      * Quality Management International uses TeamFlow to help their
        clients make ISO 9000 registration simple and certain.
      * R.T.Green & Associates is a group of experienced human resources
        professionals with broad range of accomplishments in the full
        spectrum of the Human Resources field. "Of the many productivity
        tools available we have tested, TeamFlow is the easiest to use and
        explain. Clients can see our processes and any discrete roles
        clearly laid out - the first time, every time."
      * Thousands of companies around the world use TeamFlow to help
        manage their business processes. Some of their stories and a
        listing of some of our customers are included here.


    What is TeamFlow?
      * TeamFlow is a powerful tool for team-based process management.
        TeamFlow is the only process flowcharter designed to implement the
        Deployment Flowcharting methodology invented by Dr. W. Edwards
    -more- http://www.teamflow.com/profiles.html
```

Figure 6-4:
Look, Ma,
no pictures!

Wandering around

Nearly all Lynx commands are single keystrokes. Pressing the ↑ and ↓ keys moves you from link to link on the current page. If the page fills more than one screen, the page scrolls as necessary. To move to the next screen of the current page, press the spacebar, or press the plus and minus (+ and –) keys to move forward and backward, one screen at a time.

You press the up- and down-arrow (↑ and ↓) keys to move from link to link, even when the links are next to each other on a line. For example, you may have a few lines on-screen, like this:

```
Famous philosophers:
[Moe] [Larry] [Curly] [Socrates]
```

If the highlight is on Larry, you press the ↑ key to go to Moe and press the ↓ key to go to Curly. The ← and → keys mean something else, as you will see in a second.

After you highlight a link you like, press the → key or Enter to follow that link. (Pressing → is the Lynx equivalent of clicking a link.) After Lynx fetches the new page, you can press the arrow keys to move around the new page. Pressing → takes you back to the preceding page. You can press the ← key several times to go back several pages.

Lynx just can't do some things — most notably, image maps. Although it tells you that an image exists, because you can't see the image and you can't use a mouse, you have no way to click it. Fortunately, any sensible Web page that has an image map offers some other way to get to the places the image map would otherwise take you. The page has either a set of text links under the image or, in some cases, a link that says something like "Click here for a text-only version of this page." Lynx gives you a nice, clean, image-free page from which to work.

To go to a specific URL, press g for *go-to* and then type the URL on the line that Lynx provides, then press Enter.

Leaving Lynx

When you're finished with Lynx, press q to exit. Lynx asks whether you're sure that you want to quit; press y.

Is that all there is?

Of course not. Lynx is bristling with features, just like any other modern computer program. Just about every possible keystroke means something to Lynx (we discuss some of them in Chapter 7). The arrow keys and g and q are all you really need to get going.

Chapter 7

Wrangling with the Web

. . . .

In This Chapter

▶ Window shopping

▶ Keeping track of your favorite sites

▶ Making your Web journey faster

▶ Clearing some room on your screen

▶ Filling in Web forms

▶ Saving pages for posterity

▶ Printing pages from the Web

▶ Getting plugged in with plug-ins

. . . .

*I*f you know how to find your way around the Web, you're ready for some comparatively advanced features so that you can start to feel like a Web pro in no time.

Windows on the World

Windows and Mac browsers are known in the trade as *multithreaded* programs. What this term means in practice is that the program can do several things at a time and can display several pages at once. When we're pointing and clicking from one place to another, we like to open a bunch of windows so that we can see where we've been and go back to a previous page just by switching to another window. You can also arrange windows side by side, which is a good way to, say, compare prices for *The Internet For Canadians For Dummies,* 2nd Edition Starter Kit, at various online bookstores. (The difference may be small, but when you're buying 100 copies for everyone on your Christmas list, those pennies can add up. Oh, you weren't planning to do that? Drat.)

Wild window mania with Netscape Navigator and Internet Explorer

Netscape Navigator and Internet Explorer can have several Web browser windows open at a time. To display a page in a new window, click a link with the right mouse button and select Open in New Window from the menu that pops up. To close a window, click the little X box at the top right of the window frame, or press Alt+F4, the standard close-window shortcut. Macs don't have a right mouse button, so hold down the left button to get pop-up windows. You close all Mac windows the same way — by clicking the button at the top of the window. UNIX users with three-button mice can open a link in a new window by clicking the middle button.

You can also create a new window without following a link. Press Ctrl+N or choose File⇨New⇨Navigator Window (in Netscape Navigator 4.7) or File⇨New⇨Window (in Internet Explorer 4.0 and higher). UNIX and Mac users should think "Alt" and "Apple" for "Ctrl" throughout this section.

Restrained, dignified window mania with Opera

Opera, unlike Lynx, has what's known in Windows-ese as a *Multiple Document Interface*, which means that each page appears as a sub-window inside the main Opera window. To open a link in a new window, right-click and select Get Link Document New Window. To close a window, press Ctrl+W or click the X in the top right of the document's window. To open a new empty window, press Ctrl+N or click the New Window icon (the little piece of paper) at the left end of the toolbar.

Short attention span tips

If you ask your browser to begin downloading a big file, it displays a small window in the corner of your screen. The Netscape Navigator and Opera versions of this window display a "thermometer" showing the download progress; Internet Explorer shows tiny pages flying from one folder to another. Although some people consider watching the thermometer rise or the pages fly to be quite entertaining (we do when we're tired enough), you can click back to the main browser window and continue surfing.

Doing two or three things at a time in your browser when you have a dial-up Net connection is not unlike squeezing blood from a turnip — only so much blood can be squeezed. In this case, the blood is the amount of data it can pump through your modem. A single download task can keep your modem close to 100-percent busy and anything else you do shares the modem with the download process. When you do two things at a time, therefore, each one happens more slowly than it would if done by itself.

If one task is a big download and the other is perusing Web pages, everything usually works okay because you spend a fair amount of time looking at what the Web browser is displaying; the download can then run while you think. On the other hand, although browsers let you start two download tasks at a time (or a dozen, if you're so inclined), you have no reason to do more than one at a time because it's no faster to do them in parallel than one after another, plus it can get confusing.

Lynx users are in a somewhat different situation because Lynx displays only one window at a time. In theory, you can run two copies of Lynx and switch back and forth; in practice, however, it's not worth the trouble. Because Lynx is running on your provider's system, it can take advantage of your provider's high-speed Net connection, so even large files load pretty quickly.

My Favorite Things

The Web really does have cool places to visit. Some you will want to visit over and over again. All the makers of fine browsers have, fortunately, provided a handy way for you to remember those spots and not have to write down those nasty URLs just to have to type them again later.

Although the name varies, the idea is simple. Your browser lets you mark a spot and then adds the URL to a list. Later, when you want to go back, you just go to your list and pick it out. Netscape Navigator calls these hot spots *bookmarks;* Internet Explorer calls them *favorites;* Opera calls them *hot list entries.*

Bookmarks can be handled in two ways. One is to think of them as a menu so that you can choose individual bookmarks from the menu bar of your browser. The other is to think of them as a custom-built page of links so that you go to that page and then choose the link you want. Lynx takes the latter, custom-Web-page approach. Opera leans toward the menu approach. Netscape, a prime example of the Great Expanding Blob approach to software design, does both. Internet Explorer takes yet another tack: it adds your Web pages to a folder of favorite places to which you may want to return.

Bookmarking in Netscape Navigator

Netscape bookmarks lurk under the Bookmarks Quick File button, which is located to the left of the Location box, below the Back button on the toolbar (in the two most recent versions of Netscape Navigator). To add a bookmark for a Web page, choose Communicator➪Bookmarks➪Add Bookmark, or press Ctrl+D. The bookmarks appear as entries on the menu that shows up when you click the Bookmarks Quick File button. To go to one of the pages on your bookmark list, just choose its entry from this menu.

If you're like most users, your bookmark menu gets bigger and bigger and crawls down your screen and eventually ends up flopping down on the floor, which is both unattractive and unsanitary. Fortunately, you can *smoosh* (technical term) your menu into a more tractable form. Choose Communicator➪Bookmarks➪Edit Bookmarks, or press Ctrl+B, to display your Bookmarks window, as shown in Figure 7-1.

Because all these bookmarks are "live," you can go to any of them by clicking them. (You can leave this window open while you move around the Web in other browser windows.) You can also add separator lines and submenus to organize your bookmarks and make the individual menus less unwieldy. Submenus look like folders in the Bookmarks window.

In the Bookmarks window in the two most recent versions of Netscape, choose File➪New Separator to add a separator line and File➪New Folder to add a new submenu. (Netscape asks you to type the name of the submenu before it creates the folder.) You can then drag the bookmarks, separators, and folders up and down to where you want them in the Bookmarks window. Drag an item to a folder to put it in that folder's submenu, and double-click a folder to display or hide that submenu. Because any changes you make in the Bookmarks window are reflected immediately on the Bookmarks menu, it's easy to fiddle with the bookmarks until you get something you like. Netscape preloads your bookmark window with pages they'd like you to look at, but feel free to delete them if your tastes are different from theirs.

When you're done fooling with your bookmarks, choose File➪Close or press Ctrl+W to close the Bookmarks window.

Netscape also has a cool feature that enables you to see which of the items on your bookmark list have been updated since you last looked at them. Open the Bookmarks window as described earlier in this section and then choose View➪Update Bookmarks from the menu in the Bookmarks window. You see a little box asking which bookmarks you want to check. Click the Start Checking button. When Netscape is done checking the Web pages on your bookmark list, it displays a message telling you how many have changed. The icons in the Bookmarks window reveal which pages have changed: the ones with little sparkles have new material, the ones with question marks are the ones Netscape isn't sure about, and the ones that look normal haven't changed.

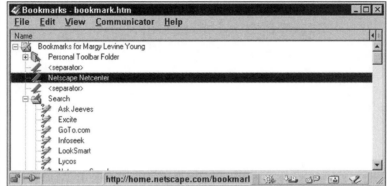

Figure 7-1:
The
Netscape
Bookmarks
window
shows the
list of Web
pages you
want to
come
back to.

Picking favorites in Internet Explorer

Internet Explorer uses a system similar to Netscape's, although it calls the saved pages "favorites" rather than "bookmarks." You can add the current page to your Favorites folder and then look at and organize your Favorites folder. If you use Windows, however, this Favorites folder is shared with other programs on your computer. Other programs also can add things to your Favorites folder, so it's a jumble of Web pages, files, and other things. (Luckily, most people use Favorites only for Web pages.)

To add the current page to your Favorites folder, choose Favorites⇨Add to Favorites from the menu. To see your Favorites folder, choose Favorites⇨ Organize Favorites from the menu. Internet Explorer also has a Favorites button on the toolbar that displays your list of Favorites down the left side of your Internet Explorer window.

Exactly how the Favorites folder works depends on which version of Internet Explorer you're running. The versions for Internet Explorer 4.0 and 5.0 for Windows 95/98 are shown in Figures 7-2 and 7-3, respectively. You can create subfolders in the Favorites folder so that you can store different types of files in different folders. (The Windows 3.1 version just lets you look at the Favorites list — you can't reorganize it.) To create a folder, click the Create New Folder button in 4.0 (the button with the yellow folder with a little sparkle, near the upper-right corner of the window) or the Create Folder button in 5.0. To move an item in the Favorites window into a folder, click the item, click the Move or Move to Folder button, and select the folder to move it to. You can see the contents of a folder by double-clicking it. When you are done organizing your favorite items, click the Close button.

In Internet Explorer 5.0 and higher, you can make pages available when you're not connected to the Internet by clicking on the page in the Favorites window and then clicking the Make available offline box. Internet Explorer immediately fetches the page to your disk and refetches it from time to time when you're connected so that you can view the page when you click on it offline.

Figure 7-2:
Internet
Explorer 4.0
shows your
favorites.

If you make a lot of pages available offline, you'll find your browser spending a great deal of time keeping them up-to-date. When you no longer need to browse a page offline, uncheck its Make available offline box or remove it from Favorites altogether.

The folders you create in the Organize Favorites window appear on your Favorites menu, and the items you put in the folders appear on submenus. To return to a Web page you've added to your Favorites folder, just choose it from the Favorites menu.

In Windows 95/98, the Favorites folder usually appears on your Start menu. Choose Start⇨Favorites and then choose items from the menu. If the item is a Web page, your browser fires up and (if you're connected to the Internet) displays the Web page.

Figure 7-3:
Explorer 5.0
lets you
access your
favorites
when you're
not con-
nected to
the Internet,
by clicking
the Make
available
offline box.

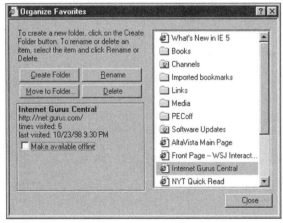

Hot, hot, hot in Opera

Opera calls its bookmark list the *hot list.* You get to it from the Lists menu item, which comes preloaded with submenus and sub-submenus full of suggested pages (pretty good ones, in fact, including the *Pacific Islands Monthly* published in Fiji). You can add and update your own as well.

To open a page in the hot list, choose Lists from the menu, select the appropriate submenu, and select a page in the submenu.

To add the current page to the hot list, choose Lists from the menu, choose the appropriate submenu, and in that submenu, select Add Current Document Here. Opera pops up a window where you can enter a nickname to use in the menu and a description (both entirely optional) and then click OK to add it.

To edit the hot list, choose View➪Hotlist or press Ctrl+2, displaying a window like the one shown in Figure 7-4. The upper portion displays all the folders in the hot list; the lower portion contains the contents of the current folder. Click any folder in the upper part of the window to open that folder. To move an item from one folder to another, open the folder where it is now, and then click and drag the item into the new folder. If you right-click on any folder or item, you get a menu of useful operations, including Delete to get rid of an item and New➪Folder to create a new folder. While the hot list is open, you can double-click any item to open it in a new window.

To close the hot list, press Ctrl+W or click the X icon at the top right of the border.

Figure 7-4:
The upper portion of the hot list window displays all the current folders in the hot list; the lower portion displays the contents of the selected folder.

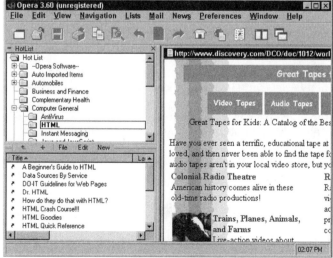

Bookmarking in Lynx

The Lynx bookmark scheme is a complete anticlimax compared to Netscape Navigator and Internet Explorer. It's controlled by two (count 'em — two) letters.

To add the current page to your bookmark list, press a. Lynx gives you the choice of adding a link to the page on-screen (d for document) or copying the highlighted link (c for current).

To look at (view) your current bookmark list, press v. When you're looking at your bookmark list, you move through it and choose links in the same way that you do on any other Web page. You can remove links from the bookmark page by pressing r.

If you're using Lynx on your own UNIX account, your bookmarks are saved in a file between Lynx sessions. On the other hand, if you're using *telnet* to connect to a Lynx system somewhere else, the bookmarks exist only through a single Lynx session, and they're discarded when you quit.

Speeding Things Up

Unless you have a high-speed dedicated connection rather than a normal dial-up account, you probably spend a great deal of time wishing that the process of getting to stuff on the Web was much faster. Here are a handful of tricks you can use to speed things up.

Where do we start?

In Netscape Navigator: When Netscape starts up, by default it loads the large and attractive Netscape home page chock full of irresistible offers (at least, Netscape's owners at AOL hope they are). After one or two times, beautiful though the home page is, you will probably find that you can do without it. You can tell Netscape not to load any Web page when you start the program:

1. **Choose E̲dit⇨P̲references.**

   You see the Preferences dialog box.

2. **Click the Navigator category in the box down the left side of the window.**

   You see a setting called Navigator starts with.

3. **To start with no Web page, click Bla<u>n</u>k Page. To choose a page to start with, click <u>H</u>ome Page, click in the box below it, and type the URL of a page you would rather see.**

You also have the option of starting where you left off last time, by clicking <u>L</u>ast page visited.

4. **Click OK.**

In Internet Explorer: Internet Explorer 4.0 and higher starts by displaying the Microsoft home page or a Web page stored on your own hard disk, depending on which version of Internet Explorer you have. You can change that start page, or you can tell Internet Explorer to load a blank page. (Loading a home page from your disk is pretty fast.) Follow these steps to change your start page:

1. **Display the Web page that you want to use as your start page.**

For example, you may want to start at the Yahoo page, described in Chapter 8, or Internet Gurus Central, at net.gurus.com.

2. **Choose <u>T</u>ools⇨Internet Options or <u>V</u>iew⇨Internet <u>O</u>ptions from the menu.**

You see the Internet Options dialog box.

3. **Click the General tab along the top of the dialog box.**

You can set the addresses of several Web pages.

4. **In the Home page section of the dialog box, click the Use <u>C</u>urrent button.**

The URL of the current page appears in the A<u>d</u>dress box. To start with no page at all, click the Use <u>B</u>lank button.

5. **Click OK.**

Choose a start page that doesn't have many pictures. By starting with a Web page that loads faster or with no start page, you don't have to wait long to start browsing.

In Opera: In Opera, the best bet is to display what you were looking at last time.

1. **Select <u>P</u>references⇨<u>G</u>eneric from the menu.**

You see the Generic Preferences box.

2. **Select the Show saved windows and history option.**

3. **Click OK.**

Switching to ugly mode

You can save a great deal of time by skipping the pictures when you're browsing the Web. True, the pages don't look as snazzy, but they load like the wind. If you decide that you want to see the missing pictures after all, you can still do so.

In Netscape Navigator: Choose Edit⇨Preferences menu to display the Preferences dialog box, click the Advanced category, and uncheck the Automatically load images check box. This change tells Netscape to load only the text part of Web pages, which is small, and to hold off on the images, which are large. At every place on the page where an image should go, Netscape displays a box with three coloured shapes. To see a particular image, click the three-shape box with the right mouse button and choose Load Image from the menu that appears.

In Internet Explorer: You can tell Internet Explorer not to bother loading images by choosing View⇨Internet Options from the menu (Tools⇨Internet Options in 5.0), clicking the Advanced tab, and scrolling down to the Multimedia section. If a checkmark or X appears in the Show pictures box, click in the box to remove the check mark or X. Then click OK. Where pictures usually appear, you see a little box with three shapes in it. If you want to see a particular picture, right-click the little box and choose Show Picture from the menu that appears.

In Opera: You can tell Opera not to load images by choosing Preferences⇨Multimedia, and checking Do Not Load and Show Images. A good compromise is Show Loaded Images Only, which displays an image if it's already available but doesn't download new ones. You can turn image loading on and off in each individual window by clicking the little frame icon at the bottom left of the window.

Cold, hard cache

When Netscape Navigator or Internet Explorer retrieves a page you have asked to see, it stores the page on your disk. If you ask for the same page again five minutes later, the program doesn't have to retrieve the page again — it can reuse the copy it already has. If you tell the program not to load images, for example, you get a fair number of them anyway because they have already been downloaded.

The space your browser uses to store pages is called its *cache* (pronounced "cash" because it's French and gives your cache more cachet). The more space you tell your browser to use for its cache, the faster the pages appear the second time you look at them.

In Netscape Navigator: To set the size of the Netscape cache, follow these steps:

1. **Choose Edit⇨Preferences from the menu.**

   You see the Preferences dialog box.

2. **Double-click the Advanced category and click the Cache category.**

   The Disk Cache box shows the maximum size of the cache in kilobytes (KB): We like to set Disk Cache to at least 4096KB (that is, 4MB). Set it to a higher number if you have a large hard disk with loads of free space — the more space your cache can occupy, the more often you can load a Web page quickly from the cache rather than slowly from the Net.

3. **Click OK.**

In Internet Explorer: To set the size of the Internet Explorer cache, follow these steps:

1. **Choose View⇨Internet Options from the menu (Tools⇨Internet Options in 5.0).**

   You see the Internet Options dialog box.

2. **Click the General tab.**

3. **Click the Settings button in the Temporary Internet Files box.**

   You see the Settings dialog box, with information about the cache. (Many versions of Internet Explorer never call it a cache — guess they don't speak French.)

4. **Click the slider on the Amount of Disk Space to use or Maximum Size line and move it to about 10 percent.**

   If you have tonnes of empty disk space, you can slide it rightward to 20 percent. If you're short on space, move it leftward to 1 percent or 2 percent.

5. **Click OK twice.**

In Opera: To set the size of the cache, follow these steps:

1. **Choose Preferences⇨Cache from the menu.**

   You see the Cache Preferences dialog box.

2. **Set the sizes of the disk cache (in the Disk Cache section) and the documents and images caches (in the RAM Cache section).**

   The default sizes are too small; try 5000 KB for the disk cache and 1000 KB apiece for the other two.

3. **Click OK.**

Some of us hardly ever exit from our browsers, which is probably not a good idea for our long-term mental stability. If you are one of us, however, remember that the pages your browser has cached aren't reloaded from the Web (they're taken from your disk) until you reload them. If you want to make sure that you're getting fresh pages, reload pages that you think may have changed since you last visited. Your browser is supposed to check whether a saved page has changed, but because the check sometimes doesn't work perfectly, an occasional Reload or Refresh command for pages that change frequently, such as stock prices or the weather report, is advisable.

Getting the Big Picture

Browsers have so many buttons, icons, and boxes near the top of the window that not much space is left to display the Web page. Here are some hints on making more space.

In Netscape Navigator: You can clear off a little more space in the Netscape window by eliminating the Personal Toolbar (the row of buttons just above the Web page area, that say "Instant Message" and "WebMail"). Choose View⇨ Show⇨Personal Toolbar to remove the check mark to the left of the command. Other commands on the View⇨Show menu let you turn off other toolbars. To restore toolbars that you just blew away, give the same command again.

In Internet Explorer: You can reclaim screen real estate by removing toolbars. If the Links toolbar appears in the Internet Explorer window, choose View⇨ Toolbars⇨Links to make it go away. Give the same command again to restore it. You can turn off the other toolbars by choosing other options on the View⇨Toolbars menu.

In Opera: The window's not as cluttered to start with, but you can unclutter it more. Choose View⇨Status bar⇨Off to remove the status bar at the bottom of the window. Choose View⇨Progress bar to toggle (interchangeably go from one window, screen or "page view" to another) the progress and status bar at the bottom of each window.

To see as much as possible of a browser window, maximize that window by clicking the maximize button near the top right of its border. This makes the window the maximum size and removes the border around it. (This same trick works in any multi-document interface program, including Word and Excel.)

Filling in the Forms

Back in the dark ages of the Web (that is, in 1993), Web pages were just pages to look at. Because that wasn't anywhere near enough fun nor complicated enough, Web forms were invented. A *form* is sort of like a paper form, with fields that you can fill out and then send in. Figure 7-5 shows a typical form.

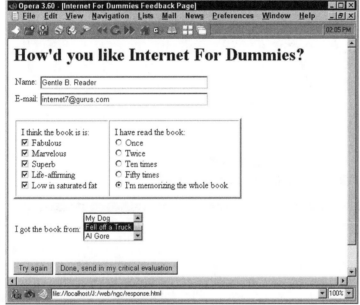

Figure 7-5:
You fill out a Web form the way you would a paper form, but on-screen, then send it in.

The top two lines in the form are fill-in text boxes in which you type, in this case, your name and e-mail address. Under that is a set of *check boxes,* in which you check whichever ones apply (all of them, we hope), and a set of *radio buttons,* which are similar to check boxes except that you can choose only one of them. Under that is a *list box,* in which you can choose one of the possibilities in the box. In most cases, more entries are available than can fit in the box, so you scroll up and down. Although you can usually choose only one entry, some list boxes let you choose more.

At the bottom of the form are two buttons. The one on the left clears the form fields and sends nothing, and the one on the right, known as the Submit button, sends the filled-out form back to the Web server for processing.

After the data is sent from the form back to the Web server, it's entirely up to the server how to interpret it.

Lynx handles forms just the way other browsers do (one of the best Lynx features), as shown in Figure 7-6. You move from field to field on a Lynx form by pressing the ↑ and ↓ keys, the same as always. To submit a form, move to the Submit button (or whatever the button is labeled) and press Enter.

Figure 7-6:
Form-ally
speaking in
Lynx.

Some Web pages have *search items,* which are simplified one-line forms that let you type some text, usually interpreted as keywords for which to search. Depending on the browser, a Submit button may be displayed to the right of the text area, or you may just press Enter to send the search words to the server.

Lower the Cone of Silence

When you are filling out a form on a Web page, you may need to provide information that you'd prefer not be made public — your credit card number, for example. Not to worry! Modern browsers can encrypt the information you send to and receive from a secure Web server. You can tell when a page was received encrypted from the Web server by an icon in the lower-left corner of your browser window. If the little lock appears open (or crossed out, in Opera), the page was not encrypted. If the little lock is locked, encryption is on. Typed-in data in forms on secure pages are almost always sent encrypted as well, making it impossible for anyone to snoop as your secrets pass through the Net.

Save Me!

Frequently, you see something on a Web page that's worth saving for later. It might be a Web page full of interesting information, or a picture, or some other type of file. Fortunately, saving stuff is easy.

When you save a Web page, you have to decide whether to save only the text that appears or the entire HTML version of the page, with the format codes. (For a glimpse of HTML, see Chapter 10.) You can also save the pictures that appear on Web pages.

In Netscape Navigator, Internet Explorer, or Opera, choose File⇨Save As, to save the current Web page in a file. You see the standard Save As dialog box, in which you specify the name under which to save the incoming file. Click in the Save As Type box to determine how to save the page. Choose Plain Text to save only the text of the page, with little notes where pictures occur. Choose HTML or HMTL Files to save the entire HTML file. Then click the Save or OK button.

To save an image that you see on a Web page, right-click the image (click the image with your right mouse button). Choose Save Image As or Save Picture As, from the menu that appears. When you see the Save As dialog box, move to the folder or directory where you want to save the image (also called a graphics file), type a filename in the File Name box, and click the Save or OK button.

A note about copyright: Contrary to popular belief, most Web pages, along with almost everything else on the Internet, are copyrighted by their authors. If you save a Web page or a picture from a Web page, you don't necessarily have permission to use it any way you want. Before you reuse the text or pictures in any way, send an e-mail message to the owner of the site. If an address doesn't appear on the page, write for permission to `webmaster@domain.com`, replacing `domain.com` with the domain name part of the URL of the Web page. For example, to reach the webmaster at Canada Post, type in `webmaster@canadapost.ca`. Hopefully, the webmaster will be awake!

Saving Lynx pages

Saving files in Lynx is a little more complicated, but still not too difficult. How you do it depends on whether you want to save a page that Lynx knows how to display or to do something else.

Whenever Lynx saves something to disk, it saves it to the disk on the computer where Lynx is running. If your Lynx session is running on your provider's computer, but you want a saved page on your own PC, you have to download it yourself.

To save a page that Lynx can display, first move to the page so that it's displayed on-screen. Then press d for download. Lynx prompts you with the various ways it knows to save the page; usually, the only option is to save to disk, which lets you specify on your provider's system a filename in which to save it. Alternatively, you can press p for print, which gives you three options:

- ✔ Save to disk, just the way d does.
- ✔ Mail to yourself (frequently the most convenient option).
- ✔ Print to screen. Turn on "screen capture" in the terminal program on your PC, which saves the contents of the page as it goes by on-screen.

Saving anything else in Lynx

Saving is the easiest part. If you choose a link that displays an image, program, or other sort of document that Lynx can't handle, it stops and tells you that it can't display this link. You press d to download it to a local file, for which you specify the name, or c to cancel and forget that link.

The Dead-Tree Thing (Printing)

For about the first year that Web browsers existed, they all had print commands that didn't work. People finally figured out how to print Web pages, and now they can all do it.

To print a page from Netscape Navigator, Internet Explorer, or Opera, just click the Print button on the toolbar, press Ctrl+P, or choose File➪Print. Reformatting the page to print can take a while, so patience is a virtue. Fortunately, each browser displays a progress window to keep you apprised of how it's doing.

If the page you want to print uses *frames* — a technique that divides the window into sub-areas that can scroll and update separately — click in the part of the window you want to print before printing; otherwise, you're likely to get the outermost frame, which usually just has a title and some buttons.

Printing in Lynx is easy in principle. You press p. If you're dialed in to your provider, however, printing on your provider's computer doesn't do you much good, so Lynx gives you some options, the most useful of which are saving to disk (so that you can download the Web page and print it locally) or e-mailing the page to yourself (so that you can download and print it locally). Are you detecting a pattern here?

Getting Plugged In: Singing, Dancing, and Chatting with Your Browser

Web pages with pictures are old hat. Now, Web pages have to have pictures that sing and dance, or ticker-style messages that move across the page, or video clips. Every month, new types of information appear on the Web. Browsers have had to evolve to keep up. You can now extend Netscape Navigator capabilities with *plug-ins*, or add-on programs, that glue themselves to Netscape and add even more features. Internet Explorer can extend itself, too, by using things called *ActiveX* controls, which are another type of add-on program. Opera uses plug-ins the way Netscape does.

What's a Web browser to do when it encounters new kinds of information on a Web page? Get the plug-in program that handles that kind of information and glue it onto Netscape or Internet Explorer. You *Star Trek* fans can think of plug-ins as parasitic life forms that attach themselves to your browser and enhance its intelligence.

A parade of plug-ins

Here are some useful plug-ins:

- ✔ **RealPlayer:** Plays audio files (sound files) as you download them (other programs have to wait until the entire file has downloaded before beginning to play). A free player is available at `www.real.com`, along with more powerful players for which you have to pay a modest amount. They also provide a list of Web sites that handle RealAudio sound files.

- ✔ **QuickTime:** Plays video files as you download them. Available at `www.apple.com/quicktime`.

- ✔ **Shockwave:** Plays both audio and video files, as well as other types of animation. Available at `www.shockwave.com`.

- ✔ **Adobe Acrobat Reader:** Displays Acrobat files formatted exactly the way the author intended. There are lots of useful Acrobat files out there, including many company annual reports (at `www.sedar.com`). Available at `www.adobe.com`.

How to use plug-ins with your browser

You can find Netscape Navigator or Opera plug-ins, and Internet Explorer ActiveX controls, at TUCOWS (`www.tucows.com`), Stroud's Consummate Winsock Applications page (`cws.internet.com`), the Netscape Web site (`home.netscape.com`), and other sources of software on the Web.

History? What history?

All three of the graphical browsers have a some-what useful feature, sometimes called *history*. Next to the box where you type a URL, there's a little arrow, which, when you click it, shows a list of recently visited URLs. Some of our read-ers have asked us how to clear out that box, presumably because they meant to type `www.disney.com` but their fingers slipped and it came out `www.hotxxx.com` instead. (It could happen to anyone.) Since some of the requests sounded fairly urgent, here are the occasionally gruesome details about how to do it.

Netscape Navigator 4.5 and later: Everything should be this easy. Select Edit⇨Preferences, select the Navigator category, click the big Clear Location Bar button.

Netscape Navigator 4.0: This starts to get more complicated, since there's no button. The list of URLs is stored in a file called prefs.js, which is probably in the folder \Program Files\Netscape\ Users\ *yourname*. (If not, use the Start menu's Find⇨File to find it.) This file contains all Netscape's preferences, and you can just delete

it; however, that will also make it forget all your other settings — so it's better to edit it. Close all Netscape windows, start up Notepad or any other text editor you like, and open prefs.js. You'll see a bunch of lines in an obscure pro-gramming language (Javascript, if you were wondering). Some of those lines have codes like `browser.url_history.URL_1`. Delete the lines with the erroneous URLs. Then save and close the file, restart Netscape, and try not to get into this situation again, okay?

Internet Explorer 4.0 and later: Select View⇨ Internet Options or Tools⇨Internet Options, click the General tab, and click the Clear History button. Click Yes when it asks if you wanted to do that.

Opera: Normally the history list is kept sepa-rately for each window, so closing the window gets rid of the history. Select Preferences⇨ Generic and make sure Global history is not checked to be sure no extra history is lurking around.

After you have downloaded a plug-in from the Net, run it (double-click its filename in My Computer, Windows Explorer, or File Manager) to install it. Depending on what the plug-in does, you follow different steps to try it out — usually, you find a file that the plug-in can play, and watch (or listen) as the plug-in plays it.

Chapter 8

Needles and Haystacks:
Finding Stuff on the Net

In This Chapter

▶ Defining some basic search strategies

▶ Finding stuff on the Web

▶ Built-in searchers

▶ Finding companies and people on the Web

▶ Finding stuff by e-mail

"*O*kay, all this great stuff is out there on the Net. How do I find it?" That's an excellent question. Thanks for asking. Questions like that are what make Canada strong and vibrant. We salute you and say, "Keep asking questions!" Next?

Oh, you want an *answer* to your question. Fortunately, quite a bit of (technical term follows) stuff-finding stuff is on the Net. More particularly, we're talking about indexes and directories of much of the interesting material available on the Net.

The Net has different types of indexes and directories for different types of material. Because the indexes tend to be organized, unfortunately, by the type of Internet service they provide rather than by the nature of the material, you find Web resources in one place, e-mail resources in another place, and so on. You can search in hundreds of different ways, depending on what you're looking for and how you prefer to search. (John has remarked that his ideal restaurant has only one item on the menu, but that it's just what he wants. The Internet is about as far from that ideal as you can possibly imagine.)

TIP

Index, directory — what's the difference?

When we talk about a *directory,* we mean a listing like an encyclopedia or a library's card catalogue (well, like the computer system that is replacing the card catalogue). It has named categories with entries assigned to categories partly or entirely by human cataloguers. You look things up by finding a category you want and seeing what it contains. In this book, we would think of the table of contents as a directory.

An *index,* on the other hand, simply collects all the items, extracts keywords from them (by taking all the words except for *the, and,* and the like), and makes a big list. You search the index by specifying some words that seem likely, and

it finds all the entries that contain that word. The index in the back of this book is more like an index.

Each has its advantages and disadvantages. Directories are organized better, use consistent terminology, and contain fewer useless pages. But indexes are larger, use whatever terms the underlying Web pages use, and are updated more often. Some overlap exists between indexes and directories — Yahoo, the best-known Web page directory, lets you search by keyword, and many of the indexes divide their entries into general categories that let you limit the search.

To provide a smidgen of structure to this discussion, we describe several different sorts of searches:

- ✔ **Topics:** Places, things, ideas, companies — anything you want to find out more about.
- ✔ **Built-in searches:** Topic searches that a browser does automatically, and why we're not thrilled about that.
- ✔ **People:** Actual human beings whom you want to contact or spy on.
- ✔ **Goods and services:** Stuff to buy, from mortgages to hockey sticks.

To find topics, we use the various online directories and indexes, such as Yahoo and AltaVista. To find people, however, we use directories of people, which are (fortunately) different from directories of Web pages. Wondering what we're talking about? Read on for an explanation!

Your Basic Search Strategy

When we're looking for *topics* on the Net, we always begin with one of the Web guides (indexes and directories) discussed in this section.

You use them all in more or less the same way:

1. **Start your Web browser, such as Netscape, or Internet Explorer, or Opera.**

2. **Pick a directory or index you like and tell your browser to go to the index or directory's home page.**

   We list the URLs (page names) of the home pages later in this section.

   After you get there, you can choose between two approaches.

3. **a. If a Search box is available, type some probable keywords in the box and click Search.**

   This is the *index* approach, to look for topic areas that match your keywords.

   After what might be a long delay (the Web is pretty big), an index page is returned with links to pages that match your keywords. The list of links may be way too long to deal with — like, oh, 300,000 of them.

   or

   b. If you see a list of links to topic areas, click a topic area of interest.

   In the *directory* approach, you begin at a general topic and drill down to get more and more specific. Each page has links to pages that get more and more specific until they link to actual pages that are likely to be of interest.

4. **Adjust and repeat your search until you find something you like.**

   After some clicking around to get the hang of it, you find all sorts of good stuff.

You hear a great deal of talk around the Web about search engines. *Search engines* is a fancy way to say stuff-finding stuff. All the directories and indexes we're about to describe are in the broad category called *search engines,* so don't get upset by some high-falutin-sounding terms. Today's latest techno-geek term, used to describe either a directory or an index, is *portal.* More on this term later.

Search-a-Roo

So much for the theory of searching on the Net. Now for some practice. (Theory and practice are much farther apart in practice than they are in theory.) We use our three favorite search systems for examples: Yahoo, which is a directory; and AltaVista and Google, which are indexes.

Yahoo!, our favorite directory

You can find stuff in Yahoo! in two ways. (Yes, it's spelled with an exclamation point. A previous fad was funny CapITallzaTion; the current fad seems to be !funny? "¿¿"¿punc@@tuation! But henceforth we leave out the "!" to avoid overexciting ourselves.) The easier way is just to click from category to category until you find something you like.

We start our Yahoo visit at the Yahoo Canada home page, at `www.yahoo.ca` (at least the page name doesn't use an exclamation point), which looks like Figure 8-1. A whole bunch of categories and subcategories are listed. You can click any of them to see another page that has yet more subcategories and links to actual Web pages. If you see a page you like, you can click on a link or on a sub-subcategory, and so on.

At the top of each Yahoo page is the list of categories and subcategories separated by greater-than symbols, that lead to that page, as in Figure 8-2. If you want to back up a few levels and look at different subcategories, just click the place on that list that you want to back up to. After a little clicking up and down, it'll become second nature. Many pages appear in more than one place in the directory because they fall into more than one category. Web pages can have an unlimited number of links referring to them.

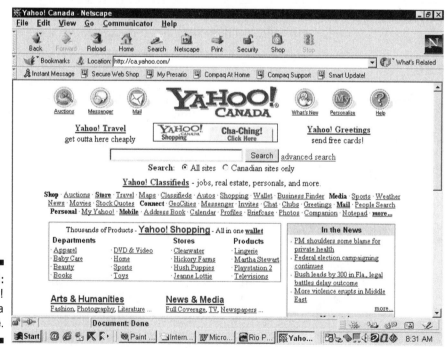

Figure 8-1:
The Yahoo!
Canada
home page.

Although all the categories in the Yahoo list have plenty of subcategories under them, some have many more than others. If you're looking for a business-related page, it helps to know that Yahoo sticks just about everything commercial under the category Business and Economy. If you were looking for something such as Canadian Children's Books, for example, you could click your way to it from the Yahoo Canada home page, at `www.yahoo.ca`, by clicking Business and Economy and then, on that page, clicking Companies, then Books, then Shopping and Services, then Booksellers, then Children's, and then Titles. Finally, on that page, you link to pages with lots of children's books.

If you know in general but not in detail what you're looking for, clicking up and down through the Yahoo directory pages is a good way to narrow your search and find pages of interest.

Searching through Yahoo

"Click on Business and Economy and then, on that page, click Companies, then Books, then Shopping and Services, then Booksellers, then Children's, and then Titles? How the heck do I know which categories to click?" you're doubtless asking. We admit it. We cheated — we searched for the page instead.

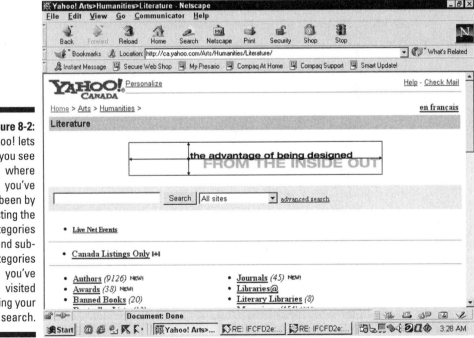

Figure 8-2:
Yahoo! lets you see where you've been by listing the categories and sub-categories you've visited during your search.

Both Yahoo (www.yahoo.com) — the U.S. version — and Yahoo Canada also let you search their indexes by keyword, which is the best way, if you have some idea of the title of the page you're looking for. Every Yahoo screen has near the top a search box in which you can type words you want to find in the Yahoo entry for pages of interest. For example, we typed Canadian Childrens Literature, clicked the Search button next to the type-in box, and got the answer shown in Figure 8-3, with several relevant entries.

Above each entry Yahoo finds, it reports the category in which it found the entry. Even if the entry isn't quite right, if you click the category, you'll find other related titles, and some of them may well do the trick.

If Yahoo finds hundreds of pages or categories, you should refine your search. One way to do that is to add extra words to specify what you're looking for. If you are looking for a key lime pie recipe and you search for baking, you get 80 fairly random pages; if you search for key lime pie, however, you get 2 pages, one of which is on the Business and Economy: Companies: Food: Baked Goods: Pies page, which has links to lots of tasty pie recipes.

You can click "advanced search," next to the Search button, to get to the slightly more advanced Yahoo search page. It lets you limit how far back you want to see pages (three years is the default), and you can tell it to look for either all the words or any of the words you typed.

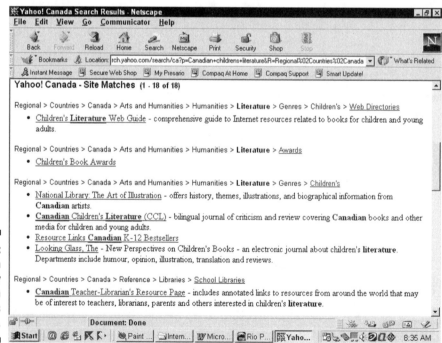

Figure 8-3: Zeroing in on quality Canadian children's literature.

Tonnes more at Yahoo

Although Yahoo is primarily a directory of resources available on the Web, it's now a "Web portal," which means that it has plenty of other databases available to encourage you to stick around inside Yahoo. Each has a link you can click just under the box in which you enter search terms:

- **Yellow Pages:** A business directory

- **People Search:** Finds addresses and phone numbers, similar to a white pages directory (see the "Finding People" section later in this chapter)

- **Maps:** Gets a more or less accurate map of a street address you type

- **Classifieds:** Lets you read and submit ads for automobiles, apartments, computers, and jobs

- **Personals:** Lets you read and submit ads for dates in all (and we mean *all*) combinations

- **Chat:** Gets you into online chat through the Web

- **Email:** Free Web-based e-mail service

- **Auctions:** Web-based auctions, similar to Bid.com or eBay

- **TV:** Impressively complete TV and cable listings, by area

- **Travel:** A link to the Travelocity reservation system (see `www.iecc.com/ airline` for our opinions and suggestions about online travel services)

- **My Yahoo:** A customized starting page just for you, with headlines, sports scores, and other news based on your preferences

- **Today's News, Stock Quotes, and Sports Scores:** News from Reuters

AltaVista and Google, our favorite indexes

Our favorite Web indexes are AltaVista and Google. Both have little robots (AltaVista's is named Scooter) that spend their time merrily visiting Web pages all over the Net and reporting back what they see. They each make a humongous index of which words occurred in which pages; when you search either index, it picks pages from the index that contain the words you asked for.

Since these systems are indexes, not directories, the good news is that they have about 10 times as many pages as Yahoo; the bad news is that finding the one you want can be difficult. Regardless of what you ask for, you probably will get 15,000 pages on your first try, but the first pages found are usually the most relevant — especially with Google.

Using AltaVista, Google, or any other index is an exercise in remote-control mind reading. You have to guess words that will appear on the pages you're looking for. Sometimes, that's easy — if you're looking for recipes for key lime pie, key lime pie is a good set of search words because you know the name of what you're looking for. On the other hand, if you have forgotten that the capital of Germany is Berlin, it's hard to tease a useful page out of AltaVista because you don't know what words to look for. (If you try Germany capital, for example, you find info about investment banking.)

Now that we have you all discouraged, try some AltaVista or AltaVista Canada searches. Direct your browser to www.altavista.com or www.altavista.ca. You see a screen like the one shown in Figure 8-4.

Figure 8-4:
The
AltaVista
home page,
ready to roll.

Type some search terms, and AltaVista finds the pages that best match your terms. That's "*best* match," not "match" — if it can't match all the terms, it finds pages that match as well as possible. AltaVista ignores words that occur too often to be usable as index terms, both the obvious ones such as *and, the,* and *of,* and terms such as *internet* and *mail.* These rules can sound somewhat discouraging, but in fact it's still not hard to tease useful results out of AltaVista. You just have to think up good search terms. Try that key lime pie example by typing key lime pie and pressing the Search button. You get the response shown in Figure 8-5.

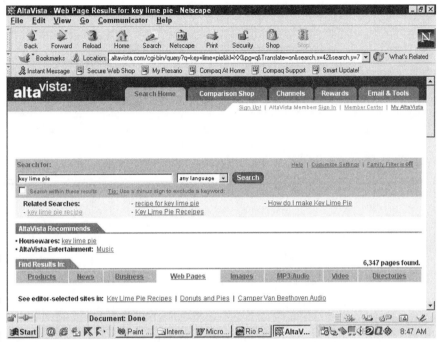

Figure 8-5:
A plethora
of pages of
pies.

Your results will not look exactly like Figure 8-5 because AltaVista will have
updated its database by the time you read this chapter. Most of the pages it
found do, in fact, have something to do with key lime pie — some even contain
pretty good recipes. AltaVista found about 6,347 matches. Although that's
probably more than you wanted to look at, if the first screen doesn't have
what you want, you should at least glance at the next couple of screens of
matches you want. Page numbers are located at the bottom of the page; click
Next in order to go to the next page.

Handy AltaVista targeting tips

AltaVista, unlike Yahoo, makes it easy to refine your search more exactly to
target the pages you want to find. After each search, your search terms appear
in a box at the top of the page so that you can change them and try again.
Here are some tips on how to change your terms:

- Type most search words in lowercase. Type proper names with a single
  capital letter, such as `Elvis`. Don't type any words in all capital letters.

- If two or more words should appear together, put quotes around them,
  as in `"Elvis Presley"`. You should do that with the pie search (`"key
  lime pie"`) because, after all, that is what the pie is called, although in
  this example, AltaVista is clever enough to realize that it's a common
  phrase and pretends you typed the quotes anyway.

The number-one reason your searches don't find anything

Well, it may not be *your* number-one reason, but it's *our* number-one reason: One of the search words is spelled wrong. Check carefully. John notes that his fingers insist on typing "Interent," which doesn't find much other than Web pages from other people who can't spell. (Thanks to our friend Jean Armour Polly, for reminding us about this problem.)

✔ Use + and − to indicate words that must either appear or not appear, such as `+Elvis +Costello -Presley` if you're looking for the modern Elvis, not the classic one.

AltaVista has a few other handy options:

✔ Rather than search Web pages, you can search Usenet, the giant collection of Internet newsgroups (online discussion groups). Simply click the box that says Search the Web and flip to Search Usenet. If a topic has been discussed recently on Usenet, this technique is the best way to find the messages about that topic.

✔ AltaVista includes a large Web directory called the Open Directory Project — sort of a giant version of Yahoo's directory — sponsored by Netscape and maintained by volunteers. The ODP is also available at Netscape's home page (`home.netscape.com`), HotBot (`www.hotbot.com`), and Lycos (`www.lycos.com`).

✔ You can limit your search to documents in a specific language. No sense in finding pages in a language you can't read, although AltaVista has a subsystem called Babelfish that can try, with mixed success, to translate pages from some other languages. Click the Translate link on a page in another language to try it.

Google smarts

Google, at `www.google.com`, is an index somewhat like AltaVista, but with some extra smarts to make it more likely that pages of interest will show up on the first page of results. When we searched for key lime pie (see Figure 8-6), all the links on the first page had pie recipes, including a copy of John's 1988 classic. The I'm Feeling Lucky button searches and takes you directly to the first link, which works when — well, when you're lucky.

Google has a couple of other useful features. If you click the Cached link on any of the pages that Google finds, it'll show you a copy of the page as of the time that Google indexed it, useful for pages that change often or have disappeared. The "Googlescout" link looks for pages related to that page, often with more useful info.

We like Google better for most searches because of its better page ranking. AltaVista still shines for obscure searches and searches for very specific key terms, like part numbers, because of its huge set of pages and its powerful search language.

Figure 8-6:
Unlike AltaVista, all of the links on the first page that Google drummed up had pie recipes.

Yahoo and more

A rather effective way to search the Web is to look in the Yahoo and Open Directory Project directories and then, if you don't find what you want, try an index. If you click "Web Pages" on a Yahoo search page, you see an index similar to AltaVista. (It's from Inktomi, the same people who provide the engine behind HotBot and other portals.) For our key lime pie example, you get a page with 20 links, at least 11 of which have pie recipes, the rest being places that will sell you ready-made pies. Here ends our survey of key lime pies. (Just a minute while we run down to the kitchen and help ourselves to another piece.)

We're from Your Browser, and We're Here to Help You

In 1998, Netscape and Microsoft both decided to crowbar their way into the search engine market. (Opinionated? Who, us?) Starting with Netscape Navigator and Internet Explorer, both will take you directly to their respective preferred search system if you give them half a chance. These search systems aren't awful, but unless you are the kind of person who turns on his TV and watches whatever is on the first channel you come to, you'll probably find that you prefer to choose your own search engine.

In both cases, you can type some keywords into the address bar where you'd normally type the URL of the Web page. The browser notices that what you typed doesn't look like a URL and sends it to a search engine instead. It displays the search result or, if there's only a single match, goes directly to the matching page.

That's okay as far as it goes, but remember that the page the browser finds is rarely the only possible match. There's some reason to believe that companies pay to get placed better, so you should search farther if you have any doubt. Also keep in mind that when you do the search, your keywords are shipped off to Netscape or Microsoft, who presumably are keeping statistical logs of what people are looking at.

The 404 blues

More often than we want to admit, when you click a link that Yahoo or one of its competitors has found, rather than getting the promised page, you get a message such as 404 Not Found. What did you do wrong? Nothing. Web pages come and go and move around with great velocity, and the various search systems do a lousy job, frankly, of cleaning out links to old, dead pages.

The automated indexes, such as AltaVista, HotBot, and Lycos, are better in this regard than the manual directories, such as Yahoo. The automated ones have software robots that revisit all the indexed pages every once in a while and note whether they still exist; even so, many lonely months can pass between robot visits, and a great deal can happen to a page in the meantime.

It's just part of life on the online frontier — the high-tech equivalent of riding your horse along a trail in the Prairies and noticing that there sure are a lot of bleached-white cattle skulls lying around.

TECHNICAL STUFF

Who pays for all this stuff?

You may be wondering who foots the bill for all these wonderful search engines. All major search sites are supported by banner advertising. On virtually every page of Yahoo, Lycos, AltaVista, Excite, and other search engines, you find lots and lots of ads. The search engine enters into agreements with banner advertising partners. One popular arrangement involves variable referral fees. Every time a visitor to Yahoo clicks on, say, Volvo's banner ad, Yahoo gets a commission. In return, Volvo gets the added exposure — and a potential sale.

To make sense of all this, and to keep the playing field fair, online "ad agencies" track the number of times a certain banner ad is clicked. These companies charge a fee in return for telling client Web sites — such as Yahoo and

Volvo — how many times a Web site was visited, from which Web sites the visitors came, how many times certain ads were clicked, and who visited the site. Unlike Big Brother, however, some Web ad agencies develop totally anonymous visitor profiles. For example, you need not worry that Engage (one of these agencies) knows that you frequently visit a Web site dedicated to the research and discussion of used purple socks! They don't even know your name.

Also, most search engines now generate additional revenues with other e-commerce initiatives. For example, AltaVista owns Shopping. com, a competitor to eBay and Bid.com. Under this type of arrangement, search engines charge a commission for brokering private purchases and sales that take place through them.

Netscape's Smart Browsing

Smart Browsing is a fairly new Netscape Navigator feature that simplifies and speeds up Internet browsing. This feature is available on Netscape 4.6 and higher. Features in Smart Browsing include *Internet Keywords*, where instead of having to remember long Internet addresses (URLs), you just type the words or names you're looking for into the location field of your browser. You'll be taken to a site for that product, company, or service. For example, instead of remembering the URL `www.chapters.ca`, simply type `Chapters` into the Location field, and you'll be taken to that address.

Smart Browsing consists of other features, too, such as *Smart Keywords*, the keywords in the address box. You can type `search word word` to search for those words using Excite, yet another AltaVista-like search engine.

Another feature, new in Netscape 4.6, is What's Related. There's a What's Related button to the right of the address box. When you click it, your browser sends your current URL to Netscape headquarters, which returns a menu of pages that seem to be on similar topics, based on pages that other people have visited in the past. We find What's Related kind of hit-and-miss, but if you're scratching your head, it's worth a click to see whether anything interesting is there.

Microsoft's AutoSearch

Microsoft's AutoSearch is not about cars. But it could be. This feature is much like Netscape's Smart Browsing. In Internet Explorer 4.0, AutoSearch lets you type your query right into the location field of your browser. In theory, Internet Explorer then jumps to a directory with a list of matching pages. In practice, you usually get a "server too busy" or "not available" error message. Like many developments in the high-tech industry, this one is a work in progress!

Internet Explorer also has the Search Bar. If you click the Search icon, a Search Bar subwindow appears to the left of your Explorer window with a small search engine page. In Internet Explorer 4.0, the page is for a specific search engine, usually AltaVista. If you prefer to use a different one, click the Choose a Search Engine button at the top of the window, and pick one of the others.

In Internet Explorer 5.0 and later versions, they've spiffed up the Search Bar. It has a bunch of buttons that let you choose one of several kinds of searches, including Web pages, people, and companies. When you search for Web pages, the Search Assistant sends it off to one of the search engines, usually HotBot. If you don't like what it finds, click the Next button at the top of the Search Bar window, and it'll try a different search engine. To start over with a new search, click New at the top of the Search Bar. You can customize which engines it uses and in which order by clicking the Customize icon, a little hammer and gear at the top of the Search Bar.

This zillion-engine search can be somewhat overwhelming, but once you're used to it, it's nice. You remain firmly in control of what searches you do, and you can certainly do a lot of searching quickly until you find what you want.

More search magic

Netscape and Microsoft remain in frantic competition, so by the time you read this, there will doubtless be even more search features in each browser. Drop by Internet Gurus Central at net.gurus.com/search to find out what's new.

The Usual Suspects

After you have surfed around Yahoo, AltaVista, and Google for a while, you may want to check out the competition.

Excite and WebCrawler

www.excite.com
www.webcrawler.com

Excite is primarily an index, like AltaVista, with a "concept search," which is supposed to find relevant pages even if you don't type exactly the same words the pages use. We don't find that the Excite concept search helps much, but perhaps we were too wordy to start with. Excite also has sections with reviews of Web pages, city directories, white pages, and more.

WebCrawler is an automated indexer that crawls around the Web cataloguing and indexing every page it comes across — again, sort of like AltaVista. It's a reasonable alternative to AltaVista. WebCrawler has been through a variety of owners, including AOL, but now belongs to Excite, although its data are different from that of Excite.

Infoseek

www.infoseek.com

Infoseek is an index similar to AltaVista, rather than a directory: You give it some keywords to look for, and it finds the pages that match the best. Infoseek also has a directory of useful Web pages, and can search the Web, Usenet, Reuters, and a few other odds and ends. Infoseek is controlled by Disney; although we haven't yet seen any mouse ears, there's supposed to be a joint portal opening soon at www.go.com.

HotBot

www.hotbot.com

HotBot is yet another index, again like AltaVista. It's affiliated with *Wired* magazine and uses — in classic *Wired* style — bright, clashing colours that make your head hurt. If you can deal with that (try sunglasses), it's not a bad index. It uses the Inktomi engine, the same as Yahoo's Web page search.

Lycos

`www.lycos.com`

Lycos is a largely automated index, sort of like AltaVista. It began as a project at Carnegie Mellon University and, like AltaVista, has gone commercial. Lycos also has a directory called Top 5% of Web Sites. Lycos was one of the earliest Web search systems, and has now surpassed Yahoo in terms of number of visitors to its network of affiliated search sites. However, in our opinion, AltaVista has a better index, and Yahoo has a better directory. Perhaps of interest is the fact that Lycos also has headline news and local pages for some North American cities.

Northern Light

`www.northernlight.com`

The Northern Light site contains an automated index of both the Web and its Special Collection, which is articles from various sources — but you must pay for them if you decide to read them. If you would rather stick with the (free) Web, you can choose to do so. The Northern Light searches also automatically categorize the pages they find, displaying a listing of "folders" from among which you can choose.

Other Web guides

Lots of other Web guides are available, including many specialized guides put together for particular interests (Femina, for example, is a feminist guide, at `femina.cybergrrl.com`).

Yahoo has a directory of other guides. Starting at the Yahoo page (`www.yahoo.com`), choose WWW (which appears under Computers and Internet) and then Searching the Web.

Finding Companies

The first way to search for companies is to search for the company name as a topic. If you're looking for the Egg Farm Dairy, for example, search for Egg Farm Dairy in Yahoo, AltaVista, or any of the other search systems. (You'll find it, too. We like the Muscoot cheese.) After you have done that, a few other places are worth checking for business-related info.

Carlson Online

www.carlsononline.com

Carlson Online is a business information company that offers free Canadian and U.S. company financial capsules, stock prices, insider trading information, and more. Company home pages vary in informativeness, but they often don't tell you much about the company itself. Basic services are free, but the all-dressed version with more frills will cost you a few dollars more.

Ask SEDAR

www.sedar.com

SEDAR (the System for Electronic Document Analysis and Retrieval) is a system that collects all the financial material that Canadian publicly traded companies have to file with the government. Filing with SEDAR started January 1, 1997, and is now mandatory for most reporting issuers in Canada. Although most of this stuff is dry and financial, if you can read financial statements and annual reports, you can find all sorts of interesting information, such as Edgar Bronfman's salary.

CDS INC., a subsidiary of the Canadian Depository for Securities Limited, manages the SEDAR system on behalf of the Canadian Securities Administrators — a regulatory body overseeing public company matters. CDS is responsible for the development and maintenance of this Web site. Access is free.

Lots of other business directories

Tonnes of business information is available on the Net. Here are a few places to begin:

Canada Stock Watch (CSW)

www.canada-stockwatch.com

CSW offers free access to Canadian company information, as well as Canadian and U.S. market information, quotes, and charts. You enter the name of a company in which you're interested, and this site tells you about it.

Canadian Business magazine

www.canadianbusiness.com

Canadian Business magazine concentrates on Canadian companies. It offers free feature articles for the month, access to archived articles, and economic and stock market predictions. Each year, its *Profit 100* features the 100 fastest-growing Canadian entrepreneurial companies that it likes the best.

Yellow Pages

canada411.sympatico.ca
yp.gte.net
www.switchboard.com

Quite a few Yellow Pages business directories, both national and international, are on the Net. The directories in this list are some of the bigger ones. We like Canada 411 the best, but they're all worth a look.

Finding People

Finding people on the Net is surprisingly easy. It's so easy that, indeed, sometimes it's creepy. Two overlapping categories of people finders are available: those that look for people on the Net with e-mail and Web addresses, and those that look for people in real life with phone numbers and street addresses. The real-life directories are compiled mostly from telephone directories. If you haven't had a listed phone number in the past few years, you probably aren't in any of these directories. The process of finding e-mail and Web addresses is somewhat hit-and-miss. Because no online equivalent to the official phone book that the telephone company produces has ever existed, directories of e-mail addresses are collected from addresses used in Usenet messages, mailing lists, and other more or less public places on the Net. And the various directories use different sources, so if you don't find someone in one directory, you can try another. Remember that because the e-mail directories are incomplete, there's no substitute for the old-fashioned alternative — calling someone up and asking, "What's your e-mail address?"

If you're wondering whether someone has a Web page, use AltaVista to search for his name. If you're wondering whether you're famous, use AltaVista to search for your own name and see how many people mention you or link to your Web pages.

Yahoo People Search

www.ca.people.yahoo.com

This is the system formerly at www.four11.com. You can search for addresses and phone numbers and e-mail addresses. If you don't like your own listing, you can add, update, or delete it.

Canada 411

www.canada411.sympatico.ca

Canada 411 is a Canadian telephone book, complete except for the provinces of Alberta and Saskatchewan, that is sponsored by most of the major Canadian telephone companies. *Aussi disponible en français,* eh? (***Note to residents of Alberta and Saskatchewan:*** Advise Telus and SaskTel to add their listings.)

American Directory Assistance

www.abii.com

Click American Directory Assistance.

This site is another white pages directory. After you have found the entry you want, you can ask for a graphical street map of the address.

Mail, one more time

Mailing lists are another important resource. Most lists (but not all — check before you ask) welcome concrete, politely phrased questions related to the list's topic. See Chapter 13 to find more information about mailing lists, including how to look for lists of topics of particular interest to you.

Getting the Goods

All the serious directories and indexes now put shopping information somewhere on their home pages to help get your credit card closer to the Web faster. Some are even sponsored by VISA. You can find department stores and catalogues from all over, offering every conceivable item (and some inconceivable items). We tell you all the do's, don'ts, and how-to's in Chapter 9.

The 10-minute challenge

Our friend Doug Hacker claims to be able to find the answer to any factual query on the Net in less than 10 minutes. Carol challenged him to find a quote she vaguely knew from the liner notes of a Duke Ellington album, whose title she couldn't remember. He had the complete quote in about an hour, but spent less than five minutes himself. How? He found a mailing list about Duke Ellington, subscribed, and asked the question. Several members replied in short order. The more time you spend finding your way around the Net, the more proficient you'll get at knowing where to go for the information you need.

Chapter 9

More Shopping, Less Dropping

● ●

In This Chapter

▶ Why shop online?

▶ Using plastic — to charge or not to charge?

▶ Step-by-step shopping

▶ Finding tickets, mutual funds, books, clothes, computers, and food (*whew!*) online

● ●

*I*f, for some reason — say, insomnia — you follow the computer trade press, you have heard far, far too much about electronic commerce (or *e-commerce*). Although e-commerce is taking a bit of time to catch on, catch on it will. In other words, much of the hype turns out to be true: An increasing number of individuals and companies are completing business transactions over the Net, in all sorts of ways.

We have bought lots of things online, from books to pants to plane tickets to stocks and mutual funds to computer parts to, uh, specialized personal products (don't read too much into that) — and lived to tell the tale.

Shopping Online: Pros and Cons

Here are some reasons why we shop on the Net:

✔ Online stores are convenient, open all night, and don't mind if you window shop for a week before you buy something.

✔ Online stores can sometimes offer great prices and a better selection than brick-and-mortar stores.

✔ Online stores offer a wider variety of items than most standard stores. (Two of the authors of this book live in small rural towns; a lot of stuff just isn't available locally.)

✔ Unlike malls, online stores don't have Muzak.

TIP

Net shopping's greatest hits

What should you buy online? Here are some good bets:

- **Books and CDs.** Online stores are fiercely competitive, and the prices can be impressively cheap.

- **Airplane tickets and other travel arrangements.** You can do as well as most travel agents.

- **Computers.** If you know what you want, online is usually cheaper and less hassle than a big computer store.

- **Stocks and mutual funds.** If you make your own investment decisions, online brokerage is much, much cheaper than a regular broker: $10 to $25 per trade rather than as much as $60 for discount or $150 for a full-service broker. Also, online brokers don't get annoyed if you check stock prices 47 times a day.

- **Anything you'd buy from a print catalogue.** Most catalogue merchants have Web sites, usually with special offers not in the print catalogue. (They'd really like you to order over the Net, rather than talk to an expensive live operator at an 800 number.)

On the other hand, here are some reasons why we *don't* buy everything on the Net:

WORLD WIDE WEB

- You can't physically look at merchandise before you buy it, and in most cases you have to wait for it to be shipped to you. (We don't expect to buy milk and bananas online anytime soon, although there may very well be a grocery service near you that does offer them.)

  Longos (`www.longos.com`) is one local Canadian grocery chain that is starting to provide online service. Grocerygateway.com (`www.grocerygateway.com`) lets you buy milk and bananas, if you like, as well as Kleenex, laundry detergent — even wine.

- You can't support your local businesses.

- You can't socialize with the staff at a Web store.

The Credit Card Question

How do you pay for stuff that you buy online? Most often, with a credit card, the same way that you pay for anything else. Isn't it incredibly, awfully dangerous to give out your credit card number online, though? Well, no.

After several years of asking for reports of card numbers being stolen from the Net, we have yet to hear of one. It doesn't happen. For one thing, most online stores encrypt the message between your computer and the store's server (indicated in your Web browser by a closed lock icon in the bottom-left corner of the window); for another, plucking the occasional credit card number from the gigabytes of traffic that flow every minute on the Net would be extremely difficult, even without encryption.

When you use your plastic at a restaurant, you give your physical card with your physical signature to the server, who takes it to the back room, does something with it out of your sight, and then brings it back. Compared to that, the risk of sending your number to an online store is remote. A friend of ours used to run a restaurant and later ran an online store, and assures us that there's no comparison: The online store had none of the plastic problems that the restaurant had.

If, after this harangue, you still don't want to send your plastic over the Net or you're one of the fiscally responsible holdouts who doesn't do plastic, most online stores are happy to have you call in your card number over the phone or send them a cheque.

Let's Go to the Store

Stores on the Web work in two general ways: with and without virtual "shopping carts." In stores without carts, you either order one item at a time or fill out a big order form with a check box for each item the store offers. In stores with carts, as you look at the items that are for sale, you can add items to your cart; when you're done, you visit the virtual checkout line and provide your payment and delivery information. Until you check out, you can add and remove items whenever you want, just like in the real world — except that you don't have to put unwanted items back on the shelf (or in someone else's basket).

Simple shopping

For a simple example, we lead you through a shopping trip at the Great Tapes for Kids Web site, a small online store for children's videotapes, audiotapes, and books, run by one of us authors. (Us, venal? Nah.) Start at the home page, www.greattapes.com, shown in Figure 9-1. It shows a featured item and has links to pages listing all the other books and tapes available. Canadian orders are airmail insured, and they'll tell you the exact shipping cost when they confirm your order.

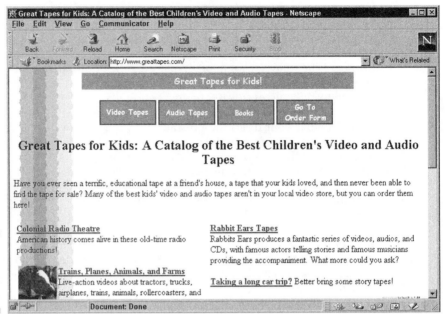

Figure 9-1:
Welcome to
Great Tapes
for Kids.

When you know what you want, you click the Go To Order Form icon on one of the Web pages to see a giant order form with a box for everything you could possibly want to order, as shown in Figure 9-2. (At large online stores, this method gets a little unwieldy.) As you continue through the form by pressing the cursor keys or clicking the scroll bar, you mark whatever it is you want to buy. At the bottom of the form, as shown in Figure 9-3, you enter the same stuff you would put on a print order form. Most forms have a place for typing a credit card number; if you're not comfortable entering it there (we are, as we describe in the section "The Credit Card Question," earlier in this chapter), leave that blank — the store invariably has a way you can call the number in. Click the Send Order button, and your order is on its way.

Fancy shopping

Although a simple store with a giant order form works okay for stores that don't have many different items in a catalogue, or businesses where you buy one thing at a time, this method is hopeless for stores with large catalogues. While writing this chapter, we decided that the Great Tapes order form had gotten hopelessly large, so we reprogrammed the Web site to provide a "shopping cart" to help track the items people order. (We would do practically anything to avoid writing. It's an author thing.)

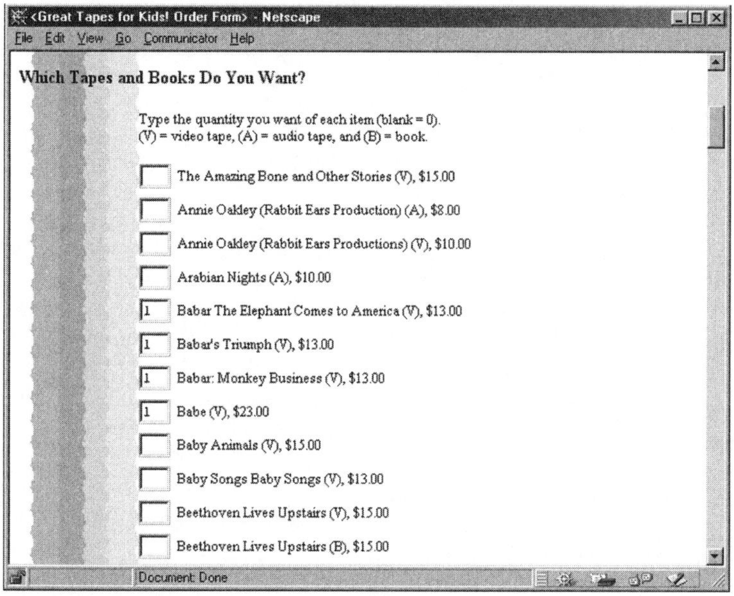

Figure 9-2:
Let's order
some animal
movies!

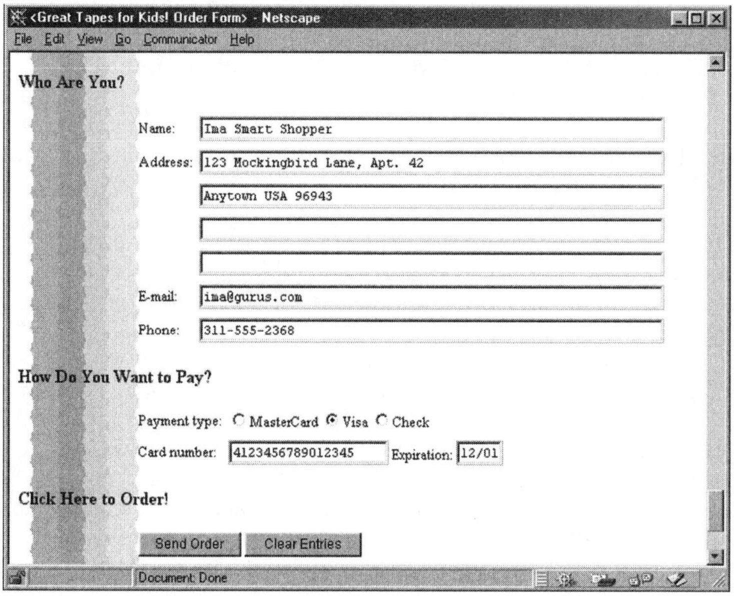

Figure 9-3:
Those last
crucial
details.

Cookie alert

You may have heard horrible stories about things called *cookies* that Web sites reputedly use to spy on you, steal your data, ravage your computer, inject cellulite into your hips while you sleep, and otherwise make your life miserable. After extensive investigation, we have found that most cookies aren't all that bad; when you're shopping online, they can even be quite helpful.

A *cookie* is no more than a little chunk of text that a Web site sends to a PC with a request (not a command) to send the cookie "file" back during future visits to the same Web site. The cookie lets you return to a Web site at a future date, and, once there, the host server remembers a few things about you. For example, you may not have to re-enter routine personal identification information every time you visit an investment Web site to get a quick real-time quote. You can see the cookies now on file in your PC in a file called something like Cookies.txt. (If you use Netscape, it's probably in your C:\Program Files\ Netscape\Users*name* folder. If you use Internet Explorer, your cookies are in the C:\Windows\ Cookies folder.) For online shopping, cookies let the Web server track the "shopping cart" of items you have selected but not yet bought, even if you log out and turn off your computer before you finish.

As you click your way around a site, you can toss items into your cart, adding and removing them as you want, by clicking a button labeled something like Add Item to Your Shopping Cart. Then, when you have the items you want, you visit the virtual checkout line and buy the items in your cart. Until you visit the checkout, you can always put back the items in your cart if you decide that you don't want them.

The cart-ized version of Great Tapes for Kids looks just like the old version, until you click the Order button on one of its pages. The giant order form is gone, and in its place is the shopping cart page, the interesting part of which is shown in Figure 9-4.

Suppose that one tape isn't enough for you because you have two nephews, so you click the Resume Shopping button, find another tape, and click Order again. Now both tapes are in your cart. (Although this process looks totally obvious, the programming required to make it work correctly on a Web server is kind of tricky. Much as we would love to share the technical details, our editor regretfully informs us that we're short of space. Phooey.)

At this point, you can continue shopping, adjust the quantities (including adjusting down to zero anything you don't want), or go to the checkout to finish your order. This example is already too long, so just go to the checkout. It looks almost the same as the page that was shown in Figure 9-3, with the same places to put your name, address, and payment details, and a button you click to confirm your order.

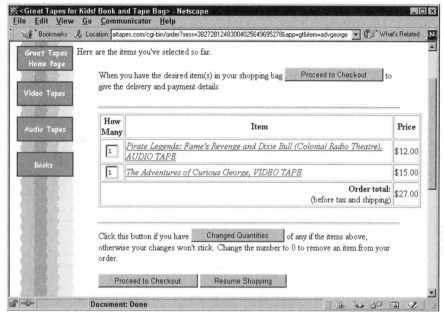

When you have the desired item(s) in your shopping bag [Proceed to Checkout] to give the delivery and payment details.

Most virtual stores use a cookie (we talk about them in the "Cookie alert" sidebar on the opposite page) to identify your personal shopping cart. The cookie lets you log off the Internet, return to the Great Tapes Web site a day or two later, and find your shopping cart still there with your stuff in it. We find this process particularly handy for book shopping — every few days, we hear about a book we want and virtually throw it into our cart. (Throwing is okay, because in cyberspace, nothing gets dented.) Then, when we have enough books to make a decent order, we submit the order and pay a single shipping charge for the whole bunch rather than ordering them one at a time.

Paying shipping charges, especially if you order goods from some U.S. online retailers, can be an eye-popping, cash-depleting experience. That's because some "shipping charges" include hidden duties that can actually exceed the price of the goods you buy. Make sure you know what the total shipping cost will be before you throw the product into your online "shopping cart"!

Up, Up, and Away

We buy lots of airline tickets online. Although the online travel sites aren't as good as really good travel agents, the sites are much better than bad travel agents. Even if you have a good agent, online sites let you look around to see what your options are before you get on the phone. We have also found some good travel agents who work via Web sites and e-mail.

The general theory of airline tickets

Four giant airline computer systems in the United States handle nearly all the airline reservations in the country. (They're known as CRSs, for Computer Reservation Systems, or GDSs, for Global Distribution Systems.) Although each airline has a "home" CRS, the systems are interlinked so that you can, with few exceptions, buy tickets for any airline from any CRS. The systems are Sabre, Apollo/Galileo (home to Air Canada), Worldspan, and Amadeus. All are American-owned.

In theory, all the systems show the same data; in practice, however, they get a little out of sync with each other. If you're looking for seats on a sold-out flight, an airline's home system is most likely to have that last, elusive seat. If you're looking for the lowest fare to somewhere, check all four systems, because a fare that's marked as sold out on one system often mysteriously reappears on another system. Some categories of fares are visible only to travel agents and don't appear on any of the Web sites, particularly if you aren't staying over a weekend, so check with a good agent before buying. On the other hand, many airlines have available some special deals that are *only* on their Web sites and that agents often don't know about.

The confusion is even worse if you want to fly outside Canada. Official fares to most countries are set via a treaty organization called the International Air Transport Association (IATA), so computer systems usually list only IATA fares for international flights. It's easy to find entirely legal "consolidator" tickets sold for considerably less than the official price, however, so an online or offline agent is extremely useful for getting the best price. Priceline.com, at `www.priceline.com`, runs regular online auctions for plane seat tickets offered by participating international airlines. You may be able to score an extraordinarily great deal if you're looking for a last-minute seat to Nepal!

Here's our distilled wisdom about buying plane tickets online:

- Check the online systems to see what flights are available and for an idea of the price ranges. Check more than one CRS.

- After you have found a likely airline, check that airline's Web site to see whether it has any special Web-only deals. If a low-fare airline flies the route, be sure to check that one, too.

- Check with a travel agent to see whether he can beat the online price, and buy your tickets from the agent unless the online deal is better. Some agents give you a small discount if you make your reservations yourself, because the agent only has to issue the ticket and mail the receipt to you.

✔ If you bid on airline tickets at a travel auction Web site, make sure that you already know the price at which you could buy the ticket, so you don't bid more.

✔ For international tickets, do everything in this list and check both online and with your agent for consolidator tickets, particularly if you don't qualify for the lowest published fare.

More about online airlines

Because the online airline situation changes weekly, anything we print here could be out of date by the time you read it. One of the authors of this book is a plane nerd in his spare time; to get a current list of online CRSs, airline Web sites, Web specials, and online travel agents, visit his Web site, at www.iecc.com/airline.

Pure Money

If you invest in mutual funds or the stock market (something that's difficult to avoid these days unless you anticipate dying at an early age), you can find a remarkable range of resources online. An enormous amount of stock information is also available, providing Net users with research resources as good as those only professional analysts had a few years ago.

The most important thing to remember about all the online financial resources is that everyone has an ax to grind and wants to get paid somehow. In most cases, the situation is straightforward; for example, a mutual fund manager wants you to invest with her funds, and a stockbroker wants you to buy and sell stocks with him. Some other sites are less obvious: some are supported by advertising, and others push other kinds of investments. Just keep a source's interests in mind when you're considering that source's advice.

Mutual funds

Mutual funds are a favorite investment vehicle for the baby boomer generation. The world now has more mutual funds than it has stocks for the funds to buy. (Kind of makes you wonder, doesn't it?) Most Canadian fund managers have at least descriptions of the funds and prospectuses online, and many now provide online access so that you can check your account and move money from one fund to another within a fund group.

Well-known Canadian fund groups include

- ✔ **Altamira:** A gorilla in Canadian mutual funds, offers a wide variety of no-load funds (www.altamira.com)
- ✔ **C. I. Mutual Funds:** A broad group of Canadian and international equity, balanced, and money market funds (www.cifunds.com)
- ✔ **Trimark:** Another broad group of funds (www.trimark.com)

Many of the online brokers listed in the following section also let you buy and sell mutual funds, although it almost always costs less if you deal directly with a fund manager. Yahoo Canada (www.yahoo.ca) has a long list of funds and fund groups; click the Business and Economy option, then Finance and Investment, then Mutual Funds.

Stockbrokers

Most of the well-known full-service brokerage firms have jumped on the Web, along with a new generation of low-cost online brokers offering remarkably cheap stock trading. A trade that may cost $100 with a full-service firm can cost as little as $8 with a low-cost broker. The main difference is that the cheap firms don't offer investment advice and don't assign you to a specific broker. For people who do their own research and don't want advice from a broker, the low-cost firms work well. For people who do need some advice, the partial- or full-service firms often offer lower-cost trades online, and they let you get a complete view of your account whenever you want. The number of extra services the brokerages offer (such as retirement accounts, dividend reinvestment, and automatic transfers to and from your chequing account) varies widely.

Here are some Canadian online brokers:

- ✔ **E*Trade Canada:** The world's fastest-growing, multi-service online brokerage (www.canada.etrade.com)
- ✔ **Charles Schwab Canada:** Another large online brokerage operation, offering full brokerage services (www.schwabcanada.com)

Many Canadian fund groups, including the ones listed above, have brokerage departments, which can be a good choice if you want to hold both individual stocks and funds.

Tracking your portfolio

Several services let you track your portfolio online. You enter the number of shares of each fund and stock you own, and at any time they can tell you exactly how much your investments are worth and (if you can handle the truth) how much money you have lost today. Some of them send by e-mail a daily portfolio report, if you want. These reports are handy if you have mutual funds from more than one group, or both funds and stocks. All the tracking services are either supported by advertising or run by a brokerage that hopes to get your trading business. The first two sites in the following list are American, and therefore track investments in U.S. dollars; the last two are Canadian.

✔ **My Yahoo:** (my.yahoo.com) You can enter multiple portfolios and customize your screens with related company and general news reports. You can also get lots of company and industry news, including some access to sites that otherwise require paid subscriptions. Advertiser-supported, very comprehensive and easy to use.

✔ **My Snap:** (my.snap.com) Snap is a clone of Yahoo. Its portfolio features are similar to and arguably better than Yahoo's.

✔ **National Post Online:** (www.nationalpost.com) You can create up to three custom portfolios for Canadian equities, and one portfolio for U.S. equities, each consisting of up to 20 stocks or mutual funds.

✔ **The Fund Library:** (www.fundlibrary.com) You can enter your Canadian mutual fund holdings into its comprehensive tracking system.

Even More Places to Shop

Here are a few other places to shop that we have visited on the Web. We've even bought stuff from most of them.

Books and such

Although you can't flip through the pages of books in an online bookstore, rubbing them between your fingers (yet), if you know what you want, you can get good deals.

Amazon.com

    www.amazon.com

Amazon.com is one of online commerce's great success stories, springing up from nothing (if you call several million dollars of seed money nothing) to become one of the Net's biggest online stores. Amazon, based in the United States, has an enormous catalogue of books, music, and a growing variety of other junk, much of which can get to you in a few days. It also has an "affiliates" program through which other Web sites can refer you to their favorite books for sale at Amazon, creating sort of a virtual virtual bookstore. Amazon sells most books at less than list price; for users in Canada, the prices are low enough that even with shipping they're sometimes cheaper than buying locally.

Chapters

    www.chapters.ca

The Chapters Web site allows you to browse through more than two million book titles that are either stocked or can be ordered within a few weeks. Chapters has a search tool to help you find books by author name, book title, or topic. You can also get videos, DVDs, popular software — even music. The list goes on and on. Chapters even lets you *return* books to them!

Indigo

    www.indigo.ca

Indigo is trying to give Chapters a run for its online money. Indigo's site offers many of the same features as Chapters, but at the moment it's not as comprehensive. Indigo is, however, less cluttered visually, and generally better organized. Indigo has recently teamed up with the gardening store, Cruickshank's. Now you can buy books and bulbs online.

Clothes

This section points out a few familiar merchants with online stores. Directories such as Yahoo have hundreds of other stores, both familiar and obscure.

Tilley Endurables

    www.tilley.com

Much of this famous Canadian store's offerings are also available online. You may even find Alex Tilley's stories to be quite entertaining.

The Gap

www.gap.com

Although this site doesn't yet have the full line of merchandise offered in the stores (for those of us who are of unusual vertical or horizontal dimension), it has jeans in sizes the stores don't stock, and the rotating 3-D pants (they don't rotate while you're wearing them, silly) are way cool.

Computers

When you're shopping for computer hardware online, be sure that a vendor you're considering has both a good return policy, in case you don't want the computer when it arrives, and a long warranty.

Dell Canada

www.dell.ca

This site has an extensive catalogue, with online ordering and custom computer system configurations. Michael Dell's company operates one of the most wildly successful and interactive e-commerce Web sites in the world.

IBM Canada

www.can.ibm.com

The world's largest computer company has what feels like the world's largest Web site, with a great deal of information about both IBM products as well as more general computing topics.

IBM sells stuff online at www.direct.ibm.com/ca. The online store sells everything from home PCs to print manuals to mid-range business systems. We got as far as putting a $1.5 million AS/400 9406-650 in our cart, but then we chickened out. We did, however, go through with the purchase of a nice manual for the 1965-era 360/67, for our vintage collection. (At IBM, nothing seems to go out of print.)

Auctions and used stuff

You can participate in online auctions for everything from computers and computer parts to antiques to vacation packages. Online auctions are like any other kind of auction in at least one respect: If you know what you're looking for and know what it's worth, you can get some great values; if you don't, you can easily overpay for, well, junk. When someone swiped our car phone handset, we found an exact replacement phone at eBay for $31, rather than the $150 the manufacturer charged for just the handset.

Many auctions, notably eBay and Bid.com, also allow you to list your own stuff for sale, which can be a way to get rid of some of your household clutter a little more discreetly than in a tag sale.

www.ebay.com
   (all sorts of neat stuff is available at this American site; see Figure 9-5)

www.priceline.com (airline tickets and more)

www.bid.com (a Canadian auction site)

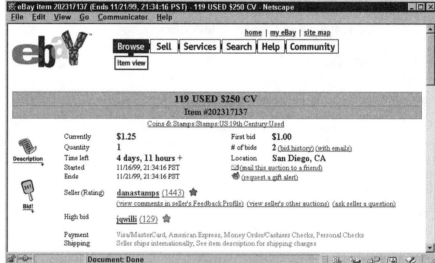

Figure 9-5:
To place a bid, scroll down, enter your top price and click the Review Bid button.

Food

There's been a recent surge in ordering groceries online. Here are two of our favorite online grocery stores.

Grocerygateway.com

www.grocerygateway.com

Grocerygateway.com sells itself mostly on convenience. You can buy everything from fresh meats and produce to household products — even beer and wine in some provinces — from this popular online grocer. This service, and others like it (you can find similar sites throughout Canada by using Google or Yahoo), lets customers shop on their own terms. Most online grocers are open 24 hours a day, 7 days a week. They have convenient delivery times, boast competitive prices, and offer a good selection of fresh produce.

You can see for yourself how online shopping works, by going to the Grocerygateway.com Web site. Once there, go to their Shopping Demo page where you'll be asked to enter only your postal code (to verify whether they currently serve your area). Handy features at this and most online grocery sites include recipe guides and saved past orders. You also get to choose a convenient date and time to accept delivery. You are usually asked to be home to accept delivery and make payment. A nominal delivery charge is usually passed on to you — about $7.50 per order, regardless of size.

Canadashop

www.canadashop.com

This online shopping Web site lets you buy products in a wide array of consumer categories, including arts and crafts, electronics, and hardware. It also lets you obtain travel and other services online. Check out its offerings by using the handy dropdown menu.

An online shopper's checklist

Here are some questions to keep in mind when you're shopping online. An astute shopper will notice that these are the same ones you keep in mind when you're shopping anywhere else.

✔ Are the descriptions clear enough for you to know what you're ordering?

✔ Are the prices competitive, both with other online stores and with mail-order and regular retail?

✔ Does the store have the products in stock, or, alternatively, does it offer a firm shipping date?

✔ Does the store have a good reputation?

✔ Can you return unsatisfactory goods?

Chapter 10

My First Home Page

In This Chapter
▶ Web page basics
▶ Up and humming
▶ Publish or perish

*A*fter a while, every Web user thinks about putting up a personal Web page. Although any Web site can consist of many Web pages, the main page of a site is generally known as its *home page*. People have home pages, companies have home pages, and groups of highly talented authors and speakers have home pages. If you're ready to have your own home page, you're in the right place.

Although creating a home page isn't difficult, it may seem complicated for a new user. But if you know how to use a word processor such as WordPerfect or Microsoft Word to type a letter, you can certainly create at least a simple home page. (Indeed, you can use either of those two word processors to do so.)

Creating a Web Page

All home pages are Web pages, although not all Web pages are home pages. We tell you how to make a Web page — whether it's a home page is up to you.

The big picture

The basic steps to creating a Web site are pretty simple:

1. **Write some Web pages.**

   One page is plenty to start with. You can use any text editor or word processor, but spiffy Web page authoring programs designed for this purpose are available and many are free, so you might as well use one. (We discuss what's available presently.) Save the pages in files on your computer's disk.

Why you don't care (much) about HTML

Just so that you know what *HTML* is, in case someone asks, it stands for *HyperText Markup Language*, and it's the language native to the World Wide Web. Web pages are made up of text and pictures that are stuck together and formatted by using HTML codes. Fortunately, you cleverly waited until now, when even more clever programs are available that let you create your pages and that write the HTML codes for you automatically. You don't have to write the codes yourself.

If you find you want to write a lot of Web pages, you should eventually learn some HTML. Although complex interactive pages require a fair amount of programming, the basics aren't all that complicated; the HTML for **complicated** is `<B>complicated</B>` (that's `<B>` for bold type). In case you decide that you want to be in the Web-page creation business, entire books have been written about how to do it. Stick to recent titles because extensions to HTML are evolving at a furious pace and the books go out-of-date in under a year.

---

2. **Test them out using your own browser.**

   Before you make your pages visible to everyone, make sure they look good! Using your Web browser, open the pages (press Ctrl+O and specify the name of the file that contains your page).

3. **Publish them on your ISP's system.**

   The rest of the world can't see Web pages in files on your disk. You have to copy them to your ISP's system so that your ISP's *Web server* can offer them to the world.

Many Web page authoring programs have an Upload or Remote Save command on their File menu that sends your creation to your provider's system. If your program doesn't have this command, you can use FTP, which we discuss in more detail in Chapter 16. In either case, you need to know these details:

✔ **The name of the computer to which you upload your files.** This isn't always the same as the name of the Web server. At one of our local ISPs, for example, the Web server is `www.lightlink.com`, while the FTP upload server is `ftp.lightlink.com`.

✔ **The user name and password to use for FTP.** Usually this is the same as the name and password you use to connect in the first place and to pick up your e-mail.

✔ **The name of the folder on the server to which you upload the pages.** At Lightlink, it's `/www/username`.

✔ **The filename to use for your home page.** Usually this is index.html or index.htm. (You can call your Web pages anything you want, but this is the page that people see first.)

✔ **The URL where your pages will appear.** It's usually `www.yourisp.com/~username` or `www.yourisp.com/username`.

You can usually find this info on your ISP's Web site or, in the worst case, you can call them or e-mail them and ask.

Picking your pen

The two general approaches to creating Web pages are the geek approach, in which you write all the HTML codes yourself, and the WYSIWYG approach, in which a program writes them for you. If you were an HTML geek, you wouldn't be reading this chapter, so we're not going to discuss that approach. The more normal approach is to use one of the WYSIWYG Web-page editors.

WYSIWYG (pronounced "whiz-ee-wig") stands for *what you see is what you get.* In the case of Web-page editors, it means that as you create your page, instead of seeing seriously unattractive HTML codes, you see what it will actually look like. HTML purists point out that WYSIWYG editors churn out less-than-elegant HTML code, but the pages they make generally look fine. If you are planning to create a large, complex Web site, WYSIWYG editors will run out of steam, but for a page or three, they're great.

Here are some of the better-known Web-page editors and where to find them:

✔ **Netscape Composer:** (`home.netscape.com`) Netscape Composer is a WYSIWYG editor that is part of Netscape Communicator and runs on Windows and Macs.

✔ **Microsoft FrontPage and FrontPage Express:** (`www.microsoft.com`) FrontPage Express comes with Windows 98. Watch out, though: FrontPage and FrontPage Express have a nasty habit of inserting Microsoft-proprietary codes that only work if your ISP runs a Microsoft Web server.

✔ **HotDog Professional:** (`www.sausage.com`) This powerful Windows-based Web editor is included on the CD-ROM in the back of this book. You can also download the program from Sausage Software's Web site.

✔ **BBEdit Lite:** (`www.barebones.com/free/free.html`) This Mac-based Web editor is also on the CD-ROM.

We like a lesser-known but just-fine-and-dandy freeware program called AOLpress, available at `www.aolpress.com`, which, despite its name, works fine whether or not you're an AOL user. AOLpress also has *templates*, pages already set up so that all you have to do is fill in your information; tutorials, more step-by-step instructions in case ours aren't enough; and clip art, images you can add to your page.

You may already have a Web-page editor — your own word processor. Both Microsoft Word (versions 97 and later) and WordPerfect (versions 8 and later) have capable Web-editing features built right in. Web page authoring tools are usually more convenient, though.

Getting started

A Web page is a file — just like a word-processing document or a spreadsheet. You begin by creating your Web pages directly on your hard disk. You can see how they look by telling your browser to view them from your hard disk. (Browsers are happy to accept filenames to display rather than URLs.) Edit and view the pages until you have something you like, and then upload them to your ISP to impress the world.

Here's our step-by-step approach to using AOLpress 2.0. If you would rather use Microsoft FrontPage or Netscape Composer, feel free, although the commands are a little different:

1. **Get a copy of AOLpress. If you would rather use your own word processor, skip this step.**

Using your browser, go to the AOLpress home page at `www.aolpress.com`. Click Download. Find the section that corresponds to the system you're using (Windows or Macintosh). If you're using AOL Canada, go to keyword *AOLPRESS*. After the download is completed, double-click the AOL Canada installation program.

2. **Run AOLpress or your word processor.**

If you run AOLpress, it displays a big welcome screen — actually, a welcome page. Because AOLpress is not only a Web-page tool but also a browser, when you wander in and around AOLpress, you're still visiting sites on the Web, which makes it easy to drop in to various sites and clip items of interest. But we digress.

At the top of your screen is the AOLpress toolbar. If you point to each icon with your mouse, AOLpress tells you what it's for. If, after you've looked around, things don't look intuitively obvious to you, we suggest that you double-click AOLpress Tutorial and use the online workbook to get started. If you're pigheaded, stick with us and we'll get you started, somewhat less graciously.

If you started Word 97 or WordPerfect, you see your usual word processing window.

3. **Create a new Web page.**

   To create a new Web page in AOLpress, choose File⇨New⇨New Page from the menu bar. In Word 97, choose File⇨New from the menu bar, click the Web Pages tab in the dialog box that appears, and choose a template (try the Web Page Wizard, which talks you through making a Web page in Word 97). In WordPerfect 8, choose File⇨New to display the New dialog box. Choose WordPerfect Web Document from the list of possible document types, and click Create. WordPerfect displays the Internet Publisher window. If you already have a document that you want to convert to a Web page, choose the View⇨Web Page command from the menu and then save the document. In WordPerfect 9, choose File⇨ Internet Publisher, click New Web Document, click Create a Blank Web Document, and click Select.

   When asked for a filename, call the document index.html or index.htm, if it's going to be your home page. These names are the names that most Web servers use.

   Once you've created your file, you're face-to-face with a big, empty page. Go ahead — make your page. Stuck for ideas or where to start? If you use AOLpress, go to the AOLpress Welcome Page, click Templates, and check out the AOLpress ready-to-fill-in forms and coordinated artsy pages that help you set up your page so that it looks spiffy.

4. **Save your work.**

   When you've done enough work that you wouldn't want to have to start over from scratch if your computer suddenly crashes, choose File⇨Save from the menu bar. In principle, when you're done with your page, you save it, but dismal experience has taught us to *save early, save often*.

Creating your first Web page is as easy as 1-2-3. Choosing what you put on your page, however, is harder. What is the page for? Who do you want to see it? Is it for your family and friends and potential friends across the world, or are you advertising your business online? If your page is a personal page, don't include your home address or phone number unless you want random people who see the page potentially calling you up. If it's a business page, by all means include your address and phone number. The content of your first page isn't all that important — we just want you to get the feel of putting it out there. You can always add to it and pretty it up, and you don't have to tell anybody about your site until you're happy with it.

Be extremely careful about putting identifying information about your children on your Web page. We each have kids whom we love dearly, but you won't read anything about them on our home pages. Just knowing your hobbies and your kids' names and where they go to school might be enough for some no-good-nik to pose as a friend of the family and pick them up after school.

Pictures to Go

Most Web pages contain graphics of some sort. Each picture that appears on a Web page is stored in a separate file. AOLpress, Word, and WordPerfect let you add images. AOLpress even provides a fair number of images to use.

Picture formats

Pictures come in dozens of formats. Fortunately, only three picture formats are in common use on the Web; these are known as GIF, PNG, and JPEG. Many lengthy. . . er, *free* and *frank* discussions have occurred on the Net concerning the relative merits of these formats. John, who is an Official Graphics Format Expert, by virtue of having persuaded two otherwise reputable publishers to publish his books on the topic, suggests that photographs work better as JPEG, while clip art, icons, and cartoons are better as PNG or GIF. If in doubt, JPEG files are smaller and download faster.

If you have a picture in any other format, such as BMP or PCX, you must convert it to GIF, PNG, or JPEG before you can use it on a Web page. Check out the Consummate WinSock Applications page, at `cws.internet.com`, for some suggestions of graphics programs that can do conversions. We like Paint Shop Pro (`www.jasc.com`), a powerful shareware graphics program on Windows, and GraphicConverter on the Mac. Paint Shop Pro and GraphicConverter are loaded on the CD-ROM in the back of this book. Go on, check it out!

Where do pictures come from?

That's a good question. You can draw them by using a paint program, scan in photographs, or use that fancy digital camera you got for Christmas. Unless you're a rather good artist or photographer, however, your graphics may not look as nice as you want them to.

Canada's role in the new JPEG2000

The International Standards Organization (ISO) recently approved the latest and greatest picture format — JPEG2000. Canadian flag-wavers will be happy to note that a wee little Canadian company called Image Power was square in the middle of the ISO standard-setting process for JPEG2000. Image Power actually led the development of the algorithms powering this new picture format!

Fortunately, you can find lots of graphic material sources on the Web:

- ✔ Plenty of freeware, shareware, and commercial clip art is available on the Net. Yahoo has a long list of clip art sites: start at `www.yahoo.com` and choose Computers and Internet, and then Graphics, and then Clip Art.

- ✔ The king of the clip art sites is Art Today (`www.arttoday.com`). There's a modest annual subscription fee, but they have hundreds of thousands of well-indexed pictures for download.

- ✔ If you see an image you want to use on a Web page, write to the page's owner and ask for permission to use it. More likely than not, the owner will let you use the image.

- ✔ Lots of regular old software programs totally unrelated to the Internet, such as paint-and-draw programs, presentation programs, and even word processors, come with clip art collections.

- ✔ You can buy CD-ROMs full of clip art, which tends to be of higher quality than the free stuff. These aren't all that expensive, particularly considering how many images fit on one CD-ROM.

Clip art, like any art, is protected by copyright laws. Whether it's already been used on a Web page or whether a copyright notice appears on or near the image doesn't matter. It's all copyrighted. If you use someone else's copyrighted art, you must get permission to do so. Whether your use is educational, personal, or noncommercial is irrelevant. If you fail to secure permission, you run the risk of anything from receiving a crabby phone call from the owner's lawyer to winding up on the losing end of a lawsuit.

Most people are quite reasonable whenever you ask for permission to use something. If an image you want to use doesn't already come with blanket permission to use it, check with the owner before you decide to add it to your own Web page.

Linking to Other Pages

The *hyper* in hypertext is the thing that makes the Web so cool. A *hyperlink* (or just *link*) is the thing on the page that lets you "surf" the Web — go from page to page by just clicking the link. A Web page is hardly a page if it doesn't link somewhere else.

The immense richness of the Web derives from the links that Web page constructors have placed on their own pages. You'll want to contribute to this richness by including as many links to places you know of that the people who visit your page may also be interested in. Try to avoid including links to places that everyone already knows about and has in their bookmarks. For example, the common Internet search engines and indexes are already well documented, so leave them off. If your home page mentions your interest in one of your hobbies, however, such as canoeing or volleyball or birding or your alma mater, include some links to related sites you know of that are interesting.

AOLpress, Word, and WordPerfect let you insert a URL and create the link for you. If you create multiple pages, you can put links among your pages; be sure to upload all the pages to ensure the links still work.

Good Page Design

After you've put together a basic Web page, use the tips in this section to avoid some mistakes that novice Websters often make.

Fonts and styles

Don't overformat your text with too many fonts, too much use of font colours, or emphasis with **bold**, *italics*, <u>underlining</u>, or some ***<u>combination thereof</u>***. Experienced designers sneeringly call it "ransom note" text. Blinking text universally annoys readers.

Background images

Tiled background images can be cool if they're subtle but as often as not make text utterly illegible. Black text on a solid white background (like the pages of this book) has stood the test of time — for thousands of years.

Big images

Many Web pages are burdened with images that, although beautiful, take a long time to load — so long that many users may give up before the pages are completely loaded. Remember that not everyone has a computer or Internet connection as fast as yours.

Take a few steps to make your Web pages load more quickly. The main step, of course, is to limit the size of the images you use, by shrinking them using a graphics editor such as Paint Shop Pro. A 20KB (20,000 bytes big) image takes twice as long to load as a 10KB image, which takes twice as long to load as a 5KB image. You can estimate that images load at 1KB per second (on a dial-up connection), so a 5KB image loads in about five seconds, which is pretty fast; a 120KB image takes two minutes to load, so that image had better be worth the wait.

Consider putting a small image on a page and giving visitors an option (via a link) to load the full-size picture. We know that you're proud of your dog, and she deserves a place of honour on your home page, but not everyone visiting your site will wait excitedly for your puppy picture to download. (We hate it when they do that on the rug.)

In GIF files, images with fewer colours load faster than images with more colours. If you use a graphics editor to reduce a GIF from 256 colours to 32 or even 16 colours, often the appearance hardly changes, but the file shrinks dramatically. Set your graphics program to store the GIF file in interlaced format; that lets browsers display a blurry approximation of the image as it's downloading, to offer a hint of what's coming.

In JPEG files, you can adjust the "quality" level, with a lower quality making the file smaller. You can set the quality quite low with little effect on what appears on users' screens.

You can also take advantage of the *cache* that browsers use. The cache keeps copies of previously viewed pages and images. If any image on a page being downloaded is already in the browser's cache, that image isn't loaded again. When you use the same icon in several places on a page or on several pages visited in succession, the browser downloads the icon's file only once, and reuses the same image on all the pages. When creating your Web pages, try to use the same icons from one page to the next, both to give your pages a consistent style and to speed up downloading.

Live and learn

If you're looking at other people's Web pages and come across one that's particularly neat, you can look at the source HTML for that page to see how the page was constructed. In Netscape Communicator 4.7, choose View⇨Page Source or press Ctrl+U; in Internet Explorer 5.0 and higher, choose View⇨ Source; and in Opera, choose View⇨Source.

Putting Your Page on the Web

After you've made some pages you're happy with (or happy enough with) and you're ready for other people to see them, you have to release your pages to the world. Although nearly every ISP has a user Web server, no two ISPs handle the uploading process in quite the same way.

Assuming that you have the server details we discussed at the beginning of the chapter, here's what to do:

1. **Run your FTP program.**

   We use WS_FTP 4.6 (described in Chapter 16), although any FTP program or even Netscape Navigator will do.

2. **Log in to your ISP's upload server, using your own login and password.**

   In Netscape Navigator, type the location `ftp://username@ftp.gorgonzola.net` into the Location box (suitably adjusting both your user name and the server name), and type your login password when it asks. Internet Explorer doesn't handle file uploads.

3. **Change to the directory (folder) where your Web home page belongs.**

   The name is usually something like /pub/elvis, /www/elvis, or /pub/ elvis/www (assuming that your user name is *elvis*). In a Web browser, just click your way to the appropriate directory.

4. **Upload your Web page(s).**

   Use ASCII mode, not binary mode, for the Web pages, because Web pages are stored as text files. Use binary mode when you're uploading graphics files. If you use Netscape Navigator, drag each file from Windows Explorer or File Manager into the Netscape window or choose File⇨Upload File.

Once you've finished uploading, if your page on the server is called mypage.htm, its URL is something like

```
www.gorgonzola.net/~elvis/mypage.htm
```

Again, URLs vary by provider. Some providers don't follow the convention of putting a tilde (~) in front of your user name.

Generally, you should call your home page — the one you want people to see first — index.html. If someone goes to your Web directory without specifying a filename, such as `www.gorgonzola.net/~elvis`, a nearly universal convention is to display the page named index.html. If you don't have a page by that name, most Web servers construct a page with a directory listing of the pages in your Web directory. Although this listing is functional enough because it lets people go to any of your pages with one click, it's not cool. If you make an index.html page and it doesn't appear automagically when you type the URL without a filename, ask your ISP if it uses a different default filename.

Be sure to check out how your page looks after it's on the Web. Inspect it from someone else's computer, to make sure that it doesn't accidentally contain any references to graphics files stored on your own computer but that you forgot to upload. If you want to be compulsive, check how it looks from various browsers — Netscape, Internet Explorer, AOL, WebTV, and Lynx, to name a few.

Shortly after you upload your pages, you'll probably notice a glaring mistake. (We always do.) To update a page, edit the copy on your own computer and then upload it to your ISP, replacing the preceding version of the page. If you change some but not all of your pages, you don't have to upload pages that haven't changed.

Be Master of Your Domain

A home page address like

```
www.people.stratford-on-avon-internet.com/~shakespeare/
PrinceOfDenmark/index.html
```

is just not going to attract as many visitors as

```
www.hamlet.org
```

Getting your own domain name is a lot easier and cheaper than you might think. There are three steps:

1. **Choose a name.**

   You'll want one that's easy to remember and to spell. Pick out a couple of alternative names in case the one you want is taken. Don't use a variation on a popular trademark such as Coke or Sony (or Dummies) unless you like dealing with lawyers.

2. **Register your name.**

   For a long time, the only game in town for registering a domain in the popular .com, .net, and .org categories was InterNIC at rs.internic.com. Several other companies are now domain name registrars, so you have more choices. You might want to give www.registrars.com a try. (We like the oddly named www.joker.com.) InterNIC's cost is $35 US per year, with the first two years paid for up front; other registrars usually charge less.

3. **Ask your ISP to "host" your name.**

   That means your ISP breathes some incantations that tell the Internet where to go when someone types in your personal Web address. Many ISPs charge a fee for this service, but a few do it for free. Your ISP may be able to handle registration for you, too.

Open a Farm Stand on the Information Superhighway

Selling stuff on the Internet used to take hundreds of thousands of dollars' worth of software and programming talent. A number of sites now let you create a Web store for very modest fees. We like Amazon.com's zStores, zstores.amazon.com, which is particularly easy to set up. They even process credit card sales for you, eliminating what was once a horrible pain in neck.

Shout It Out!

After your page is online, you may want to get people to come and visit. Here are a few ways to publicize your site:

- ✔ Visit your favorite Web directories and indexes, such as Yahoo (www.yahoo.com) and AltaVista (www.altavista.com), and submit your URL (the name of your page) to add to their database. These sites all have on their home pages an option for adding a new page. Automated indexes such as AltaVista add pages promptly, but manually maintained directories such as Yahoo may not accept them at all.

- ✔ Visit www.submit-it.com, a site that helps you submit your URL to a bunch of directories and indexes. You can get your site submitted to 20 popular searching sites for free, or pay money if you want them to submit your URL to a much larger list.

- ✔ Find and visit other similar or related sites, and offer to exchange links between your site and theirs.

Getting lots of traffic to your site takes time. If your site offers something different that is of real interest to other folks, it can build a following of its own.

Part IV
Essential Internet

The 5th Wave   By Rich Tennant

"QUICK KIDS! YOUR MOTHER'S FLAMING SOMEONE ON THE INTERNET!"

In this part . . .

If you're really going to use the Internet, you have to know the basics. In Part IV, we tell you all about electronic mail (e-mail) — how to send it and how to receive it. We tell you about electronic mailing lists so that you can meet people all over the world. We include information about instant messaging and chatting, so that you can stay in touch with the people you meet over the Net. We've re-written our chapter about downloading files, so you can get things off the Internet more easily. In addition to traditional Internet Service Providers, we also cover the use of AOL Canada and WebTV to download from the Net.

Chapter 11

Mailing Hither, Mailing Thither

● ●

In This Chapter

▶ Finding e-mail addresses

▶ Sending e-mail

▶ Receiving e-mail

▶ Following e-mail etiquette

● ●

*E*lectronic mail, or *e-mail,* is without a doubt the most popular Internet service, even though it's one of the oldest and (to some) most boring. Although e-mail doesn't get as much press as the World Wide Web, more people use it. Every system on the Net supports some sort of mail service, which means that if your computer — no matter what kind of computer you're using — has Internet access, you can send and receive mail.

Because e-mail, much more than any other Internet service, is connected to many non-Internet systems, you can exchange e-mail with lots of people who don't otherwise have access to the Internet, in addition to all the people who *are* on the Net. (See Chapter 20 for help in finding people's e-mail addresses.)

What's My Address?

Everyone with e-mail access to the Net has at least one *e-mail address,* which is the cyberspace equivalent of a postal address or a phone number. When you send e-mail, you enter the address or addresses of the recipients so that the computer knows where to send the message.

Before you do much mailing, you have to figure out your own e-mail address so that you can give it to people who want to get in touch with you. You also have to figure out some of their addresses so that you can write to them. (If you have no friends or plan to send only anonymous hate mail, you can skip this section.)

Internet mail addresses have two parts, separated by an @ (the *at* sign). The part before the @ is the *mailbox,* which is (roughly speaking) your personal name, and the part after that is the *domain,* usually the name of your Internet Service Provider (ISP), such as aol.com or fltg.net.

The username part

The mailbox is usually your *user name,* the name your provider assigns to your account. If you're lucky, you get to choose your username; in other cases, providers standardize their naming conventions, and you get what you get. Some usernames are just first names, just last names, initials, first name and last initial, first initial and last name, or anything else, including made-up names. Over the years, for example, John has had the usernames john, john1, jrl, jlevine, and jlevine3.

Back when there weren't that many e-mail users and most users of any particular system knew each other directly, figuring out who had what username wasn't all that difficult. These days, because that process is becoming much more of a problem, many organizations are creating consistent mailbox names for all users, most often by using the user's first and last names with a dot between them. In this type of scheme, your mailbox name may be something like anne.murray@snowbird.org, even though your username is something else. (If your name isn't Anne Murray, adjust this example suitably. On the other hand, if your name *is* Anne Murray, please contact us immediately. We know some people who want your autograph.)

Having several names for the same mailbox is no problem, so the new, longer, consistent names are invariably created in addition to — rather than instead of — the traditional short nicknames.

The domain name part

The domain name for commercial ISPs in Canada usually ends with two letters (called the *zone*) that give you a clue to what kind of place it is. Providers such as AOL Canada and SympaticoLycos, for example, end with .ca. Many Canadian government organizations also end with .ca. *Commercial* organizations end with .com. Examples of commercial organizations include nortel.com (Nortel Networks), and iecc.com (the Invincible Electronic Calculator Company). Educational institutions generally end with .edu (such as ubc.edu), though some end in .ca, networking organizations end with .net, United States government sites end with .gov, military sites end with .mil, and organizations that don't fall into any of those categories end with .org. Outside Canada and the United States, domains usually end with a country code, such as .fr for France or .zm for Zambia.

In 2000, an international standards group gave its stamp of approval to add some extra generic domains such as `.firm`, `.arts`, and `.web`. This will serve to help Internet users figure out, at first glance, the nature of a Web site or e-mail address.

Your mailbox usually lives on your ISP's mail server, because when you sign up for an Internet account, you almost always get one (or more) mailboxes as part of the deal. But if you don't have an ISP (say, you connect from the public library), all is not lost. Many Web sites provide free mailboxes for you to use — try Hotmail at `www.hotmail.com`, Mail.com at `www.mail.com`, or Yahoo Mail at `mail.yahoo.com`. These accounts usually use the Web site's domain name (such as `yahoo.com` or `hotmail.com`) as the second part of your e-mail address.

Putting it all together

Write your e-mail address in Table 11-1 and on the Cheat Sheet in the front of this book (then tear it out and tape it to the wall near your computer). Capitalization never matters in domains and rarely matters in mailbox names. To make it easy on your eyes, therefore, most of the domain and mailbox names in this book are shown in lowercase.

Table 11-1	Information Your E-Mail Program Needs to Know	
Information	*Description*	*Example*
Your e-mail address	Your username followed by an @ and the domain name.	jsmith@aol.ca
Password	The password for your e-mail mailbox. Don't write it here! It's a secret!	dum3my
Your incoming (POP3) mail server	The name of the computer that receives your e-mail messages. (Get this name from your ISP.)	mail.aol.ca
Your outgoing (SMTP) mail server	The name of the computer that distributes your outgoing mail to the rest of the Internet (often the same as the POP3 server).	mail.aol.ca

If you're sending a message to another user in your domain (the same machine or group of machines), you can leave out the domain part altogether when you type the address. If you and a friend both use AOL Canada, for example, you can leave out the `@aol.ca` part of the address when you're writing to each other.

If you don't know what your e-mail address is, try sending yourself a message, using your login name as the mailbox name. Then examine the return address on the message. Chapter 20 has more suggestions for finding e-mail addresses.

My Mail Is Where?

If you're the sort of person who lies awake at night worrying about obscure questions, you may have realized that your computer can only receive e-mail while it's connected to the Internet. So, what happens to mail that people send during the 23 hours a day that you're engaged in real life?

When your mail arrives, unless you're one of the few whose computers have a permanent Internet connection, the mail doesn't get delivered to your computer automatically. Mail gets delivered instead to an *incoming mail server* (also known as a *POP3 server,* for Post Office Protocol), which holds onto the mail until you dial in and run your mail program, which then picks up the mail. To send mail, your mail program has to take mail to your *outgoing mail server* (or *SMTP server,* for Simple Mail Transfer Protocol). It's sort of like having a post office box rather than home delivery — you have to pick it up at the post office and also deliver your outgoing mail there.

Unless you use your Web browser to read e-mail on a Web-based site, you have to set up your e-mail program with the name of your incoming and outgoing mail servers. When your e-mail program picks up the mail, it sucks your mail from your ISP's incoming mail server to your PC or Mac at top speed. After you've downloaded your mail to your own computer, you can disconnect, freeing up your phone. Then you can read and respond to your mail while you're *offline*. After you're ready to send your responses or new messages, you can reconnect and transmit your outgoing mail to the outgoing mail server, again at top network speed.

Keep in mind, however, that with the advent of DSL, or Digital Subscriber Line Internet access (where your Internet connection runs through the same copper wires used by your telephone), you don't have to worry about busy signals. You can use the Internet and talk on the phone at the same time. Of course, with cable Internet access, your phone is also free because a different type of connection is used altogether. Write the names of your incoming (POP3) and outgoing (SMTP) mail servers in Table 11-1 and on the Cheat Sheet (it's hanging on your wall, right?). If you don't know what to write, ask your ISP. With luck, your mail program will have the server names set automatically, but when (note we don't say "if") the setup gets messed up, you'll be glad you know what to restore the settings to.

If you use an online service such as SympaticoLycos or a UNIX shell account, the mail server is the same computer you connect to when you dial in (this statement is an oversimplification, but it's close enough). That way, when you run your provider's e-mail program, your mail is right there for you to read, your provider can drop outgoing messages directly in the virtual mail chute, and no separate POP3 or SMTP server is involved.

Too Many E-Mail Programs

It's time for some hand-to-hand combat with your e-mail system. The bad news is that countless (so many that none of us felt up to the task of counting them) e-mail programs — programs that read and write electronic-mail messages — exist. You have your freeware, you have your shareware and your commercial stuff, and you have stuff that probably came with your computer, too. They all do more or less the same thing, because they're all mail programs, after all.

Here's a quick rundown of e-mail programs:

✔ **Windows PC or Mac with an Internet account:** The most widely used e-mail programs are Eudora, Netscape Messenger (which comes with the Netscape Communicator suite), and Outlook Express (which comes with Microsoft Internet Explorer and Windows 98). Pegasus is another excellent, free e-mail program for this type of Internet account, available from the Net. See Chapter 16 to find out how to get hold of Eudora, Pegasus, Netscape, Outlook Express, and other programs from the Net. You can use any of these programs with Microsoft Network (MSN), too.

✔ **UNIX shell accounts:** You almost certainly can use Pine (see the section "Sending mail with Pine" later in this chapter). If your Internet provider doesn't have Pine, demand it.

✔ **AOL Canada:** The AOL package includes a built-in mail program, which is the *only* mail program that AOL members can use. After reading this chapter, AOL Canada members can turn to Chapter 17 for detailed instructions.

✔ **WebTV:** If you use this packaged Web connection, you also get an e-mail service. Chapter 18 has detailed instructions.

✔ **Free e-mail accounts:** At least one available service gives you free dial-up accounts for e-mail only. The price you pay is having advertisements appear on-screen as you read your messages. Juno Online (located in the United States) is this type of service. (Call 800-654-JUNO from Canada to ask for a software disk.) If you use a service such as Juno, even from Canada, you have to use its e-mail software (otherwise, the advertisements aren't displayed).

✔ **Web-based mail:** A few systems offer free e-mail accounts that you can access through the Web. The best known are Hotmail at `www.hotmail.com` and Yahoo Mail at `mail.yahoo.com`.

If you're connected in some other way, you probably have a different mail program. For example, you may be using a PC in your company's local-area network that runs cc:Mail, Lotus Notes, or Microsoft Mail, and has a mail-only link to the outside world. We don't describe local-area network mail programs here, but don't stop reading.

Regardless of which type of mail you're using, the basics of reading, sending, addressing, and filing mail work in pretty much the same way, so looking through this chapter is worth your time even if you're not using any of the mail programs we describe here.

Four Popular E-Mail Programs

After you understand what an e-mail program is supposed to do, it's much easier to figure out how to make a specific e-mail program do what you want it to. We've picked the four most popular e-mail programs to show you the ropes: Eudora, Netscape Messenger, and Microsoft Outlook Express. For UNIX account users, we picked Pine. AOL Canada and WebTV users should take a look at Chapters 17 and 18.

✔ **Eudora:** This popular e-mail program runs under Microsoft Windows (3.1, 95, and 98) and on the Macintosh, and communicates with your mail server. Eudora is popular for two reasons: It's easy to use, and it's cheap. The examples in this book apply to Eudora 3.0 and higher (for Windows) and 3.1 and higher (for the Mac). **Note:** A free mail service called Eudora Web-Mail (at `www.eudoramail.com`) is run by the authors of Eudora but has nothing to do with the Eudora mail program.

✔ **Netscape Messenger:** Yes, it's the same Netscape you meet in Chapter 6 while you're surfing the World Wide Web. All Netscape versions since 2.0 have an adequate if not superb mail program, as well as a Web browser. This chapter describes the version of Netscape Messenger that comes with Netscape Communicator version 4.7. Although we strongly prefer Eudora, some people are stuck with Netscape Messenger, so we mention it here.

✔ **Outlook Express:** Since Netscape includes an e-mail program with its browser, Microsoft does, too. Windows 95 comes with Microsoft Exchange; and Windows 98 comes with Outlook Express. When you get a copy of the Microsoft Web browser, Internet Explorer 5.0, you get Outlook Express 5.0, too. ***Note:*** Outlook Express is not the same as Outlook 97, Outlook 98, and Outlook 2000, which come with Microsoft Office.

✔ **Pine:** This nice mail program comes with a full-screen terminal interface. It's generally available from most UNIX shell providers because it's (no, wait! you guessed?) free. If you're using a UNIX shell system, Pine runs on your provider's computer, and you type commands to it by using a terminal program on your computer. There's also a PC version of Pine for people who grew up with UNIX Pine and don't want to switch.

When you install Eudora, Netscape Messenger, or Outlook Express, you have to give the program the information you wrote down in Table 11-1. When you first run these programs, they ask you various configuration questions. To tell these programs about your e-mail accounts later or to change your settings, choose Tools⇨Options (in Eudora), Edit⇨Preferences (in Netscape Messenger), or Tools⇨Accounts in Outlook Express.

Sending Mail Is Easy

Sending mail is easy enough that we show you a few examples rather than waste time explaining the theory.

Sending mail using Eudora

Here's how to run Eudora and send some mail:

1. **From your PC or Mac, start Eudora.**

   From Windows 3.1, start Eudora by double-clicking the Program Manager icon, which looks like an envelope. In Windows 95 and 98, the icon is on the desktop or on the Start⇨Programs menu. Mac users, click the Eudora icon. You should see an introductory "splash" window that goes away after a few seconds and then a window like the one shown in Figure 11-1. Exactly what's in the window varies depending on what you were looking at the last time you ran Eudora.

2. **To send a message, click the New Message button (the button with the paper and pencil) on the toolbar, or choose Message⇨New message from the menu. (If you can remember shortcut keys, you can also press Ctrl+N.)**

   Eudora pops up a new message window, with spaces in which you type the address, subject, and text of a message.

3. **On the To line, type the recipient's address (**joe.public@aol.ca**, for example).**

   For your first e-mail message, you may want to write to yourself to make sure everything's up and running (if you know what your e-mail address is). Or send a message to a friend and have them send a confirmation back to you.

4. **Press Tab to skip past the From line (which is already filled in) to the Subject line, and then type a subject.**

Make the subject line short and specific.

Figure 11-1:
Eudora says
hello.

5. **Press Tab a few more times to skip the Cc: and Bcc: fields (or type the addresses of people who should get carbon copies and blind carbon copies of your message).**

The term *carbon copy* should be familiar to those of you who were born before 1960 and remember the ancient practice, when using a typewriter, of putting sheets of carbon-coated paper between sheets of regular paper to make extra copies. (Please don't ask us what a typewriter is.) In e-mail, a carbon copy is simply a copy of the message you send. All recipients, on both the To: and Cc: lines, see who's getting this message. *Blind carbon copies* are copies sent to people without putting their names on the message, so that the other recipients can't tell who else has received it. *You* can figure out why you may send a copy to someone but not want everyone to know that you sent it.

6. **Press Tab to move to the large area, and then type your message.**

7. **To send the message, click the Send or Queue button in the upper-right corner of the message window (what the button says depends on how Eudora is set up).**

   If the button is marked Send, as soon as you click it, Eudora tries to send the message and puts up a little status window that contains incomprehensible status messages. If, on the other hand, the button is marked Queue, your message is stashed in your Outbox, to be sent later.

   The usual reason to have a Queue button is that you have a dial-up PPP connection so your computer isn't connected to the Net all the time. After you queue a few messages, you can send them all at one time.

8. **If your computer isn't already connected, dial up and connect to your provider.**

   You may be able to skip this step. Eudora tries to connect automatically when you send messages. (See Step 7.)

9. **Then switch back to Eudora and choose <u>F</u>ile⇨Send Queued Messages (Ctrl+T for the lazy) from the menu to transmit all the messages you have queued up.**

Even if you leave your computer connected while you write your mail messages, you may want to consider setting Eudora to queue the mail and not send it until you tell it to. (Choose <u>T</u>ools⇨<u>O</u>ptions from the Eudora menu, click the Sending Mail category, and be sure that the <u>I</u>mmediate Send isn't checked.) That way, you get a few minutes after you write each message to ponder whether you really want to send it. Even though we have been using e-mail for more than 20 years, we still throw away many of the messages we have written before we even send them.

After you send a piece of e-mail, you have no way to cancel it!

The same idea, using Netscape Messenger

The steps for sending mail from Netscape Messenger are almost identical to those for sending mail from Eudora (you're doing the same thing, after all):

1. **Start Netscape Messenger.**

   Click the icon on the Windows 98/95 or Mac desktop or choose Start⇨ <u>P</u>rograms⇨Netscape Communicator⇨Netscape Messenger from the Windows 98/95 taskbar. If you're already running Netscape Navigator, choose <u>C</u>ommunicator⇨<u>M</u>essenger from the menu.

   You see the Netscape Communications Services window. The first time you give the command, Netscape asks you for the password for your mailbox, which is usually the same as the password for your Internet account (refer to Table 11-1).

If you see an error message about a POP3 mailbox, Netscape is complaining that it doesn't know the name of the computer on which your mail is stored. Click OK to make the error message go away. When you see the Netscape window, choose Edit⇨Preferences from the menu and click Mail Server from the list on the left. The Incoming Mail Servers box lists all the POP3 mailboxes Netscape knows about (you can retrieve mail from more than one mailbox). To edit the information about the mailbox that appears, click the mail server name and click Edit. To add a new mail server, click Add. On the Mail Server Properties dialog box that appears, type the name of your Internet provider's incoming mail server (refer to Table 11-1) and your user name. Leave the Server Type set to POP3 Server. Click OK to return to the Preferences window, and OK again.

2. **Click the New Msg button on the icon bar, or press Ctrl+M.**

   Yet another window opens, the Composition window, with a blank message template.

   If Netscape complains that it doesn't know your e-mail address, click OK, Edit⇨Preferences, click Identity from the list of categories, fill in the first two blanks, and click OK. Then click the New Msg button again.

3. **Fill in the recipient's address (or addresses) in the Mail To or To box, type the subject, and type the message.**

4. **Click Send to send the message.**

   The message wings its way to your Internet provider and on to the addressee.

Sending mail, using Outlook Express

The first time you run Outlook Express 5.0, it asks you whether you want to sign up for an Internet account, set up an Internet connection to an existing account, or use a connection you've already set up. See Chapter 5 to find out how to set up a connection to an Internet account. Outlook Express can send and receive mail from more than one Internet account; choose Tools⇨Accounts to tell it about other accounts.

Here's how to send mail:

1. **Start Outlook Express. You don't have to connect to your Internet provider — yet — but it's okay if you're already connected.**

   Click the Outlook Express icon on your desktop, or choose it from the Start⇨Programs menu. The Outlook Express window, as shown in Figure 11-2, features a list of folders to the left, the contents of the current folder to the upper right, and the text of the current message to the lower right. (When you start the program, no folder or message is selected, so you don't see much.)

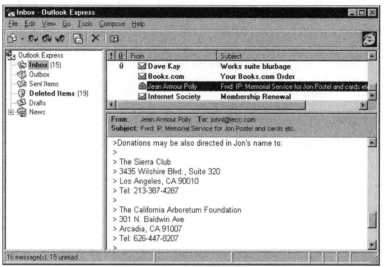

Figure 11-2:
The Outlook
Express
window is
divided into
three
sections,
showing a
list of folders,
a list of
messages in
the current
folder, and
the text of
the selected
message.

2. **Click the Inbox folder.**

   The first time you run the program, it may run the Internet Connection Wizard to ask you some questions about your e-mail account. Fill in the blanks to tell it your real name, your e-mail address, how to connect to your Internet account, and stuff like that. When it's done, you see the Inbox window again.

3. **Click the Compose Message button on the toolbar, press Ctrl+N, or choose Message⇨New Message from the menu.**

   You see a New Message window, with boxes to fill in to address the message.

4. **In the To box, type the address to which you are sending the message and then press Tab.**

   Don't press Enter unless you want to add another line to the To box so that you can type an additional address to which to send the message.

5. **If you want to send a copy of the message to someone, type that person's address in the Cc: box and then press Tab; in the Subject box, type a succinct summary of the message and then press Tab again.**

   The cursor should be blinking in the *message area,* the large empty box where the actual message goes.

6. **In the large empty box, type the text of the message.**

   After you type your message, you can press F7 to check your spelling.

7. **To send the message, click the Send button (the leftmost button) on the toolbar, press Alt+S (not Ctrl+S, for some strange reason), or choose File⇨Send Message from the menu.**

Outlook Express sticks the message in your Outbox folder, waiting to be sent. If you're connected to your Internet provider, Outlook Express sends the message, and you can skip Steps 8 and 9.

8. **Connect to your ISP, if you haven't already.**

   To send the message, you have to climb on the Net.

9. **Click the Send and Receive button on the toolbar, or choose Tools⇨Send and Receive⇨Send All from the menu.**

   Your message is on its way.

The same idea, using Pine

We presume that your UNIX shell provider has Pine all installed and ready to go (if not, call up and complain; the provider has no excuse not to have Pine available). This section tells you how to send a message.

If you have been using a PC with Windows or a Macintosh and have never experienced the utter thrill of computing without being able to point and click, you may — right this minute — be on the brink of a major trip into the past. Hide your mouse. It's of no use to you now. All the navigation you do requires you to use letters or arrow keys:

1. **Run Pine by typing** `pine` **and pressing Enter (or Return — same thing).**

   You see the Pine main menu, a list of commands that includes Compose Message.

2. **Press** `c` **to compose a new message.**

   Pine displays a nice, blank message, all ready for you to fill in.

3. **On the To: line, type the address to which you want to send mail and then press Enter.**

   At the bottom of the screen, you see a bunch of options preceded by a funny-looking caret sign and a letter. The caret sign indicates the Ctrl key on your keyboard. To choose an option, press the Ctrl key and the letter of the option that interests you (such as Ctrl+G for ^G, to get help).

4. **On the Cc: line, you can enter addresses of other people to whom you want to send a copy of this message.**

5. **Press Enter to get to the line labeled Attchmnt.**

   We don't know who came up with the idea that a good abbreviation can be constructed by leaving out all the vowels. This line is for attachments — files you want to send along with your message. You can enter the name of a file — even a file that contains stuff that isn't text — and Pine sends it along with your message. You can press Ctrl+T to choose from a list of existing files.

6. **Press Enter to get to the subject of your message, and then enter something descriptive about the content of your message.**

   Subject lines that say something like "A message from Fred" are somewhat less useful than something specific, such as "Re: Pizza dinner tomorrow (Sept. 26) at eight."

7. **Press Enter to get to the part you've been waiting for, and enter your message.**

   The message can say anything you want, and it can be as long as you want. To let you enter the message text, Pine automatically runs the simple text editor Pico, which, with any luck, you already know how to use. If you don't know how to run Pico but you know how to run another UNIX editor, ask your Internet service provider to help you set up Pine to use the editor you do know how to run. (Some providers ask you when they configure your account.) You have to be able to stumble through some type of editor, so if you don't know any, Pico is as good a place as any to start.

   Type the message. If you don't know how to use any editor features, just type your message. If you need to make changes, press the arrow keys on the keyboard to move around.

8. **When you finish, press Ctrl+X to save the message and return to Pine.**

   Pine asks whether you really want to send the message.

9. **Press** *y* **or Enter to send your message.**

   The Pine program responds with a cheery [Sending mail....] message, and you're all set.

Mail Coming Your Way

When you begin sending e-mail (and in most cases even when you don't), you will no doubt begin receiving it. The arrival of e-mail is always exciting, even when you get 200 messages a day.

Reading mail with Eudora

One seriously cool feature of Eudora is that you can do much of what you do with mail while you're not connected to your account and paying by the minute. On the other hand, when you really do want to check your mail, you have to be connected. Eudora can figure out that you're not connected and dial in for you (which, in our experience, doesn't always work).

TIP

Getting ANSI

If, when you're trying to run Pine on your UNIX shell account, you get a strange message that looks something like this:

```
Your terminal, of type "ansi,"
is lacking functions needed to
run pine
```

You have to utter a magic spell before continuing. Type this line:

```
setenv TERM vt100
```

Or, if your provider's system doesn't understand that, type this line:

```
TERM=vt100; export TERM
```

Be sure to capitalize the commands exactly as you see here. Then try again. (You're giving it some hints about which kind of terminal your computer is pretending to be. Trust us — the details aren't worth knowing.)

If you don't have a full-time Net connection, follow these steps to get your mail:

1. **Make your Net connection, if you're not already connected.**

2. **Start up Eudora, if it's not already running.**

3. **If Eudora doesn't retrieve mail automatically, click the Check Mail button on the toolbar (the button with the check mark) or choose File⇨ Check Mail (or press Ctrl+M) to retrieve your mail.**

   If you have a full-time Net connection, Eudora is probably set up to retrieve your mail automatically, in which case you only have to start Eudora for it to get your mail. (In addition, if you leave Eudora running, even hidden at the bottom of your screen as an icon, it automatically checks for new mail every once in a while.)

   If you have mail on the Mac, Eudora blows a horn and shows you a cute picture of a mailman delivering a letter. If you don't have any mail, you don't get any sound effects, although you do get a nice picture of a letter with a big, red X through it. Windows users who have a sound card hear a little song (reminiscent of Mexican jumping beans, in our opinion) to announce new mail.

   The mail appears in your Inbox, a window that Eudora labels In, one line per message.

4. **To see a message, double-click the line, or click the line and press Enter.**

   To stop looking at a message, double-click the box in the upper-right corner of the message window (the standard way to get rid of a window) or press Ctrl+W or Ctrl+F4.

Buttons at the top of the In window or at the top of your screen (depending on your version of Eudora) let you dispose of your mail. First, click (once) the message you want, to highlight it. Windows users can click the Trash Can button to discard the message or the printer icon to print it. Macintosh users can press Delete to delete it, or choose <u>F</u>ile⇨ <u>P</u>rint to print it.

Although you can do much more to messages, which we discuss in Chapter 12, that's enough for now.

If you use Windows 95 or 98, you can tell Eudora to connect to the Internet automatically when you tell it to send or fetch your mail. Choose <u>T</u>ools⇨<u>O</u>ptions from the menu, scroll the list of icons way down until you see the Advanced Network icon, and click the icon. Select the Automatically Dial and Hangup This Connection option, and choose your Dial-Up Networking connection from the list. Type your username in the box, click the Save Password option, and click OK.

The same idea, with Netscape Messenger

Reading mail with Netscape Messenger is similar to reading it with Eudora:

1. **Start Netscape Messenger.**

   Click the icon on the Windows 98/95 or Mac desktop or choose Start⇨ <u>P</u>rograms⇨Netscape Communicator⇨Netscape Messenger from the Windows 98/95 taskbar. If you are already running Netscape Navigator, choose <u>C</u>ommunicator⇨<u>M</u>essenger from the menu. You see the Netscape Messenger window, shown in Figure 11-3.

2. **Netscape may try to retrieve any waiting mail immediately; if it doesn't, click the Get Msg icon on the toolbar.**

   Incoming mail is filed in your Inbox folder. The list down the left side of the Netscape Messenger window shows your folders (indented under the Local Mail heading), with one folder (usually your Inbox) selected. The right-top part of the window shows a list of messages in that folder, and the right-bottom part shows the text of the selected message.

3. **If Inbox isn't selected on the list of folders, click it. If you can't see it, click Local Mail to display your mail folders, and then click Inbox.**

   You see the subject lines for incoming mail, listed in the right-top part of the window.

4. **Click each message to read it.**

   The text of the message is displayed in the bottom-right part of the Netscape window.

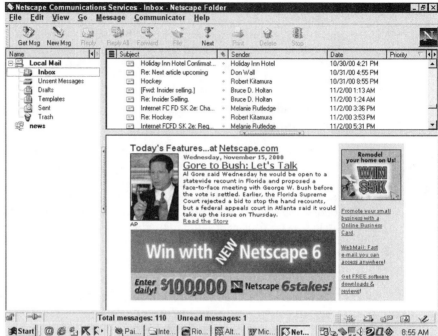

Figure 11-3:
Netscape
Messenger
shows you
your e-mail.

When you see the text of a message, you can click the Print, Delete, and other buttons to dispose of it. We discuss the other buttons in Chapter 12.

Reading mail with Outlook Express

If you have Outlook Express 5.0, here's how to get your mail:

1. **Run Outlook Express and connect to your Internet Service Provider.**

2. **Click Send and Receive All on the toolbar.**

   Outlook Express downloads your incoming mail on your computer and stashes the messages in your Inbox folder. See the list of folders on the left side of the Outlook Express window? You can choose which folder full of mail to look at. Right now, you should be looking at your Inbox.

   The box in the upper-right part of the window lists the senders and subjects of messages in the Inbox. The box in the bottom-right part of the window shows the text of the message you select.

3. **Click a message header on the list of messages to see the text of the message at the bottom of the Outlook Express window. Or double-click the message header to see the message in a new, big window.**

   If you see a message in its own window, click the Close button, choose File⇨Close from the menu, or press Alt+F4 to get rid of the window.

You can delete, reply to, forward, or print a message after you have seen it. (Chapter 12 tells you how.)

The same idea with Pine

When you log in to your shell account, you usually get a little message that says, "You have new mail" if you do, or "You have mail," if stuff you have already seen is hanging around. Depending on some obscure parameter, your mail gets checked periodically, and when you have new mail, you get the "You have new mail" message again.

Here are the steps to follow:

1. **Type the** pine **command.**

   The Pine main menu lets you choose from a variety of activities; if you have mail, the choice L (Folder List) is highlighted.

2. **Press Enter to see the list of folders you can choose from.**

   When you're just starting out, you don't have much to choose from, although that situation can change. Right now, you're interested in the folder labeled INBOX. INBOX should be highlighted. Press Enter to see your mail. Pine displays a list of messages.

3. **The message that is highlighted is the current message. To choose a different one, press the arrow keys or press P for the preceding message or N for the next message.**

   When you choose the message you want to read, press Enter. Pine displays your message.

   After reading a message, you have several choices as to what to do with it. We talk in Chapter 12 about the details of deleting, forwarding, and filing messages.

4. **To read your next message, press N; to read the preceding message, press P; to return to the index of messages in the folder you're reading (in this case, INBOX), press I.**

5. **When you finish reading your mail, press Q to quit.**

   Pine asks you whether you really want to do that. (What — leave this fabulous program? It's so wonderful!) Reassure it by pressing Y.

Not such junky mail

Outlook Express 5.0 has an optional "junk mail filter" at Tools⇨Message Rules⇨Junk Mail that attempts to detect junk e-mail and stick it in a separate folder that you can discard. We recommend that you *not* use Microsoft's junk mail filter. Why? Because it has far too many false alarms. We tried it for a while and found nearly as much real mail, including some mail we'd have been really unhappy to lose, as junk mail in the "junk" folder. Microsoft won't say what its filtering rules are, but whatever they are, they don't match the junk mail we get.

In the Junk Mail window, there's a tab labeled Block Senders in which you can list "blocked" addresses from which it should discard mail. As long as you have a firm handle on who your non-friends are, this works fine. It's particularly useful for deep-sixing those useless corporate memos and newsletters that self-impressed bureaucrats insist on sending to the entire company.

For more info on stopping junk e-mail once and for all, visit spam.abuse.net and www.cauce.org.

A Few Words from the Etiquette Ladies

Sadly, the Great Ladies of Etiquette, such as Emily Post and Amy Vanderbilt, died before the invention of e-mail. Here's what they may have suggested about what to say and, more important, what *not* to say in electronic mail.

E-mail is a funny hybrid, something between a phone call (or voice mail) and a letter. On the one hand, it's quick and usually informal; on the other hand, because e-mail is written rather than spoken, you don't see a person's facial expressions or hear her tone of voice.

A few words of advice:

✔ When you send a message, watch your tone of voice.

✔ Don't use all capital letters — it looks like you're SHOUTING.

✔ If someone sends you an incredibly obnoxious and offensive message, as likely as not it's a mistake or a joke gone awry. In particular, be on the lookout for failed sarcasm.

Flame off!

Pointless and excessive outrage in e-mail is so common that it has a name of its own: *flaming*. Don't flame. It makes you look like a jerk.

When you get a message so offensive that you just *have* to reply, stick it back in your electronic Inbox for a while and wait until after lunch. Then, don't flame back. The sender probably didn't realize how the message would look. In about 20 years of using e-mail, we can testify, we have never, ever, regretted *not* sending an angry message (although we have regretted *sending* a few — *ouch*).

When you're sending mail, keep in mind that someone reading it will have no idea what you *intended* to say — just what you *did* say. Subtle sarcasm and irony are almost impossible to use in e-mail and usually come across instead as annoying or dumb. (If you're an extremely superb writer, you can disregard this advice — but don't say that we didn't warn you.)

Keep in the back of your mind that forging e-mail return addresses is not difficult technically. If you get a totally off-the-wall message from someone that seems out of character for that person, somebody else may have forged it as a prank. (No, we don't tell you how to forge e-mail. How dumb do you think we are?)

Smile!

Sometimes it helps to put in a : -) — called a *smiley* — which means, "This is a joke." (Try leaning way over to the left if you don't see why it's a smile.) In some communities, notably SympaticoLycos and AOL Canada, <g> or <grin> serves the same purpose. Here's a typical example:

```
People who don't believe that we are all part of a warm,
caring community who love and support each other are no better
than rabid dogs and should be hunted down and shot. :-)
```

We feel that any joke that needs a smiley probably wasn't worth making — but tastes differ.

How Private Is E-Mail?

Relatively, but not totally. Any recipient of your mail may forward it to other people. Some mail addresses are really mailing lists that redistribute messages to many other people. Misrouted mail has landed in our mailbox with details of our correspondents' lives and anatomy that they probably would rather we forget. (So we did.)

If you send mail from work or to someone at work, your mail is not private. You and your friend may work for companies of the highest integrity whose employees would never dream of reading private e-mail. When push comes to shove, however, and someone is accusing your company of leaking confidential information and the corporate lawyer says, "Examine the e-mail," someone reads *all* the e-mail. E-mail you send and receive is stored on your disk, and most companies back up their disks regularly. Reading your e-mail is very easy for someone who really wants to, unless you encrypt it.

The usual rule is not to send anything you wouldn't want to see posted next to the water cooler or perhaps scribbled next to a pay phone. The latest e-mail systems are beginning to include encryption features that increase the privacy factor so that anyone who doesn't know the keyword that was used to scramble a message can't decode it.

The most common tools for encrypted mail are known as S/MIME, PEM (privacy-enhanced mail), and PGP (pretty good privacy). PGP is one of the most widely used encryption programs, both in Canada and abroad. Many experts think that it's so strong, even the National Security Agency can't crack it. (We don't know about that; if the NSA wants to read your mail, however, you have more complicated problems than we can help you solve.) S/MIME is an emerging standard encryption system that Netscape and Outlook Express both support.

PGP is available for free on the Net. To find more information about privacy and security issues, including how to get started with PGP and S/MIME, point your Web browser to `net.gurus.com/pgp`.

To Whom Do I Write?

Now that you know how to use e-mail, you will want to send some messages. Chapter 13 tells you how to find other people to write to and how to get interesting information by e-mail. See Chapter 20 to find out how to locate the e-mail address of someone you know.

Hey, Ms. Postmaster

Every Internet host that can send or receive mail has a special mail address called `post-master` that is guaranteed to get a message to the person responsible for that host. If you send mail to someone and get back strange failure messages, you can try sending a message to the postmaster. If `king@bluesuede.org` returns an error from `bluesuede.org`, for example, you may try a polite question to `postmaster@bluesuede.org`. Because the postmaster is usually an overworked volunteer system administrator, it is considered poor form to ask a postmaster for favours much greater than "Does so-and-so have a mailbox on this system?"

TIP

BTW, what does IMHO mean?

E-mail users are often lazy typists, and many abbreviations are common. Here are some of the most widely used:

Abbreviation	What It Means
BTW	By the way
IANAL	I am not a lawyer, (but . . .)
IMHO	In my humble opinion
ROTFL	Rolling on the floor laughing
RSN	Real soon now (vaporware)
RTM	Read the manual — you could have and should have looked it up yourself
TIA	Thanks in advance
TLA	Three-letter acronym
YMMV	Your mileage may vary

Chapter 12

Putting Your Mail in Its Place

. . . .

In This Chapter

▶ Deleting mail

▶ Responding to mail

▶ Forwarding and filing mail

▶ Spotting and avoiding chain letters

▶ Sending and receiving exotic mail and mail attachments

▶ Exchanging mail with robots and fax machines

▶ Dealing with spam

. . . .

Okay, now that you know how to send and receive mail, you're ready for some tips and tricks to make you into a real mail aficionado. We describe Eudora 3.0 and higher (for Windows, 3.1 and higher for the Mac), Netscape Messenger 4.7, Outlook Express, and Pine (see Chapter 11 for descriptions of these programs).

After you read an e-mail message, you can do a bunch of different things with it (much the same as with paper mail). Here are your usual choices:

- ✔ Throw it away
- ✔ Reply to it
- ✔ Forward it to other people
- ✔ File it

You can do any or all of these things to each message. If you don't tell your mail program what to do to a message, the message either stays in your mailbox for later perusal or sometimes — when you're using Pine, for example — gets saved to a Read-messages folder.

If your mail program automatically saves messages in a Read-messages, Sent, or Outbox folder, be sure to go through the folder every week or so, or else it becomes enormous and unmanageable.

Deleting Mail

When you first begin to get e-mail, you feel so excited that just throwing the message away is difficult to imagine. Eventually, however, you *have* to know how to dispose of messages; otherwise your computer will run out of room. Start early. Delete often.

Throwing away mail is easy enough that you probably have figured out how to do it already. Using the Windows version of Eudora, you click a message and then click the trash can or press Ctrl+D. In the Macintosh version of Eudora, you can click the message and press Delete. If the message file is open, press ⌘+D or choose Delete from the Message menu. In Netscape Messenger and Outlook Express, click the message and then the Delete button on the toolbar or press the Delete key. From Pine, press D for Delete.

You can often delete mail without even reading it. If you subscribe to mailing lists (described in Chapter 13), certain topics may not interest you. After you see the subject line, you may want to delete the message without reading it. If you're the type of person who reads everything Ed McMahon sends to you, you may have problems managing junk e-mail, too. Consider getting professional help.

Back to You, Sam: Replying to Mail

Replying to mail is easy enough to do. In Eudora or Netscape, choose Message⇨ Reply, click the Reply button on the toolbar, or press Ctrl+R; in Outlook Express, click the Reply to Author button on the toolbar or press Ctrl+R or choose Message⇨Reply to Sender; in Pine, press R.

Pay attention to two things in particular:

- ✔ To whom does the reply go? Look carefully at the To: line that your mail program has filled out for you. Is that who you thought you were addressing? If the reply is addressed to a mailing list, did you really intend to post to that list, or is your message of a more personal nature that may be better addressed to the individual who sent the message? Did you mean to reply to a group? Are all the addresses that you think you're replying to included on the To: list? If the To: list isn't correct, you can move the cursor to it and edit it as necessary.

- ✔ Do you want to include the content of the message to which you're replying? Most e-mail programs begin your reply message with the content of the message to which you're replying. The Netscape toolbar has a Quote button you can click to stick the quoted text of the original message into your reply. We suggest that you begin by including it and then edit the text to just the relevant material. If you don't give some context to

> people who get a great deal of e-mail, your reply makes no sense. If you're answering a question, include the question in the response. You don't have to include the entire text, but give your reader a break. She may have read 50 messages since she sent yours and may not have a clue what you're talking about unless you remind her.

When you reply to a message, most mail programs fill in the Subject field with the letters Re: (short for *regarding*) and the Subject of the message to which you're replying.

Keeping Track of Your Friends

After you begin using e-mail, you quickly find that you have enough regular correspondents that it's a pain to keep track of their e-mail addresses. Fortunately, almost every popular e-mail program provides an *address book* in which you can save your friends' addresses so that you can send mail to Mom, for example, and have it automatically addressed to chairman@exec. hq.giant-corp.com. You can also create address lists so that you can send mail to family, for example, and it goes to Mom, Dad, your brother, both sisters, and your dog, all of whom have e-mail addresses.

All address books let you do the same things: save in your address book the address from a message you have just read, use addresses you have saved, and edit your address book.

Pine doesn't have an address book feature — but never fear, there are still all kinds of things you can do to your e-mail on it (forwarding it, filing it, attaching something to it). We tell you about it later in the chapter.

Eudora's address book

Eudora has a good address book. If you're reading a message, choose Special⇨ Make Address Book Entry (or press Ctrl+K). Eudora suggests using the person's real name as the nickname, which usually works fine. Then click OK.

To use the address book while you're composing a message, you can open the address book by clicking the Address book icon or choosing Tools⇨Address Book (Ctrl+L). In the Address Book window, click the nickname to use, and then click the To:, Cc:, or Bcc: button to add the selected address to the message (close the Address Book window when you're done with it by clicking its Close or X button). Or use this shortcut: Type the first few letters of the nickname on the To: or Cc: line, enough to distinguish the nickname you want from other nicknames, and press Ctrl+ (the Ctrl key plus a comma). Eudora finishes the nickname for you.

To add someone to your address book, click the Address Book button, click the New button, type the person's name, and click OK. The name appears on your list of nicknames. Click in the Address(es) tab to its right and type the e-mail address. To make a mailing list, create a new nickname and type a series of addresses in the Address(es) box, one to a line. Alternatively, if you have received mail in your Inbox from all the people you want to put on your list, you can press Ctrl+click to highlight all those messages in the Inbox, and then press Ctrl+K to make a new address book entry that contains the addresses of all the authors.

Netscape Messenger's address book

Netscape Messenger has an adequate if uninspired address book. When you're reading a message, you can add the sender's address to your address book by choosing Message⇨Add Sender to Address Book. This action pops up a New Card window in which you can enter the nickname to use and then click OK to add the nickname to the address book. To use the address book when you're creating a message, click the Address button in the Composition window. This action pops up a window that lists the contents of your address book. Double-click the address or addresses you want, and then click OK to continue composing your message. Or type the nickname of someone in your address book; when you press Tab, Netscape replaces it with the address.

To edit your address book, choose Communicator⇨Address Book. You can create an entry for a person by clicking New Card. To create a mailing list, click the New List button, which creates an empty list, and then type the addresses you want.

Outlook Express's address book

The process of copying a correspondent's address into the address book is easy but obscure: Double-click a message from your correspondent to open that message in its own window. Then right-click the person's name in the From line, and click the Add to Address Book button. If you want to do so, you can edit the address book entry you're creating, and then click OK. Or you can skip the first step and right-click the address in the list of messages in the mailbox.

To display and edit the Address book, click the Address Book icon on the toolbar. After you manage to get some entries into your address book, you can use them while you're creating a new message by clicking on the To: or Cc: line or the little icon that looks like a Rolodex card or a book. In the Select Recipients window that appears, double-click the address book entry or entries you want to use and then click OK. If you don't know someone's e-mail address, choose Edit⇨Find⇨People from the menu to display the Find People window; you can search in your own address book or in various Internet directories, such as WhoWhere (www.whowhere.com).

Hot Potatoes: Forwarding Mail

You can forward e-mail along to someone else. It's easy. It's cheap. Forwarding is one of e-mail's best features — and one of its worst. It's good because you can easily pass along messages to people who need to know about them. It's bad because you (not you personally, but, um, people around you — that's it) can just as easily send out floods of messages to recipients who would rather not get them. Consider whether forwarding a message will actually be of use to the recipient(s).

What's usually called *forwarding* a message involves wrapping the message in a new message of your own, sort of like sticking Post-It notes all over a copy of it and mailing the copy and Post-Its to someone else.

Forwarding mail is almost as easy as replying to it. In Eudora or Netscape Messenger, choose Message⇨Forward or click the Forward button on the toolbar (or click Ctrl+L in Netscape); in Outlook Express, click the Forward message button on the toolbar or press Ctrl+F or choose Compose⇨Forward; in Pine, press F. The mail program composes a message containing the text of the message you want to forward; all you have to do is address the message, add a few snappy comments, and send it.

✔ Eudora and Outlook Express provide the forwarded text in the message part of the window. Each line is preceded by the greater-than sign (>). You then get to edit the message and add your own comments. See the nearby sidebar "Fast forward" for tips about pruning forwarded mail.

✔ Netscape Messenger doesn't show you the text of the original message — you just have to trust the program to send the text along. (Netscape treats the message as an *attached file,* which you read about later in this chapter.) The comments you type in the message box appear along with the text of the original message.

If you want Netscape to include the text of the original message in the usual way (with each line preceded by a >), choose the Message⇨ Forward As⇨Quoted command instead.

Sometimes, the mail you get may really have been intended for someone else. You probably will want to pass it along as is, without sticking the greater-than character at the beginning of every line, and you should leave the Sender and Reply-to information intact so that if the new recipient of the mail wants to respond, the response goes to the originator of the mail, not to you just because you passed it on. Some mail programs call this feature *remailing* or *bouncing,* the electronic version of scribbling another address on the outside of an envelope and dropping it back in the mailbox.

Fast forward

Whenever you're forwarding mail, it's generally a good idea to get rid of the uninteresting parts. The forwarded message often automatically includes all the glop in the message header, which is usually incomprehensible — so get rid of it, too.

The tricky part is editing the text. If the message is short, a screenful or so, you probably should leave it alone:

>Is there a lot of demand for
    fruit pizza?

>In answer to your question,
    I checked with our research
    department and found that
    the favorite pizza toppings
    in the 18-34 age group are
    pepperoni, sausage, ham,
    pineapple, olives, peppers,
    mushrooms, hamburger, and
    broccoli. I specifically
    asked about prunes, and
    they found no statistically
    significant response about
    them.

If the message is really long and only part of it is relevant, you should, as a courtesy to the reader, cut it down to the interesting part. We can tell you from experience that people pay much more attention to a concise, one-line e-mail message than they do to 12 pages of quoted stuff followed by a two-line question.

Sometimes it makes sense to edit material even more, particularly to emphasize one specific part. When you do so, of course, be sure not to edit to the point where you put words in the original author's mouth or garble the sense of the message, as in the following reply:

>In answer to your question,
    I checked with

>our research department and
    found that the

>favorite pizza toppings ...
    and they

>found no statistically
    significant

>response about them.

That's an excellent way to make new enemies. Sometimes, it makes sense to paraphrase a little — in that case, put the paraphrased part in square brackets, like this:

>[When asked about prunes on
    pizza, research]

>found no statistically
    significant response

>about them.

People disagree about whether paraphrasing to shorten quotes is a good idea. On one hand, if you do it well, it saves everyone time. On the other hand, if you do it badly and someone takes offence, you're in for a week of accusations and apologies that will wipe out whatever time you may have saved. The decision is up to you.

Eudora calls this process *redirecting;* you can redirect mail by choosing Message⇨Redirect from the menu or clicking the red-arrow-pointing-to-the-sky icon. Eudora sticks in a polite by-way-of notice to let the new reader know how the message found her. Pine uses B for Bounce. Netscape and Outlook Express have no redirection, you have to forward messages instead.

You may sometimes be tempted to forward an e-mail message to someone else. After all, forwarding e-mails is a quick and easy process. It lets you be an online gossip — in a very twisted way! However, you should first pause for a second to consider what you would do if that same e-mail message you received was in printed or voice format instead. Would the sender be offended if you photocopied their letter, or forwarded their voice-mail message to a complete stranger? A simple rule of thumb is that if a message is personal (and not business) in nature, seek the sender's permission first before forwarding that person's e-mail to someone else. This simple protocol may save you some grief later on!

Cold Potatoes: Saving Mail

Saving e-mail for later reference is similar to putting potatoes in the fridge for later. (Don't knock it if you haven't tried it — day-old boiled potatoes are yummy with enough butter or sour cream.) Lots of your e-mail is worth saving, just as lots of your paper mail is worth saving. (Lots of it *isn't,* of course, but we covered that subject earlier in this chapter.)

You can save e-mail in a few different ways:

- ✔ Save it in a folder full of messages.
- ✔ Save it in a regular file.
- ✔ Print it and put it in a file cabinet with paper mail.

The easiest method usually is to stick messages in a folder (a folder is usually no more than a file full of messages with some sort of separator between each message).

People use two general approaches in filing mail: organizing by sender and by topic. Whether you use one or the other or both is mostly a matter of taste. Some mail programs (such as Pine) help you file stuff by the sender's name. When you press S to save a message from your friend Fred, who has the username fred@something.or.other, Pine asks whether you want to put the message in a folder called *fred*. If some crazed system administrator has given him the username z921h8t@something.or.other, make up names of your own.

For filing by topic, it's entirely up to you to come up with folder names. The most difficult part is coming up with memorable ones. If you're not careful, you end up with four folders with slightly different names, each with a quarter of the messages about a particular topic. Try to come up with names that are obvious, and don't abbreviate. If the topic is accounting, call the folder *accounting*; if you abbreviate, you will never remember whether it's called *acctng, acct,* or *acntng.*

If you use Windows or a Mac, you can save all or part of a message by copying it into a text file or word-processing document. Select the text of the message by using your mouse. In Windows, press Ctrl+C (⌘+C on a Mac) or choose Edit⇨Copy to copy the text to the Clipboard. Switch to your word processor (or whatever program you want to copy the text in) and press Ctrl+V (⌘+V on the Mac) or choose Edit⇨Paste to make the message appear where the cursor is.

Filing mail with Eudora

To file a message in Eudora, click the message and choose Transfer from the menu. The Transfer menu that appears lists all your mailboxes — all the choices you have for where to file your message. Choose the mailbox in which you want to stick your message. *Poof!* — it's there.

The first time you try to file something, you may notice that you don't have anywhere to file it. Create a new mailbox in which to stick the message by choosing New from the Transfer menu. Every time you want to create a new file, choose New. Although you eventually have enough mailboxes to handle most of your mail, for a while you may feel as though you're choosing New all the time.

You can see all the messages in a folder by choosing Mailbox from the menu — a window appears listing all the messages in the folder.

If you want to save the message in a text file, click the message, choose File⇨ Save As from the menu, move to the folder you want to save the message in, type a filename, and click OK.

The same deal with Netscape Messenger

You can save a message in a folder by clicking the message, choosing Message⇨ Move Message from the menu, and choosing the folder from the list that appears. Or right-click the message, choose Move to, and pick the desired folder on the submenu. To make a new folder, choose File⇨New Folder. You can even select the message and drag it to a folder on the folder list.

To save a message or several messages in a text file, select the message or messages and choose File⇨Save As⇨File from the menu (or press Ctrl+S). Click in the Save as type box and choose Plain Text (U.txt) from the list that appears. Type a filename and click the Save button.

Filing mail with Outlook Express

To save a message in Outlook Express, you stick it in a folder. You start out with folders named Inbox, Deleted Items, Outbox, and Sent Items. To make a new folder, choose File⇨Folder⇨New Folder from the menu and give the folder a name. (Make one called Personal, just to give it a try.) The new folder appears on the list of folders on the left side of the Outlook Express window. Move messages into a folder by clicking a message header and dragging it over to the folder name or choosing Edit⇨Move to Folder from the menu. You can see the list of message headers for any folder by clicking the folder name. If you have lots of messages to file, you can even create folders within folders, to keep things really organized.

You can save the text of a message in a text file by clicking the message and choosing File⇨Save As from the menu, clicking in the Save as type box and choosing Text Files (U.txt), typing a filename, and clicking the Save button.

The same deal with Pine

To save a message in a folder, press S when you're looking at the message or when it's highlighted on your list of messages. To create a new folder, tell Pine to save a message to a folder that doesn't exist (yet). Pine asks whether you want to create the folder — press Y to do so.

Exotic Mail and Mail Attachments

Sooner or later, just plain, old, everyday e-mail isn't good enough for you. Someone's gonna send you a picture you just have to see, or you're gonna want to send something cool to your new best friend in Paris. To send stuff other than text through the mail, a message uses special file formats. Sometimes, the entire message is in a special format (such as MIME, which we talk about in a minute), and sometimes people *attach* things to their plain text mail. Attachments come in three flavours:

- **MIME:** Stands for *m*ultipurpose *I*nternet *m*ail *e*xtensions
- **Uuencoding:** A method of including information in e-mail; invented back in the days of UNIX-to-UNIX e-mail (hence the *uu* in the name)

✔ **BinHex:** Stands for *bin*ary-to-*hex*adecimal, as far as we can tell; it's popular among Macintosh users

The technical details of these three methods are totally uninteresting and irrelevant: What matters to you is that your e-mail program must be capable of attaching files by using at least one of these methods and capable of detaching incoming files that other people send you, preferably by using any of the three methods.

You can generally send a file as an e-mail attachment by using your regular mail program to compose a regular message and then giving a command to attach a file to the message. You send the message by using the program's usual commands.

When you receive a file that is attached to an e-mail message, your mail program is responsible for noticing the attached file and doing something intelligent with it. Most of the time, your mail program saves the attached file as a separate file in the folder or directory you specify. After the file has been saved, you can use it just like you use any other file.

For example, you can send these types of files as attachments:

✔ Pictures, in image files

✔ Word-processing documents

✔ Sounds, in audio files

✔ Movies, in video files

✔ Programs, in executable files

✔ Compressed files, such as ZIP files

See Chapter 20 for a more specific description of the types of files you may encounter as attachments.

If you receive a message with an attachment that uses a method (MIME, uuencoding, or BinHex) that your mail program doesn't know about, the attached file shows up as a large message in your mailbox. If the attached file contains text, about half the kinds of tarted-up text are readable as is, give or take some ugly punctuation. If the attached file contains sound or pictures, on the other hand, reading the message is hopeless because it just contains binary digitized versions of the images and no text approximation.

If you get a picture or sound MIME message and your mail program doesn't automatically handle it, clunky but usable methods may exist for saving the message to a file and extracting the contents with separate programs. Consult your Internet service provider's help desk.

Eudora attachments

To attach a file to a message with Eudora, compose a message as usual. Then choose Message⇨Attach File from the menu or click the Attach icon (a disk in front of a folder or, in newer versions of Eudora, a message clipped to an envelope) or press Ctrl+H. Eudora helps you choose the document you want to attach.

If you drag a file from Windows Explorer, My Computer, or File Manager to Eudora, it attaches the file to the message you're writing. If you're not writing a message, it starts one for you.

When Eudora receives mail with attachments, it automatically saves them to your disk (in a directory that you specify on the Options menu) and tells you where they are and what they're called.

Netscape Messenger attachments

In the Composition window, click the Attach button and choose File to attach a file to the message you're composing. Unlike most other mail programs, Netscape Messenger lets you attach any file or document you can describe with a *Uniform Resource Locator,* or *URL* (the naming scheme used on the Web, as explained in Chapter 6).

For incoming mail, Netscape displays any attachments that it knows how to display itself (Web pages and GIF and JPEG image files). For other types of attachments, it displays a little description of the file, which you can click. Netscape then runs an appropriate display program, if it knows of one, or asks you whether to save the attachment to a file or to configure a display program, which it then runs in order to display it. Netscape can handle all three-attachment methods.

Outlook Express attachments

In Outlook Express, you attach a file to a message by choosing Insert⇨File Attachment from the menu while you're composing a message, or clicking the paper-clip icon on the toolbar. Then select the file to attach. Send the message as usual.

When an incoming message contains an attachment, a paper-clip icon appears in the message on your list of incoming messages and in the message when you view it. Click the paper clip to see the filename — double-click to see the attachment.

Pine attachments

To attach stuff with Pine, you enter the filenames of whatever you want to attach, separated by commas. When you press Enter after you have entered your attachments, Pine goes and gets the file. If it can't find the file, the program enters it in your list of attachments anyway, but tells you that it can't find the file, so pay careful attention. Pine attaches files by using MIME.

When Pine reads a message with attachments, it tells you which attachments you have and displays them if they're in a format it comprehends. Generally, what happens is that you save a file with a filename of your choosing and then read it by using other software. (Chapter 20 has info about just what type of file you may have received.) Pine can handle only MIME attachments directly. If you receive a uuencoded message (it starts with `begin filename 644` or something like that), press the vertical bar key (`|`) to tell Pine to feed your message to a program, and then type `uudecode`, the name of the UNIX program that decodes uuencoded messages. The file is stored in your home directory on your provider's system.

Hey, Mr. Robot

Not every e-mail address has an actual person behind it. Some are mailing lists (which we talk about in Chapter 13), and some are *robots,* programs that automatically reply to messages. Mail robots have become popular as a way to query databases and retrieve files because setting up a connection for e-mail is much easier than setting up one that handles the more standard file transfer. You send a message to the robot (usually referred to as a *mailbot* or *mail server*), it takes some action based on the contents of your message, and then the robot sends back a response.

The most common use for mail servers is to get on and off *mailing lists,* which we explore in gruesome detail in Chapter 13. Companies also often use the lists to send back canned responses to requests for information sent to `info@whatever.com`.

One-click surfing

Recent versions of Eudora, Netscape Messenger, and Outlook Express turn all URLs (Web site addresses) they find in an e-mail message into links to the actual Web site. You no longer have to type these addresses into your browser. All you have to do is click the highlighted link in the e-mail message, and — *poof!* — you're at the Web site.

Your Own Personal Mail Manager

After you begin sending e-mail, you probably will find that you receive quite a bit of it, particularly if you put yourself on some mailing lists (see Chapter 13). Your incoming mail soon becomes a trickle, and then a stream, and then a torrent, and pretty soon you can't walk past your keyboard without getting soaking wet, metaphorically speaking.

Fortunately, most mail systems provide ways for you to manage the flow and avoid ruining your clothes (enough of this metaphor already). If most of your messages come from mailing lists, you should check to see whether the lists are available instead as *Usenet* newsgroups. (See the Web page at net.gurus. com/usenet for information about newsgroups.) Usenet newsreading programs generally enable you to look through messages and find the interesting ones more quickly than your mail program does, and to sort the messages automatically so that you can quickly read or ignore an entire *thread* (conversation) of messages about a particular topic. Your system manager can usually arrange to make particularly chatty mailing lists look like Usenet newsgroups.

Users of Netscape 4.7 and earlier versions, and, as of Version 3.0, Eudora users can create *filters* that can automatically check incoming messages against a list of senders and subjects and file them in appropriate folders. Outlook Express has the Inbox Assistant, which can sort your mail automatically. Some other mail programs have similar filtering features. (Most versions of Pine do not.)

You can, for example, create filters that tell your mail program, "Any message that comes from the POULTRY-L mailing list should be automatically filed in the *Chickens* folder."

- ✔ **Eudora:** Choose Tools➪Filters to see a window that lists filters and lets you create, edit, and delete them. (Eudora Pro has even more flexible filters, so buy Eudora Pro if you use filters frequently.) When you close the Filters window, Eudora asks whether you want to save your changes.

- ✔ **Netscape Messenger:** Choose Edit➪Message Filters from the menu to display the Mail Filters window, where you can see, create, edit, and delete filters.

- ✔ **Outlook Express:** Tell the Inbox Assistant how to sort your mail into folders by choosing Tools➪Message Rules➪Mail from the menu.

All this automatic-sorting nonsense may seem like overkill — if you get only 5 or 10 messages a day, it certainly is. After the mail really gets flowing, however, dealing with it will take more and more of your time. Keep those automated tools in mind — if not for now, for later.

Spam, Bacon, and Eggs

Pink tender morsel,
Glistening with salty gel.
What the heck is it?

— SPAM *haiku*, found on the Internet

More and more often, it seems, we get unsolicited e-mail from some organization or person we don't know. The word *spam* (not to be confused with SPAM, a meat-related product from Hormel) on the Internet now means thousands of copies of the same piece of unwanted e-mail, sent to either individual e-mail accounts or Usenet newsgroups. It's also known as "junk e-mail" or unsolicited commercial e-mail (UCE). The message usually consists of unsavoury advertising for get-rich-quick schemes or even pornographic offers — something you don't want to see and something you definitely don't want your kids to see. The message is *spam,* the practice is *spamming,* and the person sending the spam is a *spammer.*

Spam, unfortunately, is a major problem on the Internet because sleazy business entrepreneurs and occasional political lowlifes have decided that it's the ideal way to advertise. We get 50 spams a day (yes, really) and the number continues to increase.

Why call it spam?

The meat? Nobody knows. Oh, you mean the unwanted e-mail? It came from the Monty Python skit in which a group of Vikings sing the word *spam* repeatedly in a march tempo, drowning out all other discourse.

Why is it so bad?

You may think that spam, like postal junk mail, is just a nuisance that we have to live with. But it's worse than junk mail, in several ways. Spam costs you money. E-mail recipients pay much more than the sender does to deliver a message. *Sending* e-mail is cheap: a spammer can send thousands of messages an hour from a PC and a dial-up connection. After that, it costs you time to download, read (at least the subject line), and dispose of the mail. If spam volume continues to grow at its alarming pace, pretty soon e-mail will prove to be useless because the real e-mail is buried under the junk.

Not only do e-mail clients have to bear a cost, but also all this volume of e-mail strains the resources of the e-mail servers and the entire Internet. Internet Service Providers have to pass along the added costs to their users. AOL Canada has reported that an estimated 25 percent of the e-mails it processes through its system is spam, and many ISPs have told us that as much as $2 of the $20 monthly fee goes to handling and cleaning up after spam.

Spammers advertise stuff you'd never get in postal mail. It's generally fraudulent, dishonest, or pornographic. Many of the offers are for get-rich-quick schemes. No honest business would attempt to advertise by broadcasting on the Internet because of the immense bad publicity it would bring on itself.

Many spams include a line that instructs you how to get off their lists, something like "Send us a message with the word REMOVE in it." Why should you have to waste your time to get off the list? But don't bother: spammers' remove lists never work. In fact, they are usually a method for verifying that your address is real — if you do send a "remove" message, the spammer is likely to send you *more* spam.

What can I do?

The Internet tries to be self-policing; and the community of people who make up the users and inventors of this marvellous medium don't want the Internet to fall under the control of short-sighted governments or gangsters. The Internet grew from a need for the easy and free flow of information, and everyone using it should strive to keep it that way.

Check out these Web sites for information about spam and how to fight it, technically, socially, and, increasingly, legally:

- ✔ spam.abuse.net (a spam overview)
- ✔ www.cauce.org (anti-spam laws)
- ✔ www.abuse.net (a complaint forwarding service)

We believe that spam is fundamentally not a technical problem, and only non-technical, probably legal, solutions will work in the long run.

I Think I've Got a Virus

Viruses have been around the Internet for a long time. Originally, they lived in program files that people downloaded using a file transfer program or their Web browser. Now, most viruses are spread through files that are sent via e-mail, as attachments to mail messages.

The text of a plain text message can't contain a virus, because it's only text, and a virus is a (rather sneaky) program. But attachments can, and sometimes do. For the virus to work (that is, for it to run, infect your computer, and send copies of itself out to other people via e-mail), you need to actually run it.

In most e-mail programs (including Netscape Messenger and Eudora), programs contained in attachments don't run until you click them — so *don't* open programs that come from people you don't know. Don't even open attachments from people you *do* know if you weren't expecting to receive them. The Melissa virus (which got a lot of press in the spring of 1999) replicates itself by sending copies of itself to the first 50 people in your address book — people who know you.

However, if you use Microsoft's Outlook Express 5.0 or Outlook with Windows 98, the situation is more dire. Outlook (which comes with Microsoft Office) opens attachments as soon as you view the message. Outlook Express provides a *preview pane,* which displays a file and its attachments before you click it at all. Early versions of Outlook Express 5.0 and Outlook 97, 98, and maybe 2000 allowed attached programs to do all kinds of horrible things to your PC. Luckily, Microsoft has provided a patch, which is available at `www.microsoft.com/security/Bulletins/ms99-032.asp`.

Chapter 13

Mail, Mail, the Gang's All Here

· ·

In This Chapter

▶ Subscribing and unsubscribing to mailing lists

▶ Getting more or less junk mail

▶ Checking out a few interesting mailing lists

· ·

*N*ow that you know all about how to send and receive e-mail, only one thing stands between you and a rich, fulfilling, mail-blessed life: You don't know many people with whom you can exchange mail. Fortunately, you can get yourself on lots of mailing lists, which ensures that you arrive every morning to a mailbox with 400 new messages. (Maybe you should start out with only one or two lists.)

Are You Sure This Isn't Junk Mail?

The point of a mailing list is simple. The list has its own special e-mail address, and anything a person sends to that address is sent to all others on the list. Because these people in turn often respond to the messages, the result is a running conversation on a topic of mutual interest.

Lists have various styles. Some are relatively formal, hewing closely to the official topic of the list. Others tend to go flying off into outer space, topic-wise. You have to read them for a while to be able to tell which list works which way.

Mailing lists fall into three categories:

- ✔ **Discussion:** Every subscriber can post a message. These lists lead to freewheeling discussions and can include a certain number of off-topic messages.

- ✔ **Moderated:** A moderator reviews each message before it gets distributed. The moderator can stop unrelated, redundant, or clueless postings from wasting everyone's time.

- ✔ **Announcement-only:** Only the moderator posts messages. Announcement mailing lists work well for publishing an online newsletter, for example.

Getting On and Off Mailing Lists

Something or somebody has got to take on the job of keeping track of who is on the mailing list and distributing messages to all the subscribers. This job is way too boring for a human being to handle, so programs usually do the job. (A few lists are still manually managed by human beings, and we pity them!) Most lists are run by programs called *list servers* or *mailing list managers*. The most widely used list server programs are LISTSERV, Majordomo, and ListProc, which get their own sections later in this chapter.

The way you get on or off most mailing lists is simple: You send a mail message to the list server program. Because a program is reading the message, it has to be spelled and formatted exactly right. Later in this chapter, we tell you how to send the right messages to list servers.

Other lists are managed by programs with Web interfaces — to get on or off a list, you go to the Web site and click links. See the section "Clicking on and off lists" later in this chapter.

Talking to a human being

To get on or off a manually managed list, you send a nice note to the humanoid who manages the list. Suppose that you want to join a list for fans of Lester B. Pearson (a former Canadian prime minister and public speaker extraordinaire), and the list's name is `pearson-lovers@listco.com`. The list manager's address is almost certainly `pearson-lovers-request@listco.com`. In other words, just add `-request` to the list's address to get the manager's address. Because the list is maintained by hand, your request to be added or dropped doesn't have to take any particular form, as long as it's polite. `Please add me to the pearson-lovers list` does quite well. When you decide that you have had all the Pearson you can stand, another message saying `Please remove me from the pearson-lovers list` works equally well.

Subscribing from the Web

You can subscribe to a lot of mailing lists directly from Web sites. Generally you enter your e-mail address in a box on a Web page, click a Send or Subscribe button, and you're on the list. This is often more convenient than e-mailing a list manager.

But before you subscribe, be sure there is some way to get *off* the list — an option that some marketing-oriented outfits neglect to provide.

Messages to request addresses are read and handled by human beings who sometimes eat, sleep, and work regular jobs as well as maintain mailing lists. It can take a day or so to be added to or removed from a list, and, after you ask to be removed, you often get a few more messages before they remove you. If it takes longer than you had hoped, be patient. *Don't* send cranky follow-ups — they just cheese off the list maintainer.

LISTSERV, the studly computer's mail manager

Maintaining mailing lists is a great deal of work, and someone came up with the idea of letting a computer program do most of it. The first list server program was called *LISTSERV*, which originally ran on great big IBM mainframe computers. (The IBM mainframe types have an inordinate fondness for eight-letter uppercase names, EVEN THOUGH TO MOST OF US IT SEEMS LIKE SHOUTING.) Over the years, LISTSERV has grown to the point that it is an all-singing, all-dancing mailing list program with about 15 zillion features and options, almost none of which you'll care about.

Although LISTSERV is a little clunky to use, it has the huge advantage of being able to easily handle enormous mailing lists that contain thousands of members, something that makes many of the regular Internet mail programs choke. (LISTSERV can send mail to 1,000 addresses in about five minutes, for example, whereas that task would take the regular Internet sendmail program more like an hour.)

You put yourself on and off a LISTSERV mailing list by sending mail to LISTSERV@some.machine.or.other, where some.machine.or.other is the name of the particular machine on which the mailing list lives. This address — the address that includes "LISTSERV" as the username — is called the *administrative address* for the list. You send all administrative commands, like commands to get on or off the list, to the administrative address.

Because LISTSERV list managers are computer programs, they're rather simpleminded, and you have to speak to them clearly and distinctly, using standardized commands.

Suppose that you want to join a list called DANDRUFF-L (LISTSERV mailing lists usually end with -L), which lives at bluesuede.org. (This list may attract a lot of flakes.) To join, send to LISTSERV@bluesuede.org (the administrative address) a message that contains this line in the text of the message (not the subject line):

```
SUB DANDRUFF-L Roger Sherman
```

How to avoid looking like an idiot

Here's a handy tip: After you subscribe to a list, don't send anything to it until you have been reading it for a week. Trust us — the list has been getting along without your insights since it began, and it can get along without them for one more week.

You can learn a lot from just reading: what topics people really discuss, the tone of the list, and so on. It also gives you a fair idea about which topics people are tired of. The classic newcomer gaffe is to subscribe to a list and immediately send a message asking a dumb question that isn't really germane to the topic and that was beaten to death three days earlier. Bide your time, and don't let this situation happen to you.

The number-two newcomer gaffe is to send a message directly to the list asking to subscribe or unsubscribe. This type of message should go to the list manager or to a LISTSERV, Majordomo, or ListProc address, where the list maintainer (human or robotic) can handle it — not to the list itself, where all the other subscribers can see that you screwed up.

To summarize: The first message you send, to join a list, should go to a something-request

or LISTSERV or majordomo or listproc address, but *not* to the list itself. After you have joined the list and read it for a while, then you can send messages to the list.

Be sure to send plain text messages to mailing lists. Don't send "enriched" formatted messages, attachments, or anything other than text. Many e-mail programs don't handle non-text, and many people don't have the program they would need to open an attachment anyway. If you have a file you want to distribute on a mailing list, send a message inviting people interested in getting the file to e-mail you privately.

One last thing not to do: If you don't like what another person is posting (for example, some *newbie* (a newcomer to the Net) is posting blank messages or "unsubscribe me" messages or is ranting interminably about a topic), don't waste everyone's time by posting a response on the list. The only thing stupider than a stupid posting is a response complaining about it. Instead, e-mail the person *privately* and tell him to stop, or e-mail the list manager and ask that person to intervene.

You don't have to add a subject line or anything else to this message — it's better not to, so as not to confuse the LISTSERV program. SUB is short for subscribe, DANDRUFF-L is the name of the list, and anything after that is supposed to be your real name. (You can put whatever you want there, but keep in mind that it shows up in the return address of anything you send to the list.) You don't have to tell LISTSERV your e-mail address, which it can read from the automatically generated headers at the top of your message.

Shortly afterward, you should get back a chatty, machine-generated welcoming message telling you that you have joined the list, along with a description of some commands you can use to fiddle with your mailing list membership. Usually, this message includes a request to confirm that you received the message and that it was really you who wanted to subscribe. Follow the instructions by replying to this message with the single word *OK* in the body of the message. This helps lists ensure that they aren't mailing into the void. If you don't provide this confirmation, you don't get on the list.

Keep the chatty, informative welcome message that tells you about all the commands you can use when you're dealing with the list. For one thing, it tells you how to get *off* the mailing list if it's not to your liking. We have in our mail program a folder called Mailing Lists, where we store the welcome messages from all the mailing lists we join.

After you're subscribed, to send a message to this list, mail to the list name at the same machine — in this case, `DANDRUFF-L@bluesuede.org`. This address is called the *list address* (creatively enough), and it's only for messages to be distributed to the entire list. Be sure to provide a descriptive `Subject:` for the multitudes who will benefit from your pearls of wisdom. Within a matter of minutes, people from all over the world can read your message.

To get off a list, you again write to `LISTSERV@some.machine.or.other`, this time sending this line in the text of the message (not the subject line):

```
SIGNOFF DANDRUFF-L
```

or whatever the list name is. You don't have to give your name again because after you're off the list, LISTSERV has no more interest in you and forgets that you ever existed.

Some lists are more difficult than others to get on and off. Usually, you ask to get on a list and — *presto!* — you're on the list. In some cases, however, the list isn't open to all comers, and the human list owner screens requests to join the list, in which case you may get some messages from the list owner to discuss your request to join.

Urrp! Computers digest messages!

Some mailing lists are *digested*. No, they're not dripping with digital gastric juices — they're digested more in the sense that *Reader's Digest* digests. All the messages over a particular period (usually a day or two) are gathered into one big message with a table of contents added at the front. Many people find this method more convenient than getting messages separately, because you can easily look at all the messages on the topic at one time.

Some mail and newsreading programs give you the option of "dismantling" digests back into the individual messages so that you can see them one at a time yet still grouped together. This option is sometimes known as *undigestifying,* or *exploding,* a digest. (First, it's digested and then it explodes, sort of like a burrito.) Check the specifics of your particular mail program to see whether it has an option for digest exploding.

To contact the actual human being who runs a particular list, the mail address is OWNER- followed by the list name (OWNER-DANDRUFF-L, for example). The owner can do all sorts of things to lists that mere mortals can't do. In particular, the owner can fix screwed-up names on the list or add a name that for some reason the automatic method doesn't handle. You have to appeal for manual intervention if your mail system doesn't put your correct network mail address on the From: line of your messages, as sometimes happens when your local mail system isn't set up quite right, or if your address changes.

Stupid LISTSERV tricks

The people who maintain the LISTSERV program have added so many bells and whistles to it that it would take an entire book to describe them all — but this isn't that book. Here are a few stupid LISTSERV tricks. For each of them, you send a message to LISTSERV@some.machine.or.other to talk to the LISTSERV program. You can send several commands in the same message if you want to do two or three tricks at one time.

- **Temporarily stop mail:** Sometimes, you're going to be away for a week or two, and you don't want to get a bunch of mailing list mail in the meantime. Because you're planning to come back, though, you don't want to take yourself off all the lists either. To stop mail temporarily from the DANDRUFF-L mailing list, send this message:

  ```
  SET DANDRUFF-L NOMAIL
  ```

  The list stops sending you messages. To turn the mail back on, send this message:

  ```
  SET DANDRUFF-L MAIL
  ```

- **Get messages as a digest:** If you're getting a large number of messages from a list and would rather get them all at one time as a daily digest, send this message:

  ```
  SET DANDRUFF-L DIGEST
  ```

  Although not all lists can be digested (again, think of burritos), the indigestible ones let you know and don't take offence. If you later want individual messages again, send this request:

  ```
  SET DANDRUFF-L NODIGEST
  ```

- **Find out who's on a list:** To find out who subscribes to a list, send this message:

  ```
  REVIEW DANDRUFF-L
  ```

Some lists can be reviewed only by people on the list, and others not at all. Because some lists are enormous, be prepared to get back an enormous message listing thousands of subscribers.

✔ **Get or not get your own mail:** When you send mail to a LISTSERV list of which you're a member, the list usually sends you a copy of your own message to confirm that it got there okay. Some people find this process needlessly redundant. ("Your message has been sent. You will be receiving it shortly." Huh?) To avoid getting copies of your own messages, send this message:

```
SET DANDRUFF-L NOACK
```

To resume getting copies of your own messages, send this one:

```
SET DANDRUFF-L ACK
```

✔ **Get files:** Most LISTSERV servers have a library of files available, usually documents contributed by the mailing list members. To find out which files are available, send

```
INDEX
```

To have LISTSERV send you a particular file by e-mail, send this message:

```
GET listname filename
```

where *listname* is the name of the list and *filename* is the name of a file from the INDEX command. For example, to get the article about Social Security number security from the LISTSERV that hosts the privacy forum, send this message:

```
GET privacy prc.ssn-10 to LISTSERV@vortex.com
```

✔ **Find out which lists are available:** To find out which LISTSERV mailing lists are available on a particular host, send this message:

```
LIST
```

Note: Keep in mind that just because a list exists doesn't necessarily mean that you can subscribe to it. It never hurts to try, though.

✔ **Get LISTSERV to do other things:** Lots of other commands lurk in LISTSERV, most of which apply only to people on IBM mainframes. If you're one of these people or if you're just nosy, send a message containing this line:

```
HELP
```

You receive a helpful response that lists other commands.

Majordomo — an excellent choice, sir

The other widely used mailing list manager is *Majordomo*. It started out as a LISTSERV wannabe for workstations but has evolved into a system that works quite well. Because of its wannabe origins, however, Majordomo commands are almost but (pretend to be surprised now) not quite the same as their LISTSERV equivalents.

The administrative address for Majordomo lists (the address to which you send commands), as you may expect, is `majordomo@some.machine.or.other`. Majordomo lists tend to have long and expressive names. One of our favorites is called `explosive-cargo`, a funny weekly column written by a guy who is in real life a computer technical writer. To subscribe, because the list is maintained on host `world.std.com`, send this message to `majordomo@world.std.com`:

```
subscribe explosive-cargo
```

Unlike with LISTSERV, you *don't* put your real name in the subscribe command. Like LISTSERV, Majordomo will probably send back a confirmation question to make sure that it was you who wanted to subscribe. Read the confirmation message carefully and follow its instructions, since Majordomo's confirmations are more complicated than LISTSERV's.

To unsubscribe:

```
unsubscribe explosive-cargo
```

After you have subscribed, you can send a message to everyone on the mailing list by addressing it to the list address — `listname@some.machine.or.other`. (You can't post messages to explosive-cargo because it's an announcements-only list: only the guy who runs it is allowed to post messages.)

Stupid Majordomo tricks

Not to be outdone by LISTSERV, Majordomo has its own set of not particularly useful commands (as with LISTSERV, you can send in a single message as many of these as you want):

- To find out which lists at a Majordomo system you're subscribed to, send this:

    ```
    which
    ```

✔ To find all the lists managed by a Majordomo system, send this:

```
lists
```

✔ Majordomo also can keep files related to its lists. To find the names of the files for a particular list, send this:

```
index name-of-list
```

✔ To tell Majordomo to send you one of the files by e-mail, send this:

```
get name-of-list name-of-file
```

✔ To find out the rest of the goofy things Majordomo can do, ask for this:

```
help
```

✔ If you want to contact the human manager of a Majordomo system because you can't get off a list you want to leave, or have an otherwise insoluble problem, send a polite message to owner-majordomo@hostname. Remember that because humans eat, sleep, and have real jobs, you may not get an answer for a day or two.

ListProc — third-place list manager

Although ListProc is not as widely used as LISTSERV and Majordomo, its popularity is increasing because it is easier to install than LISTSERV, cheaper, and almost as powerful.

To subscribe to a ListProc mailing list, you send this message to the administrative address for the list, listproc@some-computer:

```
subscribe listname yourname
```

To subscribe to the (hypothetical) chickens mailing list at gurus.com, for example, you send this message to listproc@gurus.com:

```
subscribe chickens John A. Macdonald
```

(assuming that you have the same name as the first prime minister of Canada — and that you are not yet knighted).

To get off the mailing list, send this message to the same address:

```
signoff listname
```

You don't have to provide your name — the ListProc program should already know it.

LISTSERV, ListProc, and Majordomo: They could have made them the same, but n-o-o-o-o

Because LISTSERV, ListProc, and Majordomo work in sort of the same way, even experienced mailing list mavens get their commands confused. Here are the important differences:

✔ The address for LISTSERV is `LISTSERV@ hostname`, the address for Majordomo is `majordomo@hostname`, and the address for ListProc is `listproc@hostname`.

✔ To subscribe to a LISTSERV or ListProc list, send `sub` or `subscribe` followed by the list name followed by your real name. To subscribe to a Majordomo list, just send `subscribe` and the list name.

After you have subscribed to the list, you can send messages to everyone on the list by addressing e-mail to the list address `listname@some-computer` (`chickens@gurus.com`, for example).

To find out other things ListProc can do, send the message `help` to `listproc@ whatever`, where `whatever` is the name of the computer on which the ListProc mailing list lives.

Clicking on and off lists

A bunch of Web sites now host mailing lists, letting you join or even create mailing lists by clicking links on Web pages. These sites include Topica (`www.topica.com`), eGroups (`www.egroups.com`), Onelist (`www.onelist.com`), Coollist (`www.coollist.com`), and Listbot (`www.listbot.com`).

To subscribe to a list on one of these Web sites, just follow the instructions on the site. Some mailing list Web sites let you read the messages posted to their lists without actually subscribing — you can click links to display the messages in your Web browser.

You can set up your own mailing lists, too. It's free, because the sites display ads on their Web pages, and may even add ads to the postings on the list. If you have an unusual hobby, job, interest, or ailment, you may want to create a list to discuss it. Or set up a list for a committee or family group to use for online discussions.

Sending Messages to Mailing Lists

Okay, you're signed up on a mailing list. Now what? First, as we say a few pages back, wait a week or so to see what sort of messages arrive from the list — that way, you can get an idea of what you should or should not send to it. When you think that you have seen enough to avoid embarrassing yourself, try sending something in. That's easy: You mail a message to the list address, which is the same as the name of the list — pearson-lovers@listco.com or snufle-l@bluesuede.org or whatever. Keep in mind that because hundreds or thousands of people will be reading your inspired thoughts, you should at least try to spell things correctly. (You may have thought that this advice is obvious, but you would be sadly mistaken.) On popular lists, you may begin to get back responses within a few minutes of sending a message.

Some lists encourage new subscribers to send in a message introducing themselves and briefly stating their interests. Others don't. Don't send anything until you have something to say.

After you watch the flow of messages on a list for a while, all this stuff becomes obvious.

Some mailing lists have rules about who is allowed to send messages: Just because you're on the list doesn't automatically mean that any messages you send appear on the list. Some lists are *moderated:* Any message you send in gets sent to a human moderator, who decides what goes to the list and what doesn't. Although this process may sound sort of fascist, moderation can make a list about 50 times more interesting than it would be otherwise, because a good moderator can filter out the boring and irrelevant messages and keep the list on track. Indeed, the people who complain the loudest about moderator censorship are usually the ones whose messages most urgently need to be filtered out.

WARNING!

Boing!

Computer accounts are created and deleted often enough and mail addresses change often enough that a large list always contains, at any given moment, some addresses that are no longer valid. If you send a message to the list, your message is forwarded to these invalid addresses, and a return message reporting the bad addresses is generated for each of them.

Mailing list managers (both human and computer) normally try to deflect the error messages so that they go to the list owner, who can do something about them, rather than to you. As often as not, however, a persistently dumb mail system sends one of these failure messages directly to you. Just ignore it; you can't do anything about it.

Another rule that sometimes causes trouble is that many lists allow messages to be sent only from people whose addresses appear on the list. This rule becomes a pain if your mailing address changes. Suppose that you get a well-organized new mail administrator and that your official e-mail address changes from `jj@shamu.pol.bluesuede.org` to `John.Jay@bluesuede.org`, although your old address still works. You may find that some lists begin *bouncing* your messages (sending them back to you rather than to the list) because they don't understand that `John.Jay@bluesuede.org`, the name under which you now send messages, is the same as `jj@shamu.pol.bluesuede.org`, the name under which you originally subscribed to the list. Worse, LISTSERV doesn't let you take yourself off the list, for the same reason. To resolve this mess, you have to write to the human list managers of any lists for which this problem arises, and ask them to fix the problem by hand.

The Fine Points of Replying to Mailing-List Messages

Often, you receive an interesting message from a list and want to respond to it. When you send your answer, does it go *just* to the person who sent the original message, or does it go to the *entire list?* It depends, mostly on how the list owner set up the software that handles the list. About half the list owners set things up so that replies automatically go to just the person who sent the original message, on the theory that your response is likely to be of interest only to the original author. The other half set things up so that replies go to the entire list, on the theory that the list is a running public discussion. In messages coming from the list, the mailing list software automatically sets the Reply-To: header line to the address to which replies should be sent.

Fortunately, you're in charge. When you start to create a reply, your mail program should show you the address to which it's replying. If you don't like the address it's using, simply change the address. Check the To: and Cc: fields to make sure that you're sending your message where you want.

While you're fixing the recipient's address, you may also want to fix the Subject: line. After a few rounds of replies to replies to replies, the discussion often wanders away from the original topic, and it's a good idea to change the subject to better describe what is really under discussion.

Finding Interesting Lists

Tens of thousands of lists reside on the Internet — so many, in fact, that entire books have been written that just enumerate them. For a huge, searchable list of lists, check out one of the mailing list directory sites, such as the Liszt (bad pun) site, at `www.liszt.com`, or Topica, at `www.topica.com`. You can search for lists that include a word or phrase in the name or one-line description of the list. Once you locate a list that sounds interesting, Liszt or Topica can tell you how to subscribe.

Here are a few of our favorite lists:

Risks Digest
Majordomo@csl.sri.com
Majordomo (list name risks) moderated, news, digest

This forum discusses risks to the public in computers and related systems. It covers the risks of modern technology, particularly of computer technology (lots of great war stories).

Privacy Forum Digest
LISTSERV@vortex.com
LISTSERV (list name PRIVACY) moderated

This running discussion of privacy in the computer age has lots of creepy reports about people and organizations you would never expect were snooping on you (ambulance drivers, for example).

Tourism Discussions
LISTSERV@VM.EGE.EDU.TR
LISTSERV (list name TRAVEL-L)

The TRAVEL-L list covers travel and tourism, airlines, guidebooks, places to stay — you name it. Because participants come from all over the world (the system host is in France), you get lots of tips you would never get locally.

The Jazz Lover's List
LISTSERV@brownvm.brown.edu
LISTSERV (list name JAZZ-L)

This friendly, laid-back, ongoing discussion makes no claim to staying on topic but rather creates a salon-type atmosphere in which "like-minded, intelligent people from diverse backgrounds" can make real connections.

Liberal Judaism
Listproc@shamash.org
Listproc (list name MLJ) moderated, digest

Nonjudgmental discussions take place here on liberal Judaism (including Reform, Reconstructionist, conservative, and secular humanist), issues, practices, opinions, and beliefs. Include your real first and last name in your request — such as `subscribe MLJ yourfirstname yourlastname.`

Chapter 14

Attention, Dick Tracy

· ·

In This Chapter

▶ Instant messages with ICQ

▶ Instant messages with AOL Canada

▶ Lots of other instants

· ·

*I*nternet e-mail is pretty fast, usually arriving in less than a minute. But sometimes, that's just not fast enough. A new generation of *instant message systems* let you pop up a message on someone's screen in a matter of seconds. They also have *buddy lists* that watch to see when one of your buddies comes online so you know the instant you can instantiate an instant message to them. (Excuse us, this gives us a headache, just a moment while we get some instant coffee. Ahh, that's better.)

The good thing about instant messages is that you can stay in touch with people as fast as talking to them on the phone. The bad thing about them is that they also offer an unparalleled range of ways to annoy people. The AOL Instant Messenger, discussed later in this chapter, has about two features to send and receive messages, and about 12 features to reject, denounce, erase, and otherwise deal with unwanted messages. (This may say more about AOL Canada users than the technology, of course.)

ICQ

ICQ (which is supposed to sound like "I Seek You") is the current king of the instant messages. ICQ has about a quadrillion different features and options, but basically, you download and install ICQ, and set it up to get an eight-digit ICQ#, sort of like a phone number, that identifies you. Then you identify some buddies and start sending them instant messages and chatting with them. The ICQ program runs on Windows 98/95, Windows 3.1, Windows NT, Macs, Windows CE, Palm Pilots, and, for all we know, certain cappuccino machines.

Which instant message system should I use?

Unfortunately, the instant messaging systems don't talk to one another. Since the goal of all of these systems is to stay in touch with your friends, use whichever one they use. If you're not sure who your friends are, AOL Instant Messenger is a good bet because it's easy to set up and automatically works with any AOL user, since it's the same system that AOL Canada uses internally.

If you're really message-mad, you can run more than one system at the same time. While we were writing this chapter, we had ICQ, AOL Instant Messenger, and Yahoo! Messenger all running at once, which was an awful lot of blinking and flashing, but it did work.

Some of the distributed ICQ software out there is still *beta*, that is, it may stop working at some point, they may change the rules, ask people to pay, or something. But with more than 80 million registered users around the world, they aren't likely to make changes that will throw all those users off. This book describes ICQ version 99b beta.

Installing ICQ

First, you have to get a copy of the ICQ software and install it on your computer. Unless you already have a copy (from a friend or a CD-ROM), visit the ICQ home page at www.icq.com, a page that, if there were an Academy Award for the Most Baffling and Cluttered Home Page, would be a shoo-in for a lifetime achievement award. Squint hard at the page and look for a blob called *Download* or maybe *Get ICQ for free.* Click that and you see a much more reasonable page on which there's an area for new users with links to versions for various kinds of computers. Follow the directions that apply to you and follow the links to eventually download the ICQ program. (The program isn't all that big: Downloading it may take less time than all the rigmarole to find the download page.) Follow the instructions to install and start ICQ. After you install the software, you see the Registration Wizard window, which asks whether you already have an ICQ# or if you need a new one.

When you sign up for a new ICQ#, the ICQ Registration Wizard invites you to enter lots of personal information including e-mail address, name, nickname, city, age, phone number, home page, and more. Unless you're the kind of person who welcomes phone calls from strangers at odd hours of the night, we suggest you limit it to e-mail and name. You also have to choose a password to protect your number; all of the other options you can leave alone. When you're done, the ICQ program starts, with a small window on your screen, as shown on the left side of Figure 14-1.

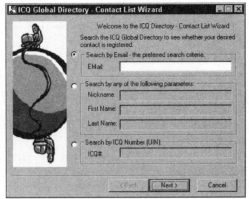

Figure 14-1:
The ICQ
window (on
the left) and
its Contact
List Wizard
are ready to
help you
find friends
to chat with.

The first time you run ICQ, the Intergalactic ICQ computer may send you a welcome message — how thoughtful! To read it, double-click the blinking icon labeled SystemMenu on the little ICQ window. Read the message in its Incoming System Request window, and then click Close.

Normally, ICQ runs all the time you're online. Minimize it using the standard minimize button and it changes the icon in the Windows toolbar and tells you over your computer's speakers when someone's trying to contact you.

When the little ICQ window is displayed, it likes to stay "on top" of all the other windows you have open, which can be inconvenient when it covers up stuff you are trying to work on. To change this behaviour, click the ICQ button in the lower-left corner of the window and choose Preferences from the menu that appears. On the Contact List tab of the Owner Prefs dialog box, click the Always On Top setting, so no checkmark appears next to it.

Getting buddy-buddy

Well, now you're set up with ICQ. Where are your friends? Click the bar in the ICQ window marked Add Users to see the Find/Add Users to Your List window. Click the topmost Search button to see the Contact List Wizard, shown on the right side of Figure 14-1. The first time you run ICQ, it may run the Contact List Wizard for you automagically.

The best ways to search for someone are by ICQ#, if you know it, or e-mail address. (We've found the name and nickname search to be unreliable.) In the Contact List Wizard window, type an e-mail address in the Search by Email box and click the Next button. If ICQ finds a match for the e-mail address or number, it displays the match(es). Click the one you want (if more than one match is displayed), click Next to add that person to your contact list.

Normally you can add the contact immediately, but some ICQ users have set their accounts with a privacy option. In that case you need their permission, in which case ICQ pops up a window like the one in Figure 14-2; type a note to plead your case and click Request.

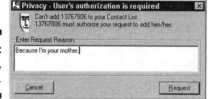

Figure 14-2:
Talk to me,
please.

If ICQ can't find a match, it offers to send the victim, uh, friend, an e-mail extolling the wonders of ICQ and encouraging your friend to sign up. Use your discretion, please.

Once you add a person to your buddies list, the ICQ window displays a bar with the buddy's nickname. You can adjust your buddies list at any time — there's no need to identify everyone right away. To add more people, click the Add Users bar again. To delete a person, click the person's entry and select Delete from the menu. To change the name that appears for a person (for example, if their ICQ number appears, and you'd like to see their name), click the entry and choose Rename from the menu.

Flashing away

When you receive a message from a person or from the ICQ system, the appropriate bar in the ICQ window flashes and the program makes a noise. (On our systems, it makes the sound of a glass breaking, or a little "Oh-oh!" Is this normal? We think so.) Double-click the flashing item to see the Incoming Message window with the message. You can write back by clicking the Reply button. To save or print the message (unlikely you'd want to), click the More Functions button.

To send someone a message, click the person's name or ICQ number on your ICQ window and select Message from the menu. Type a message (as shown in Figure 14-3) and click Send. If the person is online, you can send a message right away. If not, ICQ offers to save a message until your friend shows up.

Figure 14-3:
ICQ delivers
an important
message.

Chatting away

If you want to have an online conversation rather than just send a single message, click your buddy's name and select ICQ chat. If you just received a message from the person, you can click the Request Chat button on the Incoming Message window. Assuming that your friend is online, ICQ asks you to enter a short message to send to your friend saying why you want to chat. Click Chat to send your request.

At the receiving end, the sender's bar in the ICQ window flashes and ICQ says "Incoming chat request." Double-click the flashing bar to see the request message, and either click Accept to start chatting or click Decline to blow the sender off (you get your choice of excuses).

After both ends agree to chat, ICQ opens a chat window. The first time, ICQ asks how to arrange the window; accept its suggestion of split screen. Now each person can type and see what the other is typing. When you're done, just close the chat window.

Unless you are a very fast typist or your friend lives in Mongolia, the most effective thing to type is "What's your phone number?" and call the person on the phone.

The other 999,999 billion ICQ features

As well as sending messages and chatting, you can do a lot of other stuff with ICQ:

✔ You can send files to and receive files from your buddies. The files go directly from one person's computer to the other, so it's pretty fast. But it goes without saying that you should never accept files from people you don't know; files can contain programs with viruses, offensive pictures, or other undesirable material.

✔ You can join group chats on various topics. Click Add/Find Users and look at some of the chat options.

✔ If you're really bored, you can send messages to randomly selected people. (This also means that randomly selected people may send you messages.)

✔ In Advanced Mode, you can set up profiles, adjust your status to tell people whether you want to be interrupted, send e-mail, try to place Internet phone calls, and otherwise engage in many time-consuming communication activities. The ICQ Web site has extensive documentation on all of this.

AOL Instant Messenger

AOL Instant Messenger (AIM for short) is a lot less fancy than ICQ. Its key function is to let you type messages back and forth. But it's easier to set up than ICQ, and enables you to talk directly to AOL users across the world.

Setting up Instant Messenger

If you're an AOL Canada user, you're already set up for instant messages. If not, you have to install the AIM program. AOL Canada subscribers can also run the AIM program and use their AOL screen name when they're logged into another kind of Internet account.

AOL, being the hyper-aggressive marketing organization it is, has arranged for AIM to be bundled in with a lot of other packages. In particular, if you have a copy of Netscape Communicator 4.5 or later, you probably have AIM already. If you don't have it, visit free.aol.com/aim or www.aol.ca/aim/, and follow the directions on the Web page. You have to choose a screen name, which can be up to 16 letters long (be creative so as not to collide with one of the 61 million names already in use), and a password. You also have to enter your e-mail address. AOL, refreshingly, doesn't want any more personal information. The e-mail address you give has to be real: AOL sends a confirmation message to that address, and you must reply or your screen name is deleted.

Click the download button for Windows or Macintosh, and save the downloaded file somewhere on your computer. (C:\Windows\Temp is an okay place if you don't have another folder you use for downloads.) Then run the downloaded program to install AIM. Normally, AIM runs in the background whenever you're online. If it's not running, click the AIM icon on your desktop.

The first time you use AIM, you have to enter your AIM or AOL screen name, as in the left part of Figure 14-4. Type your screen name and password and click Sign On. If you want to use AIM every time you're online, check the Save password and Auto-login boxes before signing on, and AIM will sign you on automatically in the future. You see the AIM window, shown in the middle of Figure 14-4.

Figure 14-4:
Signing on
to AIM,
the AIM
window, and
AIM's List
Setup tab.

AIM may run the New User Wizard, which offers help getting started. Follow its instructions, or click Cancel to go it alone (you can always return to the Wizard by choosing File⇨New User Wizard from the AIM menu). A tiny Ticker window may also appear, showing a scrolling news ticker. If you don't like it, close it, or click its two buttons to see news detail or customize the Ticker.

AIM for Internet users

After creating your buddy list, you can proceed to send messages.

In the AIM window, click the List Setup tab, shown on the right side of Figure 14-4. You may want to make the window wider to make the tab visible. AOL Canada provides three groups: Buddies, Family, and Co-Workers. To add a buddy, click the group to which you want to add it, click the Add Buddy button (near the lower-left corner of the window), and enter the buddy's screen name. If you know the e-mail address but not the screen name, choose People⇨Find a Buddy⇨By E-mail Address from the menu. Doing so starts a Wizard that looks for that address and helps you add any screen names that match.

After you select your buddies, click the Online tab. AIM displays the buddies who are currently online.

To send a message to someone, double-click the buddy's name to open a message window, type the message, and click the Send button. AIM pops up a window (shown on the left side of Figure 14-5) on the recipient's machine, plays a little song, and you and your buddy can type back and forth. When done, close the message window.

 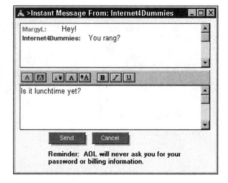

Figure 14-5:
Chatting using AIM and AOL.

AIM for AOL Canada members

AOL Canada has buddy lists and instant messages included. You need only set them up and start messaging. These instructions describe AOL Canada 6.0 (for Windows) and 4.0 (for the Mac).

The Buddy List Window, which is similar to the AIM window, appears automatically when you sign onto AOL Canada (if it doesn't, go to keyword BUDDYVIEW). You see the same three groups as in AIM: Buddies, Family, and Co-Workers. To add someone to your Buddy List or make other changes, click one of the groups and then click the Setup button. You see the Buddy List Setup window. Click the group to which you want to add the person and click Edit. Type the screen name of each buddy and click the Add Buddy button. When you're done, click Save. Note that you can enter screen names of AOL Canada users and Internet AIM users interchangeably.

In the Buddy List window, double-click the buddy to whom you want to send a message, and AIM opens a message window, shown on the right side of Figure 14-5. Type the message, click Send, and you can type back and forth with the other person. Click Cancel when you're finished.

In AOL Canada 6.0, you can use the Setup feature to easily rearrange individual screen names or entire Buddy List groups. And you can create a customized "away" message that lets your friends know when you are away from your computer. Similarly, you can tell at-a-glance which of your friends is away by looking for the yellow notepad icon next to their screen names on your Buddy List. The last new addition to instant messaging in the 6.0 software is a group of funky new icons you can use to represent yourself in cyberspace. Check them out by clicking the Setup button, then Preferences and selecting the IM tab. There' s a whole stable of wacky symbols to represent the "real you."

If you are an AOL member, an incoming message from an AIM user causes a window to pop up on your screen (AOL calls this a "knock-knock" message). Click Respond to accept the message and start a conversation, or Cancel to reject it. After the conversation, click Cancel to close the window.

Buzz off

AOL evidently has a lot of ill-mannered users, because AIM has an elaborate system for warning and blocking users you don't like.

For Internet users, the AIM window has Warn and Block buttons. Click the Warn button if you get a message that you find moderately annoying to send a warning to the sender. With enough warnings (about five), a user is blocked from sending instant messages for a while. If you find a sender to be totally objectionable, click Block to refuse all messages from that person. You can further adjust who is able to send messages and who isn't via the Controls window; choose File➪My Options➪Edit Preferences and then the Controls tab. You can limit messages to people on your buddies list, permit specific people, or block specific people. You can also add or delete people from your block list.

For AOL Canada members, go to BUDDYLIST to display the Buddy List Setup window, and click Privacy Preferences. You can permit or block specific users, block all Internet AIM users, or block all users.

Some fairly obvious rules of messaging conduct

Sending someone an instant message is the online equivalent of walking up to someone on the street and starting a conversation. If it's someone you know, it's one thing; if not, it's usually an intrusion.

Unless you have a compelling reason, don't send instant messages to people you don't know who haven't invited you to do so. (ICQ's random message feature is the most likely such invitation.) Don't say anything that you wouldn't say in an analogous situation on the street. If someone's set her ICQ status to "urgent messages only," save your non-urgent messages for later or send them as e-mail.

For some reason, AOL is plagued with childish users who now and then send rude instant messages to strangers or unwilling acquaintances, which is why AIM has its Warn and Block buttons. Not only is it rude to do that, it's silly, since AOL Canada has chat rooms full of people eager to converse on all sorts of topics, rude or otherwise.

Dozens of Other Message and Paging Systems

Instant messages are very trendy, so there are plenty of other options for instant messages. Keep in mind that on each system you can only send messages to other people on the same system, so the situation is sort of like the telephone industry in the early 1900s, with many competing companies stringing wires, but no two companies connected together. (If you're wondering why there isn't a system on the Internet that connects everyone, there is. It's called e-mail. See Chapters 11, 12, and 13.)

✔ **Yahoo Messenger:** Go to `messenger.yahoo.com` and follow the directions to download and install the program. Yahoo Messenger is available in two versions: a Windows 98/95 program, and a program that runs as a Java *applet* (a richer Web page reading application, often featuring moving images and sounds) in your Web browser, on any system that has a Java-enabled browser (including Macs or UNIX).

✔ **MSN Messenger:** Go to `messenger.msn.com` for information and downloads; the program runs on Windows 98/95, NT, and Macs. Before using the program, you have to sign up for a Hotmail account at `www.hotmail.com`. The Windows 98/95 version of MSN Messenger can send and receive messages from Outlook Express 5.0 and NetMeeting (Microsoft's online conferencing program). Early versions of Messenger could also talk to AIM users, but after about half a year of cat and mouse games where AOL blocked Messenger and Microsoft released new versions to get around the block, Microsoft uncharacteristically gave up.

✔ **UNIX talk:** UNIX systems have had a simple but functional message system called "talk" for many years. (The system is actually called ntalk for New Talk, new as of about 1981.) All UNIX and Linux systems have a talk command, and freeware WinTalk (for Windows, from `www.thoughtcraft.com/elf/wintalk`) and shareware Talk (for Mac, available at `www.macorchard.com/chat.html#Talk`) are available, too. The system is pretty basic, but if you have friends on UNIX workstations, it's the way to send them a message.

Chapter 15

Let's Face the Music and Chat

In This Chapter

▶ Getting in step with online chat

▶ Understanding chat culture, etiquette, and safety

▶ Chatting on AOL Canada and WebTV

▶ Participating in IRC (Internet Relay Chat)

▶ Playing in the MUDs (Multiple-User Dimensions and Multiple-User Dialogues)

E-mail is swell, but for some people it's just not conversational enough. Do the recipients of your witty and insightful messages neglect to answer for hours or maybe even days (what? — they have something better to do?) while you sit around looking at your empty mailbox? Maybe online chat is for you.

Online chat lets you communicate instantly with another person anywhere who is logged on to the Net, by typing messages back and forth to each other. It's much faster than regular mail and considerably faster than e-mail. And you can chat with several people at one time. Unlike instant messages (covered in Chapter 14), chatting enables you to have a conversation, rather than just sending quick notes back and forth.

Look Who's Chatting

Online chat is similar to talking on an old-fashioned party line or CB radio. In the infancy of the telephone system, people usually shared their phone line with other families, especially in rural areas, where the cost of stringing telephone lines was expensive. Everyone on the party line could join in any conversation, offering hours of nosy fun for people with nothing better to do. Today, people often arrange conference calls to have several people all talk together.

Chatting is similar to a conference call except that rather than talk, you type on your keyboard what you want to say and read on-screen what other people are saying. Although all the people participating in the chat can be typing at one time, each person's contribution is presented on-screen in order of its receipt, identified by the name of the person who typed it.

You can chat in two main ways:

- *Channels* or *rooms,* which resemble an ongoing conference call with a bunch of people. After you join a channel, you can read on-screen what people are saying and then add your own comments just by typing them and pressing Enter.
- *Direct connection,* which is a private conversation between you and another person connected to a chat system.

Who are those guys?

Which groups of people are available when you begin to chat depends on how you're connected to the Internet. If you're an AOL Canada member (where the groups are called *chat rooms*), you chat with other AOL members (and there are more than 30 million members worldwide). WebTV users have WebTV's Chat City. Users with regular Internet accounts talk to other people using the Internet's IRC (Internet Relay Chat) system — see "Chatting via IRC" at the end of this chapter. Anyone with access to the Web can use Web-based chat.

Each channel has a name; with luck, the name is an indication of what the chatters there are talking about or what they have in common. Some channels have names such as #chat, and the people there are probably just being sociable.

Who am I?

No matter which chat facility you're using, you should know that most people select a *screen name,* or *nickname,* to use before they join a group. Other members of the group know you by your screen name, a temporary name often chosen to be unique, colourful, or clever, and used as a mask. The choice of a screen name is only good for the duration of a chat session, except on AOL Canada, where you chat using your registered screen name. If you join a group and have a nice chat with someone named DrNo, the next time you see that name, you have no guarantee that it's the same person. This anonymity can make chatting a place to be careful. On the other hand, one of the attractions of chatting is meeting new and interesting people. Many warm and wonderful friendships have evolved from a chance meeting in a chat room.

When you join a group and begin chatting, you see the screen names of the people who are already there and a window in which the current conversation goes flying by. If the group is friendly, somebody may even send you a welcome message.

As in real life, a room full of strangers can have people you don't like much. Because it's possible to be fairly anonymous on the Internet, some people act boorish, vulgar, or crude. So you should be careful (to put it mildly!) about letting your children chat unsupervised (see Chapter 3). When you're new to chat, you may accidentally visit some disgusting places, although you'll soon find out how to avoid them and locate rooms that have useful, friendly, and supportive conversations.

Your First Chat Room

Your first time in a chat room can seem daunting. Here are some of the things you can do to get through your first encounter:

- ✔ Remember that when you enter a chat room, a conversation is probably already in progress. You don't know what went on before you arrived.
- ✔ Wait a minute or two to see a page full of exchanges so that you can understand some of the context before you start writing.
- ✔ Start by following the comments of a single screen name. Then follow the people that that person mentions or who reply to that original person.
- ✔ When you can follow one thread, try picking up another. It takes practice to get the hang of it.
- ✔ AOL Canada and some IRC programs can highlight the messages from selected people. This can make things easier to follow.
- ✔ You can also indicate people to ignore. Messages from these chatters no longer appear on your screen, though other members' replies to them do appear.
- ✔ Scroll up to see older messages if you have to, and remember that after you have scrolled up, no new messages appear until you scroll back down.

Figure 15-1 shows a chat in progress. Fritz is asking a German group about a phrase.

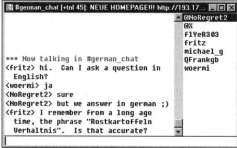

Figure 15-1:
English chat
in progress
in the
#german_
chat room.

Online etiquette

Chatting etiquette is not that much different from e-mail etiquette, and common sense is your best guide. Here are some additional chatting tips:

- ✔ The first rule of chatting is not to hurt anyone. A real person with real feelings is at the other end of the computer chat connection.

- ✔ The second rule is to be cautious. You really have no idea who the other person is. See "Safety first" later in this chapter.

- ✔ Read messages for a while to figure out what is happening, before sending a message to a chat group. (Reading without posting anything is known as *lurking*.)

- ✔ Keep your messages short and to the point.

- ✔ Don't insult people, and don't use foul language.

- ✔ Create a profile with selected information about yourself. Most chat systems have provisions for creating profiles (personal information) that other members can access. Don't give out your last name, phone number, or address. And we think that extra caution is necessary for kids. Insist that children enter neither their ages, hometowns, schools, nor their last names, phone numbers, or addresses. Try to monitor how often your kids chat on the Internet.

- ✔ Although you don't have to tell everything about yourself in your profile, what you do say should be truthful.

- ✔ If you want to talk to someone in private, send him or her a message saying hi, who you are, and what you want.

- ✔ If the tone of conversation in one chat room offends you, try another. As in real life, you may run into more people out there you *don't* want to meet than people you *do*.

For more information about the history and art of meeting people online, see Philippe Le Roux's chapter, Virtual Intimacy — Tales from Minitel and More, at net.gurus.com/leroux.phtml. For more netiquette tips, see net.gurus.com/netiquette.

Safety first

Here are some guidelines for conducting safe and healthy chats:

- ✔ Many people in chat groups lie about their occupations, ages, localities, and, yes, even genders. Some think that they're just being cute, some are exploring their own fantasies, and some are really sick.

- ✔ Be careful about revealing information that enables someone to find you personally — such as where you live or work or your phone number. This information includes your last name, phone number, mailing address, and schools your kids attend. Do not give out personal information about yourself or any member of your family, even in cases where you're offered some sort of prize for filling out a form.

- ✔ Never give your password to anyone. No one should ever ask you for it. If someone does, don't respond, but do tell your service provider about the request. (We once received a message saying, "There's been a serious threat to security, and we need your password to help determine the problem." If you ever get a message like that — anytime you're online — it's a fake. Report the incident to your Internet Service Provider.)

- ✔ If your chat service offers profiles and a person without a profile wants to chat with you, be extra cautious.

- ✔ If your children use chat, realize that others may try to meet them in person. Review the guidelines in this list with your kids before they log on. Children should never, ever meet someone in person without their parents.

If you do choose to meet an online friend in person, use at least the same caution that you would use in meeting someone through a newspaper ad:

- ✔ Don't arrange a meeting until you have talked to the person a number of times, including conversations at length by telephone over the course of days or weeks.

- ✔ Meet in a well-lit public place.

- ✔ Bring a friend along, if you can. If not, at least let someone know what you're doing and agree to call that person at a certain time (for example, a half-hour) after the planned meeting time.

- ✔ Arrange to stay in a hotel if you travel a long distance to meet someone. Don't commit yourself to staying at that person's home.

Chat abbreviations and smileys

Many chat abbreviations are the same as those used in e-mail, as we describe in Chapter 11. Because chat is live, however, some are unique. We've also listed some common *emoticons* (sometimes called smileys) — funky combinations of punctuation used to depict the emotional inflection of the sender. (If at first you don't see what they are, try tilting your head down to the left.) Table 15-1 shows you a short list of chat abbreviations and emoticons:

Table 15-1	Chat Shorthand
Abbreviation	*What It Means*
AFK	Away from keyboard
A/S/L	Age/sex/location (response may be 35/f/LA)
BAK	Back at keyboard
BBIAF	Be back in a flash
BBL	Be back later
BRB	Be right back
BTW	By the way
GMTA	Great minds think alike
IM	Instant message
IMHO	In my humble opinion
IMNSHO	In my not so humble opinion
J/K	Just kidding
LTNS	Long time no see
LOL	Laughing out loud
NP	No problem
ROTFL	Rolling on the floor laughing
RTFM	Read the manual
TOS	Terms of service (the AOL member agreement)
TTFN	Ta-ta for now!
WAV	A sound file
WB	Welcome back

Abbreviation	What It Means
WTG	Way to go!
:D	A smile or big grin
:) or :-)	A smile
;)	A wink
{{{{bob}}}}	A hug for Bob
:(or :-(	Frown
:'(	Crying
:~~(	Crying
O:)	Angel
}:>	Devil
:P	Sticking out tongue
:P~~	Drooling
***	Kisses
<——	Action marker (<——eating pizza, for example)

In addition to the abbreviations in the table, chatters sometimes use simple shorthand abbreviations, as in `If u cn rd ths u r rdy 4 chat`.

Trouble city

Some people act badly online while hiding behind the anonymity that chat provides. When this situation arises, you have four good options and one bad option:

- Go to another chat room. Some rooms are just nasty. You don't have to hang around.

- Pay no attention to the troublemaker, and just converse with the other folks.

- Make offenders disappear from your screen. On AOL Canada, double-click the jerk's screen name in the room list and then click the Ignore box.

- Complain to the individual's ISP. This technique is most effective on the value-added services. See "Calling the AOL Canada cops," later in this chapter.

> ✔ The bad option — respond in kind, which just gives the offender the attention he (it's usually a he) wants and may get *you* kicked off your service.

Let's Chat

Starting to chat using an online service, such as AOL Canada, is easy because chat service is one of their major attractions. In this section, we first cover chatting with this type of provider, and then we discuss chatting using *Internet Relay Chat (IRC)*, the Internet's chat service.

AOL Canada members can participate in IRC, too, as well as in AOL's own chat service.

Chatting on AOL Canada

When you chat on AOL Canada, you have a conversation with other AOL members — in Canada and abroad. This feature, one of the most popular at AOL, may be why AOL is the largest value-added online service in the world. Only AOL members can participate in the AOL chat rooms; the groups accessible to IRC networks are not available as AOL chat rooms.

You get started chatting in AOL Canada 6.0 — 4.0, if you're on a Mac — by clicking the People icon on the toolbar and choosing Chat Now or Find a Chat, which takes you to the chat schedule. You can also get to the chat schedule by typing the keyword CHAT.

To go to an AOL Canada "lobby room," click the People icon on the toolbar, select People Connection, and then select Chat Now. In the "lobby room," you'll see two windows; a larger one in which conversation is taking place and a smaller one that lists the people (screen names) in this room. If you're one of those people who just has to say something when you enter a crowded room, type something in the bottom area of the conversation window and click Send. In a few seconds, your comment is displayed in the window.

AOL Canada limits the number of people in a room to 23, so when a room is full and a new member wants to join in, a new (similar) room is automatically created.

Look who's here

If you want to know something about the other occupants of the room, double-click one of their names in the window labeled "people here." A little box pops up, which enables you to do one of several things:

✔ **Ignore Member:** If you check this box, no messages from this member are displayed on-screen. This technique is one way to stop receiving messages from annoying people.

✔ **Get Profile:** Click this button to retrieve the profile of this member. A *profile* is a list of information a member has supplied about her/himself. You have no guarantee that a profile has any true facts in it.

✔ **Send Message:** Click to send an instant mail message to this member. It's sort of like whispering in his ear. If someone sends you such a message (an *Instant Message* or IM), that message appears in a small window. You can ignore it or respond with a message of your own. The two of you can keep a running conversation going as long as you want.

"Who am I, and what am I doing here?"

You're identified by your screen name, the name you used when you signed on to the service. For privacy reasons, many people use a different screen name when they're chatting. AOL Canada lets each account use as many as seven different screen names, as long as no other AOL member is already using them. One of the screen names is the *master screen name*, which can never be changed. If you want to add or change other screen names, you must log on to AOL Canada under the master screen name. After you've established other screen names and passwords, you can log on to AOL Canada by using the alternative name. Each screen name has a separate mailbox. You can use screen names for either different family members or different personalities: for example, your business self and your private self.

To set your *profile* — the information that other members can see about you when you're chatting — click the Member Directory button under the "people here" window or go to keyword PROFILE. A box is displayed in which you can search the AOL membership list for names you may know. In this window is a button labeled My Profile. If you click this button, you can set or modify all your own profile settings.

Other public rooms

You probably won't find much conversation of interest in the lobby room you were thrown into when you joined the chatters. Pressing the Find a Chat button shows you the Find a Chat window with a list of the public chat rooms that are available. Two windows are displayed; the left one shows the room categories. When you double-click a category, the right window shows the room names in that category, along with the number of current occupants in that room.

The room categories are mostly self-explanatory:

✔ **Town Square:** Rooms with a restaurant, bar, or coffee house flavour

✔ **Art & Entertainment:** Hollywood, music, book, and trivia themes

✔ **Friends:** People who like to talk

✔ **Life:** All sorts of lifestyles and age groups

✔ **News, Sports, and Finance:** What you would expect

✔ **Places:** Major metropolitan areas

✔ **Romance:** Boy meets girl, in all combinations

✔ **Special Interests:** Hobbies, pets, cars, and religion

✔ **Countries:** Germany, United Kingdom, Canada, France, and Japan

Figure 15-2 shows a chat taking place in a lobby. Everything you type in the little box at the bottom, next to the Send button, is part of the conversation. You can either press the Enter key after typing your message or click Send. You can leave a room through the Main icon (just click it), or find another room (scroll through the list) and join it. Or you can close the window of the chat room to get out of the AOL People Connection.

Figure 15-2:
Chatting in
the lobby at
AOL.

Member rooms

In the Find a Chat window, click the button labeled "member chats" and the list of rooms switches over to the member rooms. Anyone can create a member room, and so can you, by clicking the Start Your Own Chat button. These rooms have the same categories as the public rooms — they're usually silly, serious, or kinky.

Private chats

The names of private rooms, unlike public or member rooms, are not revealed. To join one, you have to know its name; that is, someone must invite you to join. When you click the Enter a Private Chat button in the Find a Chat window, you're asked to name the room that you want to join. If it doesn't exist, one is created, and you're the sole occupant.

Private rooms enable people to talk more intimately — there's little danger of a stranger popping in. Two (or more) people can agree to create a private room and meet there.

Private rooms have a somewhat sleazy reputation: If you get invited to one, you should be careful about guarding your privacy. Remember that what the other people are saying about themselves may not be true.

Calling the AOL Canada cops

Another button under the "people here" window is labeled Notify AOL. If you think that someone is violating the AOL Canada terms of service (TOS) by asking you for your password or credit card number, using abusive language, or otherwise behaving badly, you can and should report them to AOL. When you press the Notify AOL button, a window pops up to help you gather all the information you want to report: for example, the chat category and room you were in, the offensive chat dialog pasted into a window, and the offender's screen name. You can then send the report to AOL Canada, and it promises to look at it within 48 hours.

Because of this policing and the power of AOL Canada to terminate (permanently) the accounts of people who don't play by the rules, the AOL chat rooms have a deserved reputation for safety and for being a good place to play. That AOL Canada has so many subscribers who like chat means you have a good chance of finding a chat room that meets your needs.

Chatting via WebTV

WebTV offers easy access to chat rooms from the WebTV home page (see Chapter 18 for details on how to navigate around the WebTV pages). Along the left edge of the home page are several buttons in a row. Click the Community button in the row and then the selection labeled Chat to display the list of rooms. WebTV offers a small list of rooms, or you can click the large TalkCity button to get the full list. The rooms New2TalkCity and New2Internet are good places to start.

To enter a chat room from the TalkCity page, click the topic to see a room list. Click the desired room. The right side of the screen displays the room's conversation, and the left side of the screen has a new sidebar. In the box below the conversation window, you can enter your contribution to the conversation. Click Send or press Enter on your keyboard to send your comment to the room. You exit a room by going to the sidebar to return to the chat page or to a previous page.

As other people enter and leave the room, you see notes in italics in the conversation window. You can find out who else is in the room by typing /whois in the box. WebTV lists the current occupants directly in the conversation window.

You leave a room by going to the sidebar to return to the Chat page or to a previous page.

Whisper in my ear

You can send a private message while you're in a chat room, by clicking Whisper in the sidebar. A new window pops up with a list of all the people in the room. You select the person or persons who you want to receive your private message and then type the message. When you send it, the message appears in the conversation window, and the recipient is indicated in parentheses:

```
KoolKatz (to Ignez): Do you like Muenster?
```

Restricting chatting

When you set up sub-accounts from your WebTV master account, you can restrict the sub-account from using the chat facilities. If you're a parent, this restriction may make sense when you're setting up accounts for your children. Each account can have its own password, so it's easy for you to keep your children from using the master account.

Chatting on the Web

Many Web sites provide a method of chatting using your browser. Some require that you download a plug-in or ActiveX control to add chat capability to your browser (see Chapter 7 for how to use plug-ins). Others have Java-based chat programs that your browser can run directly.

Here are some chat sites:

- **Talk City** www.talkcity.com (The same system WebTV connects to)
- **Yahoo Chat** chat.yahoo.com (Includes former Geocities users)
- **Snap Chat** chat.snap.com

Many other Web sites have chats on the specific topic of the site.

Chatting via IRC

IRC (Internet Relay Chat) is available from most Internet Service Providers as well as from AOL Canada. To use IRC, you have to install an *IRC client* program on your computer. An IRC client (or just *IRC program*) is another Internet program, much like your Web browser or e-mail program, and freeware and shareware programs are available for you to download from the Net. If you use Windows, use a Winsock-compatible program; if you use a Mac, use a MacTCP-compatible program.

Two of the best shareware IRC programs are the following:

- ✔ **mIRC** for Windows
- ✔ **Ircle** for the Macintosh

You can find these IRC programs, along with others, at shareware Web sites, such as TUCOWS (www.tucows.com), or at the mIRC home page (www.mirc.com) and the Ircle home page (www.amug.org/~ircle).

The information in Chapter 16 can help you download and install the IRC client program. For more detailed information about setting up mIRC, point your browser to www.mirc.com. You can also find a great deal of useful information about IRC there.

Although most of our examples are from mIRC, Ircle is very similar. You can read the Ircle Help file by choosing Help from the Apple menu.

Check with your Internet Service Provider for any additional information you may need to use IRC. If you have a direct link to the Internet, ask your system administrator whether the link supports IRC.

Firing up IRC

To start chatting using IRC, start up your IRC program. If you're using a PPP account, double-click the program's icon. From a UNIX shell Internet provider that offers IRC, type ircii or irc at the UNIX prompt.

Getting connected

To use IRC, your IRC program has to connect to an *IRC server* — an Internet host computer that serves as a switchboard for IRC conversations. Although dozens of IRC servers are available, many are full most of the time and may refuse your connection. You may have to try several servers, or the same one dozens of times, before you can connect.

When you're choosing a server, pick one that's geographically close to you (to minimize response lag, as explained in the following sidebar, "Lags and netsplits") and on the IRC network you want.

To connect to a server:

- ✔ **Using mIRC:** Choose File⇨Setup (or press Alt+E) to display the mIRC Setup window, and then click the IRC Servers tab. When you start mIRC, it gives the Setup command for you automatically, so you see the mIRC Setup window right away. Double-click a server on the list to attempt to connect to it.

- ✔ **Using Ircle:** Choose File⇨Preferences⇨Startup. Select a server and then choose File⇨Save Preferences.

At peak times, the servers can be extremely busy. If at first you don't connect, try, try again.

Choosing a network

IRC servers are organized into networks. Although servers within each network talk to each other, servers on one IRC network don't connect to servers on other networks. Someone on EFnet can't talk to someone on Undernet, for example.

The four biggest networks and their home pages are listed here (in descending order):

- ✔ **EFnet:** www.irchelp.org
  (The original network of servers, with the most users)
- ✔ **Undernet:** www.undernet.org
- ✔ **IRCnet:** www.funet.fi/~irc
- ✔ **DALNet:** www.dal.net

Most people on IRC eventually develop a preference for one network. It's usually the one where their friends hang out.

Lots of smaller IRC networks exist. Here are some, with their home pages:

- ✔ **Kidsworld:** www.kidsworld.org
- ✔ **StarLink:** www.starlink.org

If you use mIRC, you can find a list of servers it knows about by choosing File⇨Setup (or pressing Alt+E) and clicking the tab labeled IRC Servers. Because each server entry notes its network and location, you can easily choose one near you.

Commanding your IRC

You control what is happening during your chat session by typing IRC commands. All IRC commands start with the slash character (/). You can type IRC commands in upper- or lowercase or a mixture — IRC doesn't care. If you use the mIRC client program, many commands are available directly from the menu or by clicking or double-clicking items you see in the mIRC window.

If anyone ever tells you to type in IRC any commands you don't understand, *don't do it — ever.* You can unwittingly give away control of your IRC program and even your computer account to another person. (No, we don't tell you the commands!)

The most important command for you to know gets you out of IRC:

```
/quit
```

The second most important command gives you an online summary of the various IRC commands:

```
/help
```

Here are a few of the most useful IRC commands:

- ✔ `/admin server`: Displays information about a server.
- ✔ `/away`: Tells IRC that you will be away for a while. You don't have to leave this type of message; if you do, however, it's displayed to anyone who wants to talk to you.
- ✔ `/clear`: Clears your screen.
- ✔ `/join channel`: Joins a channel. See "Group chat" later in this chapter.
- ✔ `/leave`: Leaves a channel. Typing `/part` does the same thing.
- ✔ `/me action`: Sends a message that describes what you're doing and is used to punctuate your conversation with a description of gestures. If you're Mandrake, for example, and type `/me gestures hypnotically`, other users see `UMandrake gestures hypnotically` on-screen.
- ✔ `/msg name message`: Sends a private message to `name` (only `name` can see it).
- ✔ `/nick newname`: Changes your name to *newname*.
- ✔ `/ping #channelname`: Gives information about the lag (delay) between you and everyone on that channel.
- ✔ `/topic message`: Sets the topic message for the current channel.

✔ `/who channel`: Lists all the people on a channel. If you type `/who U`, you see displayed the names of the people on the channel you're on.

✔ `/whois name`: Lists some information about the user `name`. You can use your own name to see what other users can see about you.

Remember: Lines that start with a slash are commands to the IRC program; everything else you type is conversation and gets put in the chat box.

If you use mIRC or Ircle, you can achieve most of the same effects controlled by IRC commands by choosing commands from the menu bar or clicking icons on the toolbar. These IRC commands work, too, however, and some IRC programs don't have menu bar or toolbar equivalents.

Group chat

The most popular way to use IRC is through *channels.* Most channels have names that start with the # character. Channel names are not case-sensitive. Numbered channels also exist (when you type a channel number, you don't use the # character).

Thousands of IRC channels are available. You can find an annotated list of some of the best by visiting `www.funet.fi/~irc/channels.html`. Each channel listed there has its own linked home page that tells you much more about what that channel offers.

To find out how to see a list of channels, see the section "Channel surfing," later in this chapter.

Some good channels to know about:

✔ **#irchelp:** A place to ask questions about IRC

✔ **#newbies:** All your IRC questions answered

✔ **#21plus and #30plus:** Age-appropriate meeting places

✔ **#41plus:** A more mature channel (with many people on it younger than 41)

✔ **#teens:** For teenagers — chill and chat

✔ **#hottub:** A "rougher" meeting place

✔ **#macintosh:** Meeting place for Mac users

✔ **#windows98:** Meeting place for Windows users

✔ **#chat:** A friendly chat channel

✔ **#mirc:** A help channel for mIRC users

You can also try typing # followed by the name of a country or major city.

Channeling

You join a channel by typing:

```
/join #channelname
```

To join the #dummies channel, for example, you type `/join #dummies` and press Enter. Don't forget the / before the command or the # before the channel name.

In mIRC, you can click the Channels Folder icon on the toolbar and then double-click one of the channels listed. In Ircle, choose Command⇨Join from the menu.

Remember: After you join a channel, everything you type that doesn't start with a slash (/) appears on the screen of everyone on that channel after you press Enter. The text of your messages is preceded by your nickname.

In mIRC, you can join several channels at a time. Each channel has its own window, with a list of the participants on the right side and the conversation on the left, with a box at the bottom in which you type your messages.

You leave a channel by typing this:

```
/leave
```

In mIRC, you can leave a channel by simply closing the window for that channel. In Ircle, choose Commands⇨Part from the menu.

Lags and netsplits

Two phenomena, lags and netsplits, are the bane of an IRCer's existence. A *lag* is the delay between the time you type a message and the time it appears on other people's screens. Lags foul up conversations. Sometimes, one group of people on a channel is lagged while another group is not, and the first group's messages appear after delays of several minutes. You can check on the amount of time a message takes to get from you to another person and back again by typing the command `/ping nickname`.

A *netsplit* breaks the connection between IRC servers — the network of connected IRC servers gets split into two smaller networks. A netsplit looks like a bunch of people suddenly leaving your channel and then reappearing en masse sometime later. Although all the people who are connected to the IRC servers in one half of the network can chat among themselves, they can't communicate with the people connected to the IRC servers in the other half. Eventually (after minutes or hours), the two networks reconnect and the netsplit is over.

Channel surfing

To see available channels in mIRC, click the List Channels icon on the toolbar. If you're looking for a particular channel name, type in the <u>M</u>atch text box the text you're looking for. If you want to see channels with at least several people on them (rather than the hundreds of channels with one bored, lonely, or lascivious person waiting), type a number in the Mi<u>n</u> box. Then click <u>G</u>et List. Because the list of channels can be extremely long, you may have to wait a few minutes for the list to be displayed. If you want to see the channels listed in your Channels folder (the list of channels you visit frequently), click the Channels Folder icon instead.

In any IRC program, you can find out all the public and private channels by typing the following command:

```
/list
```

Figure 15-3 shows an mIRC window after a /list command has been given. The window shows the channel name, number of current chatters, and the channel topic.

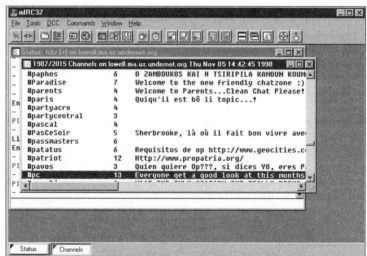

Figure 15-3:
A heap o' channels to choose from!

In Ircle, you choose Commands⇔List from the menu.

Before typing /list to see all the available channels, type the following line:

```
/set hold_mode on
```

This phrase keeps the names from flying by so fast on-screen that you can't read them. Don't forget to type `/set hold_mode off` after you finish reading the list.

You can also limit the number of channels listed by typing

```
/list -min 8
```

Only channels with at least eight people on them are listed when you type this phrase.

In the listing, `Pub` indicates a public channel. You may see `Prv`, which means a private channel. The @ sign indicates a channel operator *(chanop)*, who is in charge of managing the goings-on of the channel.

Picking a nickname

Everyone using IRC needs a *nickname*. This name is unique within the network: No two people connected to the same IRC network can use the same nickname at the same time. If you attempt to connect to a network and your chosen nickname is already in use, you cannot join a channel. The name can be the same as the username in your e-mail address, although most people pick a different name. To choose a nickname, type the following command:

```
/NICK thenameyouwant
```

Nicknames can be as long as nine characters. Because common names will already be in use, obviously, you have to choose something distinctive.

Unlike e-mail addresses, nicknames can change from day to day. Whoever claims a nickname first on an IRC server gets to keep it for as long as she is logged in. Nicknames are good for only a single session on IRC. If you chatted with someone named ElvisPres yesterday and then run into someone named ElvisPres today, you have no guarantee that it's the same person.

If you use Ircle or mIRC, you can tell it your preferred nickname so that it doesn't ask you each time you run it:

- ✔ **mIRC:** Choose File➪Setup or press Alt+E and click the IRC Servers tab. mIRC lets you specify an alternative nickname also in case the first one is in use when you start.
- ✔ **Ircle:** Choose File➪Preferences➪Startup. Enter your name and then choose File➪Save Preferences.

To find out more about the person behind a nickname, type the following command:

```
/whois nickname
```

The two ways to find someone's nickname are to see it on a channel or to have another user reveal it to you.

Just between us

To send a message to someone whose nickname you know, type the following line:

```
/msg nickname whatyouwanttosay
```

This method becomes tiresome, however, for more than one or two lines of text. You can instead start a longer conversation by typing this line:

```
/query nickname
```

Now, whenever you type something that doesn't start with /, it appears on *nickname*'s screen, preceded by your nickname, immediately after you press Enter.

Your "private" conversation can go through many IRC servers, often in different countries, and the operators of any of these servers can log all your messages.

A more private way to chat is via Direct Client Connections, or DCC. You don't have to be on the same channel as the person you want to talk to; you just have to know the person's nickname. You type this line (assuming that you want to talk to Shirley):

```
/dcc chat shirley
```

When someone tries to start a DCC chat with you, mIRC asks whether you want to chat with the other person. If you click Yes, mIRC opens a window for the discussion. Your DCC chat window is just like a minichannel, with only two people in it.

You can also use DCC commands to send files to other people. For example, you can send a picture of yourself to a person you have just met. If someone offers to send you a file, however, consider declining unless you know the person. Unsolicited files can be unbelievably rude and disgusting, as well as dangerous because they may be infected with a virus.

Operating your own channel

Each channel has its own channel operator, or *chanop,* who can control, to some extent, what happens on that channel. In the list of nicknames on a channel, operators' nicknames are preceded by an @ sign. You can start your own channel and automatically become its chanop by typing this line:

```
/join #unusedchannelname
```

As with nicknames, a channel name belongs to whoever asks for it first. You can keep the name for as long as you're logged on as the chanop. You can let other people be chanops for your channel — just make sure that they're people you can trust. A channel exists as long as someone is on it; when the last person leaves, the channel winks out of existence.

As chanop, you get to use special commands. The main one is /kick, which kicks someone off your channel, at least for the three seconds until he rejoins the channel. Kicking someone off is a thrill (although a rather small one), sort of like finding a penny on the sidewalk. People usually get kicked off channels for being rude or for sending so many garbage messages that they make the channel unusable.

Server operators manage entire servers and can kick unruly users off a server permanently or temporarily. The really big thrill occurs when a server operator temporarily kicks off an unruly — or better yet, polite — chanop, especially moments after the chanop himself kicked someone else out. Now that's more like finding a toonie on the sidewalk!

Channel types

The following three types of channels are available in IRC:

- ✔ **Public:** Everyone can see them, and everyone can join.
- ✔ **Restricted (lurk only):** Although everyone can see them, you can join them only by invitation.
- ✔ **Secret:** They don't show up by typing the /list command, and you can join them only by invitation.

If you're on a private or secret channel, you can invite someone else to join by typing the following:

```
/invite nickname
```

If you get an invitation from someone on a private or secret channel and want to join, you just type the following:

```
/join #invite
```

Reporting bad guys

Compared to AOL Canada, IRC is a lawless frontier. Few rules, if any, exist. If things get really bad, you can try to find out an offender's e-mail address by using the /whois command. If you type the command

```
/whois nickname
```

you will receive a bundle of information about that person, including, perhaps, his e-mail address — say it's badguy@gurus.com. You can then send an e-mail complaint to postmaster at the same host name; in this example, postmaster@gurus.com.

Get Down in the MUDs

MUD, which originally stood for Multiple-User Dungeon, was invented to let Internet users play the fantasy role-playing game *Dungeons and Dragons*. MUDs have evolved from those beginnings, however, into a whole new way for people to interact electronically; so much so that the name MUD is usually defined as *Multiple-User Dimension* or *Multiple-User Dialogue*. Many MUDs are based on the worlds created in popular films and novels, including *Star Wars*, *Star Trek*, J.R.R. Tolkien's *Lord of the Rings*, Douglas Adams's *Hitchhikers' Guide to the Galaxy*, and especially Anne McCaffrey's *Dragonriders of Pern*.

Another kind of MUD is called a *MOO* — an "object-oriented" version of a MUD. (The much shorter MOO sounded better than OOMUD, which in some countries is also a hex word meaning, "Wish you a slow death!") In a MOO, you not only interact with the other characters residing there; you can also program new rooms and implements. For example, you can create a new chamber of horrors, thereby expanding the confines and landscape of the game. You can even add new weapons and hazards. If you liked pulling wings off flies as a youth, you'll love MOOs and MUDs. On second thought, maybe OOMUD was a better name after all!

MUDs and MOOs are Internet chat taken to a whole new dimension. You don't just pick a nickname; you take on a whole new identity — a fantasy role you want to play in the MUD.

Many MUDs are battle-oriented with simulated combat and even wars. Your virtual identity can be gruesomely killed online. Some people find this amusing.

Using MUDs

Most MUDs are text-based, with little or no graphics. You type messages to the MUDs, such as "open door" or "pick up the cat," and you get a message back. Different MUDs have different commands.

There are many MUDs out there, each with its own personality. Here are some good places to look for one that may interest you:

✔ **The MUD Resource Collection:** www.godlike.com/muds

✔ **The MUD Connector:** www.mudconnect.com

The `rec.games.mud` hierarchy of Usenet newsgroups includes groups for each major type of MUD. A `rec.games.mud.misc` group also exists. Each newsgroup offers, of course, a FAQ for its type of MUD. We found this question in the FAQ for one group: "Is MUDing a game or an extension of real life with gamelike qualities?" And you thought AOL chat was intense!

If the idea of acting out a fantasy life on the Internet appeals to you, here's how to get started:

✔ Find a MUD that seems interesting to you at one of the MUD Web sites listed above.

✔ Visit that MUD; read its help files, and try out its guest area, if it has one.

✔ If the MUD you pick is based on a book or movie, read the book or see the movie. If you read the book or saw the movie a while back, read or see it again. The folks on the MUDs are into the details.

✔ Read the MUD FAQ posted regularly to the newsgroup `rec.games.mud.announce`. The FAQ is also available from `ftp://rtfm.mit.edu/pub/usenet-by-group/rec.games.mud.announce`.

✔ Set aside a big block of time for yourself — a few hours at least — and plunge in.

Chapter 16

Swiping Files from the Net

● ●

In This Chapter

▶ Downloading — why do it?

▶ Using your Web browser to swipe files

▶ Finding out about FTP

▶ Using WS_FTP to swipe files

▶ Installing software you've swiped from the Net

● ●

*T*he Internet is chock full of computers, and those computers are chock full of files. What's in those files? Programs, pictures, sounds, movies, documents, spreadsheets, recipes, *Anne of Green Gables* (the entire book) — you name it. Some computers are set up so that you can copy some of the files they contain to your own computer, usually for free. In this chapter, we tell you how to find those files and how to copy and use them. For a list of the types of files you may want to download and what to do with them after you have them, see Chapter 20. As a free added bonus, we also tell you how to copy files from your own computer to another computer, most often a Web page you've just made to a server that makes your page available to the rest of the Net.

Downloading means copying files from a computer Up There on the Internet "down" to your computer on or under your desk. *Uploading* is the reverse — copying a file from your computer "up" to a computer on the Internet.

You probably won't be surprised to hear that there are at least two different ways to download and upload files:

✔ *HTTP* is the *HyperText Transport Protocol* that your Web browser uses to retrieve Web pages, and your browser turns out to be just as good at using it to retrieve any other kind of file.

✔ *FTP* stands for *File Transfer Protocol*, an older but still very popular way that computers transfer files across the Internet.

FTP both downloads and uploads; HTTP in principle does both but in practice mostly downloads. You can also transfer files by using e-mail attachments to other e-mail users, but we don't discuss that here (see Chapter 12).

Getting Files over the Web

Getting files over the Web is simplicity itself. You probably have been doing it for ages and didn't even know. Every Web page, every icon or image on a Web page, every ornate Web background is a file. Every time you click a link or type a URL to go to a Web page, you're getting at least one file. (If it's a page with many graphics, you're getting many files, one per picture. Regardless of how many files it is, your Web browser manages the space it uses for automatically downloaded files so that it doesn't fill up your disk.)

Getting the picture

To download a picture over the Web, first display the picture in your Web browser. When you see a picture you want to save on your hard disk, right-click the picture. From the menu that appears, choose Save Image As or Save Picture As. Tell your browser where to save the picture. That's all it takes!

Graphics files have special filename extensions that identify what graphics format the file is in. When you download a picture, you can change the name of the file, but don't change the extension. See Chapter 20 for details.

Just because a picture is now stored on your hard disk doesn't mean that you own it. Most pictures on Web pages are copyrighted. Unless a picture comes from a site that specifically offers pictures as reusable "clip art," you have to get permission to reuse the picture for most purposes or even to upload it to your own noncommercial Web page.

Getting with the program

Downloading a program file over the Web is also easy — you click a link to it — frequently a link that says either Download or the name of the program. Your Web browser stops and asks you what to do with the file. If it's a program (a Windows with the extension .exe, .com, or .dll) or a ZIP file, the most reasonable thing for your browser to do is to save it to disk so that you can run it or unzip it later. If it's a ZIP file and you have WinZip (mentioned later in this chapter) installed, you can also tell the browser to run WinZip directly; we find that method less handy than it might seem.

If you're interested in downloading an Internet program, for example, you can go to TUCOWS, The Ultimate Collection of Windows (and Mac) Software, at www.tucows.com. After you're at the site, click links to choose a site near you, choose the operating system you use (Windows 3.1, Windows 95 or Windows 98, or Mac), and choose the type of programs you want to download. TUCOWS displays a Web page like the one shown in Figure 16-1, with a list of programs available for downloading. To download a program file, just click the name of the program or the Download Now button.

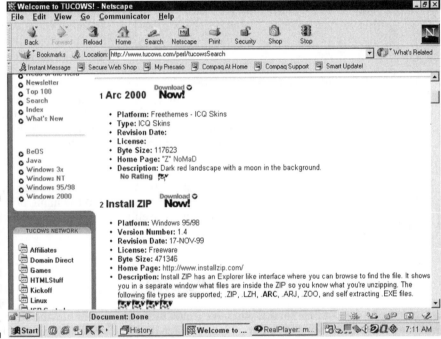

Figure 16-1: Click the Download Now button in TUCOWS to download the program file.

Want to make absolutely sure that your browser downloads a file for which you have a Web link to the disk? Rather than try to run it, display it, or otherwise get clever, hold down the Shift key while you click the link. You see the Save As dialog box, and the name of the file you're saving.

Getting other files

To download other types of files — sound files, video files, whatever — you follow the same steps as for downloading a program. Find a Web page that contains a link to the file you want. Then click the link for the file you want and tell your browser where to store it. Many of these files can even be downloaded into a Palm handheld computer. Check out the Palm Web site at www.palm.com to see how.

How FTP Works

Being able to download files from the Web is great, but not all files are available over the Web. You may need FTP — File Transfer Protocol.

Transferring a file via FTP requires two participants: an FTP client program and an FTP server program. The *FTP client* is the program that we, the Joe Six-Pack Users of the world, run on our computers. The *FTP server* is the program that runs on a huge mainframe somewhere (or, these days, likely as not, on a PC under someone's desk) and stores tens of thousands of files. The FTP server holds an online library of files. The FTP client can *upload* (send) files to the FTP server or, more commonly, *download* (receive) files from the FTP server.

Thousands of publicly accessible FTP servers exist; they store millions of files. Many of the files are freeware or shareware programs. Some FTP servers are so popular that they can't handle the number of file requests they receive. When FTP servers are inundated, *server managers* set up other FTP servers called *mirrors*, which have copies of the same files, to handle the overflow traffic.

More and more FTP sites are converting to Web sites, so that you can download the file with your browser. When someone gives you the name of an FTP site (like `ftp.iecc.com`), try the matching Web site (`www.iecc.com`) with your browser first.

Hello, this is anonymous

To use an FTP server, you have to log in with a user name and password. What happens if you don't have an account on the FTP server machine? No problem, if it's a publicly accessible FTP server. You log in as anonymous and type your e-mail address as your password. *Voilà!* You have access to lots of files! This method of using public FTP servers is called, quite logically, *anonymous FTP*. There's nothing sleazy about it; public FTP sites expect you to use anonymous FTP to download files.

When is a file not a file?

When it's a text file. FTP can download six different types of files, of which only two types are useful: ASCII and binary. An *ASCII file* is a plain text file; a *binary file* is anything else. FTP has two modes, *ASCII mode* and *binary mode* (the latter is also called *image mode*), to transfer the two types of files. When

A few anonymous FTP tips

Some FTP servers limit the number of anonymous users or the times of day that anonymous FTP is allowed. You may be refused access, but don't gripe about it — no law says that the owner of the system has to provide any access at all.

Don't store (upload) files on the FTP server unless the owner invites you to do so. A directory called INCOMING or something similar is sometimes available in which you can put stuff.

Some FTP servers allow anonymous FTP only from host computers that have names. That is, if you try to FTP anonymously from a host that has a number but no name, these hosts don't let you in. This problem occurs most often with Internet dial-up accounts, which, because they generally offer no services that are useful to other people, don't always have names assigned. If you have this problem, complain to your provider, who can fix it easily.

---

you transfer an ASCII file between different types of computers that store text files differently, ASCII mode automatically adjusts the file during the transfer so that the file is a valid text file when it's stored on the receiving end. (Because Macs, Windows, and UNIX all have slightly different conventions for storing text files, this automatic conversion can save a great deal of hassle.) A binary file is left alone and transferred verbatim.

Note that a document from Microsoft Word, WordPerfect, or any other word-processing program is *not* a text file for FTP purposes because the file contains non-text-formatting codes. Text here means plain unadorned text, like you'd view with Simpletext on a Mac or Notepad on a Windows machine.

Getting your FTP client

If you want to get files by FTP, you need an FTP client program. Luckily, you have several excellent ones to choose from:

✔ **Use your Web browser.** Most browsers can handle anonymous FTP for downloading files (no anonymous uploading — you probably didn't want to do that anyway). See the next section, "Your Web Browser Is an FTP Client, Too."

✔ **With an Internet account, you can use a Winsock or MacTCP FTP program.** The most popular freeware FTP program that's Winsock-compatible is WS_FTP, and you find out how to use it in this chapter (in the section "Hard-Core FTP-ing Using WS_FTP"). The CD-ROM in the back of this book contains WS_FTP Pro, a shareware version of the program.

If you have a Mac, you can use shareware programs called Fetch or Interarchy, which used to be called Anarchie. These programs can handle both the uploading and downloading of files by using either anonymous FTP or private accounts on an FTP server.

✔ **If you use AOL Canada, it's easy to get files via anonymous FTP. Use the keyword ftp.** See the section in Chapter 17 about grabbing files from FTP servers.

Your Web Browser Is an FTP Client, Too

To get your Web browser to transfer files by using FTP, you use a special kind of URL: an FTP URL. (Too many TLAs — Three Letter Acronyms.) Usually, browsers are smart enough to tell which files are ASCII and which are binary. You don't have to worry about it.

The URL of FTP

When you've used your Web browser as a Web browser, you have probably typed URLs that begin with `http`, the abbreviation for the way that browsers talk with Web servers (Hypertext Transport Protocol, if you must know). Most browsers expect URLs to start with `http://`, so you can leave it off and let the browser add it for you. To tell your Web browser to log in to an FTP server, you tell it a different kind of URL — an FTP URL. An FTP server's URL looks like this:

```
ftp://servername/directoryname/filename
```

You can leave out the directory name and filename, if you like, to get the top-level directory of that FTP server. For example, the URL of the Microsoft FTP server (at `ftp.microsoft.com`) is

```
ftp://ftp.microsoft.com/
```

This URL has no filename part. If you omit the filename, the server displays the top-level directory to which you have access.

Browsing with an FTP URL

No matter which Web browser you use, you follow the same general steps to retrieve files via FTP:

1. **Run the Web browser as usual.**

2. **To tell your browser to load the URL of the FTP server, type the FTP URL in the Address, URL, or Netsite box just below the toolbar, and then press Enter.**

   The browser logs in to the FTP server and displays its home directory, as shown in Figure 16-2. Each file and directory in the current directory appears as a link. Depending on the Web browser you use, the format may differ from the one shown in this figure (Netscape Navigator).

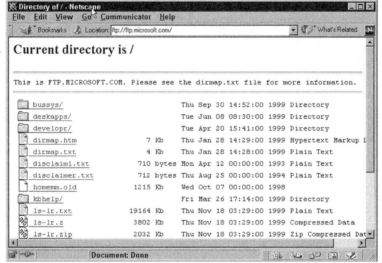

Figure 16-2: Each file and directory in the FTP server your browser logs in to appears as a link.

3. **Move to the directory that contains the file you want, by clicking the directory name.**

   When you click a directory name, you move to that directory and your browser displays its contents.

4. **Download the file you want by clicking its filename.**

   If you download a text file or another file that your browser knows how to display, the browser displays it after it downloads. If you click the filename Readme.txt, for example, the browser displays the text file. If you want to save the file after you look at it, choose File⇨Save As from the menu and tell your browser the filename to use.

   If you download a file your browser *doesn't* know how to display, such as a program, it usually asks you what to do. The various versions of Netscape Navigator and Internet Explorer display different dialog boxes, but the key question is this: Do you want to save this file on disk, or do you want to run a program to open the file? If you have a recent version of Netscape Navigator, it may run its Smart Download utility, which usually saves the file in your C:\My Download Files folder. Opera pops up a box with a variety of options, with the useful one being Save.

Hey, it's me!

Most Web browsers can handle more than just anonymous FTP; they can also access FTP files from sites on which you have to have an account. To download a file from a password-protected FTP server, assuming that you have an account on the server, you can include your account name by typing the account name followed by an @ sign immediately before the FTP server name.

If your account name is elvis, for example, you type a URL like this:

```
ftp://elvis@ftp.gurus.com
```

When it logs in to the server, your browser asks you to type your password, which on your provider's system is probably the same password that it uses when you first connect.

5. **If your browser asks what to do with the file, tell it to save the file, and then choose the directory and filename in which to save it.**

   Your browser downloads the file. Most browsers display a pop-up box that reports the status of the download process. In the case of Opera, it then shows you a Transfer Window that tracks the files you've downloaded, and lets you open them by clicking the desired file.

If you use a Web browser other than Netscape Navigator, Internet Explorer, or Opera, the browser may download files differently. Check your browser's documentation to find out how to save files that are downloaded. Or just try it — click the filename of a file that looks interesting and see what happens. If you don't like what happens, try holding the Shift key and clicking again.

Hardcore FTP-ing Using WS_FTP

So you want to use a real FTP program? The basic steps you follow to use your FTP client program, no matter which program you use, are more complicated than using a browser:

1. **Log in to the FTP server by using your FTP client program.**

2. **Move to the directory on the server that contains the files you want to download, or move to the directory to which you want to upload files.**

3. **Tell the program which type of files (ASCII or binary) you will be moving.**

4. **Download or upload the files.**

5. **Log off the FTP server.**

If you use an Internet account, you can use any Winsock (for Windows users) or MacTCP (for Mac users) FTP client program. Many good freeware and shareware FTP programs are available right off the Internet. Our favorites are WS_FTP for Windows and Fetch for the Mac. This section describes how to use WS_FTP Pro, which is included on the CD-ROM at the back of this book.

Here are some handy features of WS_FTP:

✔ Scrollable and selectable windows for the names of local and remote files and directories

✔ Clickable buttons for such common operations as connecting and setting binary mode

✔ Connection profiles, which save the host name, login name, password, and remote host directory of your favorite FTP sites; comes with a bunch of useful profiles already set

Getting WS_FTP

Our favorite Winsock FTP program is called WS_FTP. The freeware version, WS_FTP LE, for *Limited Edition*, is available by (what else!) FTP from a variety of places, including its "home," the United States Military Academy. (Doubtless there's a connection between FTP and national security.) An evaluation (shareware) version of WS_FTP Pro is loaded on the CD-ROM that comes with this book, but you can also download it from the Web.

Attention, UNIX shell account users!

If you use a UNIX shell account, FTP transfers files to and from your ISP's computer, not your own computer. You need to add two extra steps to your FTP procedure:

✔ **If you want to upload files using FTP, first upload the files from your own computer to the ISP's computer.**

Before you can upload files from your ISP's computer, you have to get them there! Consult your terminal program's documentation

(or your Internet Service Provider) to find out how to transfer files from your computer to your UNIX shell provider's.

✔ **If you downloaded files from an FTP server, download them to your own computer from the ISP's computer.**

After you download using FTP, the files are sitting on your ISP's computer. Use your terminal program to transfer them to your own computer.

FTP-ing Web pages

If you maintain a Web site, you use FTP to upload to the Web server the Web pages you create or edit. You can use WS_FTP or another FTP program to transfer the pages, although you have to keep track of which Web pages you created, changed, or deleted on your computer and remember to do the same on the Web server computer. The larger your Web site grows, the worse your headache.

There's a better way: Use an FTP program designed just for maintaining Web sites. Margy uses NetLoad, a nifty program that can compare the files (by checking file sizes and dates) on your computer and on your Web site to see which files need to be uploaded or deleted. One click of a button, and NetLoad transfers all the necessary files. You can get NetLoad, or one of a number of similar programs, from TUCOWS (at www.tucows.com) on the Net.

Because we get a little better service from a mirror site, that's what we encourage you to use:

1. **In My Computer or Windows Explorer (in Windows 95 or Windows 98) or File Manager (in Windows 3.1), make a folder (directory) in which to put WS_FTP.**

2. **Use your Web browser to go to The Ultimate Collection of Winsock Software (TUCOWS), at** www.tucows.com. **Click the mirror site closest to you, and then click Windows 95/98 or Windows 3.1. Then click the link for FTP programs.**

   You see a long list of freeware and shareware FTP clients. Cool!

3. **Scroll down to WS_FTP LE and click the program name. Tell your browser to store the file in the folder you created in Step 1.**

   Your browser downloads the file. It's time to install it.

4. **Run the Ws_ftple.exe installation program.**

   The installation program asks a bunch of questions, such as whether you agree to the terms for noncommercial use (if you're a home user, you probably do), which directories to use, and which version of the program to use. In each case, the suggested answer is fine.

You're ready to FTP by using WS_FTP LE!

Dial "F" for files

Here's how to use WS_FTP Pro or WS_FTP LE to swipe files from or put files on an FTP server:

1. **Run the WS_FTP program by double-clicking its icon.**

   You see the Session Properties dialog box, as shown in Figure 16-3. This dialog box lets you enter information about the FTP server that you want to connect to. After you have entered this information, WS_FTP saves it so that you can easily connect to the saved FTP server again.

2. **In the Profile Name box, enter the name you want to use for this FTP server.**

   If you want to FTP to rtfm.mit.edu, for example, which contains FAQs for all the Usenet newsgroups, you might enter Usenet FAQ Central.

3. **In the Host Name/Address box, enter the name of the FTP server.**

   This name can be a regular Internet name (such as bc.ubc.edu, another useful FTP server) or a numeric address.

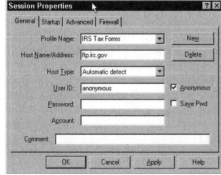

Figure 16-3:
Which FTP
server do
you want
to talk to
today?

4. **Leave the Host Type box set to Automatic detect.**

   This step tells WS_FTP to guess which operating system the FTP server is using.

5. **If you really have a user name on the FTP server, enter your user name and password in the User ID and Password boxes.**

   Otherwise, click the Anonymous box. WS_FTP asks for your e-mail address, which it uses as your password (the usual thing to do when you FTP anonymously).

If you want WS_FTP to store the password in the Password box rather than ask you for it every time you connect to the FTP server, click the Sa̲ve Pwd box so that it contains a checkmark.

6. **Click the Startup tab along the top of the dialog box.**

The top two boxes, Profile Na̲me and Host N̲ame/Address, are where you can specify the directories on the FTP server and on your own computer to and from which you'll transfer files.

7. **In the Initial R̲emote Host Directory box, enter the directory in which you want to look on the FTP server.**

Alternatively, you can leave this box blank and look around on your own.

8. **In the Initial L̲ocal Directory box, enter the directory in which you want to store downloaded files on your own PC.**

9. **Click OK.**

WS_FTP tries to connect to the FTP server.

"It won't speak to me!"

If you have a problem connecting to the FTP server, messages appear in the two-line box at the bottom of the WS_FTP window. You can scroll the little window up and down to see what happened. For example, `rtfm.mit.edu` is frequently overloaded and doesn't let you log on. When this situation happens, some helpful messages are displayed about other FTP sites that may have the information you want. You can see these messages in this box.

To see the messages the FTP server sent, double-click them. WS_FTP opens a big window so that you can see them better. To close the window, click the Close button. Frequently the FTP server sends messages explaining access policies, how to find the file you want, or other useful information.

Do you copy?

After you're connected to the FTP server, you see the WS_FTP window, as shown in Figure 16-4. (Some versions of WS_FTP arrange the window a little differently.) WS_FTP displays information about the files on your own computer on the left side of the window (labeled Local System) and the directories and files on the FTP server on the right side (labeled Remote System). On each side are buttons that enable you to change directories (ChgDir), make directories (MkDir), delete directories (RmDir), view files, and so on. Naturally, you don't have permission to delete or change anything on most FTP servers, so don't even try. The little arrow buttons between the two sides of the window are for transferring files.

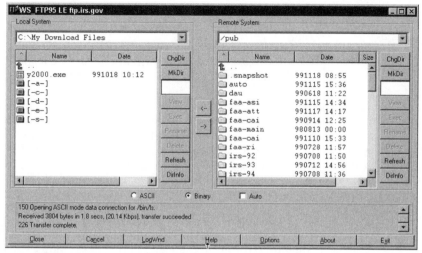

Prepare to
receive
some files!

To move from directory to directory on the FTP server, choose directory names from the file name and date box. Or you can click the ChgDir button and enter the full pathname of the directory to go to.

Here's how to copy a file:

1. **Choose ASCII or Binary by clicking the radio buttons at the bottom of the window.**

   For files that consist entirely of text (such as HTML files), choose ASCII. For anything else (such as graphics files), choose Binary. Click the Auto box if you want WS_FTP to guess based on the file extension.

2. **Choose the file you want on the FTP server.**

   Click the filename on the list on the Remote System side of the window.

3. **Choose the directory to put it in on your own computer.**

   On the Local System side of the window, move to the directory where you want to store the file.

4. **Click the left-pointing arrow button in the middle of the window.**

   WS_FTP downloads the file. For large files, this step can take some time; WS_FTP displays your progress as a percentage completed.

Hang up!

To disconnect from the FTP server after you're finished, click the Close button at the bottom of the WS_FTP window.

Connecting again

To call someone else, click the Connect button in the upper-right side of the screen. You see the Session Properties window again (see Figure 16-3). Fill in different information and click OK to make the connection.

To call an FTP server you have called before, click Connect. In the Session Properties window, click the downward-pointing arrow button to the right of the Profile Name box. You see a list of the FTP servers you've entered (along with a bunch of FTP servers that come pre-entered into WS_FTP). Choose one and then click OK.

How to foul up your files in FTP

The most common error inexperienced Internet users (and experienced users, for that matter) make is transferring a file in the wrong mode. If you transfer a text file in binary mode from a UNIX system to an MS-DOS or Macintosh system, the file looks something like this (on a DOS machine):

```
This file
      should have been
             copied in
                 ASCII mode.
```

For Mac users

It's not that we want you to feel slighted by the in-depth coverage of WS_FTP. It's just that things on the Mac are a little simpler, and we have a tight page budget.

When it comes to FTP, we like the excellent shareware program Fetch, by Jim Matthews. The problem, of course, is figuring out how to get it before you have FTP. Using your handy browser software, go to this site:

    www.dartmouth.edu/pages/
        softdev/fetch.html

where you can find complete information about Fetch, and instructions for downloading.

Fetch gives you a choice between downloading files as raw data or MacBinary. The *MacBinary* format combines the parts (*forks*) of Macintosh files into one file so that they can travel together when they're being FTP'd. Use MacBinary for Mac-specific stuff that only other Macs can understand, such as Macintosh software. When you download Mac software from a Mac software archive, for example, use MacBinary. Don't use MacBinary for text files, graphics files, and other non-Mac-specific stuff. MacBinary-formatted files usually have the filename extension .bin.

Patience is a virtue

The Internet is pretty fast, although not infinitely so. When you're copying stuff between two computers over a local area network (LAN), information can move at about 200,000 characters per second. When the two machines are separated by a great deal of intervening Internet, the speed drops — often to 1,000 characters per second or fewer. If you're copying a file that's 500,000 characters long (the size of your typical inspirational GIF image), it takes only a few seconds over an LAN, although it can take several minutes over a long-haul connection.

It's often comforting to look at the directory listing before retrieving a file so that you know how big the file is and can have an idea of how long the copy will take. Because programs get inexorably larger, even with faster modems, patience remains the key to successful downloading.

On a Mac, the entire file looks like it's on one line. When you look at the file with a text editor on a UNIX system, you see strange ^M symbols at the end of every line. You don't necessarily have to retransfer the file. Many networking packages come with programs that do ex post facto conversion from one format to the other.

If, on the other hand, you copy something in ASCII mode that isn't a text file, it gets scrambled. Compressed files don't decompress; executable files don't execute (or they crash or hang the machine); images look unimaginably bad. When a file is corrupted, the first thing you should suspect is the wrong mode in FTP.

If you're FTP-ing (Is that a verb? It is now!) files between two computers of the same type, such as from one Windows system to another, you can and should make all your transfers in binary mode. Because neither a text file nor a non-text file requires any conversion, binary mode does the right thing.

About Face!

Okay, now you know how to retrieve files from other computers. How about copying the other way? If you write your own Web pages and want to upload them to your Internet Service Provider's computer, here's how you do it: FTP them to your ISP's Web server.

Uploading with your browser

In Netscape Navigator 4.7 and Internet Explorer 4.0 or later, you can log in to the Web server as yourself by using an FTP URL, something like this:

```
ftp://yourid@www.yourprovider.com/
```

Use your login ID rather than *yourid* and the name of your ISP's Web server, which most likely is `www` followed by the ISP's name but may also be something like `ftp.www.fargle.net`. (If this info isn't in the sign-up packet your ISP gave you, ask for it.)

The browser asks for your password; use the same one you use when you dial in. If this password works, you see your home Web directory listed on-screen. If you want to upload files to a different directory, click that directory's name so that you see that directory.

After you have the directory you want on-screen, just drag the file to upload from any other program (such as File Manager or Windows Explorer) into the browser window. *Poof!* (It may be a slow poof, depending on how big the file is.) In Netscape, you can also choose File⇨Upload File from the menu if you find dragging to be a drag.

Uploading with WS_FTP

In WS_FTP, log in as we just described in the preceding section, using your login ID and password. After you have the local and remote directories you want in their respective windows in WS_FTP, just click the local file you want to upload, and then click the right-pointing arrow button (pointing to the Remote System part of the window).

If you're uploading a Web page to a Web server, be sure to upload the page itself (in ASCII mode because the HTML file that contains the Web page is a text file) as well as any graphics files that contain pictures that appear on the page (in binary mode).

It's Not Just a File — It's Software

Using your Web browser or FTP, you can download freeware and shareware programs and install and use them. You need a few well-chosen software tools, including a program to decompress compressed files. (Useful little programs like this one are called *utilities* in the jargon.)

Installing downloaded software usually requires three steps:

1. **Using FTP or your browser, download the file that contains the software.**

2. **If the software isn't in a self-installing file, it's usually in a compressed format, so decompress it.**

3. **Run the installation program that comes with it, or at least create an icon for the program.**

The first part of this chapter describes how to do Step 1, the downloading part. The rest of this chapter describes Steps 2 and 3: uncompressing and installing. Here goes!

Decompressing and unzipping

Most downloadable software on the Internet is in a compressed format, to save both storage space on the server and transmission time when you download the file. An increasing amount of software is self-installing — the file is a program that does the necessary decompressing and installing. Self-installing Windows files have the extension .exe, and non-self-installing compressed files have the extension .zip.

If a file is compressed, you need a program to deal with it. Files with the file extension .zip identify compressed files (these files are called, amazingly, *ZIP files*). Programs with names such as PKZIP, PKUNZIP, and UNZIP have been around for years to allow DOS users to zip and unzip files. Although UNZIP and its brethren work fine, they're DOS programs and not really convenient to use from Windows. It's annoying to use the MS-DOS icon every time you want to run one. Luckily, someone (a guy named Nico Mak, actually) wrote a nice little Windows program called WinZip that can both unzip and zip things for you, directly from Windows. We also like ZipMagic (available from www.mijenix.com), which makes ZIP files look like Windows folders. Mac users can get a program named unzip. WinZip 8 for Windows 95/98 is available on the CD-ROM that accompanies this book.

If you already have WinZip (which is also available from retail outlets as well as on the Web as shareware), skip this entire section. If you have and love PKZIP and PKUNZIP or UNZIP and don't mind running them from DOS, you too can skip this section. You can get a Windows version of PKUNZIP, which isn't as nice as WinZip, although some people like it. It works fine.

To get WinZip from the Web, go to www.winzip.com, a page full of pictures of outer-space-type blobs. Click the blob marked Download Evaluation to get to the download page. On that page, download either the Windows 3.1 or Windows 95/98 version, as appropriate.

To install WinZip:

1. **Run the file you just downloaded.**

   Depending on which version of Windows you use, the file is named Winzip80.exe or Winzip31.exe.

2. **Follow the installation instructions WinZip gives you.**

   Although you have a bunch of options, you can accept the suggested defaults for all of them.

Mac users say StuffIt

Mac users can download an unzip program from `ftp.uu.net` in the /pub/ archiving/zip/MAC directory or from `ftp.doc.ic.ac.uk` in the /packages/ zip/MAC directory or from `quest.jpl.nasa.gov` in the /pub/MAC directory. The file that contains the unzip program is called something like unz530x.hqx. (The exact name depends on the latest version number.)

More popular than zip and unzip for the Mac crowd is a shareware program, by Raymond Lau, known as StuffIt. StuffIt comes in many flavours, including a commercially available version called StuffIt Deluxe. StuffIt files of all varieties generally end with the extension .sit.

For decompression, you can use the freeware programs UnStuffIt and StuffIt Expander. You can get StuffIt Expander from The Mac Orchard (`www.macorchard.com`): click Other on the list of categories, then scroll down to file the program. Stuffit Expander 5.5 and DropStuff 6 are also loaded on the CD-ROM that accompanies this book.

Running WinZip

Give it a try! Double-click that icon! Take a look at Figure 16-5 to see what WinZip looks like.

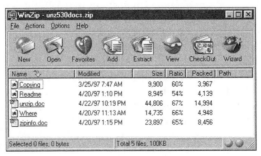

Figure 16-5:
WinZip is
ready to
unzip your
ZIP files.

To open a ZIP file (which the WinZip folks call an *archive*), click the Open button and choose the directory and filename for the ZIP file. And there you have it! WinZip displays a list of the files in the archive, with their dates and sizes.

Unzip it!

Sounds suggestive, we know, although it's not as much fun as it sounds. If you want to use a file from a ZIP file, after you have opened the ZIP file, you *extract* it — that is, you ask WinZip to decompress it and store it in a new file.

To extract a file:

1. **Choose it from the list of files.**

   You can choose a group of files that are listed together by clicking the first one and then Shift+clicking the last one. To select an additional file, Ctrl+click it.

2. **Click the Extract button.**

   A dialog box asks in which directory you want to put the file and whether you want to extract all the files in the archive or just the one you selected.

3. **Select the directory in which you want to store the unzipped files.**

4. **Click OK.**

   WinZip unzips the file. The ZIP file is unchanged, and now you have the decompressed file (or files) also.

Zipped out?

Although WinZip can do a bunch of other things, too, such as add files to a ZIP file and help you create your own ZIP files, you don't have to know how to perform these tasks in order to swipe software from the Net — so we skip them. (We bet that you can figure them out just by looking at the buttons on the WinZip toolbar.)

Now that you know how to unzip software you get from the Internet, you're ready for the next topic: safe software.

Scanning for viruses

We all know that you practice safe software. You check every new program you get to make sure that it doesn't contain any hidden software viruses that may display obnoxious messages or trash your hard disk. If that's your habit, you can skip this section.

For the rest of you, it's a good idea to run a virus-scanning program. You never know what naughty piece of code you may otherwise unwittingly download to your defenseless computer!

It's a good idea to run a virus scanner after you have obtained and run any new piece of software. Although the Web and FTP servers on the Internet make every effort to keep their software archives virus-free, nobody's perfect. Don't get caught by some prankster's idea of a joke!

If you use WinZip, you can configure it to run your virus scanner before you even unzip the ZIP file containing a program. Choose Options⇨Program Locations from the menu and in the Scan program box type the pathname of your virus scanner program.

Although Windows 98 and 95 don't come with a virus scanner, several commercial ones are available, including the McAfee VirusScan program, which you can download from the McAfee Web site, at www.mcafee.com. Another good virus scanner is Norton AntiVirus, at www.symantec.com.

If you use Windows 3.1 with DOS 6.2, you have a somewhat out-of-date virus scanner built right in to File Manager. Because so many viruses have been invented and released since Windows 3.1 was written, the virus scanner doesn't do you much good. Download a virus checker that detects more recent viruses. TUCOWS (www.tucows.com) lists a several Windows 3.1 virus scanners.

Installing the program you downloaded

After you have downloaded a program from the Net and unzipped it (if it's a ZIP file), the program is ready to install. To install the program, double-click its name in Windows Explorer, My Computer, or File Manager. If it's an installation program, it installs the program. In the process, the installation program probably creates an icon for the program. In Windows 95 or Windows 98, it may also add the program to your Start menu.

Some programs don't come with an installation program — you just get the program itself. To make the program easy to run, you need an icon for it. You can actually create your own icon or menu item for the program.

In Windows 95/98, follow these steps:

1. **Run either My Computer or Windows Explorer, and select the program file (the file with the extension .exe, or occasionally .com).**

2. **Use your right mouse button to drag the filename out on the desktop or into an open folder on the desktop.**

   An icon for the program appears.

Here's how to make one in Windows 3.1:

1. **Open both Program Manager and File Manager and arrange the screen so that you can see the program group in which you want to put the icon (in Program Manager) and the program name (in File Manager).**

2. **Drag the program name from File Manager into Program Manager, and place it in the program group where you want it.**

   You see a new icon in the program group.

To run your new program, you can just double-click the icon. Cool!

Configuring the program

Now you can run the program by double-clicking its icon. Hooray!

You may have to tell the program, however, about your Internet address or your computer or who knows what before it can do its job. Refer to the text files, if any, that come with the program, or choose Help from the program's menu bar to get more information about how to configure and run it.

Where Is It?

"Downloading programs sounds fine and dandy," you may say, "but what's out there, and where can I find it?" One of the best places to find software is www.tucows.com. It has a great collection of FTP sites grouped by platform and category of program.

Chapter 17

Can Two Hundred Thousand Users All Be Wrong? It's AOL Canada!

In This Chapter

▶ Using AOL Canada

▶ Using AOL Canada e-mail

▶ Web surfing with AOL Canada

▶ Pulling files from FTP servers

▶ Trying other things

Can more than 200,000 users really be wrong? Sure they can. But if you're brand-new to the world of computers as well as to the world of the Internet, you may find using AOL Canada — the Canadian arm of AOL International — easier than starting off with a traditional Internet Service Provider. Also, if you're interested in online chatting, AOL is the world capital of chat. (In his book *Burn Rate,* Michael Wolff claims that AOL's success is primarily due to online chat.)

You can access AOL Canada with a dial-up connection by using AOL Canada's very own local access phone numbers. You can find these numbers at `www.aol.ca/access.adp` (if you can access the Net through a friend or at work) or by calling 1-888-AOL-HELP (1-888-265-4357). Another way to access AOL Canada is through a TCP/IP connection — the type you get when you use a local ISP — or other network access point.

The services provided by AOL Canada are much the same as those provided by AOL's other international sister sites. For example, at AOL Canada, you get seven e-mail addresses for every account, free instant messaging (described in Chapter 14), personal home pages (described in Chapter 10), private chat rooms, personalized news, and the ability to connect to your AOL Canada account in more than 100 countries around the world.

AOL Canada also has a distinctly Canadian flair. For example, it has partnered with other Web sites like SamtheRecordMan.ca, Tribute.ca, TD Waterhouse, Canada Trust, Royal Bank, FiftyPlus.net, Canadian Press, The Weather Network, and EUTrade Canada. Together, this partnership tries to give AOL Canada members the best value for their time — and their loonie.

This chapter tells you how to use e-mail, the World Wide Web, and FTP — all from AOL Canada. Because chatting is extremely popular all over the Net, chat has its own chapter, Chapter 15. You probably also want to read through Chapters 6 to 13, which describe e-mail and the World Wide Web — all the conceptual information there applies to you, too. In this chapter, we give you the specifics for using AOL Canada.

Hello, AOL Canada

If you've decided to join the AOL Canada ranks, we tell you how to sign up and then install AOL Canada and connect to it in Chapter 5. After you have the AOL Canada software running, how do you do all those Internet tricks? We take you on a tour of AOL Canada features using the recently introduced Version 6.0 of the AOL Canada software for Windows. Mac users use Version 4.0 of the software. The CD-ROM at the back of this book includes both. If you are already an AOL Canada member and have been using Version 5.0 (or 4.0), don't worry. The instructions that follow generally apply to all recent versions.

When the AOL Canada software has successfully connected, you see a row of icons under the top File menu. This is called the Toolbar. Some Toolbar buttons display their own little menus when you click them. An arrow brings up the word "more" when you move your mouse over these sections, which have drop-down menus offering more menu choice. Below the Toolbar is yet another row of buttons with a white Web address box in the middle of the row. The Search and Keyword buttons are on the far right-hand side. You can enter a Web address or an AOL keyword in the address box and then click Go to get anywhere fast and more importantly — directly! The browser navigation buttons are on the far left-hand side of the address window; these are for moving forwards and backwards between AOL or Web screens, as well as stopping or refreshing your Web pages. The AOL Canada Welcome window looks something like Figure 17-1.

One way to get around in AOL Canada is to "go to" a *keyword*: you either enter the keyword in the white address window, or you can bring up a separate keyword window by clicking on the keyword button (on the far right, just beside the Search button). Once you have the keyword box open, enter the keyword and click Go. Those with control function keys on the brain can click "Ctrl + K" and get that same keyword box. In the rest of this section about AOL Canada, we just say "go to **keyword**."

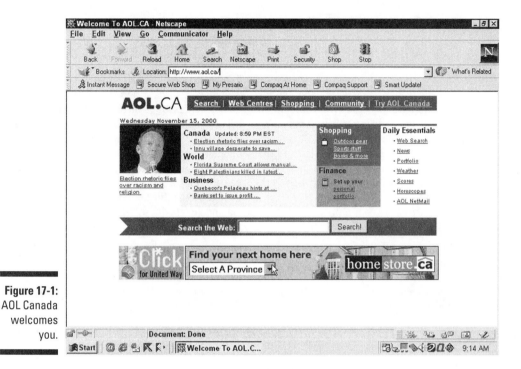

Figure 17-1:
AOL Canada
welcomes
you.

Using E-Mail from AOL Canada

The first thing to do is send mail to all your friends to let them know that you have successfully installed AOL Canada and tell them your e-mail address. You can send messages to other AOL Canada members and to folks on the Internet.

Your Internet mail address is your screen name (omitting any spaces) plus @aol.com. Your screen name is the user name you use when you log on. If your screen name is John Smith, for example, your Internet address is JohnSmith@aol.com.

"Do I have mail?"

Every time you connect to AOL Canada, it tells you whether you have mail. The leftmost icon on the toolbar is a little mailbox, and in the lower-left corner of the Welcome window you see a similar mailbox with some writing nearby. If the little red flag is *up,* you have mail. The message says, "You've Got Mail," just in case you're from a part of the world where mailboxes don't have little red flags. If your computer has speakers, a voice may also say, "You've Got Mail!"

So what's new with AOL Canada Version 6.0?

AOL Canada 6.0 for Windows boasts a new look and extra features. A new toolbar organizes your favorite AOL features with rearranged icons and colour-coded, drop down menus. The Channel Guide is now part of the AOL toolbar, and gives you one-click access to the best of AOL's content. You can now customize your Welcome Screen with links to five areas you visit most often.

Version 6.0 also introduces "My Calendar" — a free calendar tool that helps you keep track of all the important dates in your life. The new Groups@AOL feature lets you customize private online areas with your own group of family and friends where you can share photos, plan events, post quick notes, and more.

E-mail improvements let you sort messages in your mailbox by date, e-mail address, or subject and save messages directly to folders in your Filing Cabinet. You can personalize the instant messages you send with buddy icons, and choose to display text-based "smileys" like this :), as yellow smiley face graphics. Finally, you can now locate and open files attached to e-mail immediately after the file has finished downloading. (In previous versions, the process was more tedious and time-consuming.)

For instructions on how to download AOL Canada 6.0 software, see the "Web Browsing from AOL Canada" section later in this chapter. Or just download Version 6.0 onto your hard drive from the CD-ROM in the back of this book.

Reading your mail

You probably *do* have mail, in fact, because every new member gets a nice note from the CEO of AOL Canada and because AOL Canada members tend to get mountains of junk mail, much more than people with other types of accounts. To read your unread mail, follow these steps:

1. **Click any mailbox you can find.**

   Start with the Read icon in the Mail section of the toolbar. Alternatively, you can click the Mailbox on the bottom left of your Welcome Screen or press Ctrl+R. All of the above will bring up your New Mail window.

   In the New Mail window, each line on the list describes one incoming mail message with the date it was sent, the sender's e-mail address, and the subject.

2. **To read a message, double-click it or highlight it on the list and then either click Read or press Enter.**

   You see the text of your message in another cute little window.

3. **To reply to the message, click the Reply button. Type the text of your message in the box in the lower part of the window that appears. Then click the Send or the Send Later button.**

4. **To forward the message to someone else, click the Forward button. Fill in the e-mail address to which you want to forward the message. You can add a message to go along with the original message, too, by typing it in the large message area box. It will appear above the forwarded message. Then click Send Now (if you're online) or Send Later (if not).**

   If you get annoying or unwanted mail from another AOL Canada member, forward it to TOSspam, a special mailbox at AOL Canada set up to investigate junk e-mail.

5. **To see the next message, click the Next button; to see the preceding message, click the Prev button.**

6. **When you finish, click the Close button (in Windows 95 and higher), which is the X button in the upper-right corner. For Macs, it's the icon in the upper-left corner.**

It's not always a good idea to respond to aggressive or otherwise offensive messages right away. You may have to get some information or cool off after reading the brainless message some jerk sent you.

Saving a message on your PC

If you get a message on AOL Canada that you want to save in your AOL Filing Cabinet, choose the Save to Filing Cabinet button on the bottom of your e-mail screen and either put the message in an existing folder, create a new folder to save it to, or just save it directly to the Filing Cabinet.

If you want to save your e-mail someplace other than your Filing Cabinet (for example, as a separate text file), that's easy too. Display your e-mail on-screen as described in the preceding section, "Reading your mail." Then choose File⇨Save from the menu bar or press Ctrl+S. AOL Canada lets you choose the directory and filename in which to save the file on your computer. When you click OK, the e-mail message is saved as a text file. Nice and easy!

Composing a new message

You don't have to only reply to other messages — you can begin an exchange of messages, assuming that you know the e-mail address of the person to whom you want to write:

1. **Click the Write button — the second icon from the left on the Toolbar, the picture of a pencil and paper.**

   Alternatively, you can choose Write Mail from the Mail drop-down menu or press Ctrl+M. You see the Write Mail dialog box, shown in Figure 17-2.

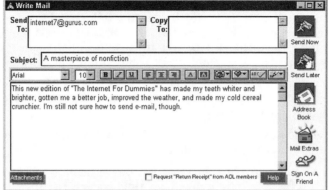

Figure 17-2:
Send a
message to
anyone with
an AOL or
Internet
account.

2. **Enter the recipient's address in the Send To box.**

   For AOL members, just enter the screen name. For others on the Net, type the entire Internet address, which includes the @such-and-such.com.

3. **In the Copy To box, enter the addresses of everyone to whom you want to send a copy.**

   You don't have to send a copy to yourself — AOL Canada keeps copies of mail you have sent.

4. **Enter a brief subject line in the Subject box (Optional).**

5. **In the box with no name, type the text of your message.**

   Don't press the Tab key, because it moves your cursor from one box to the next in the dialog box. You can press Enter, though, to begin a new paragraph. If you're sending a message to another AOL member, you can use the buttons above the text box to add underlining, italics, colour, and other whizzo formatting to your message. There's even a button called Greetings which gives you a whole library of AOL pictures and graphics you can insert easily into the body of your e-mail. However, don't bother formatting messages to the Internet, because the formatting doesn't work on non-AOL e-mail programs.

6. **When you like what you see, click the Send Now or the Send Later button.**

   AOL Canada confirms that the mail is winging on its way.

7. **Click OK.**

Attaching a file to your message

If you want to send a file from your computer to someone as an e-mail message, AOL Canada makes this process easy. When you're writing the message, click the Attachments button. You see the Attachments dialog box, which lets you choose any file from your PC. Click Attach, select a file, and click OK.

AOL Canada attaches the file by using MIME, a method that most other e-mail programs can deal with. (It's still a good idea to ask first before sending attachments, to make sure that the recipient has the necessary program to read the file you want to send.)

Keeping an address book

Of course, you can't remember all your online friends' Internet addresses; AOL Canada provides you with an address book to keep track of them. And with version 6.0, you no longer have to type long e-mail addresses into your e-mails. Once you've entered someone into your address book, it will automatically fill in the address once you start typing it.

Adding names to your book

You get to the AOL Address Book from the Mail drop-down menu on the AOL toolbar. Or, click the Address Book icon on the right-hand side of your e-mail screen while you're composing a message. The Address Book window shows the current contents of your address book.

Click the New Person button to create a new entry and then fill out the first name, last name, and e-mail address of the person to whom you want to write. You can also create an entry for a group of people (your special friends, for example) by clicking the New Group button instead. Give the group a name, such as Cabal, and then list in the Addresses box their mail addresses separated by commas.

Using the black book

When you compose a message, you can bring up the address book by clicking its icon on the right side of the Write Mail window. In the Address Book window, select the person you want to write to and click the Send To button. To send the person a copy of the message, click Copy To or (for a blind copy) Blind Copy. After you have put addresses in the message, you can remove them by ordinary methods.

There are additional fields in the 6.0 software Address Book for you to keep track of each person's home and work mailing addresses and multiple phone and cell numbers. It also allows you to view, edit, search, and print contact information for people you know online and offline.

Your Address Book is still accessible when you sign on to AOL Canada from another computer (as a Guest). Very handy when you're on the road.

"What if I get an attachment?"

Sometimes, when people send you e-mail, they send along an attachment. If you don't know the person who sent you the message, do not download the attachment, in case it contains a virus or an offensive picture or document.

The name of the attached file is noted in the message as well as its size and estimated time to download. Two extra buttons are at the bottom of the message window: Download File and Download Later. The attachment is not in your computer until you download it from AOL Canada Central. If you choose to download the file immediately, you get a chance to choose the folder to save it in. If you choose Download Later, the file gets added to the Download Manager list of tasks to do. You can call up the file by clicking the File section of the very top grey File Menu and then choosing Download Manager; it can get all your attachments at one time. With 6.0, you can download any file immediately and you have the option of viewing it wherever you've placed it. In fact, AOL prompts you with this choice.

Stop the junk mail!

AOL Canada members get more junk e-mail messages than users of any other online system. Most of the messages are for fraudulent (in our opinion) get-rich-quick schemes and offers to advertise *your* product by e-mail to millions of people who are just as unenthusiastic about getting those types of messages as you are.

As you can imagine, AOL Canada has gotten many complaints about the level of junk mail, especially from users who have to pay by the hour to read it. (Even with the new flat rates, members in Europe still pay by the minute for phone calls.) The folks at AOL Canada have been fighting the junk e-mailers for some time, including trying to block their messages. Because many junk e-mail messages have forged return addresses, however, it isn't always easy to trace or block them. What's an e-mail reader to do?

Go to the keyword **mail controls**, that's what. For each screen name on your account, you can block all incoming e-mail, e-mail from sites you select, or only e-mail attachments. AOL Canada also has an area called Neighbourhood Watch (go to keyword: Neighbourhood Watch) that gives you recent updates on the latest scams and viruses and information on how to avoid them. It's a good resource tool.

Mail on the road

AOL Canada members can send and receive mail via the Web without using the AOL Canada software — it's called (naturally) "AOL Mail on the Web." On any computer with a Web browser such as Netscape, Opera, or Internet Explorer, go to www.aol.ca/aolmail. On that page, enter your AOL screen name and password, and you'll get a window similar to the AOL mail program where you can send, receive, and respond to mail.

This is a handy way to keep up with your mail on a computer at the office if you normally use AOL Canada at home, or when you're travelling via a friend's computer, a Web kiosk at an airport, or a computer at a cybercafé.

Don't download files, especially program files, from people you don't know. Even if you do know the sender, never run a program you received by e-mail unless you have confirmed that the sender meant to send it to you (that is, that the program isn't a virus that sent itself to you).

Going Offline

You can work *offline* with AOL Canada; that is, you can disconnect from AOL Canada and read your downloaded e-mail or compose new messages or replies. You may want to work offline to avoid tying up your phone line and give some other AOL Canada-deprived individual a shot at getting connected. In fact, when you first run the AOL Canada software program, you're not online yet; you can minimize the sign-on window and start composing messages or reading old ones. All the features of AOL Canada that you cannot access because you're not connected are greyed out so that you can't use any features that require you to be online. If you're online and want to go offline without exiting AOL Canada, choose Sign Off➪Sign Off from the menu bar.

Using AOL Canada to Connect to the Net

In version 6.0, AOL Canada has more or less merged AOL-specific content screens with any Internet content you may be looking for. There are many access points on the Toolbar that take you to both AOL-specific content and general Internet content: the white address window and browser navigation buttons (back, forward, refresh, stop); the keyword button; the search button and the Internet icon all help direct you to what you're looking for quickly, regardless of whether it's within the AOL world or on the Internet at large.

Web Browsing from AOL Canada

The AOL Canada software includes a built-in Web browser, so it's easy to find out how to use it. You can save the addresses of Web pages in your Favorite Places list. You can have a Web browser window open at the same time that other AOL Canada windows are open.

The Web browser requires that you use AOL Canada Version 3.0 or higher. If you don't yet have Version 6.0, the latest version, you should download it — the built-in Web browser is much better than earlier versions. Go to keywords **preview** or **upgrade**, and follow the directions on-screen; or go to www.aol.ca/software.adp. The good news is that it's easy and that AOL Canada doesn't charge you for the connect-time while you're downloading the Web browser program. The bad news is that it takes a while (several minutes to a half-hour, depending on your modem speed) to download the program. For example, with a 56K modem, it will take about 170 minutes to download the latest version. Make sure you have a magazine handy while you wait!

Starting the Web browser

Here are two ways to start the AOL Canada Web browser:

- ✔ Choose the Internet icon on the AOL Services (mauve) section of the Toolbar (or go to keyword **internet**). Unless you configured your AOL browser differently, this method brings you to the AOL Canada home page.

- ✔ Click in the white address window on the bottom (middle) of the Toolbar and type the URL of the Web page you want to see (rather than a keyword), and press Enter or click Go.

To use the browser, click any picture that has a blue border or any button or any text that appears underlined. (Chapters 6 through 8 tell you how to find information on the World Wide Web.)

Protecting your kids

In Chapter 3, we talk about the need for parents to be involved with their kids' online experience. Because you're using AOL Canada, you may want to take advantage of its parental controls. You can create up to six separate screen names for your children and set separate levels of access and control for chat, e-mail, instant messaging, and more so that your kids see age-appropriate content and don't go to places you don't want them to! Go to keyword **parental controls**, or click Parental Controls on the AOL Canada Welcome Screen to set them up for your kids.

You can also order a free video about online safety for kids from the Safe Surfin' AOL-sponsored site. There's a link to it from the aol.ca home page.

Creating your own Web page

Although it's fun to look at Web pages that other people have created, what about making your own? AOL Canada lets you create your own *home page* (a page about you).

Go to keyword **123publish** and follow the instructions to create your own home page on the Web. AOL Canada uses a Web-authoring tool called Personal Publisher II that generates HTML 3.2 with some Netscape extensions. AOL Canada gives you two megabytes of space to save your Web pages at keyword **my FTP space.** Check out Chapter 10 for help in writing your first home page.

Grabbing Files from FTP Servers

AOL Canada lets you download files from FTP servers on the Internet. AOL Canada can do anonymous FTP, in which you connect to an FTP server that you don't have an account on, or FTP-ing, in which you do have an account. To use the AOL Canada FTP service, you have to know which file you want to download, which FTP server has it, and which directory the file is in. For information about FTP, see Chapter 16.

Most people now download software via the Web. Links on Web pages may be FTP links — that is, you click a link to start downloading a file.

If you need to use FTP directly, here's how to download a file:

1. **Click in the keyword box (or press Ctrl+K), type ftp, and click Go.**

   You see the FTP–File Transfer Protocol window.

2. **Click the Go To FTP button.**

   The Anonymous FTP dialog box appears.

3. **If the FTP server that has the file you want is listed, select it and click Connect. If not, click Other Site, type the Internet name of the FTP server, and click Connect.**

   When you have connected to the FTP server of your choice, AOL Canada may display an informational message about it — click OK when you have read it. Then you see a list of the contents of the current directory on the FTP server.

4. **To move to the directory that contains the file you want, double-click the directory names.**

   AOL Canada shows little file-folder icons by directory names and little sheet-of-paper icons by filenames. For files, look at the size of each file (in bytes, or characters) — the larger the file, the longer it takes to download.

5. **To download a file to your computer, choose the file and click Download Now.**

   The Download Manager dialog box appears, asking where to put the file on your computer.

6. **Choose the directory in which you want to put the file on your own computer and edit the filename. Then click OK.**

   AOL Canada downloads the file to your computer's disk. Depending on the size of the file and the speed of your modem, this step can take seconds, minutes, or hours. Make sure you know how long it will take in advance of downloading the file. Do something else — like make another cup of coffee.

7. **Close dialog boxes in AOL Canada when you're finished.**

   You can even close dialog boxes while AOL Canada is transferring the file.

If you have an account on the FTP server (and therefore have access to files not available to the public), use the Other Site button and click the button named Ask for login name and password.

Some FTP servers are extremely busy, and you may not be able to connect. Try again during off-hours or try another server. AOL Canada keeps cached copies of most or all of the files on separate storage servers, to alleviate the traffic jams online.

Using AOL Canada as an Internet Account

It's a tough decision, choosing between a commercial online service, such as AOL Canada, and an Internet account. Although AOL Canada has lots of "exclusive" AOL-only information, an Internet PPP account lets you use all that snazzy, new Winsock software, such as Netscape Navigator. What's a cybernaut to do?

Now you don't have to choose — you can have it all. AOL Canada has created a special version of the Winsock.dll program that all Winsock programs use to talk to PPP accounts. (See Chapter 5 for an explanation of Winsock and PPP accounts.) Using the AOL Canada Winsock.dll program, your Winsock programs talk to your AOL Canada account.

Confused? So were we. Here's how it works: When you run the AOL Canada program, it checks to see whether a Winsock.dll is loaded in your computer's memory. If it isn't, AOL Canada loads its own Winsock.dll. Either way, you're now ready to run Winsock software. (Older versions of AOL Canada software require you to download and install the Winsock.dll program yourself.) Users of Windows 95/98 already have a Winsock.dll, so they don't need to do a thing.

Getting Winsock-compatible programs

Lots of freeware and shareware Winsock software is available from AOL Canada and from the World Wide Web. Here are places to look for Winsock programs:

- ✔ Go to Winsock Central in AOL Canada (keyword **winsock**) and click the Software Library button. You see a list of Winsock programs that AOL Canada promises work with its Winsock software.

- ✔ Look at the TUCOWS (The Ultimate Collection Of Winsock Software) Web site at this Web address:

  ```
  www.tucows.com
  ```

  In TUCOWS, click on United States and then Virginia to choose a server. (Regardless of where you live in Canada, AOL connects from headquarters in Virginia.) You see an extensive list of Winsock programs. Click the type of program you want, Web browsers or newsreaders, for example, and you see names, descriptions, and even reviews of the programs. Click the Location section of the program description to download the program.

Using a Winsock program

Suppose that you want to use Netscape Navigator rather than the AOL Canada Web browser. Assuming that you're running a new version of the AOL Canada software that includes a Winsock.dll and you have downloaded the Netscape Navigator program (or bought a commercial version), here's all you have to do:

1. **Run it.**

   That's it. That's all you do. To be specific, run AOL Canada and log in to your account. Then run Netscape Navigator (or any other Winsock-compatible program). It works, using your AOL Canada account as its connection to the Internet. The Winsock application will run in its own window, even though it's sharing AOL Canada's connection to the world.

When you finish, exit from your program. Then log off from AOL Canada.

For more information about where to get nifty Winsock programs that you may want to use, see Chapter 16.

Doing Other Things

Because AOL Canada offers tonnes of information that has nothing to do with the Internet, after you sign up, you may as well check it out. The Computing and Games channel (department) lets you exchange messages with others about the software you use or download shareware. Learning & Reference offers all kinds of online reference materials, including the Library of Congress database of books, *Compton's Encyclopedia,* and *Webster's Dictionary of Computer Terms.* The Kids Only channel has fun and educational stuff for kids, including games, homework help, and AOL Canada-supervised chat rooms. The Travel channel lets you make and check your own airline reservations.

It can be hard to *cancel* an AOL Canada account if you decide that you don't want it. You may have to make several phone calls and let your credit card company know that you refuse any additional charges from AOL Canada.

Connecting to AOL Canada via your Internet account

If you have an existing Internet account, you can use AOL Canada via the Internet. This technique is really useful if no AOL Canada access number is available in your local calling area, or your computer is already directly connected to the Net via a fast network at school or work or a cable modem — connect to your local Internet account and then connect to AOL Canada over that account.

Start up the AOL Canada software, but *don't* connect yet. Go to the Edit Location menu and change the Network setting to TCP/IP. It doesn't matter what the telephone number is set to because AOL Canada doesn't dial it. Connect to your Internet Service Provider in the usual way and, after that connection is made, connect to AOL Canada. AOL Canada connects via your ISP as just another Winsock program, and you can start any other Internet programs you want and

click back and forth between AOL Canada and the other programs. When you're finished with AOL Canada, disconnect from it and then disconnect from your ISP. When you use AOL Canada this way, it's running as a Winsock program, and you can run other Winsock programs at the same time if you want.

If your Internet Service Provider charges by the hour, you probably don't want to connect this way because you'll pay its hourly charges. On the other hand, it could be the better way to go because your ISP may provide a faster connection than your local AOL Canada access number. This might especially be the case if you live in a rural area and don't have a local AOL Canada dial-in. AOL Canada has a special "bring your own access" price of $13.95 per month if you always connect via an Internet account instead of dialing into AOL Canada.

Chapter 18

Not Just "I Love Lucy," It's WebTV

*W*ebTV is introduced in Chapter 5, where we tell you where you can get one and how to connect it. In this section, we tell you what to do with WebTV.

On Your Mark, Get Set, Click

We make the bold assumption that if you've chosen WebTV as your way of getting on the Net, you already know how to use a remote control. The WebTV remote has a few special functions. The green buttons at the top turn on the power to your TV and WebTV. Turn on your TV first and then press the TV/Video button at the top to select video mode (you see the word *Video* on the screen). Then power up WebTV. The "thermometer bar" is there to let you know that something is happening. We hope you find it reassuring.

After you're connected, press the up and down arrows on the remote to select the account you want to use (assuming that you have more than one account), and then press the Go or Select button (in the middle of all the arrows) to activate your selection. Pressing this button is equivalent to clicking with the mouse button or pressing the Return or Enter key on a computer keyboard. To help you tell what's what as you move up or down on the screen, WebTV draws an orange border around the portion of the screen that is "active." You can always use the arrow keys to move the active area left, right, up, or down. If you try to move off the screen, you hear a little *thunk*. In the following sections, whenever we say *select an icon or a button on the screen,* we mean that you navigate the orange border to the correct place and then press the Go or Select button on the remote or, if you've hooked up a keyboard, press Enter.

You can buy WebTV without a keyboard, although we don't think that's a good idea. Without a keyboard, you have to pull up an image of a keyboard and use the remote to select each letter you want to type — the '90s equivalent of setting type 19th-century style, by picking individual metal letters out of a type case. (One author of this book actually did that. It was fun for the first 20 minutes.) You can get the remote keyboard from WebTV for $70, or buy a computer keyboard for about $15 and plug it in to the back of the WebTV terminal. If you like your couch, buy the remote keyboard (with a long cable).

Getting E-Mail on Your WebTV

Until you *tell* someone, nobody, except for the folks at WebTV, will know your e-mail address. If you want to get mail, spread the word.

Your e-mail address is `accountname@webtv.net`. (Replace *accountname* with your WebTV account name.) You can prove that this statement is true and make sure that your mail is working by sending a message to our robot at `internet7@gurus.com`. You can tell us what you think of WebTV and, while you're at it, what you think of this book, because we peek over the robot's shoulder and read its mail, too.

Sending mail

When you sign on to WebTV, you get a nice welcome e-mail from the president of WebTV. To send mail, select the Mail icon. Then choose Write to begin writing your message. Be sure to fill in the To: and Subject: lines. To use the address book, press the Select button while you're in the To: or CC: fields. The address book opens, and you can select an entry from the book.

Watch those phone bills

When you first sign up for WebTV, your WebTV box calls an 800 number at WebTV headquarters and looks up local access numbers that you can call for free. At least, that's what it tries to do. We've heard at least one report where it guessed wrong and a large phone bill arrived at the end of the month.

To see which phone numbers WebTV is using in Canada, visit WebTV's home page by pressing Goto and then typing `www.webtv.net` and pressing Return. Select the small "local access" link at the left side of the page and then enter your area code and the first three digits of your own phone number. WebTV shows you the numbers it's dialing. If any of those numbers are not a local call for you, call WebTV on the phone and see if it can straighten the problem out before you run up a huge phone bill.

Select the Send button in the lower-right corner to mail your message. Watch WebTV stuff an envelope into a mailbox and slam the mailbox door shut. *Klunk.*

Reading your mail

If you have unread messages, the Mail icon on the Home Page shows an envelope sticking out of the mailbox. To read your mail, select the Mail icon. Your mail is always kept at WebTV Central. The WebTV e-mail program displays a list of the messages you have, showing whom the message is from along with the subject of the message and the date received. Messages you have not yet read are highlighted. To read a message, select it.

When you select a message to read, the body of the message is retrieved from WebTV Central, and a new table of options appears on the left. You can discard, save, reply to, or forward the message. Or you can move to the next or preceding message, or return to the List of Messages page.

WebTV keeps four folders of messages: current messages, saved messages, sent messages, and discarded messages. Messages you discard are kept for a week before they are permanently erased.

To see if new mail has arrived, press the Mail button on the keyboard, or press Home on the remote and select the mailbox.

Where's the Web in WebTV?

To get to a Web site from WebTV, press the GoTo button on your keyboard, or the Options button on your remote control, and GoTo on the panel of choices that slides onto your screen. Another panel slides in with a place to type an address, already started with `http://`. Type the URL and press the GoTo button. (Don't know what a URL is? Read Chapter 6.)

To search for something special, click the Search button on the WebTV home page. It takes you to the Infoseek search system (the same one that the rest of the world finds at `www.infoseek.com`).

The bottom of the WebTV home page has links to select from a list of topics, such as Economy and Sports.

Traditionally designed Web pages look a little different on WebTV from the way they look on a computer. On your WebTV, you may have to scroll to see a whole page. Links are highlighted with an orange border, and you can move from link to link by pressing the arrow keys on your remote. Press the Select button to follow a link.

Keep pointers to your favorite Web sites by pressing Save on the options panel, which puts links to them in your Favorites pages.

Press the Recent button on the remote or keyboard to view the last dozen or so pages you've visited; select any of those pages to return to it.

Chatting on WebTV

Like every other Internet Service Provider, WebTV provides online chat. On the WebTV home page, select Community and from there select Chat, then the TalkCity box on the chat page.

WebTV's chat is provided by a service called TalkCity, which any Internet user can get to via www.talkcity.com. You can join any of the chats that WebTV's chat page suggests, or you can go directly to www.talkcity.com and choose from a larger set of chats there.

On normal Internet accounts, TalkCity has a fancy Java-based talk program that requires Netscape Navigator or Internet Explorer, but it recognizes when you're connecting from WebTV and automatically uses WebTV's simpler but adequate chat scheme. Either way, it's the same set of chats, so WebTV users can chat with anyone they like.

Although in theory you can chat without a keyboard, it's hard to imagine anyone patient enough to do it (and other chatters willing to wait while you pick the letters out of the virtual type case).

All in the family

When you first sign up with WebTV, you create a master account (the one that gets the bill for the service). From this account, you can create other accounts, each of which can have its own password and receive its own e-mail. You can bar sub-accounts from using e-mail or chatting.

To protect your kids, you can set up sub-accounts to use Internet screening programs. Choose from two screening levels: SurfWatch, which restricts access to pages it considers inappropriate, and Kid friendly, which allows access to approved pages only.

Part V

The Part of Tens

It started as a wrap-around porch, and then Stuart found a section on medieval architecture on the Internet.

In this part . . .

Because some things just don't fit anywhere else in this book, we've grouped them into special lists. By the strangest coincidence, exactly *ten* facts happen to be in each list. We even gave these lists a distinctly Canadian flair! (*Note to the literal-minded:* You may have to cut off or glue on some fingers to make your version of ten match up to ours. Perhaps it would be easier just to take our word for it.)

Chapter 19

Ten Frequently Asked Questions

In This Chapter

▶ Answering some important Internet questions

▶ Our opinions about computers, Internet Service Providers, and other favorite things

We get lots of questions in our e-mail every day. In this chapter, we've responded to some of the most common queries, in the hope that the answers can help you, too.

If you have more than ten remaining questions after you read this book, surf to our Web site, at `net.gurus.com`, where we tell you where to find answers.

Why can't you just give me step-by-step instructions?

We get this question by e-mail all the time. Other *...For Dummies* books give detailed, step-by-step instructions, although this book can be frustratingly vague.

Two reasons spring to mind. One is that we don't know what kind of computer you use or what programs you use. We've tried to give you lots of general background so that you have a good idea about how the Internet works, in addition to specific instructions wherever possible for the most commonly used systems. You can always search the Web for handy primers by typing in the word `primer` followed by the topic on which you want information. The best part about this is that the information is free!

The other reason is that the programs change continually. By the time you read this chapter, even newer versions may appear and may work a little differently from the way we describe. We hope you learn enough from reading this book to help you negotiate the inconsistencies you're bound to run into as you begin to explore the Net.

If you're using Windows 98, you might check out *The Internet For Windows 98 For Dummies* (published by IDG Books Worldwide, Inc.), which does have steps for many of the Internet programs that come with Windows 98.

Are the Internet and the World Wide Web the same thing?

Nope. The Internet started out in 1969 and is a network of networks. The World Wide Web, born in 1989, is a system of interconnected Web pages that you can access via the Internet. In the past couple of years, the Web has become the most common way of using the Internet, and, more and more, Web browsers include traditional Internet technology. For example, you can send and receive e-mail from Netscape Navigator, and you can find Usenet newsgroups at www.dejanews.com. On the other hand, you can find plenty of goodies other than the Web on the Net, such as instant message systems, multi-user games, and plain old e-mail.

What's the difference between a browser and a search engine?

A *browser* is the software program that lets your computer show you pages on the World Wide Web. The most commonly used browsers are Netscape Navigator and Internet Explorer. A *search engine* (or directory or index) helps you find pages (on the Web) about specific topics of interest to you. Netscape Navigator and Internet Explorer are browsers — programs you install on your own computer. AltaVista, Yahoo, Lycos, Excite, and a host of other search engines are Web sites that can help you find stuff on the Web. Think of the browser as the telephone and the search engine as the phone book.

How can I erase my browser's list of the Web pages I've been looking at?

Gee, why would you want to do that? Aren't you proud of the fascinating and intellectual sites you've been visiting? *No?*

We get this question often, almost always from persons of the male persuasion. Here's how to clear the list of Web sites that appears in your Address or Location bar: In Netscape Navigator 4.7, choose Edit➪Preferences, choose Navigator from the list of categories, and click the Clear History button. In Internet Explorer 5.0 and higher, choose Tools➪Internet Options, click the General tab, and click the Clear History button.

Should I buy WebTV?

Maybe, if you don't own a computer. Visit a consumer electronics store and get a demonstration. If e-mail and Web surfing are all you want to do on the Internet, WebTV may be adequate. WebTV is certainly cheap, and it does get you on the Net for about $100 plus $75 for a remote keyboard and $20 per month to actually connect (assuming that you already own a TV and a telephone); if you use WebTV much, however, you will soon pine for a real computer with a real monitor.

As digital high-definition TV (HDTV) — which acts more like a computer screen and less like a TV — becomes mainstream in the near future, Web TV will become especially attractive. That's because the picture you see on your HDTV screen will be as sharp as the picture you see on a good-quality PC monitor. When the computer you're using today is ready for the scrap heap — say, in two years — you may want to revisit the WebTV option. See Chapters 5 and 18 for details about WebTV.

Can I change my e-mail address?

It depends. (Don't you hate it when we say that?) On most systems, you can't just change your e-mail address. Your e-mail address is usually your *username* on your Internet Service Provider's system. Most ISPs let you choose any username you want, as long as it's not already taken. If you want to be called SnickerDoodles, that's okay with the ISP. And your e-mail address may be something like `snickerdoodles@furdle.net`.

Later, when it occurs to you that SnickerDoodles will not look real great on your business card, you may want to change your e-mail address. If you're using a small, local provider, you can probably call up and ask politely, and the company will grumble and change the name. If the company doesn't change it, or if you like being SnickerDoodles to your friends, you can usually get a *mail alias* for a small extra charge.

No law says that each address corresponds to exactly one mailbox, and having several *aliases,* or mail addresses, that put all the mail in one mailbox is a common practice. In other words, if your true mailbox name is `john1`, for example, mail addressed to `john`, `john1`, and a couple of other misspellings are all aliased to `john1` so that the mail is delivered automatically.

Ask your Internet Service Provider whether it will give you a mail alias. Most will — it's just another line in a file full of mailing addresses. After your ISP does that, you can set or alter your return address (in Eudora, for example) to the alias, so that your address contains your new alias name, rather than your original name.

If your ISP can't or won't give you a mail alias, you can check out some third-party e-mail alias services. One is PoBox, which likens itself to a post office box service. It gives you, for a modest fee, any addresses you want at `pobox.com`, which it then forwards to your true e-mail address. Contact PoBox at `www.pobox.com`, or you can send a message to `info@pobox.com`. Zillions of Web sites, including Raging Bull and Hotmail, also offer free, Web-based mail addresses. Visit `www.ragingbull.com` and `www.hotmail.com`.

AOL Canada is a special case because its users can change their e-mail addresses on a whim — and at a moment's notice. When you sign up for AOL Canada, you choose a screen name, which is your username and e-mail address. Each AOL Canada user can choose as many as four extra screen names, ostensibly for other family members, and can change them at any time. The good news is that AOL Canada users can have any addresses they want (as long as they don't conflict with any of the 17 million AOL International addresses already assigned); the bad news is that it's practically impossible to tell who's sending any particular piece of mail from AOL Canada. WebTV uses the same scheme as AOL Canada and allows as many as five extra accounts.

How can I get a file from my word processor into e-mail?

It depends. (Oops, we said it again.) Do you want to send the contents in just plain text or do you want to send them in pretty, formatted text — what some people call *rich text*. It depends, too, on whom you're sending the file to and what that person is able to receive.

Everyone can always read plain text, and if that's all you need, the process is easy. Use simple copy and paste commands, either from the Edit menu in your word-processor and e-mail programs or by pressing Ctrl+C (⌘+C on the Mac) and Ctrl+V (⌘+V). Select and copy the text of the document in your word processor and then paste it into your e-mail message.

If you and your recipient both use e-mail programs that support rich text, you can include rich text in your message. But be sure about this before you send, or the result will be very different from what you intend. What you think is going to look beautiful will be filled with illegible formatting codes.

If both your e-mail program and that of your recipient can handle attachments and your recipient uses the same word-processing software as you do, you can attach the word-processing file to your e-mail message (see Chapter 12 for details).

Is it safe to use my credit card on the Net?

Everyone's idea of what is safe is different. Some people say that using a credit card is a lousy idea — period. Others think that the Net is full of people trying to steal credit card numbers and that under no circumstances should you ever send your card number across the Net. We think that the risks of online credit card use have been overblown. See Chapter 9, in which we address this topic in detail.

How important is this Internet stuff?

Very important. OK, make that *extremely* important. We're here to tell you that ignoring the Internet is not an option anymore. If you don't go to the Internet, it won't be long before the Internet will come to you. That's because the Internet is in the process of converging with your TV, phone, cellphone, Palm Pilot, and other electronic appliances that can access it. In other words, you'll be hard-pressed to avoid the Internet — it will be everywhere. Know how to use it. Ask your kids — or your neighbour's kids — to show you how!

What's the best Internet Service Provider?

It dep— oh, you know. Do you want the cheapest? The best user support? The fastest?

If all you want is e-mail and access to the World Wide Web, almost any account will do, although the price varies widely. How easy it is to get started may be the deciding factor for you. If you have never used a computer in your life and get frustrated easily, we recommend choosing a service that puts a great deal of effort into making your life easier. Look at the services with access numbers that are a local call from where you are. Assuming there's more than one, find out how much help is available from your Internet Service Provider (ISP). Talking to someone from an ISP before you begin, and then asking your online friends how they like its services, can give you valuable insight. In the end, you have to decide which one is best for you. These days, the biggest difference between ISPs isn't technical — it's the level of service. Don't waste time with one that doesn't offer good service. Shopping around is key.

How can I make money on the Net?

We can't remember exactly how many trillions of dollars of business opportunity the Internet represents, according to the people who claim to know about these things. However, we do see that the marketplace relies on communication — and as a new medium of communication, the doors of the Internet are being flung open for new ways of doing business.

We recommend that rather than try to figure out how to make money in the Internet business, you spend time getting to know the Net extensively — by checking out newsgroups and mailing lists in addition to exploring the World Wide Web. The more you see, the more you can think about effective ways that your business can use the Net.

We have found that the best way to make money on the Internet is to invest in the companies building the Net (or to write books about it!). We're inclined to look at companies engaged in Internet infrastructure (they supply the Internet's building blocks), and business-to-business e-commerce (they develop and sell software that manages a product-and-service supply chain).

This should go without saying, but remember that anyone who tells you that you can make big bucks on the Net without working hard and being creative and determined is lying to you. Keep in mind this maxim: If it sounds too good to be true, it probably is. However, if your idea works, you can have the world at your Web doorstep.

What type of computer should I buy to use the Internet?

You can guess what we're going to say, right? It depends. For many people, the Internet is the first good reason they have for buying a computer. Which type of computer you buy depends on how you expect to use it.

You don't absolutely *have* to have a computer to use the Internet. You can get WebTV instead (see "Should I buy WebTV?" earlier in this chapter, for details). But if you think you're gonna buy a computer eventually, and you can afford to do it now, keep reading.

If you want to buy a computer to use the Internet, buy a new computer, or, at worst, one that's no more than a year old. New computers come with Internet software already installed and are often under $1,000. By the time you add whatever you need to an old computer, you will probably spend just as much money, invest more time, and get something not as useful.

If you're purchasing a new computer primarily to surf the Net, you can buy a reasonably fast computer — a Pentium III with a colour monitor — for between $1,000 and $1,400. The World Wide Web is a fascinating place; to get the real effect, you have to see it in colour.

Pardon our limited vision — we tend to talk about only two categories of computers: IBM PC clones and Macintoshes. Which one is for you? Either is okay; they both work. Our advice: Buy what your friends have so that down the road you can ask them for help.

When you're trying to decide what to buy, talk to people who do the same kinds of things you do, not just other people who happen to have computers. When you evaluate price, don't forget the value of your own time spent learning how to set up and use a computer and its software programs, not to mention your own nature when it comes to mechanical devices.

What's your favorite Web application?

Our favorite is the application that allows us to download digital music from the Web that we can play back on our computer. At `www.mp3.com`, you can find links to some of the more popular Web-based musicians and MP3 sites endorsed by record companies.

Although this Web site is very controversial, check out the infamous Napster site at `www.napster.com`. Just about any popular song can be downloaded for free from this Web site. Only one problem — Napster is being sued for possible copyright violations. While the record companies — and rock stars — are screaming, "Thief!" techies are replying, "New economy, new rules, mate!"

Stay tuned (pun totally intended) to see how technology's David fares against the recording industry's Goliath.

Chapter 20

Ten Killer Applications on the Net

- -

In This Chapter

▶ Finding addresses

▶ Your family tree

▶ Still and moving images

▶ Music and your PC

▶ Speech-to-text devices

▶ E-books

▶ Fax-to-e-mail services

- -

*E*very once in a while, a new *killer application* is born. A killer application is a techno-geek term used to describe a new technology that is so absolutely cool, it's certain to appeal to the masses. Technology that we take for granted today — such as basic e-mail — was at one time itself considered to be a killer application. So let's take a look at today's hottest technologies, which even by next week may be considered old news!

Ways to Find E-Mail Addresses

Trying to find an e-mail address you don't know can be a lot harder than you think. However, since your ability to fire off e-mail to someone is a fundamental use of the Net, you should know about some of the great tools available that help you find someone on the Net.

The Net provides you with many different ways to look for e-mail addresses. We save you the trouble of reading on by starting out with the easiest, most reliable method:

Call them on the phone and ask them.

Pretty low-tech, huh? For some reason, this technique seems to be absolutely the last thing that people want to do. Try it first. If you know or can find out the phone number, this method is much easier than any of the others.

Search for people on the Web

The world is changing. Perhaps your friend has created a home page. Use your favorite Web directory or index to search by using your friend's name in quotes (" ") as the keyword for your search. If your friend does have a home page, an e-mail address is probably somewhere on the page.

Search for people in newsgroups

If your friend participates in any Usenet newsgroups (online discussions), you can use AltaVista to search Usenet (rather than the Web) or check out the Web page at www.deja.com. Remember that although your friend may not use his full name or anything resembling his name, it's worth a quick try.

Online directories

Wouldn't it be cool if some online directory listed everybody's e-mail address? Maybe, but the Internet doesn't have one. For one thing, nothing says that somebody's e-mail address has any connection to his name. For another, not everybody wants everybody else to know his e-mail address. Although lots of directories in progress are attempting to accumulate e-mail addresses, none of them is complete, and many work only if people voluntarily list themselves with the service.

Some of the directories you can use to find people do provide an e-mail address, if it's known. Although we talk about these directories in Chapter 8, it's worth pointing out here which ones \ can be helpful.

Yahoo People Search

Chapter 8 tells you all about Yahoo People Search, formerly called the Four11 directory service. Go to ca.people.yahoo.com and try its e-mail search. If you want other people to find you, this is a good place to list yourself.

Canada 411

Go to www.canada411.sympatico.ca to find the telephone numbers of people and businesses. Remember what we said at the outset? To get a person's e-mail address, try calling that person first. That's where Canada 411 really comes in handy. Unfortunately, this service has not yet incorporated a comprehensive e-mail address feature.

Online services directories

AOL Canada boasts a member directory. If you don't have an account with AOL Canada but someone you know does, you can ask your acquaintance to look up an address for you.

Alumni directories

Canadian universities and community colleges have embraced the World Wide Web; you'd be hard-pressed to find one without an extensive, informative Web site. Many are choosing to include some sort of alumni directory. Check your alma mater, and see whether it has a place for you to list yourself, your e-mail address, or your home page.

The Missing Link

Some of the most popular Web sites on the Net are those that deal with genealogy. If you're trying to find a missing link in your family tree, or want to see if you're related to Queen Elizabeth, the Net can provide you with a road map to find some answers.

Tracing your genealogy on the Net is first and foremost a research exercise. In other words, don't expect to just enter your name, push a button, and have your family tree bloom before your very eyes. There's more work involved. The real power of the Net as a tool for genealogical research resides in its ability to bring together several genealogy resources into one spot — your home computer. This can translate into real time savings for you.

So where do you start? The Genealogy Home Page (GHP) at www.genhomepage.com and Ancestry.com at www.ancestry.com are probably the only two sites you need to know about when starting to grow your family tree. Each boasts well over a million visits since its inception. Predominantly American Web sites, GHP and Ancestry.com nonetheless have extensive resources that Canadians can use. At these sites, you can access archives, deeds, maps, and other tools of the genealogical trade. Related newsgroups and mailing lists are also listed. Both sites provide loads of relevant Web site links — key ingredients to any good genealogy Web resource. Finally, both list directories of local genealogy societies across the United States and Canada.

A distinctly Canadian genealogy resource is the Canadian Genealogy and History site at www.islandnet.com/~jveinot/cghl/cghl.html. It provides you with useful links to provincial resources — census data, provincial and national archives (church affiliations, marriage and death certificates, and deeds), and referrals to local genealogical organizations. From this site, you can access and draw information from a database of historical data and statistical overviews. Like GHP and Ancestry.com, it's a "how to find" genealogical resource more than it is one that actually "finds" a long-lost relative for you.

For the Artistically Inclined

Internauts tend to love online pictures. After all, it's one of the key attractions of the Web. So not surprisingly, a large and growing fraction of all the bits flying around the Internet is made up of increasingly high-quality digitized pictures. About 99.44 percent of the pictures are purely for fun, games, and worse. We're sure that you're in the 0.56 percent of users who need the pictures for work, so here's a roundup of picture formats. Knowing about these formats will make your Net surfing experience a lot more fun.

The most commonly used graphics formats on the Net are GIF and JPEG. You almost never find GIF or JPEG image files compressed or archived. The reason is that these formats already do a pretty fair job of compression internally, so compress, zip, and the like don't help any.

I could GIF a . . .

The most widely used format on the Internet is *GIF* (Graphics Interchange Format). This format is well matched to the capabilities of a typical PC computer screen — no more than 256 different colours in a picture and usually 640×480, 1024×768, or some other familiar PC screen resolution. Because GIF is well standardized, you never have problems with files written by one program being unreadable by another. GIF files have the extension *.gif*.

Dozens of commercial and shareware programs on PCs and Macs can read and write GIF files. Netscape and Internet Explorer can display them as well; just choose Open from the File menu.

The eyes have it

A few years back, a bunch of digital photography experts got together and decided that it was time to have an official standard format for digitized photographs but that none of the existing formats was good enough. They formed the *Joint Photographic Experts Group (JPEG),* and after extended negotiation, the JPEG format was born. JPEG is designed specifically to store digitized, full-colour or black-and-white photographs, not computer-generated cartoons or anything else. As a result, JPEG does a fantastic job of storing photos and a lousy job of storing anything else.

JPEG files can be *any* size because the format allows a trade-off between size versus quality when the file is created. The main disadvantage of JPEG is that it's slow to decode. Most programs, including Netscape and Internet Explorer, now handle JPEG. JPEG files usually have filenames with the extension *.jpeg* or *.jpg*.

JPEG2000 — the millennium snapshot

In December 2000, the new JPEG2000 still-image compression standard was adopted by the International Standards Organization (ISO). We expect to see a gradual replacement of the original JPEG standard with JPEG2000 — a far superior still-image compression algorithm. JPEG2000 handles the same kinds of images that JPEG does, only faster and better. It compresses more densely, and provides improved quality images.

Many programs that can handle (encode and decode) JPEG will soon be updated for JPEG2000. JPEG2000's superior compression technology and faster download times should also make it useful for countless Internet imaging applications on the desktop, in a digital camera, or in an Internet appliance such as the Palm Pilot.

Ready, Aim, Click, and Clip

More and more Canadians use Internet e-mail as a way of staying in touch with family and friends who live far away. But it's surprising how few people we meet realize that they could attach JPEG or other format picture files to their regular e-mail. With a digital camera, you could photograph your children or your new home, and then e-mail the pictures away the same day!

Digital cameras create an electronic digital image instead of a film copy. Most digital cameras have cute little "memory" cards that you can remove and re-use. Others accept totally uncute — because we're all tired of seeing them — floppy disks. Once memory is full, pictures can be transferred to your PC, where special software "develops" the image. Just think — no more darkrooms and their migraine-inducing red lightbulbs!

Digital cameras are fast and convenient, and, over the long haul, using memory cards or disks is loads cheaper than using film. A good camera averages about $350, but others can easily exceed that amount. Many offer LCD screen, flash, auto-focus, and light-sensing features. Although digital image quality is almost always inferior to traditional photographs, digital cameras are gradually getting cheaper in price and better in quality.

So how is a digital image attached to e-mail? Simple. The image you transferred and saved in your PC is already in digital format, and has a name. When you want to e-mail an image, simply find the file and attach it the same way you would attach, say, a Microsoft Word file. Chapter 12 discusses e-mail attachments.

Matinée, Anyone?

As networks get faster and disks get bigger, people are starting to store entire digitized movies (albeit still rather *short* ones, at this point). The standard movie format is called *Moving Picture Experts Group (MPEG)*. MPEG was designed by a committee down the hall from the JPEG committee and — practically unprecedented in the history of standards efforts — was designed based on earlier work.

MPEG viewers are found in the same places as JPEG viewers. You need a reasonably fast server-based workstation or a top-of-the-line Pentium III PC (or fast Macintosh computer). A computer with a powerful processor will let you see MPEG movies in clear real-time resolution, instead of in fuzzy and jerky images.

A few other competing movie formats are also used — notably, Shockwave and Apple QuickTime — and appear on Web pages. You can get Web browser plug-ins that run the movies for you. For Netscape Navigator plug-ins, visit home.netscape.com/plugins. For Internet Explorer add-ons, visit www.microsoft.com/msdownload/default.asp and click Internet Explorer under Windows Update.

As with JPEG, MPEG is going the way of the dodo bird. As you might have expected, Motion JPEG2000, or MPEG2000, will be much faster and better performing than its predecessor!

The Sound of (Digital) Music

Audio files — files that contain digitized sound — can be found all over the Web. If you like to listen to CBC Radio, for example, but can't get around to tuning in when it's on, you can listen to major news and special interest stories from the CBC Web page (at www.cbc.ca) at any time — totally cool. We also like some of the live concerts and radio stations at www.broadcast.com.

You can listen to sounds from the Web in two ways:

- ✔ **Download an entire audio file, and then play it.** This method has the advantage that you can play the file as many times as you want without downloading it again. Downloading an audio file can take quite a while.

- ✔ **Play the audio file *as you download it* so that you don't have to wait for the whole file to arrive before starting to hear it.** This method involves *streaming audio.* Although the quality isn't as good, some sound on the Net isn't worth waiting to download, anyway.

Nonstreaming audio files have extensions such as *.wav, .mp3,* and *.au.* MPLAYER, which comes with most versions of Windows, can play *WAV* files. MP3 (MPEG Layer 3) is a new standard that is currently taking the Internet-based music industry by storm and is posing a serious threat to the bottom line of traditional record companies. MPEG is versatile in that it handles both image and sound files. More on MP3 shortly.

The most popular system for playing streaming audio files is RealAudio, and files in its format have the extension *.ra* or *.ram.* To play RealAudio files, you need the RealPlayer plug-in, which you can download from `www.real.com` or from software archives such as TUCOWS (`www.tucows.com`). The RealAudio player also handles RealVideo, which has small, blurry moving pictures to go with your sound. RealAudio has recently introduced RealJukebox, which allows you to transfer music from your favorite CD into your PC while you play the song. The best part of all is that you can download RealJukebox for free!

MP3, C3PO, and R2D2

The Internet has opened a pretty interesting window on the world of music. Record companies, however, liken it to opening Pandora's box! That's because you can now download free music you like and play it on your PC or a portable digital player. MP3 technology enables you to quickly download music from the Internet by compressing music and other audio data to $\frac{1}{12}$ its original size. Music in MP3 format is near CD-quality, and there are more than 500,000 songs on the Internet to choose from.

Unfortunately, MP3 has also spawned a thriving, and illegal, music pirating industry. You can find free and legitimate MP3 songs (typically from special genres such as gospel, hip-hop, and swing) at `www.mp3.com` — and a host of similar Web sites proliferating on the Net. You can also access more popular MP3 songs at "pay-per-listen" Web sites that are hosted by some Net-based record companies or distributors. Links to such places can be found at many MP3 Web sites.

To decode and play MP3 songs on your PC, you'll need player software, which you can get for free at www.winamp.com. If you prefer your music on the go, you can buy a portable digital music player at most large electronics stores. Check out the Nomad Jukebox at www.creative.com. These are typically smaller than audiocassettes, and have easy interfaces to transfer digital files from your PC to the devices. Most come with player software, and mix and store up to 60 minutes of downloaded CD-quality music or up to eight hours of voice audio. Memory cards (digital cassettes) are also available.

Buying Tailored CDs and Other Music

You can buy canned music CDs at CDnow (www.cdnow.com), Chapters.ca (www.chapters.ca), or Canada's own Tower Records (www.towerrecords.com). Boring.

What is more exciting is that at Musicmaker (www.musicmaker.com) and CustomDisc (www.customdisc.com) you can buy CDs that are customized to your taste.

Dictatorship on the Go

Portable recording devices — such as the Dragon Systems *Naturally-Speaking Mobile* — are now available to record your spoken words and convert them to digital text with the help of some nifty software.

If you're a teacher, student, contractor, professional, or someone who simply enjoys writing, you can dictate almost an hour of speech — to automatically write notes, quotes, letters, or reports. You can also save the file you created into WAV or MP3 format — in other words, not have to bother transcribing it to text — and attach it to your e-mail as is.

These portable devices are easy to hook up. You basically use a cable to connect the recorder to the serial port of your PC. Then, you run the voice-recognition software, which transcribes the data to text. (There's something really neat about watching a string of spoken words quickly turn into text right before your eyes!) From there, you'll probably have to fine-tune the text layout a bit and make a few typo corrections before saving the file as a Word, WordPerfect, or other document. Some software developers boast results of up to 95-percent transcription accuracy.

Be aware that getting started takes some time. You first have to "train" the software by reading a boring story into the recorder for about half an hour.

Most portable recorders weigh about 4 ounces and fit in the palm of your hand. They have LCD screens and a series of buttons that let you organize your recordings into folders and files, replay a recording, and edit text verbally. Packages that include both portable recorder and the software cost about $450 and are available in major Canadian electronics stores.

E-Books

Most booksellers on the Internet give you access to traditional print editions via the Internet. In other words, the book that you order over the Internet is sent to you by mail. A second book "selling" approach allows for online browsing and downloading of digital text — sometimes for free. Once downloaded, you can read the new text on your PC. But now, you can also download it to an e-book!

E-books are small portable devices that display electronic pages in an illuminated, hand-held box built to hold several digital novels. To turn a page, simply press a button! Batteries on most e-books are intended to last continuously for over one day between recharges. After you buy an online book (digital text), you can download it into your PC for future transfer to your e-book.

E-books are available from more than 25 major publishers, or from one of hundreds of specialized Web sites (you can use a portal such as Lycos to find a site). NuvoMedia (www.nuvomedia.com) offers its Rocket eBook for about $600. Softbook (www.softbook.com) has a similar offering for a little less money. You can get all the details, including where to obtain downloadable "books," at their Web sites.

One specialized Web site that any self-respecting e-book owner should visit is The Online Books Page at www.cs.cmu.edu/books.html (administered by Carnegie Mellon School of Computer Science, in Pittsburgh, Pennsylvania). This site allows for online browsing or file downloading and contains a searchable index of thousands of online books that can be read completely for free. You'll likely need Adobe Acrobat Reader to be able to read online publications in proper format (it's on the CD in the back of this book). You can also download the software for free (go to www.adobe.com).

Fax–to–E-Mail

A new type of Web-based service exists that provides you with a free personal inbound fax number and the security you need to be sure that inbound faxes are being sent directly to you. All faxes received through your fax number are sent directly to your specified e-mail address for your private viewing. A viewer program is included. The viewer program allows you to see the text and images on the fax through your PC screen. You can also print it out, of course.

Most fax–to–e-mail services allow for an unlimited number of free fax transmissions. Outbound faxing — whereby you send a fax through your e-mail — is also available. Outbound faxing usually involves a fee, depending on the destination of your fax. Check out Canada's own FaxPC site at www.faxpc.com.

Chapter 21

Ten Practical Ways Canadians Use the Net

*E*veryone who uses the Internet does so in a very personal way. Some use it as a tool. Others use it as a form of recreation. But when we talked to Canadians, we found that common themes and preferences emerged. This chapter highlights some of those themes.

Turning Sense into Dollars

You may just have doled out some cash for a new computer system, Internet connection, and even a *...For Dummies* book! Do you feel a bit poorer? You can't be blamed. The average Canadian spends virtually all his or her disposable annual income on one thing or another. Many people, perhaps even you, can use a few extra cash-making or cash-saving tips. Enter the Net.

As briefly covered in Chapter 8, many of today's financial gurus and investment houses have jumped on the Internet in a big way. For example, from an assortment of financial planning Web sites, you can learn how to manage your bank accounts and investments, plan your estate, use Internet resources at tax time, determine your insurance needs, and tap into government financial program information.

As for your investments, several Canadian Web sites exist to help you

✔ Educate yourself about the world of investments

✔ Research companies

- ✔ Obtain advice from online periodicals
- ✔ Obtain live stock price data and company press releases
- ✔ Access discussion forums about specific companies
- ✔ Trade securities
- ✔ Track and chart your investments over time

Check out Canoe Money, at `www.canoe.ca/money`, a one-stop financial super-market catering to most of the financial information needs of Canadians. If you'd prefer to step away from your computer screen, check out *Investing Online For Canadians For Dummies* (published by CDG Books Canada), which shows you the nuts and bolts of investing online in Canada. Trust us, it's a good book. One of us co-wrote it!

To Your Health!

Canadians love to stay healthy and fit, whether they prefer to run, bike, swim, skate, or ski. In Vancouver, you can do all these activities in one day! Canadian climate and topography make exercise easy and fun, since you have so many recreational activities to choose from. Canadians are also fairly healthy compared to many other developed countries, as poll after poll suggests. But at the end of the day, the maintenance of your good health, or a speedy recovery from ill health, is based on two things: access to information about healthcare and access to healthcare itself.

There is a wealth of medical information available on the Internet. Doctors and medical institutions now share information that used to reside, for the most part, in their professional — and rather exclusive — territory. Now that you can access this information, you are in a much better position to become a good consumer of healthcare information.

While the Internet cannot, and should not, replace a visit to your doctor, its vast resources *can* assist you in accessing quick, useful, and current health-related information. You can obtain information and advice on your current symptoms, find out about alternative treatments, get second opinions, and access advice on staying healthy. The information you get from the Net can also increase your overall knowledge of your own body — which is always a good thing!

Check out AltaVista's Health "channel" at `www.altavista.ca` to access a complete repository of health-related links and information. Find out, for example, about the possible cause and cure of a sickness, or about the side effects of a certain drug.

Home Sweet Home

Did you know that Canadians move more often than do citizens of any other country in the Western Hemisphere? The Internet can play an important role in the housing decisions you make. The Net can help you decide whether to move or to stay where you are; it can also help you decide when and where to move. Many real estate Web sites exist that can show you what the housing and rental markets are doing. Other Web sites let you access demographic information about particular neighbourhoods, towns, or cities. The Net also allows you to see, on your PC monitor, what a listed house, condo, or apartment on the market looks like. Although you can't usually get a property directly through the Internet, some Web sites connect you with the brokers, vendors, or lessors of properties. You can also devise a tailored search of online listings of homes for sale or units for rent. Finally, you can educate yourself about real estate by perusing the many online primers on how to make or assess an offer.

An example of a good real estate resource on the Internet is the well-known Multiple Listing Service (MLS) at `www.mls.ca`. On any given week, there are 120,000 to 160,000 Canadian properties listed there. The site also features relevant links, news stories, and statistics built to dazzle. At the MLS site, you can select your desired home's features and price range, and even see a picture of a listed property.

Pack Your Bags!

As Canadians, we are also known for our penchant for traveling. What with frosty Canadian winters and our infatuation with southern climes no one could blame us for having the travel bug.

Whether you plan to stay in Canada or travel abroad, you want to know, before you go, more about your destination. You also want to know the most cost-effective and efficient way to get there. The Internet can help on these and many related fronts.

Most Internet travel Web sites allow you to access information about tour packages, discounts, travel insurance, special regulations, photography tips, travel and health alerts, vehicle rental, exchanging cash, traveler's cheques, and more.

Most airlines, railways, hotels, cruise lines, coach lines, bed-and-breakfast inns, and recreational vehicle destinations have their own Web sites, and allow you to make actual bookings online.

One Canadian Web site that you can visit before planning your vacation is Uniglobe Travel Online at www.uniglobe.com, one of the biggest travel agencies in the world. Uniglobe's Web site provides both trip planning information and trip booking capabilities. You can access pictures of cruise liners, cities, resorts, and loads of neat attractions. Also check out www.travelocity.com and www.expedia.ca.

Painting the Town

Arts and entertainment is something that almost everyone enjoys taking in once in a while. A portal (such as SympaticoLycos [www.lycos.ca]) is probably a good first stop for local information on stage, dining, and theatre. Keep clicking through the portal's Arts sub-directories until you're "local" enough to actually browse the details of the show you may want to see. Since many portals also have a link to the City Guide www.cityguide.com or City.Net www.city.net Web sites, click the link to access information about what's happening in your neck of the woods. The City Guide and City.Net sites exist solely to provide you with pointers to arts-related information.

Charge It!

Shopping on the Internet has revolutionized the way Canadians spend their hard-earned loonies. In fact, on a per capita basis, Canadians use the Internet to shop more often than Americans do! The convenience, occasional discounts, and variety of choice are why the *e-commerce* aspect of the Net is exploding today.

You can shop on the Internet in several ways. For example, you can browse the Web sites of The Bay or Canadian Tire, where you can see — from the comfort of your home — what's offered behind the actual bricks and mortar.

You can also tour an online mall, something that exists only in cyberspace. Offerings are organized by product and service categories. Check out Imall www.imall.com for an example of this type of shopping experience.

Some Internet shopping sites are specialized. For example, there are Web sites that exist for only one purpose: to help you buy a car! A good car site should allow you to do the research, decide on the model, and select a buying service. Check out www.autobytel.ca for a sample of this type of specialized service.

Finally, if auctions are your cup of tea, you can try your hand on Bid.com (www.bid.com), a Canadian auction site, to get your hands on that purple dinnerware set you absolutely must have! You can participate in a standard (increasing bid) or Dutch-style (decreasing bid) auction.

You Only Live Twice

The Internet also offers some edifying spiritual resources.

The Bible Gateway at www.gospelcom.net is the most popular Web site of its kind in the world, "accessed monthly by millions." Through this Christian gateway, you can access Web pages from more than 80 Christian organizations and groups. The site boasts a searchable online Bible in multiple versions and in seven languages. You can browse the site's extensive index by subject or service provided. You can also search for a well-known biblical quote or browse their compelling Reasons to Believe pages. Several of its resources are presented in RealAudio, making the learning experience even easier.

Extra, Extra!

Canadians love their news. A good online starting point is Publisher Interactive, a Canadian Web site (www.mediainfo.com) that has about 1,200 links to publications organized by country. Canadian newspapers are organized by province. And don't forget that you can bypass this site to search the Net directly for your very own local paper's Web site.

Thirty Percent Chance of Rain

When you want to know what the weather is going to be — whether it's in your own backyard or across the world — check out Environment Canada's Web site at www.ec.gc.ca. Nothing spoils a golf game or a picnic like an uninvited and unanticipated rainy day.

He Shoots, He Scores!

Whether you're an armchair quarterback or an active triathlete, the Web has the sports information you crave. CANOE Slam Sports (www.canoe.ca/Slam) is one of Canada's largest repositories of sports information. Other sites you may want to check out include TicketMaster Canada Online (www.ticketmaster.ca) and TSN (www.tsn.ca).

Chapter 22

Ten Ways to Avoid Looking Like a Klutz

In This Chapter

▶ Tips for suave, sophisticated Net usage

▶ Some bonehead moves not to make

Gosh, using the Internet is exciting. And gosh, it offers many ways to make a fool of yourself — heaven forbid that you should act like a *clueless newbie*. In this chapter, we round up the usual suspects of unfortunate moves so that you can be the coolest Web surfer on your block.

Read Before You Write

The moment you get your new Internet account, you may have an overwhelming urge to begin sending out lots of messages right away. *Don't do it!* Read discussion forums, Web pages, and other Net resources for a while before you send out *anything*. You will figure out where best to send your messages, which makes it a) more likely that you will contact people who are interested in what you say, and b) less likely that you will annoy people by bothering them with something directed to an inappropriate site. If you see a FAQ (Frequently Asked Questions) section, read it to see whether your question has already been answered.

Netiquette matters

What type are you? On the Net, the impression you create depends on *what* you type. The messages you send are the only way that 99 percent of the people you meet on the Net will know you.

Speling [sic] counts

Many Net users feel that because Net messages are short and informal, spelling and grammar don't count. Some even think that strange spelling makes them E133T K00L D00DZ. If you feel that wey, theirs' not much wee can do abowt it. We think that a sloppy, misspelled message is like a big grease stain on your shirt — your friends will know that it's you, but people who don't know you will conclude that you don't know how to dress yourself.

Many mail programs have spell checkers. Eudora Pro (the commercial version of Eudora) checks your spelling after you click the dictionary icon (the *ABC* one) on the toolbar or choose Edit⇨Check Spelling from the menu. In Netscape Messenger Version 4.0 or higher, which also comes with a spell checker, you choose Tools⇨Check Spelling from the menu when composing a message. In Outlook Express, you can elect, via the Options menu, to have your outgoing messages checked or choose Tools⇨Spelling to check any message in progress. In Pine, you check your spelling by pressing Ctrl+T. Although spell checkers aren't perfect, at least they ensure that your messages consist of 100-percent genuine words.

DO NOT SEND YOUR ENTIRE MESSAGE IN CAPITAL LETTERS. This technique comes across as shouting and is likely to get you some snarky comments suggesting that you do something about the stuck Shift key on your keyboard. Now and then we get mail from someone who says, "i dont use capital letters or punctuation its too much work." Uh-huh.

If you don't have anything to say, don't say it

Avoid trying to sound smart. When you do, the result is usually its opposite. One day on Raging Bull — a popular Web-based discussion forum on invest-ments and investing — someone asked for a link to a certain *Wall Street Journal* story about Microsoft. Then came the edifying comment "Sorry, Too Busy to Help You." Well, duh. We hoped that people who didn't know anything could keep their mouths shut, but clearly we were wrong. Each message you post to a discussion forum is read by all participants in that forum. Each participant is there on a voluntary basis. Like us, they only have so much time to spend reading posts. Does the good content of the discussion forum outweigh the noise and inanity? The more inanity, the more likely it is that sensible participants will leave and the forum will deteriorate. If you're going to participate, find a constructive way to do so.

Keep your hands to yourself

Another stupidity we witnessed involved someone subscribing his arch enemy — or friend — to a mailing list or Web-based newsletter against the recipient's wishes. Okay, folks — this is not kindergarten. When you start to abuse public lists and newsletters, they go private or start charging fees. Lists that are unmoderated turn moderated. Moderated lists welcome people "by invitation only." Newsletters that were once free now charge token amounts to force subscribers to give away only their own credit card numbers — effectively blocking out unwanted subscriptions to friends and foes.

Subscription inscription (and defection)

Signing up for a mailing list is a cool thing. We tell you all about how to do it in Chapter 13. Still (or maybe this advice is just for people who aren't reading our book), a classic way to look like a klutz is to send to the list itself a message asking to be added to or taken off a list, where all the people on the list have to read it, but it doesn't actually get the sender subscribed or taken off. Subscribe and unsubscribe requests go to the list server program in a particular format or, in the case of lists that are not automated, to the list owner.

Read the rules

When you first subscribe to a mailing list, you usually get back a long message about how this particular list operates and how to un-subscribe if you want. *Read this message. Save this message. Print this message.* Before you go telling other people on the list how to behave, read the rules again. Some officious newbie, newly subscribed to JAZZ-L, began flaming the list and complaining about the off-topic threads. JAZZ-L encourages this kind of off-topic discussion — it says so right in the introduction to the list. Can't say that she made herself real welcome with that move.

Edit yourself

When you're posting to a mailing list, remember that your audience is the entire world, made up of people of all ethnicities and races speaking different languages and representing different cultures. Work hard to represent yourself and your culture well. Avoid name-calling and disparaging comments about other peoples and places. Read several times through whatever you intend to post before you send it. We have seen inadvertent typos change the entire meaning of a message.

Discretion is the better part

Sooner or later, you see something that cries out for a cheap shot. For example, on the Raging Bull Web site, some Internet sleuth with nothing better to do with his time revealed the multiple aliases of another board member who simply wanted to be creative with screen names. Soon, other members descended on this multiple-alias individual with hostile and taunting comments usually reserved for death row convicts. Similarly, someone may send you something you shouldn't have seen, and you want to pass it on. Don't do it. Resist cheap shots and proliferating malice. The Net has plenty of jerks — don't be another one. (See the suggestion later in this chapter about what to do when you're tempted to flame.) Be tolerant of newbies — you were once one yourself.

Keep it private

Okay, someone makes a mistake, such as sending to the entire mailing list a message that says, "subscribe," or posting a message that says, "Gee, I don't know!" in response to a request for help in a discussion forum such as a newsgroup. Yes, it's true, someone made a dumb move. Don't compound it, however, by posting additional messages complaining about it. Either delete the message and forget about it, or respond privately, by e-mail addressed only to the person, not to the mailing list. The entire mailing list doesn't want to hear your advice to the person who blew it. For example, you can send a private e-mail message saying, "In the future, send subscription and un-subscription messages to eggplants-request, not to eggplants, okay?" or "This is a list about domestic laying hens, so could you post your message about cats somewhere else?"

Signing off

All mail programs let you have a *signature,* a file that gets added to the end of each mail or news message you send. The signature is supposed to contain something to identify you. Snappy quotes quickly became common, to add that personal touch. Here's Andrew's signature, for example:

```
Regards,
Andrew Dagys, aj-dagys@home.com, Technology Stocks Fan
        (and guru)
```

Some people's signatures get way out of hand, though, going on for 100 lines of "ASCII art," or containing long quotations, extensive disclaimers, and other allegedly interesting stuff. Although this type of signature may seem cute the first couple of times, it quickly gets tedious — and marks you as a total newbie.

Keep your signature to four lines or fewer. All the experienced Net users do.

Don't get attached

Attachments are a useful way to send files by e-mail. But they work only if the person on the receiving end has a program that can read the files you are sending. For example, if you send a WordPerfect document to someone who doesn't have a word-processing program, the file is unreadable. Ditto for graphics files, sound files, and other files that you may want to send around. Indeed, some older mail systems can't handle attachments at all. Ask *first,* before sending an attachment.

Flame Off!

For some reason, it's easy to get VERY, VERY UPSET ABOUT SOMETHING SOMEONE SAYS ON THE NET. (See, it happens even to us.) Sometimes it's something you find on the Web, and sometimes it's personal e-mail. You may be tempted to shoot a message right back telling that person what a doofus he is. Guess what? He will almost certainly shoot back. This type of overstated outrage is so common that it has its own name: *flaming.* Now and then, it's fun if you're certain that the recipient will take it in good humour, but it's completely unnecessary. For one thing, e-mail messages always come across as crabbier than the author intended; for another, crabbing back will hardly make the person more reasonable. A technique we often find helpful is to write the strongest, crabbiest response possible, full of biting wit and skewering each point in turn. Then we throw it away rather than send it. But if you absolutely, positively have to reply to a hostile message — and will lose sleep if you don't — an effective reply is "Duly noted and ignored; I wish you well."

Antisocial Mail

Although we mention this subject in Chapters 11 and 12, it's worth mentioning here, too. There are a few kinds of messages you should never, ever send. Most are not illegal (at least, not in most places), but your mailbox will quickly fill with displeased responses, and your Internet Service Provider will eventually cancel your account.

The chain gang

Sending a chain letter on the Net is easy: Just click the Forward button, type a few names, and send your letter off. It's a lousy idea. We have never, ever gotten a chain letter that was worth passing along. Bunches of classic chain letters have been circulating around the Net for a decade. Regardless of where the messages come from, even if they seem to be for a good cause, please just throw them away.

Some of the online chain letters started as paper letters. We once got a paper version of the Make Money Fast chain letter from Guam. We did the same thing with it that we do with computer chain letters — threw it in the trash.

Spam, spam, horrible spam

One of the least pleasant online innovations in recent years is *spamming,* or sending the same message — usually selling something that was rather dubious in the first place — to as many e-mail addresses or Usenet newsgroups as possible. This practice is annoying, illegal in some places, and the spammer is usually liable for her Internet Service Provider's costs in cleaning it up. Spamming is also ineffective because automatic systems identify and cancel most Usenet spams within minutes of their occurring, an increasing number of ISPs offer e-mail filtering, and most recipients, including us, automatically presume that anything advertised by spam must be fraudulent. For more information about this topic, see Chapter 12.

Don't Be a Pig

An unbelievable amount of material is on the Net: programs, documents, pictures, and megabyte after megabyte of swell stuff — all free for the taking. You can download it all. *Don't.* Go ahead and take whatever you're likely to use, but don't download entire directories or leave your computer online for hours at a time "just in case."

Your Internet Service Provider sets its charges based on the resources a typical user uses. A single user can use a substantial fraction of the provider's Net connection by sucking down files continuously for hours at a time. ISPs typically "overcommit" their Net connection by a factor of three or so. That is, if every user tried to transfer data at full speed at the same time, it would require three times as fast a connection as the provider has. Because real users transfer for a while and then read what's on-screen for a while, sharing the connection among all the users works out okay. (You're not being cheated by this method; it's a sensible way to provide access at a reasonable cost.

Although you can get guaranteed connection performance if you want it, the price is horrifying.) If users begin using several more connections than the ISP budgets for, prices will go up.

Hang up, already!

This advice applies particularly to those of you with accounts that offer unlimited connect time per month. Don't leave your computer connected if you're not using it. Most Net software packages have a time-out feature that hangs up automatically if no data is transferred to or from the Net for a specified period. We leave ours set to 15 minutes — enough time to change our toddlers' diapers and to make some coffee — on our dial-up connections; otherwise, other users may get a busy signal when they try to connect.

Audio and video pigs

Internet telephony transmits audio and video data over the same communications backbone as the one used by your Internet Service Provider, but presents a particular type of problem. This type of data puts a much, much heavier load on both the local Internet Service Provider and the Net in general than do other Internet services. When you're transferring audio information over the Net, you're pumping data through as fast as your connection will let you. Video connections are even worse: When sites with fast Net connections begin sending video programs around to each other, the entire Net slows down.

For the moment, few enough people are using Internet telephony that it hasn't become a big problem. If it becomes popular enough, though, ISPs will have to provide "no phone" and "phone" accounts, with the latter costing much more, to maintain reasonable access for all their users.

Cybercafé Etiquette

Although cybercafés have been around for some time now, we think it never hurts to repeat a few helpful tips on how to comport yourself while you're there. Look sharp! You're not in the comfort of your own home, and there are some definite rules to keep in mind (we don't want you to embarrass yourself).

No gawking over other people's shoulders

Okay, we understand that you're curious — that's why you're here, to find out about the Internet. Great. Cool. Rent some time, and get some help. Don't stand over another person, reading her screen over her shoulder. It's just plain rude.

Clean up after yourself

We mean not just the trash around your computer but also the trash you probably left *on* the computer. Many folks don't seem to be aware that most mailer programs keep copies of messages that are sent. If you don't want someone to read your mail, make sure that you find the sent-message folder and delete your mail. Then take the next step and empty the trash. There are many examples of people finding all kinds of interesting goodies that the sender wouldn't have wanted to share.

Don't order stuff from a public PC

Normally, we think that ordering over the Web or by e-mail is perfectly safe — much safer than handing your credit card to some waiter you've never met! Some shopping sites store information about you, however (including your mailing address and payment info), in a file on your computer. This arrangement works perfectly when you are ordering from your own computer — you don't have to type all that info when you visit the site the next time you place an order. When you order stuff at a cybercafé, however, this personal information may be stored on the cybercafé's computer instead. Better not chance it.

Some Web Wisdom

Most Internet providers let you put your own private pages up on the World Wide Web. (Chapter 10 helps you get your Web page going.) Again, because what you put on your Web page is all that most people will know about you, this section provides a few suggestions.

Small is beautiful, Part I

Most people who look at your Web page are connected by using a dial-up line and a modem, which means that big pictures take a long time to load. If your home page contains a full-page picture that takes 12½ minutes to load, you may as well hang up a Keep Out sign. Keep the pictures small enough so that the page loads in a reasonable amount of time. If you have a huge picture that you think is wonderful, put a small "thumbnail" version of it on your home page and make it a link to the full picture for people with the time and interest to look at the big version.

Small is beautiful, Part II

Small pages that fit on a screen or two work better than large pages. Small pages are easier to read, and they load faster. If you have 12 screens full of stuff to put on your Web page, break up your page into five or six separate pages with links among them. A well-designed set of small pages makes finding stuff easier than does one big page because the links can direct readers to what they want to find.

If we want the Microsoft Web site, we know where to find it

No Web page (or set of Web pages, as we just suggested) is complete without some links to the author's other favorite pages. For some reason, every new user's Web page used to have a link to `www.microsoft.com` and maybe to Yahoo, Netscape, and a few other sites that every Net user already knows about. Cool Web sites give you links to interesting pages you *don't* already know about.

Let a hundred viewers blossom

Whenever you create a new Web page, look at it with as many Web browsers as possible. Yes, most people use some version of Netscape Navigator or Internet Explorer, but AOL members (more than 200,000 possible AOL Canada members and 20 million possible American AOL members) use the browsers that come with those services, and users with dial-up shell connections use the text-only browser Lynx. Take a look at your pages to make sure that they're at least legible, regardless of which browser people are using.

Don't be an open book, er, Web page

We know that sounds self-evident, but it's not. Don't put information on your Web page that you don't want everyone in the world to know. In particular, don't include your home address and phone number. We know at least one person who received an unexpected and unwelcome phone call from someone she met on the Net. Why would Net users need this information about you, anyway? If they want to reach you, there's e-mail.

Appendix

About the CD

*I*n this Appendix, we tell you how to install and get more information about the programs on *The Internet For Canadians For Dummies,* 2nd Edition Starter Kit CD-ROM.

We first provide brief descriptions of each program. We then explain how to run and use the CD-ROM's Installer to copy the programs to your hard disk. Finally, we provide more details about each program, such as installation and usage tips and pointers on where to get additional information.

The program lists are organized into two groups: software for Microsoft Windows and software for the Macintosh. Within each group, the programs are listed alphabetically.

The Windows programs on the CD-ROM are as follows:

- ✔ **Adobe Acrobat Reader 4.0:** An evaluation version that lets you view and print Portable Document Format, or PDF, files.

- ✔ **AOL Canada 6.0:** Software to sign you up for an Internet account with AOL Canada, a commercial Internet Service Provider (ISP) available locally for many Canadian cities, as well as a large set of Internet software.

- ✔ **Eudora 5.0.2:** An excellent trial version of an electronic-mail program that lets you send and receive e-mail messages over the Internet.

- ✔ **Free Agent 1.21:** A first-rate, freeware *newsgroup* reader (or *newsreader*) program that lets you participate in thousands of online discussions over the Internet.

- ✔ **HotDog Professional 6.0:** A trial version that enables you to create your own World Wide Web pages without having to become an HTML programming whiz.

- ✔ **Microsoft Internet Explorer 5.5:** The Web browser from Microsoft as well as related Internet utility programs (for Windows 95 and 98).

- ✔ **mIRC 5.82:** A shareware Internet Relay Chat, or IRC, program that lets you interact live with a group of people on the Internet via your keyboard.

- ✔ **Netscape Communicator 4.7:** The Web browser from Netscape, along with related programs for mail, news, and Web page editing.

- **Paint Shop Pro:** An evaluation version of a graphics program you can use to view virtually any image you're likely to encounter on the Web. It also lets you create and edit images and convert them into different file formats, which is useful if you want to make your own Web pages.

- **WinZip 8.0:** An invaluable shareware utility you can use to compress and decompress files.

- **WS_FTP Pro:** An evaluation version (for noncommercial use) File Transfer Protocol, or FTP, program you can use to copy files between your PC and a computer on the Internet.

The Macintosh programs on the CD-ROM are:

- **Adobe Acrobat Reader 4.0:** An evaluation version that lets you view and print Portable Document Format, or PDF, files.

- **AOL Canada 4.0:** Software to sign you up for an Internet account with AOL Canada, a commercial Internet Service Provider (ISP) available locally for many Canadian cities.

- **BBEdit Lite 4.6:** Software that enables you to create your own World Wide Web pages without having to become an HTML programming whiz.

- **Eudora 5.0.1:** An excellent trial version of an electronic-mail program that lets you send and receive e-mail messages over the Internet.

- **GraphicConverter 4.0.1:** A shareware graphics program you can use to view virtually any image you're likely to encounter on the Web. It also lets you convert images from one file format to another, which is useful if you want to make your own Web pages.

- **Interarchy 4.0:** A shareware version of a File Transfer Protocol, or FTP, program you can use to copy files between your Macintosh and a computer on the Internet.

- **InterNews 2.02:** A shareware newsgroup reader (or newsreader) program that lets you participate in thousands of online discussions over the Internet.

- **Ircle 3.0.4:** A shareware Internet Relay Chat, or IRC, program that lets you interact with a group of people on the Internet via your keyboard.

- **Microsoft Internet Explorer 5.0:** The Web browser from Microsoft, as well as related Internet utility programs.

- **NCSA Telnet 2.6:** A freeware program that lets you log on to other computers at a terminal via a slightly old-fashioned method called telnet.

- **Netscape Communicator 4.7:** The Web browser from Netscape, along with related programs for mail, news, and Web page editing.

- **StuffIt Expander 5.5 and DropStuff 6 with Expander Enhancer:** Invaluable decompression utilities you can use to make compressed files useable again.

A few words about shareware: Shareware programs are available to you for an evaluation period (typically, anywhere from 30 to 90 days). If you decide that you like a shareware program and want to keep using it, you're expected to send a registration fee to its author or publisher, which entitles you to technical support and notifications about new versions. (It also makes you feel good.)

Because most shareware operates on an honour system, the programs continue working even if you don't register them. It's a good idea, however, to support the shareware concept, and to encourage the continued production of quality, low-cost software, by sending in your payment for the programs you use.

If you don't know the letter of your PC's CD-ROM drive: Most PCs assign the letter D to a CD-ROM drive. Here's how to find out which letter your CD-ROM drive uses:

- ✔ If you use Windows, double-click the My Computer icon on your desktop. A window appears that lists all your drives, including your CD-ROM drive (which is usually represented by a shiny disk icon), and shows you the letter of each drive. When you're done examining the My Computer display, exit by clicking the window's Close button in its upper-right corner or choosing File⇨Close from its menu.

- ✔ If you use a Macintosh, you don't have to worry about it; simply double-click the icon on your desktop that looks like a CD and is named Internet For Dummies.

System Requirements

Make sure that your computer meets the minimum system requirements listed below. If your setup doesn't match up to most of these requirements, you may have problems using the contents of the CD.

- ✔ A PC with a Pentium or faster processor, or a Mac OS computer with a 68040 or faster processor. Netscape Communicator 4.7 and Internet Explorer for the Mac require a PowerPC.

- ✔ Microsoft Windows 95 or later, or Mac OS system software 8.0 or later. Netscape Communicator 4.7 for the Mac requires Mac OS System 7.6.1.

- ✔ At least 16MB (32MB recommended) of total RAM installed on your computer if it's running Windows or a Mac. (Netscape Communicator 4.7 for the Mac requires 24 MB.)

- ✔ At least 130MB of free hard drive space to install all the software from this CD. (You need less space if you don't install every program.)

> ✔ A CD-ROM drive, double-speed (2X) or faster.
>
> ✔ A monitor capable of displaying at least 256 colours or greyscale.
>
> ✔ A modem with a speed of at least 14,400 bps, but preferably 33,000 or 56,000 bps; or a cable modem, ISDN modem, or DSL modem.

If you need more information on the basics, check out *PCs For Dummies,* 7th Edition, by Dan Gookin; *The iMac for Dummies,* by David Pogue; *Macs For Dummies,* 6th Edition, by David Pogue; *Windows 95 For Dummies,* 2nd Edition, by Andy Rathbone; *Windows 98 For Dummies,* by Andy Rathbone (all published by IDG Books Worldwide, Inc.).

Installing the Programs from Microsoft Windows

If you are using a PC running any flavour of Microsoft Windows, follow these steps to install any program from *The Internet For Canadians For Dummies,* 2nd Edition Starter Kit CD-ROM:

1. **Insert the CD-ROM into your CD-ROM drive. Be careful to touch only the edges of the CD-ROM.**

   If your CD-ROM drive requires a caddy (a protective plastic holder), insert the CD-ROM into an empty caddy and then place the caddy into your drive; otherwise, simply insert the CD-ROM directly into the holder provided by your drive. In either case, be sure to insert the CD-ROM with its printed side up.

2. **If you use Windows, click the Start button (located in the bottom-left corner of your screen) and choose the Run option.**

3. **In the Run dialog box that appears, type** d:\start.htm **(the letter** d, **a colon (:), a backslash (\), and the word** start**). If your CD-ROM drive isn't drive D, type the letter appropriate for your drive rather than** d.

   If you're not sure which letter to type, see the paragraphs that begin "If you don't know the letter of your PC's CD-ROM drive," earlier in this appendix.

4. **Press Enter or click OK.**

   In a few moments, you see a Licence Agreement.

5. **Read the CDG Books Canada, Inc., agreement, to see if you can abide by its terms. When you're ready, click the Agree button. (After you click Agree, you'll never be bothered by the Licence Agreement again, but if you don't click Agree, you can't use the Installer program, although you can use the individual programs.)**

After you click Agree, an opening screen appears.

6. **Admire the attractive screen and then click anywhere to continue.**

A menu displays two software categories: Windows Programs, for Windows-compatible programs; and Macintosh Programs, for Mac-compatible programs. A submenu in each displays three more software categories: Connecting, for programs that get you connected to the Net; Communicating, for programs that let you interact on the Net; and Working Offline, for programs that help you deal with files you've downloaded from the Net. This menu is the Installer's *main menu* (so named because all your other selections stem from this initial menu).

7. **Click a program in which you're interested.**

A description of the program appears. Notice that in addition to an Install button, the screen displays buttons labeled Back (go back one level), Main (return to the Main Menu), Help, and Quit.

8. **If you want to copy the program to your hard disk, double click the hotlinks (name or bullet). (Otherwise, skip to Step 11.)**

After you click Install, the installation program runs for the program you selected.

9. **Follow the prompts that appear on-screen to complete the installation of the program.**

Although some installations of a more complicated nature have to restart your computer, don't worry. If this happens, the program's installation screen might come back, or the program may simply be ready to run. Look for it on your Start menu or in a Program Group. If you want to install more software, start the CD installer program up again, the way you did in Step 2, and pick up where you left off.

10. **Click the Go Back button to return to previous menus and explore the other contents of the CD-ROM.**

Because the Go Back button is available on every screen (except the first one), you can always use it to retrace your steps to the main menu.

11. **When you're done examining all the options you're interested in and installing all the programs you want, click the Exit button.**

The Installer program closes. You can now start using the new software you've installed on your hard disk.

To run the Installer program again: If you've exited the Installer program and then want to run it again while *The Internet For Canadians For Dummies,* 2nd Edition Starter Kit, CD-ROM is still in your drive, simply return to Step 2 of the preceding list of steps.

To examine *The Internet For Canadians For Dummies,* **2nd Edition Starter Kit CD-ROM's contents:** You can use the *Internet For Canadians For Dummies* Installer program to install all the software on the CD-ROM. If you're simply curious about the CD-ROM, however, you can examine its contents after you exit the Installer. If you're using Windows, open a Windows Explorer window (as opposed to a My Computer window) and double-click the CD-ROM's icon. If you're using a Macintosh, double-click the Internet FC folder that looks like a CD on your desktop.

Installing the Programs from a Macintosh

To install the items from the CD to your Mac hard drive, follow these steps:

1. **Insert the CD into your computer's CD-ROM drive.**

   In a moment, an icon representing the CD you just inserted appears on your Mac desktop. Chances are, the icon looks like a CD-ROM.

2. **Double-click the CD icon to show the CD's contents.**

3. **Double-click the Start.htm icon.**

4. **Read the CDG Books Canada, Inc., agreement, to see if you can abide by its terms. When you're ready, click the Agree button. (After you click Agree, you'll never be bothered by the Licence Agreement again, but if you don't click Agree, you can't use the Installer program, although you can use the individual programs.)**

   After you click Agree, an opening screen appears.

5. **Admire the attractive screen and then click anywhere to continue.**

   A menu displays two software categories: Windows Programs, for Windows-compatible programs; and Macintosh Programs, for Mac-compatible programs. A submenu in each displays three more software categories: Connecting, for programs that get you connected to the Net; Communicating, for programs that let you interact on the Net; and Working Offline, for programs that help you deal with files you've downloaded from the Net. This menu is the Installer's *main menu* (so named because all your other selections stem from this initial menu).

6. **Click a program in which you're interested.**

   A description of the program appears. Notice that in addition to an Install button, the screen displays buttons labeled Back (go back one level), Main (return to the Main Menu), Help, and Quit.

7. **If you want to copy the program to your hard disk, click the Install button. (Otherwise, skip to Step 10.)**

   After you click Install, the installation program runs for the program you selected.

8. **Follow the prompts that appear on-screen to complete the installation of the program.**

   Although some installations of a more complicated nature have to restart your computer, don't worry. If this happens, the program's installation screen might come back, or the program may simply be ready to run. Look for it on your Start menu or in a Program Group. If you want to install more software, start the CD installer program up again, the way you did in Step 2, and pick up where you left off.

9. **Click the Go Back button to return to previous menus and explore the other contents of the CD-ROM.**

   Because the Go Back button is available on every screen (except the first one), you can always use it to retrace your steps to the main menu.

10. **When you're done examining all the options you're interested in and installing all the programs you want, click the Exit button.**

    The Installer program closes. You can now start using the new software you've installed on your hard disk.

To run the Installer program again: If you've exited the Installer program and then want to run it again while *The Internet For Canadians For Dummies,* 2nd Edition Starter Kit, CD-ROM is still in your drive, simply return to Step 2 of the preceding list of steps.

To examine *The Internet For Canadians For Dummies,* 2nd Edition Starter Kit CD-ROM's contents: You can use the *Internet For Canadians For Dummies* Installer program to install all the software on the CD-ROM. If you're simply curious about the CD-ROM, however, you can examine its contents after you exit the Installer. If you're using Windows, open a Windows Explorer window (as opposed to a My Computer window) and double-click the CD-ROM's icon. If you're using a Macintosh, double-click the Internet FC folder that looks like a CD on your desktop.

Windows Programs

Here's a run-down of the Windows-compatible programs on the CD-ROM:

Adobe Acrobat Reader

Acrobat Reader 4.0, from Adobe Systems, is a free program that lets you view and print Portable Document Format, or PDF, files. Many programs that you find on the Internet for storing documentation use the PDF format, because it supports the use of such stylish elements as assorted fonts and colourful graphics (as opposed to plain text, or ASCII, which doesn't allow for any special effects in a document).

To install Acrobat Reader, follow Steps 1 through 6 in the section "Installing the Programs from Microsoft Windows," near the beginning of this Appendix. When you see the main menu, click the Working Offline category, click the Acrobat Reader option, click the Install button appropriate for your version of Windows, and follow the prompts that appear on-screen to complete the installation.

You can now run Acrobat Reader at any time by clicking the Start button, choose Programs and then Adobe Acrobat, and then click the Acrobat Reader icon.

To find out more about using Acrobat Reader, choose Reader Online Guide from the Help menu. You can also get more information by visiting the Adobe Systems Web site at www.adobe.com.

AOL Canada

AOL Canada is a commercial Internet Service Provider (ISP) that has local telephone access from most areas of Canada. The software provided by AOL Canada on the CD-ROM (Version 6.0 for Windows) includes an easy-to-use interface to the Internet programs you will want to use, as well as a large selection of the Internet client programs.

Before you sign up for an account with AOL Canada, check whether it's accessible from your location as a local telephone call. If you have access to the Web, you can check the AOL Canada Web site, at www.aol.ca or call 1-888-AOL-HELP to speak to a customer service representative. While you're on the phone with AOL Canada, ask about local phone numbers and check to see whether its pricing has changed.

Some of the programs on the CD-ROM can also be found in the AOL software. In most cases, the ones on the CD-ROM are more recent versions, so you may want to install them rather than the versions from AOL Canada.

To install the AOL Canada programs, follow Steps 1 through 6 in the section "Installing the Programs from Microsoft Windows" near the beginning of this Appendix. On the main menu, choose the Connecting category and then the

AOL option, click the Install button appropriate for your version of Windows, and follow the prompts that appear on-screen to complete the installation.

The installation program asks whether you want to make a New or Custom installation. A New installation installs all the programs in the preceding list; a Custom installation enables you to pick the ones you want. The installation program prompts you for all the information necessary to open an account with AOL Canada, including a credit card number. The program checks your modem, dials a toll-free or local number to register you, and returns with your password and other groovy information.

The AOL Canada installation reboots your computer. Make sure that you're not running any other applications while you're installing it.

To run the AOL Canada program in Windows 95 or Windows 98, press the Start button, then choose Programs and then AOL Canada.

Notice: While AOL Canada 6.0 for Windows or AOL Canada 4.0 for the Macintosh should work for most users, in the event that you are unable to install either of these, please call AOL Canada Member Services at 1-888-AOL-HELP (1-888-265-4357) or 1-506-853-3801 to request a new CD-ROM that contains other versions of the software, which should be compatible with your system configuration.

Eudora

Eudora 5.0.2, from QualComm, Inc., is a trial version of a powerful electronic-mail program. If you have an Internet e-mail account, you can use Eudora to send e-mail to and receive e-mail from any of the tens of millions of other people around the world who are connected to the Net. In addition to text messages, Eudora lets you attach files to e-mail, so you can use it to transmit electronic pictures, sound clips, or any other kind of data stored in files. To install Eudora, follow Steps 1 through 6 in the section "Installing the Programs from Microsoft Windows," near the beginning of this Appendix. When you see the main menu, choose the Communicating category and then the Eudora option, click the Install button, and follow the prompts that appear on-screen to complete the installation of the version of Eudora appropriate for your version of Windows.

To run the program, click the Start button, choose Programs, and click the Eudora icon.

For information about how to use Eudora see Chapters 11 and 12. You can also find out more about Eudora by choosing options from its Help menu and by visiting its Web site at www.eudora.com.

Free Agent

Free Agent 1.21, from Forté, Inc., is a freeware Windows program that lets you read and participate in ongoing group discussions that take place on the Internet via Usenet newsgroups. Tens of thousands of newsgroups exist, devoted to virtually every topic under the sun, ranging from knitting to high finance, from dating to decoding DNA, and Free Agent is one of the best programs available for accessing them. Among the great features of Free Agent is its capability to let you read newsgroup articles offline, which could conceivably save you Internet connection charges and phone charges.

To install Free Agent, follow Steps 1 through 6 in the section "Installing the Programs from Microsoft Windows," near the beginning of this Appendix. When you see the main menu, choose the Communicating category and then the Free Agent option, click the Install button appropriate for your version of Windows, and follow the prompts that appear on-screen to complete the installation.

To run Free Agent, click the Start button, choose Programs, and click the Agent icon.

You can also find out more about Free Agent by choosing Contents from its Help menu to launch its online manual and by visiting the Free Agent Web site at www.forteinc.com/agent/freagent.htm.

HotDog Professional

HotDog Professional 6.0, from Sausage Software, is a trial version of a powerful but easy-to-use Windows program that helps you create Web pages.

To install HotDog, follow Steps 1 through 6 in the section "Installing the Programs from Microsoft Windows," near the beginning of this Appendix. When you see the main menu, choose the Communicating category and then the HotDog Professional option, click the Install button appropriate for your version of Windows, and follow the prompts that appear on-screen to complete the installation.

To run the program, click the Start button, click Programs, click HotDog Professional, and then click the HotDog icon.

When the program starts, it gives you several ways to get help, including through tutorials. For more information about HotDog, visit the program's witty Web site at www.sausagetools.com.

Microsoft Internet Explorer

Internet Explorer 5.5, from Microsoft, is one of the best-known Web browsers available. Chapters 6 and 7 describe in some detail how to use it. In addition to the browser, this software includes other Internet tools from Microsoft: Outlook Express 5, a mail and news reading program; Windows Media Player, a program that can display or play many types of audio and video files; and NetMeeting 3, a video conferencing program.

If you have Windows 95 or a version of Windows 98 that came with Internet Explorer 4.0, here's what you do to install Internet Explorer 5.5:

Follow Steps 1 through 6 in the section "Installing the Programs from Microsoft Windows," near the beginning of this Appendix. When you see the main menu, choose the Communicating category and then the Internet Explorer option, click the Install button, and follow the prompts that appear on-screen to complete the installation.

You are given a choice of installing only the browser, or the browser and other components. Choose whichever option you think is best (and for which you have room on your disk). If you choose not to install some parts at this time, you can go back later and get the pieces you missed.

To run Internet Explorer, click the Start button, choose Programs and then Internet Explorer, and then click the Internet Explorer icon or double-click the Internet Explorer icon on the desktop.

You can find information about Internet Explorer and other Microsoft Internet programs at its Web site at `www.microsoft/windows/ie/default.htm`.

mIRC

mIRC 5.82 is a shareware Windows program from its author, Khaled Mardam-Bey. mIRC lets you participate in Internet Relay Chat (IRC), a worldwide system that enables you to receive messages over the Internet within seconds of when other people type them, and vice versa. Chapter 15 has detailed instructions for using IRC.

To install mIRC, follow Steps 1 through 6 in the section "Installing the Programs from Microsoft Windows," near the beginning of this Appendix. When you see the main menu, choose the Communicating category and then the mIRC option, click the Install button appropriate for your version of Windows, and follow the prompts that appear on-screen to complete the installation.

To run mIRC, click the Start button, choose Programs, click mIRC, then click the mIRC582 icon.

For more information about mIRC, click its Introduction button in the first window that appears. You can get additional information after you're past the opening window by pressing F1, clicking a Help button that looks like a life preserver, or choosing the Contents option from the Help menu. The mIRC home page is a good source of information, too; you can reach it at www.mirc.co.uk.

Netscape Communicator

Netscape Communicator, from Netscape Communications, is one of the best-known Web browsers available. Chapters 6 and 7 describe in detail how to use this powerful tool. *The Internet For Canadians For Dummies,* 2nd Edition Starter Kit CD-ROM installs Netscape Communicator 4.7. You also have the option of installing RealPlayer G2 (to play streaming audio and video files) and Winamp (to play MPEG3 files).

To install Netscape Communicator, follow Steps 1 through 6 in the section "Installing the Programs from Microsoft Windows," near the beginning of this Appendix. When you see the main menu, choose the Communicating category and then the Netscape Communicator option, click the Install button, and follow the prompts that appear on-screen to complete the installation.

To run Netscape Navigator, click the Start button, choose Programs and then Netscape Communicator, and choose Netscape Navigator. You can find information about Netscape Navigator from its Help menu or at its Web site at home.netscape.com.

Paint Shop Pro

Paint Shop Pro, from JASC, Inc., is an evaluation version of a multipurpose graphics tool for Windows. This superb shareware program lets you view images in virtually any graphics format you're likely to encounter on the Internet. In addition, it lets you edit and crop images, convert images from one file format to another, and even create pictures from scratch, which all can be useful in helping you to create your own World Wide Web pages.

To install Paint Shop Pro, follow Steps 1 through 6 in the section "Installing the Programs from Microsoft Windows," near the beginning of this Appendix. When you see the main menu, choose the Working Offline category and then the Paint Shop Pro option, click the Install button appropriate for your version of Windows, and follow the prompts that appear on-screen to complete the installation.

To run Paint Shop Pro, click the Start button, choose Programs and then Paint Shop Pro, and click the Paint Shop Pro icon.

For more information about Paint Shop Pro, click the floating question mark icon on the program's toolbar or choose Help Topics from its Help menu. You can also visit JASC's Web site at www.jasc.com.

WinZip

WinZip 8.0, from Nico Mak Computing, is a shareware version of an invaluable file compression and decompression Windows shareware utility. Many files you find on the Internet are *compressed,* or shrunken in size via special programming tricks, both to save storage space and to cut down on the amount of time required for their downloading. You may also occasionally receive compressed files (ZIP files) as e-mail attachments. If you have a compressed file on your hard disk, you can use WinZip to decompress it and make it useable again.

To install WinZip, follow Steps 1 through 6 in the section "Installing the Programs from Microsoft Windows," near the beginning of this Appendix. When you see the main menu, choose the Working Offline category and then the WinZip option, click the Install button appropriate for your version of Windows, and follow the prompts that appear on-screen to complete the installation.

To run WinZip, click the Start button, choose Programs and then WinZip, and click the WinZip icon.

The first time you launch WinZip, it displays a bunch of messages and configuration questions. When you're asked whether you want the program to operate in WinZip Wizard or WinZip Classic mode, we recommend that you choose WinZip Classic, which we consider easier to use. After you've answered all the questions, WinZip is ready to go.

For information about using WinZip, see Chapters 16 and 20 or choose the Contents option from the program's Help menu or double-click the program's Online Manual icon in its folder. To find out even more about WinZip, visit the program's Web site at www.winzip.com.

WS_FTP

WS_FTP Pro, from Ipswitch, Inc., is an evaluation version (for noncommercial use) of a Windows File Transfer Protocol (FTP) program you can use to copy files between your PC and a computer on the Net. FTP programs were more useful before the World Wide Web took hold and made finding and downloading files a snap. FTP programs are still handy, however, for activities not supported by the Web, such as uploading your own files and Web pages.

To install WS_FTP, follow Steps 1 through 6 in the section "Installing the Programs from Microsoft Windows," near the beginning of this Appendix. When you see the main menu, choose the Communicating category and then the WS_FTP option, click the Install button appropriate for your version of Windows, and follow the prompts that appear on-screen to complete the installation.

To run the program, click the Start button, choose Programs and then WS_FTP, and click WS_FTP95.

For information about using WS_FTP, see Chapter 16. You can also find out more by clicking the Help button from the program's main window or Session Profile dialog box or by double-clicking the WS_FTP Help icon from the WS_FTP folder. You can also visit the WS_FTP Web site at www.ipswitch.com.

Macintosh Programs

Here are the programs you get if you've got a Macintosh:

Adobe Acrobat Reader

Acrobat Reader 4.0, from Adobe Systems, is a free program that lets you view and print Portable Document Format, or PDF, files. Many programs you find on the Internet for storing documentation use the PDF format, because it supports the use of such stylish elements as assorted fonts and colourful graphics (as opposed to plain text, or ASCII, which doesn't allow for any special effects in a document).

To install Acrobat Reader, follow the steps in the section "Installing the Programs from a Macintosh," near the beginning of this Appendix. When you see the main window, choose the Working Offline folder and then the Acrobat Reader folder. Open the Reader folder first and then double-click the Reader 4.0 Installer icon. Follow the prompts that appear on-screen to complete the installation. If you would like to add the capability to search for specific words or phrases in PDF documents to your version of Acrobat Reader, open the Search folder and double-click the Search Installer icon.

You can now run Acrobat Reader at any time by clicking the Start button, choose Programs and then Adobe Acrobat, and then click the Acrobat Reader icon.

To find out more about using Acrobat Reader, view the Acrobat.pdf file that was installed in the same folder as the program. You can also get more information by visiting the Adobe Systems Web site at www.adobe.com.

AOL Canada

AOL Canada is a commercial Internet Service Provider (ISP) that has local telephone access from most areas of Canada. The software provided by AOL Canada on the CD-ROM (Version 4.0 the Mac) includes an easy-to-use interface to the Internet programs you will want to use, as well as a large selection of the Internet client programs.

Before you sign up for an account with AOL Canada, check whether it's accessible from your location as a local telephone call. If you have access to the Web, you can check the AOL Canada Web site, at www.aol.ca, or call 1-888-AOL-HELP to speak to a customer service representative. While you're on the phone with AOL Canada, ask about local phone numbers, and check to see whether its pricing has changed.

Some of the programs on the CD-ROM can also be found in the AOL software. In most cases, the ones on the CD-ROM are more recent versions, so you may want to install them rather than the versions from AOL Canada.

To install the AOL Canada components, follow the steps in the section "Installing the Programs from a Macintosh," near the beginning of this Appendix. When you see the main window, open the Connecting folder and then the AOL folder. Double-click the AOL Install.1 icon and follow the prompts that appear on-screen to complete the installation.

The installation program asks whether you want to make a New or Custom installation. A New installation installs all the programs in the preceding list; a Custom installation enables you to pick the ones you want. The installation program prompts you for all the information necessary to open an account with AOL Canada, including a credit card number. The program checks your modem, dials a toll-free or local number to register you, and returns with your password and other groovy information.

The AOL Canada installation reboots your computer. Make sure that you're not running any other applications while you're installing it.

Notice: While AOL Canada 6.0 for Windows or AOL Canada 4.0 for the Macintosh should work for most users, in the event that you are unable to install either of these, please call AOL Canada Member Services at 1-888-AOL-HELP (1-888-265-4357) or 1-506-853-3801 to request a new CD-ROM that contains other versions of the software, which should be compatible with your system configuration.

BBEdit Lite

BBEdit Lite 4.6, from Bare Bones Software, Inc., is a Macintosh lite version of a program that helps you create Web pages. Chapter 10 tells you all about how to do that. We also include a demo of BBEdit 5.1, the not-free version of BBEdit Lite, for you to check out.

To install BBEdit Lite, follow the steps in the section "Installing the Programs from a Macintosh," near the beginning of this Appendix. When you see the main window, choose the Communicating folder. Click and drag the BBEdit Lite 4.6 folder and drop it on your hard drive icon. You can run the program by double-clicking the BBEdit Lite 4.6 icon in its folder.

If you'd like to install the BBEdit 6.0 Demo, open the Connecting folder and double-click the Install BBEdit Demo icon. Follow the prompts that appear on-screen to complete the installation. After the installation is finished, you can run the program by double-clicking the BBEdit icon in its folder. With this demo, you will not be able to save anything you create.

For more information about BBEdit Lite, visit the program's Web site at `www.barebones.com/free/free.html`.

Eudora

Eudora 5.0.1, from QualComm, Inc., is a trial version of a powerful electronic-mail program. If you have an Internet e-mail account, you can use Eudora to send e-mail to and receive e-mail from any of the tens of millions of other people around the world who are connected to the Net. In addition to text messages, Eudora lets you attach files to e-mail, so you can use it to transmit electronic pictures, sound clips, or any other kind of data stored in files.

To install Eudora, follow the steps in the section "Installing the Programs from a Macintosh," near the beginning of this Appendix. When you see the main window, choose the Communicating folder. Double-click the Eudora Installer icon and follow the prompts that appear on-screen to complete the installation. After the installation is finished, you can run the program by double-clicking the Eudora icon in its folder.

For information about how to use Eudora see Chapters 11 and 12. You can also find out more about Eudora by choosing options from its Help menu and by visiting its Web site at `www.eudora.com`.

GraphicConverter

GraphicConverter 4.0.1, by shareware author Thorsten Lemke, is a Macintosh program that lets you view images in virtually any graphics format you're likely to encounter on the Internet. It lets you convert the most common Windows, DOS, Amiga, and Atari computer images to Macintosh formats and vice versa; and it provides a rich set of image-editing options. The latter two features are especially useful if you're interested in creating your own Web pages.

To install GraphicConverter, follow the steps in the section "Installing the Programs from a Macintosh," near the beginning of this Appendix. When you see the main window, choose the Working Offline folder and then double-click the GraphicConverter Installer icon. Follow the prompts that appear on-screen to complete the installation. After the installation is finished, you can run GraphicConverter by double-clicking the GraphicConverter icon in the GraphicConverter 4.0.1 folder.

For more information about GraphicConverter, double-click the Documentation icon in the program's folder, or visit the Web site at www.lemkesoft.de.

Interarchy

Formerly called Anarchie, Interachy 4.0, from Stairways Software, is a Macintosh shareware File Transfer Protocol (FTP) program you can use to find files on the Net and to copy files between your Mac and a computer on the Net. FTP programs were more useful before the World Wide Web took hold and made finding and downloading files a snap. FTP programs are still handy, however, for activities not supported by the Web, such as uploading your own files and Web pages.

To install Interarchy, follow the steps in the section "Installing the Programs from a Macintosh," near the beginning of this Appendix. When you see the main window, choose the Communicating folder and then double-click the Interarchy Installer icon. Follow the prompts that appear on-screen to complete the installation. After the installation is finished, you can run the program by double-clicking the Interarchy icon in its folder.

To use Interarchy to find a file on the Internet, first choose File from the menu, and then choose the Search Internet option. Type part of the name of the file you want and then click the Find It button. If a matching list of files is displayed, double-click the one you're after; the file is then downloaded to your hard disk. After the file is saved, if it turns out that it's compressed, use StuffIt Expander 5.5 (which is also on the CD-ROM) to decompress the file and make it useable. More on Stuffit Expander a little later in this section.

For more information about downloading and uploading files, see Chapter 16; for more information about Interarchy, visit its Web site at www.share.com/peterlewis/anarchie.

InterNews

InterNews 2.02, from Moonrise Software, is a shareware Macintosh program that lets you read and participate in ongoing group discussions that take place over the Internet via Usenet newsgroups. Tens of thousands of newsgroups exist, devoted to virtually every topic under the sun, ranging from knitting to high finance, from dating to decoding DNA. InterNews is one of the best Mac programs available for accessing them. Among this program's charms is that it's trim and quick — it doesn't require a great deal of memory or a superfast Mac to operate effectively. In addition, because it's highly customizable, you can tailor it to your tastes.

To install InterNews, follow the steps in the section "Installing the Programs from a Macintosh," near the beginning of this Appendix. When you see the main window, open the Communicating folder and then double-click the InterNews 2.02 FAT.sea icon. Follow the prompts that appear on-screen to complete the installation. To run InterNews, double-click the program's icon in its folder.

For more information about InterNews, visit the program's Web site at www.dartmouth.edu/~moonrise.

Ircle

Ircle 3.0.4 is a Macintosh shareware program from MacResponse that lets you participate in Internet Relay Chat (IRC), a worldwide system that enables you to receive messages over the Internet within seconds of when other people type them and vice versa. For a detailed discussion of IRC and chatting, read Chapter 15.

To install Ircle, follow the steps in the section "Installing the Programs from a Macintosh," near the beginning of this Appendix. When you see the main window, open the Communicating folder and click and drag the Ircle US folder to your hard drive icon. To run Ircle, double-click its icon.

For more information about Ircle, choose the Help option from the program's Apple menu, and visit the Ircle Web site at www.ircle.com.

Microsoft Internet Explorer

Internet Explorer, from Microsoft, is one of the best-known Web browsers available. Chapters 6 and 7 describe in some detail how to use it. In addition to the browser (version 5.0), this package includes other Internet tools from Microsoft: Outlook Express, a mail and news reading program; Windows Media Player, a program that can display or play many types of audio and video files; and NetMeeting, a video conferencing program.

To install Internet Explorer, follow the steps in the section "Installing the Programs from a Macintosh," near the beginning of this Appendix. When you see the main window, open the Communicating folder and then the Internet Explorer folder. Double-click the Installer icon that is correct for your computer and follow the prompts that appear on-screen to complete the installation.

To run Internet Explorer, click its icon on your desktop.

You can find information about Internet Explorer and other Microsoft Internet programs at its Web site at www.microsoft.com/mac/products/ie.

NCSA Telnet

NCSA Telnet 2.6, from NCSA Software Development, is a freeware telnet program for the Macintosh that lets you connect to other computers over the Internet when more modern routes (such as the World Wide Web) aren't feasible or available.

Telnet lets you log on to another computer as though your PC were a terminal attached to that computer. In the old days (like, way back in 1992), telnet was the way to get lots of information; for example, libraries let you telnet into their card catalogues.

Although Telnet is more of a techie tool now, it still has its uses. For example, you may be able to telnet into your PPP and SLIP account (to get access to a UNIX shell) to periodically change your password. If you're on the road and you want to check your mail, you can telnet in via a UNIX shell and run Pine or elm or mail (UNIX mail programs) to read your e-mail without downloading it, which is handy if your disk space is limited or you're on someone else's computer at the time. Also, many people participating in multi-user games (such as MUDs and MOOs) connect via telnet.

To install NCSA Telnet, follow the steps in the section "Installing the Programs from a Macintosh," near the beginning of this Appendix. When you see the main window, open the Communicating folder and click and drag the Telnet-2.6 folder to your hard drive icon.

To run the program, make sure that your modem is turned on and your phone line is hooked in, and double-click the NCSA Telnet icon in the Telnet folder.

For more information about NCSA Telnet, double-click the icon MacTelnet.pdf, which is a PDF document that must be viewed with the Adobe Acrobat Reader program (see the "Acrobat Reader" section). You can also visit the program's site at `www.ncsa.uiuc.edu/SDG/Software/MacTelnet/Docs/index.html`.

Netscape Communicator

Netscape Communicator 4.7, from Netscape Communications, is one of the best-known Web browsers available. Chapters 6 and 7 describe in detail how to use this powerful tool.

To install Netscape Communicator, follow the steps in the section "Installing the Programs from a Macintosh," near the beginning of this Appendix. When you see the main window, open the Communicating folder and then the Communicator 4.7 Complete folder. Double-click the Start Here icon and then follow the prompts that appear on-screen to complete the installation.

To run Netscape Communicator, double-click the Netscape icon in its folder. You can find information about Netscape Communicator from its Help menu or at its Web site at `home.netscape.com`.

StuffIt Expander and DropStuff

StuffIt Expander 5.5, from Aladdin Systems, Inc., is an invaluable freeware file-decompression utility for the Macintosh. Many files you find on the Internet are *compressed,* or shrunken in size via special programming tricks, both to save storage space and to cut down on the amount of time they require to be downloaded. You may also occasionally receive compressed files as e-mail attachments. After you have a compressed file on your hard disk, you should use StuffIt Expander to decompress it and make it useable again.

DropStuff 6 with Expander Enhancer is a complementary product that enables StuffIt Expander to handle a wider variety of compression formats and to decompress files more quickly on Power Macintosh computers.

To install these programs, follow the steps in the section "Installing the Programs from a Macintosh," near the beginning of this Appendix. When you see the main window, open the Working Offline folder and double-click the StuffIt Expander 5.5 Installer icon. Follow the prompts that appear on-screen to complete the installation. After you have installed StuffIt Expander, go back to the Working Offline folder and double-click the Install DropStuff 6 icon, and once again, follow the prompts to complete the installation.

You typically run StuffIt Expander indirectly because it activates automatically when you download a compressed file or double-click a compressed file. When StuffIt has finished its work, you can toss the compressed file in the trash can and use the normal files that have been generated.

 For more information about decompressing files, see Chapters 12 and 18. For more information about StuffIt Expander and DropStuff, visit the Web site of these two programs, at `www.aladdinsys.com`.

Supporting the Shareware Concept

A final note: Although some of the programs on *The Internet For Canadians For Dummies,* 2nd Edition Starter Kit are free, many of them are shareware. As we mention near the beginning of this Appendix, shareware programs are available to you for an evaluation period, after which you're expected to either stop using them or pay for them. Sending a registration fee to a shareware publisher typically entitles you to technical support and notifications about new versions — and it also makes you feel good. Most shareware operates on an honour system, and it's just plain sensible to support the shareware concept and encourage the continued production of quality, low-cost software by sending in your payment for the programs you use. You can typically get information about where to send your payment for a shareware program by checking its online help system or visiting its Web site.

If You've Got Problems (of the CD Kind)

We tried our best to compile programs that work on most computers with the minimum system requirements. Alas, your computer may differ, and some programs may not work properly for some reason.

The two likeliest problems are that you don't have enough memory (RAM) for the programs you want to use, or you have other programs running that are affecting the installation or running of a program. If you get error messages such as `Not enough memory` or `Setup cannot continue`, try one or more of these methods and then attempt again to use the software:

- **Turn off any antivirus software that you have on your computer.** Installers sometimes mimic virus activity and may make your computer incorrectly believe that a virus is infecting it.

- **Close all running programs.** The more programs you're running, the less memory is available to other programs. Installers also typically update files and programs; if you keep other programs running, the installation may not work properly.

✓ **In Windows, close the CD interface and run demos or installations directly from Windows Explorer.** The interface itself can tie up system memory or even conflict with certain kinds of interactive demos. Use Windows Explorer to browse the files on the CD and launch installers or demos.

✓ **Add more RAM to your computer.** This is, admittedly, a somewhat expensive step. However, if you have a Windows 95/98 PC or a Mac OS computer with a PowerPC chip, adding more memory can really help the speed of your computer and enable more programs to run at the same time.

If you still have trouble installing the items from the CD, please call the IDG Books Worldwide Customer Service phone number: 800-762-2974.

Glossary

ActiveX A Microsoft standard for computer program building blocks, known as *objects*.

address Internet users encounter two important types of addresses: e-mail addresses (for sending e-mail to someone; e-mail addresses almost always contain an @) and Web page addresses (more properly called URLs).

ADSL (Asymmetric Digital Subscriber Line) A technology that lets you transmit data over phone lines faster in one direction (as much as 7 million bps) than in another. A bit expensive, but nice, if you can get it.

AltaVista A search engine used for finding things on the World Wide Web. Its URL is www.altavista.com.

anonymous FTP A way of using the FTP program to log on to another computer to copy files, even though you don't have an account on the other computer. When you log on, you type anonymous as the username and your e-mail address as the password.

AOL Canada A value-added online service that provides content and many features in addition to Internet access, including access to popular chat groups.

applet A small computer program written in the Java programming language. You can download applets by using a Web browser. Applets must obey special rules that make it difficult for the programs to do damage to your computer.

archive A single file containing a group of files that has been compressed for efficient storage. You have to use a program such as WinZip or StuffIt to get the original files back out.

ARPANET The original ancestor of the Internet, funded by the United States Department of Defense.

ASCII (American Standard Code for Information Interchange) The predominant character set encoding of present-day computers. It tells computers how to read alphabetic characters. The most recent standard uses 7 bits for each character and allows for the inclusion of lowercase letters.

attachment A computer file electronically "stapled" to an e-mail message and sent along with it.

backbone The high-speed communications links that connect Internet Service Providers and other large Internet sites.

bandwidth The capacity level of a fibre-optic, wireless, or other data network to carry digital information.

baud The number of electrical symbols per second that a modem sends down a phone line. Often used as a synonym for bps (bits per second); although this usage is incorrect, only 43 people on the entire planet know why or care. Named after J.M.E. Baudot, inventor of the teletype.

BCC *B*lind *c*arbon *c*opy. BCC addressees get a copy of your e-mail without other recipients knowing about it. See also *CC.*

beta A term used to describe a version of developed software that is still in a testing stage. Beta copies of software are often released to the public for free as a way of obtaining feedback on the software's effectiveness. This process is called *beta testing.*

binary file A file containing information that does not consist of text only. For example, a binary file may contain an archive, a picture, sounds, a spreadsheet, or a word-processing document that includes formatting codes in addition to text characters.

BinHex A file-encoding system popular among Macintosh users.

bit The smallest unit of measure for computer data. Bits can be *on* or *off* (symbolized by 1 or 0) and are used in various combinations to represent different types of information.

bitmap Little dots put together to make a black-and-white or colour picture.

bookmark The address of a Web page to which you may want to return. Netscape Navigator lets you maintain a list of bookmarks to make it easy to go back to your favorite Web pages.

bounce To return as undeliverable or redeliver to the appropriate address. If you mail a message to a bad address, it bounces back to your mailbox. If you get e-mail intended for someone else, you can bounce it to her.

bps (bits per second) A measure of how fast data is transmitted. Often used to describe modem speed.

browser A super-duper, all-singing, all-dancing program that lets you read information on the World Wide Web.

byte A group of eight bits, enough to represent a character. Computer memory is usually measured in bytes.

cache Pronounced "cash." A special high-speed storage mechanism. It can be either a reserved section of main memory or an independent high-speed storage device. Two types of caching are commonly used in personal computers: *memory caching* and *disk caching*. Both types serve to reduce the time it takes to retrieve frequently used computer instructions.

CC *C*arbon *c*opy. CC addressees get a copy of your e-mail, and other recipients are informed of it if they bother to read the message header. See also ***BCC.***

CCITT The old name for ITU-T, the committee that sets worldwide communication standards.

channel In IRC, a group of people chatting together. Called "rooms" by value-added providers who use "channel" to mean a major interest area you can get to easily, such as a TV channel. In Windows 98, a Web site to which you have subscribed.

chanop In IRC, the *chan*nel *op*erator is in charge of keeping order in a channel. The chanop can throw out unruly visitors. (We also wonder if visitors can throw out unruly chanops.)

chat To talk (or type) live to other network users from any and all parts of the world. To chat on the Internet, you use an Internet Relay Chat (IRC) program such as mIRC or Microsoft Chat.

client A computer that uses the services of another computer or server (such as Usenet, Gopher, FTP, or the Web). If you dial in to another system, your computer becomes a client of the system you dial in to. See also ***server.***

client/server model A division of labour between computers. Computers that provide a service other computers can use are known as *servers*. The users are *clients*. See also ***client, server.***

com When these letters appear as the last part of an address (in `net.gurus. com`, for example), it indicates that the host computer is run by a commercial organization, probably in the United States.

communications program A program you run on your personal computer that enables you to call up and communicate with other computers. This type of program makes your computer pretend to be a terminal (that's why it's also known as a *terminal program* or a *terminal emulator*).

cookie A small text file stored on your computer by a Web site you have visited, used to remind that site about you the next time you visit it.

country code The last part of a geographic address, which indicates the country in which the host computer is located, such as *us* for the United States. Country codes are always two letters.

cyber- A prefix meaning the use of the computers and networks that make up the Internet, as in *cyber*space or *cyber*cop.

DES (Data Encryption Standard) A United States government standard for encrypting unclassified data. Breakable at some expense, although a newer version, triple-DES, is probably safe.

Dial-Up Networking The built-in Internet communication program in Windows 95 and Windows 98.

digest A compilation of the messages that have been posted to a mailing list during the past few days.

directory A special kind of file used to organize other files, such as lists of Web sites, into a hierarchical structure. Directories contain bookkeeping information about files that are, figuratively speaking, beneath them. You can think of a directory as a folder or cabinet that contains files and other folders. In fact, many graphical user interfaces, such as Windows, use the term *folder* instead of *directory*. Related to ***index***.

domain Part of the official name of a computer on the Net, for example gurus.com. To register a domain name, go to www.internic.net.

domain name server (DNS) A computer on the Internet that translates between Internet domain names, such as xuxa.iecc.com, and Internet numerical addresses, such as 208.31.42.42. Sometimes just called a *name server*.

download To copy a file from a remote computer "down" to your computer.

dummies People who don't know everything but are smart enough to seek help. Used ironically.

edu When these letters appear as the last part of an address (in www.middlebury.edu, for example), it indicates that the host computer is run by an educational institution.

e-mail Electronic messages sent via the Internet.

emoticon A combination of special characters that portray an emotion, such as :-) or :-(. Although hundreds have been invented, only a few are in active use, and all are silly.

encryption A process of encoding (scrambling) sensitive or personal data into a secure, unreadable format for transmission. When the encrypted data arrives at its destination, it is decoded back into readable form.

Eudora A popular e-mail program that runs on the Macintosh and under Windows.

extranet An Internet technology used to connect a company with its customers and business partners.

FAQ (Frequently Asked Question(s)) A list that answers questions that come up often. Many mailing lists and Usenet newsgroups have FAQs that are posted regularly. To read the FAQs for all newsgroups, FTP to rtfm.mit.edu.

Favorites A list of files or Web pages you plan to use frequently. Internet Explorer lets you maintain a list of your favorite items to make it easy for you to see them again.

fax–to–e-mail An Internet-based document messaging service where users are provided with a local or toll-free fax number. Faxes sent to your number are forwarded to your e-mail address. The attached fax (usually in JBIG2 or JPEG format) can be printed and viewed with special viewer software. Outbound faxing (e-mail–to–fax) is also available, but is usually fee-based.

firewall A specially programmed computer that connects a local network to the Internet and, for security reasons, lets only certain kinds of messages in and out.

flame To post angry, inflammatory, or insulting messages. Don't do it!

flame war Far too much flaming between two or more individuals.

freeware Copyrighted software given away for free by the developer. Although it's available for free, the author retains the copyright, which means that you can't do anything with it that is not expressly allowed by the developer. Usually, the developer allows people to use the software, but not sell it.

FTP (File Transfer Protocol) A method of transferring files from one computer to another over the Net.

FTP client The client part of FTP server architecture. Typically, an FTP client is an application that runs on a personal computer or workstation and relies on a server to perform some operations. For example, an FTP client application lets you send (upload) and receive (download) FTP files, much the way an e-mail client lets you send and receive e-mail.

FTP server A computer on the Internet that stores files for transmission by FTP.

gateway A computer that connects one network with another, where the two networks use different protocols.

GIF (Graphics Interchange Format) A patented type of graphics file originally defined by CompuServe and now found all over the Net. Files in this format end in .gif and are called GIF files or just GIFs. Pronounced "jif" unless you prefer to say "gif."

giga- Prefix meaning one billion (1,000,000,000).

gov When these letters appear as the last part of an address (in cu.nih.gov, for example), it indicates that the host computer is run by a government body.

handle A user's nickname or screen name.

header The beginning of an e-mail message containing To and From addresses, subject, date, and other gobbledygook important to the programs that handle your mail.

home page The entry page, or main page, of a Web site. If you have a home page, it's the main page about you. A home page usually contains links to other Web pages.

host A computer on the Internet.

hostname The name of a computer on the Internet (chico.iecc.com, for example).

HTML (HyperText Markup Language) The language used to write pages for the World Wide Web. This language lets the text include codes that define fonts, layout, embedded graphics, and hypertext links. Don't worry; you don't have to know anything about it to use the World Wide Web. Web pages are stored in files that usually have the extension .htm or .html.

HTTP (HyperText Transport Protocol) The way in which World Wide Web pages are transferred over the Net.

HTTPS A variant of HTTP that encrypts messages for security.

hyperlink A digital element or bookmark in an electronic document that links to another place in the same document or to an entirely different document. Typically, you click on the hyperlink to follow the link. Hyperlinks are the most essential ingredient of all hypertext systems, including the World Wide Web.

hypermedia Like hypertext, but including all types of information, such as pictures, sound, and video, not just text. See also *hypertext*.

hypertext A system of writing and displaying text that enables the text to be linked in multiple ways, to be available at several levels of detail, and to contain links to related documents. The World Wide Web uses both hypertext and hypermedia.

ICQ "I Seek You," a popular paging and instant message system that lets users track friends who are online and exchange instant messages with them.

IETF (Internet Engineering Task Force) The group that develops new technical standards for the Internet.

index A digital bookmark that links files or Web sites in a *directory* and sub-directories. Acts in a similar way to a file number found on the side of a doctor's patient folder.

instant messaging systems Types of communications services that let you create a private chat room with another individual. Typically, the instant messaging system alerts you whenever somebody on your private buddy list is online. You can then initiate a chat session with that particular individual. There are several competing instant messaging systems. AOL's system is the most popular in terms of number of users. Since there's no common standard, anyone you want to send instant messages to must use the same instant messaging system that you use.

Internet All the computers that are connected together into an amazingly huge global network so that they can talk to each other. When you connect your puny little computer to your Internet Service Provider, your computer becomes part of that network.

Internet Explorer A Web browser vigorously promoted by Microsoft that comes in Windows, Mac, and (arguably) UNIX flavours.

Internet Relay Chat (IRC) A system that enables Internet folks to talk to each other in real time (rather than after a delay, as with e-mail messages).

Internet Society An organization dedicated to supporting the growth and evolution of the Internet. You can contact it at www.isoc.org.

InterNIC The Internet Network Information Center, a central repository of information about the Internet. To register a domain name, go to www.internic.net.

intranet A private version of the Internet that lets people within an organization exchange data by using popular Internet tools, such as browsers.

IRC client An application that runs on a computer and relies on a server to perform some operations. An IRC client application/program lets you engage in Internet chat.

IRC server A high-memory capacity and very fast central computer that handles a multitude of IRC users at virtually the same time. An IRC server handles Internet chat, whereas an FTP server handles file uploads and downloads.

ISDN (Integrated Services Digital Network) A faster, digital phone service that operates at speeds as high as 128 kilobits per second.

Java A computer language invented by Sun Microsystems. Because Java programs can run on many different kinds of computers, Java makes it easier to deliver application programs over the Internet.

JBIG2 A new-generation, black-and-white image file format. This highly compressed format is already embedded in many new fax machines and scanners, and reduces transmission and scanning times.

JPEG A type of still-image file found all over the Net. Files in this format end in .jpg or .jpeg and are called JPEG (pronounced "JAY-peg") files. Stands for Joint Photographic Experts Group.

JPEG2000 A next-generation colour still-image file set to replace its predecessor — JPEG. This high-quality format is more highly compressed and will reduce image download times.

Kbyte 1,024 bytes. Also written *KB* or just plain *K*. Usually used as a measure of a computer's memory or hard disk storage, or as a measure of file size.

kilo- Prefix meaning one thousand (1,000) or often, with computers, 1,024.

link A hypertext connection that can take you to another document or another part of the same document. On the World Wide Web, links appear as text or pictures that are highlighted. To follow a link, you click the highlighted material. See also *hypertext, WWW.*

Linux A freeware version of the UNIX operating system that runs on personal computers and is supported by a dedicated band of enthusiasts on the Internet.

ListProc Like LISTSERV, a program that handles mailing lists.

LISTSERV A family of programs that automatically manages mailing lists, distributing messages posted to the list, adding and deleting members, and so on, which spares the list owner the tedium of having to do it manually. The names of mailing lists maintained by LISTSERV often end with -L.

lurk To read a mailing list or join a chat group without posting any messages. Someone who lurks is a *lurker*. Lurking isn't great, but it's nowhere near as bad as flaming.

Lynx A character-based World Wide Web browser. No pictures, but it's fast.

MacBinary A file-encoding system that's popular among Macintosh users.

MacTCP TCP/IP for the Macintosh. You can't put your Mac on the Internet without either it or a newer product called Open Transport. Comes with System 8.

mail server A computer on the Internet that provides mail services for mail clients.

mailbot A program that automatically sends or answers e-mail.

mailing list A special type of e-mail address that re-mails all incoming mail to a list of subscribers to the mailing list. Each mailing list has a specific topic, so you subscribe to the ones that interest you. Often managed using ListProc, LISTSERV, or Majordomo.

Majordomo Like LISTSERV, a program that handles mailing lists.

MBone The multicast backbone. A special Internet *multicast* subnetwork that transmits live video and other multimedia to many different places on the net simultaneously.

mega- Prefix meaning one million (1,000,000).

Microsoft Network (MSN) A commercial online service that provides many Internet services, including e-mail and access to the World Wide Web.

mil When these letters appear as the last part of an Internet address or domain name (the zone), it indicates that the host computer is run by some part of the United States military.

MIME (Multipurpose Internet Mail Extension) Used to send pictures, word-processing files, and other nontext information through e-mail.

mirror An FTP or Web server that provides copies of the same files provided by another server. Mirrors spread out the load for more popular FTP and Web sites.

modem A gizmo that lets your computer talk on the phone or cable TV. Derived from *mo*dulator/*dem*odulator.

moderated mailing list A mailing list run by a *moderator*.

moderator The person who looks at the messages posted to a mailing list or newsgroup before releasing them to the public. The moderator can nix messages that are stupid, redundant, off topic, or offensive.

Mosaic An older Web browser, now supplanted by Netscape Navigator, Internet Explorer, Opera, and other browsers.

MPEG A type of video file found on the Net. Files in this format end in .mpg. Stands for Moving Picture Experts Group.

MP3 file A highly compressed music or voice sound file. This very popular format is used mostly for downloading music over the Net. MP3 stands for MPEG Layer 3. Files in this format end in .mp3.

MUD (Multi-User Dimension or Multiple-User Dialogue) Started as a *Dungeons and Dragons* type of game that many people can play at one time; now, it's an Internet subculture. For information about joining a MUD, consult the Usenet newsgroup `rec.games.mud.announce`.

multicast To send the same network information simultaneously to multiple places on a network. Currently only used by the MBone and a few network routing schemes.

multiple document interface The part of a computer program that electronically connects documents with other documents. There are also interfaces to connect programs, devices, and to connect programs to devices.

net A network, or (when capitalized) the Internet itself. When these letters appear as the last part of an address (in `www.abuse.net`, for example), it indicates that the host computer is run by a networking organization.

Netscape Navigator A popular Web browser that comes in Windows, Mac, and UNIX flavours. Part of the Netscape Communicator suite of programs.

network Computers that are connected together. Those in the same or nearby buildings are called local-area networks; those that are farther away are called wide-area networks; and when you interconnect networks all over the world, you get the Internet!

network computer A computer that lacks a hard disk and gets all its data instead over a computer network, like the Internet.

newbie A newcomer to the Internet (variant: *clueless newbie*). If you have read this book, of course, you're not a clueless newbie anymore!

news server A computer on the Net that receives Usenet newsgroups and holds them so that you can read them.

newsgroup A group of Internet users who discuss a topic area in the Usenet news system. (See the Web page `net.gurus.com/usenet` for a description of Usenet newsgroups.)

newsreader A program that lets you read and respond to the messages in Usenet newsgroups.

NIC (Network Information Center) Responsible for coordinating a set of networks so that the names, network numbers, and other technical details are consistent from one network to another. The address of the NIC for names ending in .com, .org, .net, and .edu is `rs.internic.net`.

nickname In IRC, the name by which you identify yourself when you're chatting, synonymous with *screen name* or *handle.*

node A computer on the Internet, also called a host.

Opera A small, fast Web browser from Opera Software, in Norway, available at `www.operasoftware.com`.

org When these letters appear as the last part of an e-mail address or URL (in `www.uua.org`, for example), it indicates that the host computer is run by a noncommercial organization.

packet A chunk of information sent over a network. Each packet contains the address that it's going to and the address from which it came.

page A document, or hunk of information, available by way of the World Wide Web. Each page can contain text, graphics files, sound files, video clips — you name it.

parity A simple system for checking for errors when data is transmitted from one computer to another. Just say "none" when you're setting up a communications program.

password A secret code used to keep things private. Be sure to pick one that's not crackable, preferably two randomly chosen words separated by a number or special character. Never use a single word that is in a dictionary or any proper name.

path In Windows operating systems, a path is a list of directories where the operating system looks for executable files if it is unable to find the file in the working directory.

PDF file A method for distributing formatted documents over the Net. You need a special reader program called Acrobat. Get it at `www.adobe.com/acrobat`.

PGP (Phil's Pretty Good Privacy) A program that lets you encrypt and sign your e-mail, written by Phil Zimmerman. Check out `comp.security.pgp.discuss` for more information or point your Web browser to `web.mit.edu/network/pgp.html`.

PICS (Platform for Internet Content Selection) A way of marking pages with ratings about what is inside. Designed to keep kids from getting at the racy stuff, although it has other applications as well.

Pine A popular UNIX-based mail program. Pine is easy to use (for a UNIX program).

plug-in A computer program you add to your browser to help it handle a special type of file.

POP (Post Office Protocol) A system by which a mail server on the Net lets you pick up your mail and download it to your PC or Mac. A POP server is the computer from which you pick up your mail. Also called POP3.

port number An identifying number assigned to each program that is chatting on the Net. You hardly ever have to know these numbers; the Internet programs work this stuff out among themselves.

posting An article published on or submitted to a mailing list or Usenet newsgroup.

PPP (Point-to-Point Protocol) A scheme for connecting your computer to the Internet over a phone line. Like SLIP, only better.

protocol The agreed-on rules that computers rely on to talk among themselves. A set of signals that mean "go ahead," "got it," "didn't get it, please resend," "all done," and so on.

public key cryptography A method for sending secret messages whereby you get two keys: a public key that you give out freely so people can send you coded messages and a second, private key that decodes them.

push technology A way for other computers to send information to you rather than wait for you to ask for it. Push technology enables you to subscribe to channels of information that get updated automatically on your computer. Not that popular (yet?). See also *channel.*

QuickTime A video and multimedia file format invented by Apple Computer and widely used on the Net.

RealAudio A popular streaming audio file format that lets you listen to programs over the Net. You can get a player plug-in at `www.real.com`.

RC4 A simple but powerful encryption algorithm developed by Ron Rivest, widely used on the Internet.

RFC (Request for Comment) A numbered series of documents that specify how the different parts of the Internet work. For example, RFC-822 describes the Internet e-mail message format.

router A computer that connects two or more networks.

RTFM (Read The Manual) A suggestion made by people who feel that you have wasted their time by asking a question you could have found the answer to by looking it up in an obvious place. A well-known and much-used FTP site named `rtfm.mit.edu` contains FAQs for all Usenet newsgroups.

search engine A program used to search the Web. A search engine can access a *directory* or *index,* which are organized lists of Web sites.

search part A URL suffix that directs the host computer to retrieve a certain file on a Web site.

secure server A Web server that uses encryption to prevent others from reading messages to or from your browser. Web-based shopping sites usually use secure servers so that others cannot intercept your ordering information.

serial port The place on the back of your computer where you plug in your modem. Also called a *communications port* or *comm port.*

server Also known as a Web server. A computer that provides a service such as e-mail, Web data, Usenet, or FTP to other computers (known as clients) on a network. See also ***client.***

shareware Computer programs that are easily available for you to try, with the understanding that if you decide to keep the program, you will send the requested payment to the shareware provider specified in the program. This works on an honour system. A great deal of good stuff is available, and people's voluntary compliance makes it viable.

Shockwave A program for viewing interactive multimedia on the Web. For more information about Shockwave and for a copy of the program's plug-in for your browser, go to `www.macromedia.com/shockwave`.

SLIP (Serial Line Internet Protocol) An obsolete software scheme for connecting your computer to the Internet over a serial line. See also ***PPP.***

S/MIME (Secure Multipurpose Internet Mail Extension) An extension to MIME that includes encryption (to keep mail confidential) and authentication (to prove who sent a message).

SMTP (Simple Mail Transfer Protocol) The optimistically named method by which Internet mail is delivered from one computer to another. An SMTP server is the computer that receives incoming e-mail.

socket On a UNIX or Windows system, a logical "port" that a program uses to connect to another program running on another computer on the Internet. You may have an FTP program using sockets for its FTP session, for example, and have Eudora connect by way of another socket to get your mail. Winsock is the standard way that Windows Internet programs use sockets.

spam E-mail sent to thousands of uninterested recipients or Usenet messages posted to many uninterested newsgroups or mailing lists. It's antisocial, ineffective, and often illegal. Sending spam is called *spamming*; if you are the sender, you're known as a *spammer*.

SSL (Secure Socket Layer) A Web-based technology that lets one computer verify another's identity and allows secure connections.

stop bits Just say "1" when you're setting up your communications software.

streaming audio A system for sending sound files over the Net that begins playing the sound before the sound file finishes downloading, letting you listen with minimal delay. RealAudio is the most popular.

StuffIt A file-compression program that runs on Macs. StuffIt creates an SIT file that contains compressed versions of one or more files. To restore these files to their former size and shape, you use UnStuffIt.

surfing Wandering around the World Wide Web and looking for interesting stuff.

T1 A telecommunications standard that carries 24 voice calls or data at 1.544 million bps over a pair of telephone lines.

TCP/IP (Transfer Control Protocol/Internet Protocol) The way networks communicate with one another on the Net.

telnet A program that lets you log in to some other computers on the Net.

terminal In the olden days, a computer terminal consisted of just a screen and a keyboard. If you have a personal computer and you want to connect to a big computer somewhere, you can run a program that makes it *pretend* to be a brainless terminal. The program is called a *terminal emulator*, *terminal program*, or *communications program*.

text file A file that contains only textual characters, with no special formatting, graphical information, sound clips, video, or what-have-you. Because most computers, other than some IBM mainframes, store their text by using a system of codes named ASCII, these files are also known as ASCII text files. See also *Unicode.*

thread A message posted to a mailing list or Usenet newsgroup, together with all the follow-up messages, the follow-ups to follow-ups, and so on.

Unicode An up-and-coming extension of ASCII that attempts to include the characters of all active written languages.

UNIX A geeky operating system originally developed at Bell Labs. Used on many servers on the Net. Linux is now the most popular version.

upload To transmit data from a computer to a bulletin board service, mainframe, server, or network. For example, if you use a personal computer to log on to a network, such as Napster, and you want to send files across the network, you must upload the files from your PC to the network.

URL (Uniform Resource Locator) A Web page address.

URN (Uniform Resource Name) A Web page name that doesn't change when the page is moved to a different computer. Proposed as a solution to the broken-link problem.

Usenet A system of thousands of newsgroups. You read the messages by using a *newsreader*. See the Web page `net.gurus.com/usenet` for a description of Usenet newsgroups. See also ***newsreader***.

uucp An elderly and creaky mail system still used by a few UNIX systems. Stands for *U*NIX-to-*U*NIX *copy*.

uuencode/uudecode A method of sending binary files as e-mail. Older and cruddier than MIME.

viewer A program to show you files that contain stuff other than text.

virtual reality A 3-D visual computer simulation that responds to your input so realistically that you feel you are inside another world.

VRML A language used for building virtual reality pages on the Web.

VT100 The model number of a very popular terminal made in the early 1980s by Digital Equipment Corporation that became a de facto standard. When you run a terminal emulator you may be asked what type of terminal you have; generally, saying you have a VT100 works just fine.

WAV A popular Windows format for sound files (.wav files) found on the Net.

Web page A document available on the World Wide Web.

WebTV A type of Internet access that includes hardware (an Internet terminal and remote control) that you connect to your TV.

Winsock A standard way for Windows programs to work with TCP/IP. You use it if you connect your Windows PC directly to the Internet, with either a permanent connection or a modem, by using PPP or SLIP.

WinZip A file-compression program that runs under Windows. It reads and creates a ZIP file that contains compressed versions of one or more files.

WWW (World Wide Web) A hypermedia system that lets you browse through lots of interesting information. The Web will be the central repository of humanity's information in the 21st century.

X.400 A cumbersome, ITU-blessed mail standard that competes, not very successfully, with the Internet SMTP mail standard.

X.500 A standard for white-pages e-mail directory services. It isn't quite as broken as X.400, and Internet people are trying to use it.

Xmodem A protocol for sending files between computers; second choice after Zmodem.

XON/XOFF One way for your computer to say "Wait a sec!" when data is coming in too fast; the other way is usually called *hardware flow control*.

Yahoo! An Internet directory made up of a set of Web pages that provide a subject-oriented guide to the World Wide Web and many other kinds of information. Go to the URL www.yahoo.ca.

ZIP file A file with the extension .zip that has been compressed using WinZip or a compatible program.

Zmodem A protocol for sending files between computers; one of the best to use, if it's available.

zone The last part of an Internet host name. If the zone is two letters long, it's the country code in which the organization that owns the computer is located. If the zone is three letters long, it's a code indicating the type of organization that owns the computer.

Index